Financing and Managing State and Local Government

Financing and Managing State and Local Government

Richard W. Lindholm
University of Oregon

Hartojo Wignjowijoto
Massachusetts Institute of
Technology

Lexington Books
D.C. Heath and Company
Lexington, Massachusetts
Toronto

Library of Congress Cataloging in Publication Data

Lindholm, Richard Wadsworth, 1914–
    Financing and managing state and local government.

    Includes index.
    1. Finance, Public—United States—States.   2. Local finance—United
States.   I. Wignjowijoto, Hartojo, joint author.   II. Title.
HJ275.L55   352.073   78-19227
ISBN 0-669-02434-1

Published simultaneously in Canada.

Printed in the United States of America.

International Standard Book Number: 0-669-02434-1

Library of Congress Catalog Card Number: 78-19227

Contents

List of Figures
and Tables

Preface and Acknowledgments

State and local government is entering a new phase of management and finance that demonstrates a strong likelihood of producing a workable combination of additional citizen participation and reduced reliance on revenues and programs from the federal government. A tax revolt and a public program revolt is underway.

The aim of 'nis book is to provide a concise and accurate account of the development, current position, and future opportunities for change in the major state and local government action areas. Each topic discussed is accompanied by a list of in-depth analyses of programs along with more general but related information sources. Particular attention is given to modeling implementation as stimulated by the work undertaken at Massachusetts Institute of Technology and the Urban Institute.

This book includes discussions of both the allocation and collection of funds. By being presented in the context of management of state and local government resources, these analyses develop an integrated picture that permits the reader and student to enjoy the breadth of understanding so badly needed to make intelligent decisions, both broadly based policy decisions and the most specialized and on the surface, at least, the most inconsequential decision.

The active participation of citizens in government increases the need for both convenient sources of alternative approaches and summaries of traditional procedures and estimations of importance of new developments. This book has kept this need in the forefront and by using a minimum of technical language and abstract analyses has made the existing state-of-the-arts available to the nonspecialist and to students of public sector management and economics.

The format of this book is aimed at providing a readily understood description and analysis of the basics as well as observed trends and new technical developments.

Financing and managing state and local governments has in the recent past taken on new and expanded dimensions. The evolution of existing institutional patterns is continuing in a variety of ways. These new approaches cannot possibly be included in the discussions carried out under each of the book's ten parts and forty-six chapters. To stimulate the inclusion of such approaches, and to improve the usefulness of this book as an educational tool, questions aimed at greater in-depth as well as in-breadth analysis have been formulated for each chapter. In addition, special reference sources are given that relate to each chapter.

More than five hundred questions and nearly three hundred references, divided by chapter, provide a base for expanded study and interpretation of conditions existing today in your state, county, or urban area. References, notes, and questions are at the end of the book, permitting the reader to proceed uninterrupted by chapter-end materials or notes.

We wish to acknowledge the assistance received from G.W. Atkinson of the University of Nevada, T.M. Calmus of the University of Oregon, and C.C. Cook and Arlo Woolery of the Lincoln Institute of Land Policy. Appreciation is also expressed to the editors of Lexington Books who gave additional strength to many of our paragraphs. Finally, we wish to thank our secretary, Susan Drake, who typed most of the manuscript and was most helpful and cooperative, and Dean J.E. Reinmuth and the Bureau of Business Research of the University of Oregon for providing needed resources.

The views expressed are our own and all errors arose from our shortcomings.

Part I
General Environment

1 Responsibility Diffusion under Federalism

When the new state constitutions that set the stage for the development of the American federation were adopted, the ideas of popular sovereignty and limited government were very strong. This point of view was carried forward in the Articles of Confederation. A central government that could deal directly with the people was not acceptable and was not established. It was not until the "firm league of friendship" concept envisaged in the articles had been badly damaged that an amending convention was called. The purpose of the meeting was expanded into a Constitutional Convention that drafted an entirely new document.

The central authority granted in the Constitution was needed to relieve the existing economic problems. The limited political power bestowed on any one government level has meant a mutual dependence. Local governments are created by state legislation and are provided for only in state constitutions and are not mentioned in the federal Constitution. The powers of home rule granted by states to local governments are often so comprehensive that local governments operate with as much relative independence from the state as states do from the national government.

The governments of the world are either predominantly unitary or federal in form. Under a unitary system, governments below the central level are completely dependent. Lower level governments do not collect their own revenues nor select their own judges and they have no power of legislation. A unitary government system operates on the theory that uniformity established at the top best advances the interests of citizens.

Where the federal form of government is in use there is a constant pressure to both reduce decentralization and to increase it. The relationship existing between the powers to be exercised by the citizens directly and by different governments of all sorts is never settled. Constant attempts to bring about an upward and downward flow of power is the order of the day.

The unitary government worries about coups that will place a new group in complete control of the levers of government. Federal governments are constantly threatened with loss of one or more of their components, and day after day lower levels of government press for fiscal assistance without a reduction in independence. Each level of government under the federal system is bound to carry out certain duties established in its charter or constitution. However, to force a government to carry out the type of action required at an acceptable level often becomes enormously complex, particularly when funds are not specifically distributed to perform the task. Consequently, the central

3

government of a federation is always tempted to induce a lower level government through grants (bribes) to carry out a designated activity.

Away from Federalism

The current federal programs to aid urban areas continues the practice introduced in the 1972 federal revenue sharing legislation of going directly to local governments and abandoning the state pass-through. The current federal program to aid urban areas is described as the "New Partnership to Conserve America's Communities." The partnership between the federal government and communities resembles the way a unitary government operates more than a federation. The federal government, by assuming more urban responsibility, reduces the close relationship of the state to local government envisaged when states were allocated the power to create local governments and generally accept responsibility for the actions of local government.

The nation has become basically urban. Over two-thirds of the population live in Standard Metropolitan Statistical Areas (SMSAs). By surrendering control and responsibility for urban areas, states are abandoning a basic aspect of rational federalism as envisaged in the Constitution.

The federal government first got its nose in the urban tent in the 1930s by providing financial aid for public housing projects. Its next major intrusion was made in 1949 when the urban renewal program was initiated. The federal government began to take over responsibility for the urban areas in earnest in the 1960s, however, when the Department of Housing and Urban Development (HUD) was created. Along with HUD virtually every major domestic federal department or agency has programs that affect the economic soundness of urban enclaves.

Direct federal control over the use of funds made available to local and state governments was reduced during the New Federalism of the early 1970s. Currently the federal government is busy attempting to draw up a national urban policy. All its past efforts have been expensive and generally appear to have weakened the acceptance of responsibility by the states and local governments. In 1979 a federal urban development bank was proposed and a portion of the debt of the City of New York has been guaranteed. Both these actions push toward reduced responsibility diffusion under the American federalism.

The Urban and Regional Policy Group (URPG), which is the coordinating agency for federal action to meet urban problems, has excluded from its area of responsibility education, crime, and energy problems. The federal government has run into money shortages and serious disagreements on priorities in URPG. As a result the federal government has encouraged states to place more resources into assisting their creations, the cities, counties, school districts, and other local governments. Incentive grants have been offered to encourage renewed state effort.

National Urban Policy

The national urban policy now being considered is a giant step toward a unitary government and in the process will certainly develop additional confusion. Counties, for example, have been excluded from the definition of urban, yet counties perform many urban government functions. Another aspect of the confusion certain to develop, as the halfway house of federalism is constructed, is what allocation formulas will be introduced. Some national agency will have to interpret any formula established, so that it can be applied to a poverty neighborhood in rich San Francisco as well as in poor Buffalo.

All of the shortcomings and waste of previous federal efforts to "solve urban problems" and the large federal deficits and the state surpluses cause a rational observer to conclude the state level of government is the proper locus for urban stimulation and management. States, after all, have the basic power allocation to carry out domestic policies in our federal system. States have an abundance of tax powers and have historically stimulated many social programs, including health care and assistance to the poor.

Nevertheless, the federal government has not turned over the guidance and financing of urban efforts to the states. The success enjoyed by such states as Massachusetts, Michigan, and California has not convinced the federal government that the diffusion of responsibility envisaged by the authors of the Constitution is the right way to go. As a result, the states waffle between waiting to see what they can get out of "Uncle Sugar" to going ahead on their own without trying to work out sensible programs with the federal government.

Under modern conditions, with the growth of cities to a size never envisaged by the framers of the Constitution, the federal system has moved toward a three-layer cake—federal, state, and urban. The need to develop new diffusion of responsibility appropriate to this new population distribution is not recognized at the decision level of our society. Instead, for the past forty years, government leadership has continued to attempt to bring about improved urban conditions by moving toward an unitary government system. Apparently, uniformity of social services throughout the nation has been the driving force, although it is seldom admitted. The attractiveness of industrial location because of social costs is an important cause of the support of social spending uniformity in the progressive states—that is, high per capita expenditures.

Tax Power Diffusion

The federal Constitution restricts states and local governments from taxing interstate commerce. The Constitution also prohibits states and local governments from taxing the income or property of the federal government. The federal government is prohibited from taxing exports and cannot tax property unless the tax liability is allocated on the basis of population. Finally, state and local governments must use a generally accepted fair allocation formula in the distribution of income or profits to be used as a tax base.

The separation of revenue sources developed after the adoption of the Sixteenth Amendment to the federal Constitution in 1913. This amendment extended the power to levy income taxes to the federal government. The revenue source under revenue allocation granted to the federal government was income taxes, to the states, sales taxes and to local government property taxes. Separation never was complete but the federal government has stayed very closely with income taxes. Although states have largely abandoned the property tax, recently they have been expanding their use of the income tax. Local communities continue to rely heavily on property taxes but they have, also, been rather active in introducing a variety of taxes including income and sales taxes.

The federal Constitution limits federal taxation to enumerated powers. The residual taxation power rests with the states. All the taxation powers of local government are the result of grants of power by the states. State constitutions frequently contain provisions limiting legislative power of taxation below the broad sweep extended in the federal constitution.

Shared taxes or the application of a special additional rate or the only rate to a base established by the state is relatively common between state and local governments. The federal income and corporate tax base is used by many states to apply their state or local government rates. Often the base is somewhat adjusted. A few states apply a legislated rate to the federal tax liability. The federal government does not share its income tax collections with the state from which they are collected, as is the general practice in Canada, for example.

The federal government's income tax law permits deducting all kinds of taxes paid to state and local governments from taxable income. Income taxes paid to foreign governments are treated as a tax credit and are deductible from federal tax liability.

The diffusion of tax power resulting from state grants of taxation powers to local governments has permitted additions to the breadth of urban taxation power and increased the potential for independent urban action. Governments at both the federal and state levels have not exercised much initiative in making local revenue raising more attractive. For example, fees and service charges are not deductible from federal taxable income of households and this is also generally true under state legislation.

A major advantage of the diffusion of a federation's tax power, and a very important justification for its encouragement, is that tax diversity and spending efficiency are encouraged. Recent Supreme Court action points toward limitation of federal established standards as a prerequisite for receiving federal funds (*National League of Cities v. Usery*, 1976). This decision is a good example of the Supreme Court acting to preserve the diffusion of federalism.

The Constitution gave the power "to coin money and declare the value thereof" exclusively to the federal government. When the federal government extends financial aid to state and local governments, while it is running a deficit that is ultimately financed with additional federal reserve credit, then state and local governments have been granted access to the federal powers of money coinage and creation. Generally speaking, federal grants to state and local governments from any source other than federal tax collections, amounts to an allocation of some federal money powers to state and local governments.

Summary

The functioning of a truly federal form of government has many built-in weaknesses that make for the appearance of inefficiency. There are also checks and balances that prevent loss of citizen power and the creation of the dictatorship of the bureaucracy.

The federal Constitution retains opposition to central government dealing directly with the people, which was the lynchpin of the American Revolution. Starting in the 1930s the federal government has increasingly moved away from the Constitution. The justifications for the trend have been numerous but the two basic reasons for the move to unitary government have been federal financial strength and need for uniformity of social benefits. Federal financial strength has been dissipated. Social uniformity has proved to be too expensive and inefficient when provided through revenue sharing and grants procedures.

Current tendencies point toward new methods of public sector financing and a shift in the allocation of service provision responsibility. Federalism is a form of government that is always in a precarious balance.

2 Economic Support of Citizens

State and local government expenditure levels have been growing more rapidly than those of the federal government. The relationship has arisen because of two quite different but still relevant developments. First, the baby boom following World War Two greatly expanded the need for state and local support of education, a traditional state and local government function. Second, the federal government substantially increased its grants-in-aid and revenue sharing to state and local governments. These federal revenues permitted state and local governments to expand their levels of services offered beyond the limits of their own revenues.

The level of government spending is perhaps ultimately determined by the willingness of citizens to make economic resources available to government so that they can benefit from services they want and which they believe government can best provide. In the United States, in addition to deciding they want government to do something, citizens must decide which level of government should be given the responsibility. Also, to a degree, they must decide how the activity is to be financed. In a few areas, such as foreign relations and defense, the federal government is allocated the function by the Constitution. Basically, the designation of certain taxes or certain services to a particular level of government has become blurred through time. As a result, which level of government should perform a particular task has become largely a conscious decision.

Division between Public and Private Sectors

Many needed services can be provided by either the public or the private sector. The advantage of public provision is the availability of the service largely on the basis of need demonstrated when requesting it. The advantage of private sector provision is that each user largely makes his own economic resources available to acquire the service, and therefore the quantity and cost of the service are determined largely by his own need.

Sometimes public services are divided into social wants and merit wants. Social wants are met by services that are consumed equally by all to the extent they enjoy satisfaction from using the facility. A street lighting system is a good example of a social good; a drinking fountain is another. To a considerable extent, all police and fire protection services are also taking care of social wants. These services can be only partially or not at all included under the exclusion principle; that is, enjoyment cannot be limited to those selected by price or in some other manner.

Merit wants, on the other hand, are services of greater benefit to the public than to the individual using the service. These services are subject to the exclusion principle and therefore those using them can be required to pay a price. However, the charge is best set below cost or provided free. The provision of education, at least at the precollege level, is an example of a public service provided to meet a merit want.

One way of looking at the pricing and provision of services is to allocate to the private sector all services that can be subject to the exclusion principle. If these services also turn out to be meeting merit wants, then legislation requiring a certain level of consumption would be adopted. In Sweden, for example, primary education is required by law, as in the United States, but the attending student in Sweden must pay tuition and such schooling is not basically free as it is in the United States. Another example is legally required vaccinations that must be paid for when given. Under this approach society meets the cost only if the user is unable to meet the expense.

Price Subsidy or Income Support

The expenditures of governments in the United States continue to face the choice that the British and Americans discussed when welfare and employment-related spending was expanding during the 1930s. The choice is whether incomes should be set high enough through government assistance so that acceptable transportation, housing, food, education, and other basic needs can be purchased at market prices or whether services should be subsidized or provided free. If the answer to this broad question is that income should be adequate, then the question of what is adequate must be answered. Adequate in New York City may be lower than adequate in Minneapolis. More laws requiring minimum expenditure levels for certain services with large externalities are needed. The list of shortcomings in providing adequate income is nearly limitless. However, this procedure has the advantage that individuals can judge the price-benefit relationship, and quantities to be produced are determined by sales levels at prices covering costs.

If the answer is subsidized or free services, the list of possible abuses and administrative difficulties is comparable with that in the adequate income approach. In addition, this approach has all the problems associated with allocation of resources when prices set within a relatively competitive market are not available.

The actual program that has gradually evolved in the United States and other Western industrial nations has been a combination of income supports and subsidized services. The welfare payment program has the goal of establishing minimum incomes; unemployment payments to those under the unemployment insurance program has the same objective. However, the income levels of these recipients, and of most of those under income maintenance programs, make them eligible for subsidized housing and food stamps that sharply reduce the cost of food and housing. Consequently, one family without accumulated wealth and unable to earn enough to cover minimum living costs frequently benefits from both income payments and subsidized prices.

The use of public funds to support an acceptable living standard by the poor plus medical attention has become an accepted very large government program. However, the expense of this government function and the need for a degree of national and state uniformity have together pushed this responsibility from the traditional county and city levels to the federal and state levels of government.

The combined effects of much larger consumption maintenance programs and the shift in the level of control and financing is one of the continuing revolutions going on in the United States. It has been the prime element in the explosive mixture that is destroying the traditional American separation of revenue sources and control over expenditure policies. The separation has always been more of a marble cake than a layer cake but now it is becoming nearly a loaf cake, at least in the area of consumption maintenance (welfare) spending.

Welfare Provision

The poverty of the nation is not evenly distributed and never has been. The Southeast and certain areas of the Southwest were considered poverty concentration areas in the 1930s when this aspect of government responsibility began expanding. Gradually, poverty in the cities has become the dominant element in policy consideration aimed at meeting the consumption maintenance aim.

Although it is sometimes said that the new type of cooperative federalism has made locally acceptable income equalization federal legislation aimed only at where needed, the actual legislation does not yet substantiate this position. The federal government finds it very difficult to pass legislation that would relieve poverty only where the burden is too heavy to bear locally. To fund desperately needed welfare programs, federal legislation must distribute funds equitably around the nation, even to areas where state governments are running surpluses and local resources are adequate to meet poverty relief needs. Under these circumstances, the federal government must use a sledge hammer to accomplish a task requiring only a carpenter's hammer. The approach is obviously wasteful and results in efforts that would be unnecessary if the programs were locally financed and carried out.

Transfer Payments

The national social security program has the potential of sharply reducing state and local government welfare responsibilities. It is often argued that social security taxpayers cannot receive full value for their money when the collections are skewed towards payments to the poor. This argument gives the impression that the social security system is a procedure for redistributing income from the retiree with a record of high earnings to one with a record of low earnings. This is only partially the reality of the economic relationship.

The income transfer brought about by social security is more one between generations than between different earning levels. The average recipients of social security retirement and disability benefits pay in only about one-third of their lifetime benefits. The remainder is a subsidy provided by the generation of payers of social security tax during the period the retiree is receiving benefits.

There are two basic differences between a social security approach and a welfare approach. First, welfare payments are not related to prior contributions or tax payments as are social security payments. Second, unlike welfare payments social security eligibility does not require investigation to determine whether poverty levels required for eligibility have been reached.

The use of welfare-type payments to reduce poverty places a heavy burden on local administration to determine if restrictions on eligibility are being met. These difficulties are largely eliminated in a social security program that goes one step beyond the present United States program. In Western Europe, a two-step social security program pays everyone a minimum subsistence benefit at retirement or disability. Income level is not ascertained, because income does not affect payment. The second step consists of payments based on salary and wage levels that have been used as the base to which payroll taxes have been applied. One tier prevents poverty; the second tier recognizes prior earnings or standards of living.

Under the two-step approach for social security, the government subsidy is limited to financing the minimum benefit. The subsidy from general revenues is not spread over the entire social security benefit payment schedule as it is in the United States. The development of social security in America along the two-level approach would relieve state and local government from the burden of determining eligibility.

The elimination of the means test also avoids the creation of a welfare class separate from the rest of the population. While the rest of society operates within a society basically of free market hiring and pricing, the welfare class operates in a quite different social milieu.

The economic world of the underclass is a portion of what is sometimes called the "grants" economy. The economic requirements of life come from operating within a system of regulations that when met provide food stamps, reduced rents, medical attention, reduced tuition, and free transportation. The civil servant takes on an adversary posture with the beneficiaries of his activities under these conditions. Most observers agree that a two-class society along these lines is inappropriate for a democracy.

Summary

The provision of needed goods and services to the poor, the aged, and others in need has become a major government responsibility. Although this has been generally accepted for some forty years, the problems of efficient delivery and the allocation of costs plus the difficulties encountered in preserving a society that encourages private initiative and individual responsibility remain.

New approaches are needed. The Western European use of a pay-as-you-go basic income guarantee plus an actuarially sound pension program for middle- and upper-income earners offers one alternative.

Another consumption maintenance choice still unresolved is whether income should be made adequate to cover the costs of a basic living standard, or whether subsidized housing, food stamps, and other direct services and goods be provided. It is more than likely that the existing compromise approach will be continued, because the once-popular negative income tax alternative has declined as a result of the New Jersey and other experiments.

3 Economic, Political, and Social Trends in Land Control

Political and social trends apparent in proposed and enacted legislation affect the distribution of income and the concentration of wealth by taxing land. All economic, political, and social activities require the use of land, water, and various quantities of other natural resources that can be allocated for private and monopoly use. To a lesser degree this control also extends to the atmosphere. The value of ownership and control of land and natural resources rests on the basic shortage of supply that cannot be stimulated as readily through higher prices as can the supply of manmade goods.

As the world's natural resources, particularly land surface, for each individual decline, the value of control over land increases. The increasing value of land, due basically to its limited quantity and multiple uses, has caused changes in land use and ownership to be one of the basic trends affecting the financing and management of state and local government.

The analysis and selection of economic policies during the 1946–1978 period of macroeconomic dominance emphasized the effect of determined actions on the level of savings and aggregate demand. When economic development and planning is examined in these terms, the differing effects of the tax package selected is not allocated a high priority. The analyses are concerned only with the aggregate revenues raised and the manner of raising them is given slight attention.

The macroeconomic approach to economic policy has through the years frequently emphasized fiscal policy. The Keynesian revolution has sometimes been described as the introduction of fiscal policy into the economic policy process, because monetary policy had failed in the 1930s. The word "fiscal" in the macroeconomic literature is not concerned with how government revenues are raised and certainly not with how they are spent, except to favor investment. Fiscal policy, in being concerned nearly entirely with aggregate government revenues and collections, was really a type of monetary policy. The approach fails to utilize the impact potential inherent in the specific, selective, and varied characteristics of the variety of fiscal actions available.

A new economic revolution is developing. The emphasis is moving away from aggregate and macroeconomic policy analyses toward disaggregated and microeconomic analyses. The new economic revolution continues to recognize—as did the old—that market decisions within an aggregate purchasing power framework cannot be relied on to put a price on important side effects (externalities) of economic actions. The two approaches differ in attitude toward government and the market. Formerly, improvement was always seen to require corrective action through government regulation. Under the revived new approach, corrective action through the pricing alternative is always seriously considered and used where appropriate. As a result, user charges to finance government services have gained support and the difference between homestead and business capital gains are being recognized.

If a nonsovereign government wishes to provide services not available from the central government, it must develop a revenue system capable of meeting these costs as they occur. Some flexibility exists if the credit standing of the government allows some revenue flow through borrowing.

The expenditure to be financed will cost the same whatever the revenue source. The aggregate revenues required remain the same whether source A, B, or C is used. Under the aggregate and macroeconomic approach, the fiscal portion of the decision consisted of determining the portion to be borrowed and the portion to be raised through taxes. Making this choice continues to be important under the new revolution, but in addition, the choice of the revenue source to use is an important component of the policy decision.

In making a revenue source choice, the incidence or economic burden of the collection must be considered. How will tax A affect so and so? If it has a number of undesirable effects then tax A is not likely to be the public choice. The best tax to finance an activity can only be decided in a very general and uncertain way because identifying and measuring incidence (that is, economic effects) is a very uncertain business.

Social Land Use and Taxation

Currently, a number of programs are actively utilized, largely in urban fringe areas, that combine the public revenue potential of the land tax with the improvement of the degree to which land use fosters greater livability and productivity. The programs we selected for brief consideration vary considerably in the degree to which they emphasize revenue or land use.

One aspect of these programs that we do not evaluate is the perception the community has of the fairness of the approach. Certain industries, such as agriculture, timber, and recreation, feel that they are being asked to bear too large a portion of the environmental preservation and local revenue burden. Two businesses with the same level of profits may be asked to contribute very differently under a program of improved land use and the capture of land rents for social use.

Development Land Tax in the United Kingdom

Real estate put to a higher use in the United Kingdom after May 1, 1977, is subject to the Development Land Tax (DLT). This tax is payable at an 80 percent rate on the difference at the date of disposal between the value on April 6, 1965, or the date of acquisition, whichever is later.

The DLT is paid by the person making the disposal. DLT is payable when a material development takes place without change of ownership. For example, improvement of the land beyond that authorized in original planning document is a material development. To be a material development, a building improvement must increase its dimensions. The value of the development must be more than £5000 to become a material development and subject to DLT. In theory, this approach means that property enjoying material development has been sold at the market price and reacquired at that same price.

The aim of the British DLT legislation is to help bring about a higher level of accomplishment in meeting the goals of town and country planning. It is believed that DLT will eliminate most of the problems of compensation and betterment because the payment, directly or indirectly, of compensation to prevent the development of land will not increase, but government will be able to benefit up to 80 percent in betterment arising from public expenditures and planning controls.

The writers of the DLT legislation have attempted to establish a tax and benefit system that does not destroy the efficiency of the market in determining the selection of sites for business development. On the other hand, the DLT legislation accepts the proposition that the free market is not efficient in taking externalities of land use choices into account. The market is seen to be unable to give proper weight to the desertion of the central business district (CBD) and to the breakdown of old established communities.

The DLT, or betterment approach to the capture for social use of the increase in the value given to land in the market due to inflation, population growth, cheap energy, and urbanization, is quite different from that of the land value tax (LVT). DLT does not provide the steady source of government revenues for local governments covering relatively small geographical areas that is possible under LVT. Also, DLT does not provide an annual pressure for efficiency as does the annual LVT payment. The role of government in decision making under DLT is concentrated during the period when a change—that is, material development—in land use is being considered. Under LVT the possibility of making large errors is reduced because the LVT tax is constantly pressing the owners and managers of land to move toward full use within zoning restrictions.

The advantage of DLT is in its apparent greater public acceptance than LVT and because it substantially reduces the pressure of landowners to change zoning restrictions. Although LVT is not as effective in reducing market pressures to changes in zoning, it does, of course, make preservation of zoning boundaries somewhat easier. However, the market pressures to change zoning decisions are not always entirely undesirable. The market pressures may exist because the original zoning decision was basically unsound. When this is the case, the DLT approach makes correction nearly impossible, whereas LVT allows a persistent market pressure for change. The market price appreciation during a land use correction benefits the social organization through the added tax payments arising under LVT. The DLT approach does not provide for additional society benefits in the form of tax payments until a change in use has been consummated.

Hawaii and New Jersey Plans

Legislation has been proposed and actually enacted in several states, including Hawaii, Massachusetts, and New Jersey, that follow the betterment and the UK land development philosophy. Such legislation provide for setting aside land for particular uses, such as agriculture.

The owners of the land are free to use the land for agricultural purposes and to sell it to others for use as agricultural land. The value of the land in the market and on the property tax rolls is determined on the basis of agricultural use.

When the designated government level decides a better or different use of the land is appropriate, the land is purchased from the owner at its market value. The governmental unit then changes the use to which the land can be put, such as an industrial park, and sells the land at auction to the highest bidder for the land in this new use. The difference between the market purchase price of land for agricultural use and the price received when the land was auctioned becomes government revenue to be used in meeting public sector needs.

Sweden's Preemptive Purchase of Real Estate

The concept of preemptive purchase has been discussed along with the right of eminent domain and other procedures for the government to acquire land. Under eminent domain, landownership is necessary to carry out a determined government program. The unique characteristic of preemptive purchase in Sweden is that the government makes an investment that will provide revenues for financing public services. The preemptive purchase is a procedure allowing governments to acquire control over the economic rent being earned by lands and to direct the use to which the land is to be put. Both the control over use and the revenue base acquired are important aspects of the preemptive purchase approach to taxation and land policy.

The Swedish legislation gives municipalities the power to purchase any property that comes on the market at the price agreed on between prospective buyers and sellers of real estate. The sale of any piece of real estate is not final for a three-month period while the municipality decides whether to use its preemptive purchase right and acquire the property. After three months the deed of sale becomes effective and the municipality's power of preemptive purchase has expired.

The municipalities cannot forecast what properties will be sold. In effect, they only have the power to take the "pick of the litter." As a result, the procedure does not permit the full initiation of a land use plan but, through the acquisition of certain key properties, it does affect the basic character of development. Even this opportunity to direct land use while acquiring control over land rents depends on municipalities' assets for making actual purchases. A number of financial procedures can be legislated depending on how active a program is considered appropriate.

The Swedish plan for giving the power of preemptive purchase to local governments has stimulated local interest in ownership and use of land within municipal borders. The residents of several urban areas have acquired considerable amounts of land that can be used more intensively or shifted to meet new needs.

While providing a growing municipal revenue base, and setting a general direction of development, the preemptive purchase of real estate develops a public understanding of the social qualities of income from land ownership and of land use decisions. Another desirable quality of the preemptive purchase is its local control and its contribution to a community attitude of being able to solve problems through community action. The preemptive purchase avoids nearly all national control and the making of decisions by a faceless and often heartless bureaucracy.

Korea's Land Readjustment

Korea's rapid development during the past twenty years has led to an expanded use of the land readjustment approach developed in Germany under the name *Lex Adickes.* This approach has been adopted in Japan and Taiwan as well as Korea. Basically, it provides for financing relatively large new housing developments out of increased land value arising when agriculture use is no longer required. *Lex Adickes* was formalized in law by Frankfurt-am-Mein, Germany, in 1902 and in Japan in 1919. The British improvement trusts in its colonies, which is still used in India, operate along similar lines.

Land readjustment in Korea functions under detailed legislation, unlike the Japanese approach, which provides for voluntary associations formed to carry out land development projects. Current land prices are rising so rapidly that voluntary associations are not needed to realize urban values on suburban land in Japan.

In Korea the title to the land of an area to be developed for urban use is transferred to a government agency. All costs for streets, sewers, schools, and other public improvements are paid by government sale of some lots in the developed area. When these improvements are completed, each former landowner receives title to developed lots that now have a considerably greater market value than agricultural land. However, property owners receive considerably fewer square feet of land than their original holdings. The government, through its sales of withheld lots, can frequently make earnings above total development costs. These funds can be used to subsidize housing for the poor.

The Netherlands

In 1970, the Dutch decided not to continue a group of taxes used by urban centers to meet a traditional group of government services financed at the local level beyond 1979. A new type of real estate tax was made available to municipalities to replace the unrenewed revenue sources. The new real estate tax can be levied either on a value basis or on the surface basis.

By 1977, many municipalities had changed to the new revenue source and abandoned their old sources. (The former taxes included a land tax, duty on houses, street tax, building site tax, insurance tax, and entertainment tax. About 17 percent of all the municipalities, including both Amsterdam and Rotterdam, which include 27 percent of the total population, adopted the new surface real estate tax. The surface approach to taxing real estate is based on dividing up the urban area into sections that have been given tax payment levels per square meter based on the location and use of the real estate.

The total square meters within a real estate holding is reduced by 300 square meters of land not covered by the structure. The next step, after this exemption to encourage small gardens, is to establish the number of square meters covered with a building and the additional square meters of bare land.

The tax per square meter of land is calculated from a table developed by the Union of Netherlands Municipalities—that is, the Bouwcentrum foundations. Each square meter of land is included within blocks that are given a single location coefficient. The taxable surface is divided into two parts—land on which a structure rests and land not covered by a building.

The square meters of land not covered by a structure is multiplied by three coefficients based on desirability of the area. The result is the adjusted number of meters used to apply the rate established in that city.

The meters covered by a building is adjusted by application of the same coefficient of location as on bare land. In addition, it is multiplied by the coefficient of kind and use and the coefficient of the quality of the building.

The total meters of bare land plus the square meters covered by a building, as adjusted, are taxed separately on the basis of the adjusted square meters. The tax per adjusted square meter of surface in Rotterdam is about $1 and in Amsterdam about $1.50 (in 1975 figures). The substantially higher tax in Amsterdam is partially the result of exemptions of many historical buildings and the greater revenues Rotterdam collects from its port.

The total tax levied on the property is divided into two parts, based on the concepts of legal user and legal owner. The adjusted square meters are subject to both the legal user tax rate and the legal owner tax rate. The legal owner's tax rate is typically several times higher than the legal user tax rate. Both taxes are paid by the same taxpayer on owner-occupied property.

The revenues provided by the new tax approach are proving to be adequate. The varying rate applied to legal owners and legal users has permitted Amsterdam to favor legal users (renters) to a greater extent than does Rotterdam.

Value of Buildings and Land

Assessors and economists have frequently attempted to define the "equal rate of assessment" mentioned in many state constitutions. Their doubts and final conclusions after examining a number of procedures for setting the base or "assessed value" to which the tax rate is to be applied are of interest in developing an understanding of the relationship between the unrefined concepts of market and of use value methods of assessment. In addition, their definitions provide a start toward a relatively sophisticated understanding of the two concepts of the real estate base to be developed through actual appraisals.

One approach starts with the original value of land before improvements but including the potential value of the land. The emphasis is on urban areas, but reference is made to rural practices. It is usually concluded that efforts to outforecast sales values as a measure of potential value is not likely to be helpful. For example, the multivariate analysis procedure is seen to fail to develop useful potential value forecasts. When income of some sort is used to set the value of land, the difficulty of establishing the capitalization rate (that is, the interest rate) is too fundamental to be dismissed and impossible to resolve. Efforts to arrive at a better measure of value than the market selling price are not helpful except in separating the value of improvements from the total market value of a property.

The sources of the relative usefulness of the "appraisal" approach in setting the value of a building, that are not available in the case of land, are often neglected by assessors. The failure to adequately consider these differences is not unlike the typical tendency to treat the tax on real estate as a single tax, and not as a tax on structures, a tax on land, and often a tax on commercial and industrial personal property. For example, relatively substantial depreciation is a current deductible expense for owners of a building. This deduction has the effect of increasing the immediate aftertax income. A similar deduction from taxable income is not available to the owner of land. This depreciation relationship encourages investors to purchase or to build structures.

On the other hand, depreciation as a cost is appropriate because a building is to a degree a depreciating asset, because it does wear out or become outmoded, and the demand for the particular service a building was built to provide often declines. These qualities give a building a life expectancy—that is, a point in time when it becomes valueless. As a result errors that are made in setting the interest rate used to calculate the capitalized value of income are much less important because the capital base is declining—in real terms—year by year through the operation of depreciation. The decline in capital value from physical deterioration reduces the applicableness of the concept of capitalization of a permanent annual income.

Land is not a deteriorating asset like a building. Also, land, generally speaking, cannot be produced and does not have a cost of production like a building. It is also true the quantity available does not change. As a result, the price the market sets for land is a price that allocates land to those bidding for control. The price set in the market is demand determined.

Agriculture Profits and Land Values

The substantial increases in land prices in real terms throughout the world during the past ten years has been caused by a number of factors, particularly an expanding need for food and fiber. In the United States, the liberalization of lending terms offered through FHA (Farmers Home Administration) and the FLB (Federal Land Banks) is an additional factor.

FLB loan limits, for example, were increased from 65 percent of normal agricultural value to 85 percent of market value. When some value was provided by recreation and urban influences, the borrowing ability of a landholder and prospective land buyer very substantially increased. The effect has been higher land prices arising from increased demand and a fixed supply. In time, these higher land prices became a cost of production that must be covered by market prices set on products and services of the land.

The FHA has provided liberalized credit terms by increasing the debt limit for individual farm ownership borrowers. Debt from all sources has been increased from $100,000 to $225,000. The FHA may loan or guarantee up to $100,000 of the amount borrowed from all sources.

In 1978, U.S. Department of Agriculture (USDA) market condition reporters felt that interest rates paid on loans to purchase land would increase. They also believed land prices would increase. That is, land prices will continue to be sufficiently strong to absorb the expected rising cost of borrowing.

Summary

As all societies have become more urban and as population increases have reduced the land available to meet individual needs, land use, taxation and management policies have come to the forefront. Who controls the land and how the control is modified by government and private actions have long been basic questions. Including the protection of private property in the federal Constitution and in state constitutions sets the basic approach in this fundamental area in the United States.

A social problem requiring careful consideration has arisen because efforts to assure the benefits of private ownership of real estate, and particularly of land, conflict with use and monopoly limitation goals. The United Kingdom, Korea, Sweden, The Netherlands, and several U.S. states are developing techniques to meet today's requirements. The aim of all the programs and analyses considered in this section is to develop procedures to supplement decisions of the market in a manner that takes account of many of the externalities of land use choices.

4 Current Tax Developments

In the United States local governments have always been bigger spenders than state governments. Local governments had neared the level of state tax collections until relatively recently when the states moved substantially ahead. In fact, during recent years the states have been more aggressive in developing and using tax resources than either the federal or local governments.

The explanation for the original growth of state fiscal activity has its roots in the great depression of the 1930s; however, some demonstrations of how an expanded state fiscal activity could be used to meet public service needs arose in the 1920s. At that time, the states actively used new taxes—that is, the gasoline tax—and old taxes—corporate franchise tax—to finance highway and higher education spending expansions.

Urban Crisis

The decline of the American city from the efficiency developed around the streetcars, subways, and train terminals of the 1920s has emerged from our inability to manage the combustion engine and cheap gasoline. Our cities are crowded with expensive automobiles while buildings crumble and roads deteriorate.

An inefficient urban area is unable to hold its affluent residents and its prosperous industries. The loss of these groups sharply reduces tax collection ability without bringing about a commensurate reduction in expenses. In fact, without a complete reorganization of the city, costs increase as efforts are made to meet human needs and subsidies are offered to induce industries to stay or to attract new industries.

Most urban fiscal problems have been created out of declining economic efficiency. When these urban deficits occur states must increase intergovernment grants in a variety of forms. These grants are largely used to permit the declining cities to meet basic needs while initiating adjustment programs.

In the 1930s state expenditures expanded largely from the failure of the property tax to provide the revenues needed to cover the costs of primary and secondary education. In both rural and urban areas, properties were abandoned and property taxes unpaid. The states stepped in and assisted the school districts. This state help frequently came from funds raised by new state retail sales taxes. Other revenue sources included state income taxes. Frequently, some help came through state abandonment or reductions in use of the property tax.

The rather widespread introduction of the retail sales tax as a state revenue source provided a revenue base for state fiscal growth. The economic potential of this tax was increased as a local revenue source when the property tax was given up by many states. This new equilibrium with expanded state revenue raising and spending level and expanding federal grants worked rather well; for example, it helped meet the education cost bulge of the early 1960s. The state and local revenue raising and spending system proved to have many flaws; these flaws, along with a decline in social and moral standards, caused the current urban crisis. The result has been rapidly expanding state intergovernmental transfers and troubled cities that are receiving as much in assistance payments as they are collecting in taxes.

An important aspect of the downward cycle in which some cities find themselves arises from the high property tax rates needed to meet even basic operating costs plus a minimum of capital improvements. The high rates stimulate the downward cycle, discouraging new construction and property developments.

To prevent ever-rising property taxes, cities have increased their revenues from sales and income taxes and have relied more on user charges; nevertheless, property taxes continue to dominate own-source revenues. During the past ten years, the total from all own-source revenues has actually been increasing at less than the inflation rate. This has not been enough to meet identified local expenditure needs and quite inadequate to cover expenditures stimulated largely by federal programs. As a result, intergovernment revenues and grants have skyrocketed to become by far the greatest revenue source of American cities.

The higher general education of the population and the large number of well-trained people available for employment by state and local government has increased the actual and potential efficiency of these governments. It is no longer true, as was largely the case in the 1930s when the federal government actively entered the area of social public expenditures, that the competence of civil service employees decreased sharply outside the federal arena. Competency today exists at all levels of government. This new situation, plus computer development, provide the potential for much greater decentralization of government. The centralization potential is, of course, also there. With planning, the new relationships developing will use both opportunities to improve the sensitivity and efficiency of government spending and revenue raising.

Tax Source and Spending Benefits

Public finance literature reports an old controversy: Should particular revenue sources be dedicated to the finance of particular expenditures? The outstanding success story of taxes tied to expenditures has been the gasoline tax and the finance of highways.

The expenditures made by local governments and to a considerable degree by the states directly benefit the people as members of households and of business and agricultural establishments. According to those who believe that government decision making should be similar to the market procedure, better tax level decisions would be made if collections were closely tied to expenditures.

Others hold that in government revenue raising and spending decisions should be entirely separate. General tax should be allocated to various purposes through the budgetary process. The willingness of taxpayers to pay higher taxes to assure more of a certain government service should not enter into either the expenditure process or into tax collection decisions (see Chapter 30).

The local property tax provides a revenue raising procedure of great flexibility. The property tax is a general revenue source. The base of the tax, property, has not been generally used to push aggressively for the use of all the revenues to directly benefit property, and that, perhaps, is as it should be.

The property tax has, in addition, a particular expenditure aspect that state and local governments find both useful and often exasperating. The rate that is applied to the taxable property base is often made up of a number of rates that are added together for each tax code area. The sum of these rates is the rate that is applied in calculating the tax due.

Each rate that is included in the total property tax rate has resulted from a decision of the voters or another authority to spend a certain amount for a certain purpose. The property tax is therefore made up of a number of special taxes to finance particular expenditures. How closely the benefit to be gained from the expenditures equals property taxes paid varies widely. In some cases—for example, when the benefit is irrigation works—the relationship is very close. In other instances—for example, education—the benefit is only related to the property tax base in a very general way.

The property tax could be used to levy a special tax rate to finance each service provided in various areas by different levels of government. Although this extreme has not been reached, the growth of special districts in some places is approaching this potential. Special districts are formed to finance a special service such as sewage or water. These special districts for different purposes may overlap geographically but they do not overlap with other districts providing the same service. The most important special district is the school district.

Grant Management

In developing special intergovernmental programs, both federal and state governments find it convenient to establish and later work with special districts. State and federal agriculture departments have found their purposes are better met by creating a special soil conservation district, for example, than by working through the county commissioners. The same relative situation has resulted in a group of special districts dealing with urban renewal and housing development.

The special district, with its own programs and financing that includes portions or all of a number of communities, is a blood relative of taxation dedicated to accomplish a particular purpose. The existing tendency to relate a tax collection to a service provision has been strengthened by the rapid growth of intergovernment programs. Along with this good aspect, at least to the eyes of those favoring market-type decisions by the government, has come a negative effect—greater confusion about how the local government is run.

The Bureau of the Census divides city government expenditure by function into seventeen groups:

Education, highways, public welfare, hospitals, and general expenditures; health, police, fire, sewage, and other sanitation; parks and recreation, housing and urban renewal, airports, water transport, parking, libraries, and finance administration.

Perhaps each functional expenditure group has, at one time or another, been financed and managed through a special district. Each has also been stimulated or turned in some direction by a state or federal agency offering financing.

The four biggest spenders of the seventeen functional areas are general expenditure, education, highways, and police protection. These areas are, of course, very traditional; they are also areas that are criticized for the quality of their performance. Perhaps education, highway construction, and police protection could have been performed more effectively and imaginatively at the state or even federal level. In most nations, both education and police activities are national functions with some local government input. The desirability of splitting up the highway functions of a state between counties, townships, and municipalities and then the state itself must be questioned.

Fragmentation provides a basic protection for democratic procedures and citizen government; that is, a balance against the probable greater efficiency of state performance and maybe even direct national performance of many major local government revenue-raising and expenditure activities. Today, inter-governmental spending is a third possibility that must be considered in evaluating state and local government expenditure and revenue developments. Intergovernmental programs, which have complicated financing and spending control, have demonstrated serious weaknesses; yet their growth continues. And each time a new intergovernmental program is initiated, it is emphasized that no strings will be attached and that all the goodies are free—or nearly so.

Summary

One part of the property tax is basically a payment for government services received. Another portion finances education and other merit goods and services at a higher level than private expenditure decisions would support. In both of these financing functions, the property tax has proven to be a revenue source of great adaptability and flexibility.

The great depression of the 1930s pushed government financing and, to a lesser extent, service provisions up to the state and federal levels. This shift has not proved to be entirely satisfactory. One loss, which shows signs of being regained, is that of democratic procedures. Another loss, that of citizen government, also shows signs of revival. An important lasting change that has proved to be very helpful was the adoption of broadbased income and sales taxes, at the state level in particular.

Intergovernmental programs financed by the federal government are now offered with the promise of no strings attached. The promise has proven to be illusive.

Part II
Budgeting and
Planning

5 Forecasting and Planning

Since World War II, the United States has experienced a virtual explosion of unexplored local government growth and change patterns. This unprecedented development must be understood by those attempting to produce helpful forecasts for use by city budget offices. In addition, rampant inflation and evident shifts in economic conditions make today's best program tomorrow's disaster.

Budget officers expecting to find a fundamental explanation in economic literature that will enable their staffs to develop projections based on widely accepted relationships will be disappointed. The available studies go very little beyond reporting the growth or decline rates.

In a projection published in 1966, using data through 1965, the Tax Foundation concluded that revenues and expenditures of state and local governments would increase at an annual rate of about 7 percent during the decade ending in 1975. Its projection also envisaged a surplus of revenues. The effort was way off the mark.

A new projection through 1975 by the Tax Foundation, which was based on data through 1969, set a 72 percent state and local government spending increase and a 66 percent revenue expansion from local sources, plus an 85 percent federal grant expansion for a "deficit on general accounts of around $5 billion in 1975." The expenditure projections for 1975 were 40 percent higher than those made by the Tax Foundation in its 1966 forecasts; revenue projections, however, were only about a third higher. The new projected total revenues again exceeded the actual growth, but this time by only 17 percent. The growth rates of federal assistance and revenues from all other sources other than major taxes was larger than the growth trend of previous years.

Undoubtedly, the underlying forces causing city revenue and expenditure changes have not been discovered; projections are less likely to be called forecasts today than in the past. The degree of inflation and the level of the birth rate—two broad explanations of the height of city expenditure and revenue levels—both reflect yet unidentified conditions. Nevertheless, each city budget department desiring more completely to follow the requirements of sound budgetary procedures developed around the concept of a Planning Programming Budget (PPB) system must make a four- or five-year expenditure and revenue forecast.

Basic Decisions

The type of dollar—current or constant purchasing power—is an early decision to be made in developing the four- or five-year forecast. The preferred procedure is to completely work out the forecast with constant dollars and then re-estimate the forecast using the price changes expected in each category. Applying some general inflation or deflation percentage to the budget total should be avoided. For example, if a three-year wage contract has just been negotiated, the level of change in the cost of a given sized work force can be calculated with great accuracy. This is not the case when forecasting the cost of purchases of materials and vehicles during the projected period.

Individual calculations, rather than mere projections of a percentage change based on previous experience, are also needed in the area of revenues. For example, if the city uses an income tax largely based on wages, and if the demand for labor is weak as evidenced by wage contracts coming into effect, then the future growth of income tax collections must be slowed down from what it was in the immediate past.

Demographic expectation is a basic element in all forecasts, particularly of a people-service organization like a city. The number of children in the education system will directly affect the ability of the city to use the property tax to meet its own needs. In turn, this will affect such policy decisions as use of service charges and special business taxes. Also, the developing age and racial mixture of the population will affect expenditure trends of different city departments. For example, more young people and minorities may require more uniformed police on patrol.

A four-year forecast, to be sufficiently realistic and useful, requires continual attention. Something is happening everyday—from the popularity of a parking lot resulting from a change in the one-way direction of a street to the bankruptcy of a major employer. The effect of such shifts is a legitimate portion of the information input used in developing the budget projections of a city. It is very complex and perhaps impractical to attempt to develop a system of equations that can use econometric techniques to assess the impacts of the changes on the need for welfare generally or the level of tax receipts.

Ideally, the blocks of services and revenue sources making up the budget would be parameters that could be changed as required within a general equilibrium model. Under these circumstances, the changes envisaged or experienced could be plugged into the model and the effect on expenditures and revenues would be calculable. The set of equations such a model would require have not yet been formulated by any city budget department. (See chapter 33.) However, many budget and planning departments have prepared four- and five-year budget estimates; they have also developed performance goals and detailed cost and revenue estimates, plus the use of trade-off analyses—that is, they have determined what has to be given up to gain a desired goal. Progress here will eventually make possible the overall model that will permit all impacts of a change to be identified.

Restricted Impact Forecast

A simple example of a five-year expenditure forecast that deals with work units as well as manhours and projected cost is given in table 5–1. It is one block of a PPB system. The interactions between this block (fire inspections) and the rest of the economy including city activities are not considered. In other words, the illustration is not the ideal but at the same time it is very helpful to city management. For example, the failure to provide benefit estimates looms immediately as a shortfall. Also, a new type of program that might even provide rather than use revenue is more likely to be identified through this sort of analysis. For example, could a system of fines and sample inspections plus a checklist sent to property owners be initiated?

Table 5–1
Fire Inspections (Public Safety):
Function—Protection of Persons and Property

Fiscal Year	Man Hours	Current Tax Dollars	Inspections Made	
			Units	Unit Cost
1976–77 Actual	11,493	80,311	6,159	13.04
1977–78 Actual	15,774	78,331	5,297	14.79
1978–79 Actual	9,488	72,623	6,861	10.59
1979–80 Estimated	9,839	85,125	6,763	12.58
1980–81 Proposed	17,721	169,029	12,000	14.09
1981–82 Projected	17,721	176,780	12,000	14.73
1982–83 Projected	17,721	184,223	12,000	15.85
1983–84 Projected	17,721	190,248	12,000	16.37
1984–85 Projected	17,721	196,450	12,000	16.87

Source: Werner Z. Hirsch, *The Economics of State and Local Government* (New York: Appleton, 1971).

In summary, table 5–1 indicates a proposed doubling of an activity. It then predicts that this activity will remain at this height for the next four-year period. If this city is experiencing some growth, then the need for the activity or the service level declines during the next four-year period. However, if activity is declining, the level of this service by remaining constant is forecasted to increase. In other words, the projection of no change in activity generally does not mean no change in service level. In this instance, however, the prediction of no change does demonstrate that the future level of the activity has been considered and the new proposed expansion for the next four-year period has been accepted. The decisionmakers are granted assurances the expansion is not a foot-in-the-door operation.

The gradual year-by-year expansion of unit costs in table 5–1, as well as the increase of total cost accompanied by no increase in number of work hours, may demonstrate a number of elements. For example, it could be the result of assuming that the fire inspectors will remain relatively constant and will gradually move towards the top end of their wage bracket. Or, it could mean an assumed rate of inflation and a policy of moving wages up as the value of the dollar declines. Or, it could represent an assumed level of general expansion of productivity in which these city workers share through a gradual increase in wages. Or, of course, it could reflect any combination of the elements mentioned.

An important aspect of the forecasting process is that it forces decision-makers to consider the money costs of the program during the next four years, by setting down the money costs of inflation, a more experienced labor force, and a share in the nation's expanding productivity. This causes all parties to the operation to include these numbers in their thinking.

Revenue Forecasting

The basic data required to make useful forecasts of collections from various taxes and other revenue sources vary from tax to tax. It is also true, however, that basic information such a personal income, demographic data and industrial trends are needed to understand the basic elements affecting the economic base available to all taxes.

Property Tax

The property tax base consists of various elements; by far the most important is the assessed value of real estate. Future trends in assessed values in different areas can be forecast by using sale prices of existing properties, building permits, and new developments in the planning stage. Sales data are most useful in forecasting assessed values of nonfarm residences and smaller commercial properties. Large industrial, mineral, timber, and ranch properties need to be valued by using sales data from other, rather similar communities. General trends in the price of materials, construction labor, and land are, of course, useful in setting values on real estate.

Assessments can be adjusted annually on the basis of a selected index such as the consumer price index. In addition, however, a careful reassessment must be undertaken on a five- or seven-year cycle. Under stable prices values do not change substantially until the reassessment cycle is completed. To the extent that all properties are changing in values at approximately the same rate as those included in the current reassessment cycle, the reassessment data provide a basis for forecasting general assessment levels five years ahead. The usefulness of this forecasting technique depends on good valuation data and the applicable legal restrictions on levies. (See chapter 19.)

New construction activity can be estimated by using projections of income and population as a base for estimating new construction. An income or population elasticity multiple is helpful only in estimating value of new housing and commercial construction. New real estate industrial investments are related to growth and decline trends of the particular industries that find an area to be an attractive location. When information from such sources is understood, decisionmakers can make an educated guess about the relative desirability of their industrial parks and other factors such as labor and transportation.

Personal property, such as machinery, inventories, or furniture, has become a smaller share of the property tax base as legal and administrative adjustments have reduced the coverage. These trends vary with different types of industries and can be forecast on the basis of application dates of legislated changes in coverage.

The property tax, because it is a wealth tax and the base varies depending on prevailing interest rates as well as portion of income dedicated to holding real estate and certain types of personal property, cannot be treated like income and sales taxes. The tax-base elasticity of the property tax is very difficult to approximate through yield data. Collections are basically determined by need to balance budgets and not by shifts in the size of the base. Expansion of the base results largely in lower rates and not in expanded revenues.

Other Taxes

The great variety of sales and income taxes all have one common element: the collections vary almost directly with shifts in the tax base. The quantity of sales tax collections depends on the level of taxable sales and the applicable rate. The rate is typically relatively constant. As a result, forecasting depends nearly entirely on projecting per capita personal income. Personal income is estimated monthly by the federal government at the state and national levels; it is also forecast, but much less frequently, for SMSAs, and even less frequently for census tracts within SMSAs.

Although personal income is not a measure of available income for spending on goods and services, it is the only measurement of spending ability available on a continuing basis. General sales tax collections can be readily projected by using a simultaneous equation model.

Revenues from taxation of sales can be projected through the interreactions of three endogenous variables (per capita disposable income, distribution of income, and population), plus some exogenous and random factors. A separate forecast, including family formation and automobile sale expectations, might be needed for durable consumer goods.

Income taxes can be estimated largely on the basis of salary and income projections. Gross receipt taxes can be estimated by using about the same procedures as used in estimating the retail sales tax.

Expenditure Projections

The level of expenditures of state and local governments is determined by the level of federal revenue sharing and grants for which the government unit can qualify, the quantity of debt the voters will support, and the amounts collected from various taxes. The types of services and products allocated to the public sector remain relatively constant. When welfare, and social spending generally, were substantially increased in the mid-1960s through federal grants, a new phase of state and local government activity was initiated. To this new social activism was added the high level of education and highway expenditures that were traditional public sector activities. The result of this double-barreled expansion was an unusually rapid growth of public sector state and local government expenditures. Education, police, and fire protection costs have nearly tripled during the past ten years, while public welfare outlays have increased fivefold and highway expenditures have only doubled. At the same time, all prices approximately doubled, so highway expenditures in real terms have remained constant.

Expenditure levels of the private sector are always a trade-off between the pain of the tax payments and the pleasure offered by the service or good. Some predict that the dissatisfaction with the types of services being financed with general taxes, as greater relative attention is paid to welfare and social expenditure goals, and less to highways and police, will reduce the growth of expenditures and the need for revenues. Current data point somewhat in this direction.

If we are entering a new phase in the public's attitude toward supporting state and local government spending, then projections based on former trends can be in serious error. Two types of adjustments can be expected. One approach would keep taxes at levels approximating the current portion of GNP being paid in taxes. Welfare and social expenditures would decline and traditional expenditures would grow. The other adjustment would cause a decrease in state and local revenues, with the greatest reduction in the welfare and social areas. Because the property tax is a residual tax, an expenditure growth slowdown or an expenditure decline is likely to result in another reduction in the share of local public sector expenditures funded with property tax collections.

Summary

Projections of tax collections and other revenues can be rather readily performed with conventional simultaneous equation analysis. A projection is not a forecast but an extension into the future of the trends experienced in the past, modified by some secular and other trend assumptions. Forecasting requires careful analysis of the data developed by the projections and making appropriate modifications. These expert contributions will play a less important role when the underlying political and economic forces causing state and local government revenue and expenditure shifts are understood.

The development of expenditure projection blocks in the application of the PPB system helps analysts to understand the forces affecting expenditure levels. Along with this understanding will surface weaknesses in the program. One positive result may be the development of service-related financing opportunities so that less reliance need be placed on general revenues. This development of pressures to raise revenues as a portion of department operations is apt to increase internal pressures to increase efficiency.

6

The Budgetary Process

The budget stands in the center of the organization and management of resources received and utilized by state and local governments. The skill with which the financial manager, in association with the chief administrative officer and other elected officials and advisers, develops and presents the budget sets the pattern for failure or success. Skill is measured by the degree to which the historical, social, political, economic, and financial basis of the community are recognized and dealt with.

The budgetary procedures to be followed, in moving from a general citizen environment and consensus of what should and can be accomplished, are rather uniformly used by government units. They are conventionally divided into six steps.

Development and Application

The first step is to establish the expenditure levels required to meet new and expanded needs and to reach goals that have gained visibility and citizen support, plus the costs of continuing old programs at their accustomed levels. The second step is to develop a revenue estimate from all sources. The third step is to review both the expenditure and revenue estimates to determine an appropriate balance between them. A third step, closely associated with the second, but still a separate procedure, is the development of a forecast for a period of years. A five-year time span is frequently adopted. The fourth step is the preparation of the budget document. The fifth step is the presentation of the budget to the legislative body for formal acceptance. The sixth and final step in the budgetary process is the administration of the provisions of the budget adopted.

Accountability Management

The administration of the budget is nearly always done by allotments to the different departments for purposes established in the budget and in other similarly legislated expenditure documents. These allotments are nearly always for periods shorter than the budget year. Frequently, they are for a quarter of a year, and sometimes monthly allotments are used. One purpose of the allotment system is to keep control over the relationship between the use of funds and the accomplishment of budgetary goals. Allotment procedures also assist management to make certain expenditures are proper and legal.

Management controls exist to husband the resources of the government unit, to develop performance reports, to encourage the efficient, and to eliminate ineffective activities. Management control goes beyond the purely financial controls and includes digging down into the organization to learn how much work is actually being performed that pushed budget goals forward. As attention is given to progress toward budget goals rather than to operations within line-item boundaries, the government unit progresses toward a variety of a planning-programming-budgeting (PPB) system called performance budgeting or program budgeting.

Performance Budgeting

The use of goal-oriented budgetary procedures, often called performance budgeting, has resulted in many government units developing data that permit citizen groups and management to learn what is happening to the funds allocated to do a particular job. The performance budget is an accountability budget that goes one step beyond making certain a particular type of person is hired and a particular product is purchased. This additional step brings together into one section of the budget document the personnel and materials to be used to carry out a particular function.

Frequently, the expenditures related to carrying out a particular activity are divided into five categories of functions—for example, (1) personal services, (2) fringe benefits, (3) contractual services, (4) materials and supplies and (5) capital outlay-equipment.

The contractual services category, for example, may be itemized into printing and binding, telephone and telegraph, travel and subsistence, and miscellaneous contractual expenses. The expenditure for personal services frequently dominates state and local government project costs. This dominance often justifies establishing personnel on a line-item basis—for example, three secretaries at level 2 and ten earthmoving machine operators.

The weakness of both the performance and the accountability budgetary procedures is that they do not come to grips with the basic budgetary problem of setting priorities. The well-administered accountability budget makes certain the money provided hires the people and purchases the materials the budget executive wants. The performance budget organizes these goods and personnel into groups to carry out a purpose decided upon as proper. The PPB makes the ultimate budget step. It compares the productivity of various types of uses of government revenues.

PPB

To be operative, the PPB must first provide top elected officials with information and analyses that can be used to decide resource allocation between a number of claimants. Second, the elected officials must use this information to allocate resources. The true functioning of PPB makes careful marginal cost and marginal benefit and incremental benefit analyses fundamental. (See chapter 7.)

PPB can only be effective if decisionmakers want to make decisions based on in-depth information. The desire, for example, must be at least strong enough to adequately fund a PPB operation. In addition, the determination must exist to do battle with the forces of tradition, special interest, and inertia. Although PPB is not dead, its use has not spread as anticipated when introduced in the Department of Defense and other divisions of the federal government. Another approach with PPB elements, called "sunset legislation" or zero-based budgeting (ZBB), has gained more support than PPB.

Sunset and ZBB Laws

The first sunset measure was adopted by Colorado. This April 1976 legislation applied to all 43 commissions and boards with the Department of Regulatory Agencies. The law as originally written limited the life of each regulatory board and commission to six years. A review schedule provided for termination of one-third of the regulatory agencies every two years.

The first ZBB legislation was adopted in 1972 by Georgia. The system establishes a financial planning phase to precede actual budget preparation. This procedure also improves the quality of management information and expands the budgetary process to include more management personnel.

The Georgia program and others adopted by states since then call for the creation of program groupings or "decision packages." These packages are further divided into separate groupings for different levels of effort, including line-item descriptions and measures of performance. The primary purpose of this process is to force all program managers at *every level* to justify their entire budget requests. Experience with the ZBB system is expected to result in sounder and more compact decision packages.

The New Jersey legislation adopted in 1974, another pioneer state in this budgeting process, added ZBB to a rather highly developed PPB system. The ZBB was introduced to increase the action orientation of the PPB system. When ZBB was adopted, Governor Brendan Byrne directed all state agencies to assign a priority ranking to each program and activity. The ZBB legislation has provided the governor with budget options. Necessary services were demonstrated to be functional through a more efficient and different approach from that previously developed and being followed.

Incremental Budgeting

The current method of developing service cost estimates where PPB, ZBB, or sunset laws are not in effect relies largely on the previous year's costs. Such incremental budgeting is defended on the grounds that it avoids much complexity, uncertainty, and needless repetitive estimating.

Because the departments largely consume general government revenues and not special services or use charges, they are largely expenditure budget-oriented. Department directors often look to the finance department for the funds required to finance a consensus level of services. A result of this approach to departmental budgeting is very little emphasis on how the department through its own actions could provide a portion of its operating costs. Of course, the procedure also assumes general acceptance of the current level of expenditures and services. These basic aspects of conventional incremental budgeting are coming under general scrutiny.

Summary

Budgeting and management are becoming close allies. Out of this relationship improved cost-benefit analyses and more efficient use of government resources is developing. This evaluation shows signs of becoming nationwide and of carrying with it increased consideration of relating revenue sources to service provision.

The accountability function and performance grouping of yesterday's state and local government budgets provide the base for PPB, ZBB, and sunset laws, with a concurrent appreciation of the need for citizen participation.

7 The Planning-Programming-Budgeting (PPB) System

Modern municipal budget procedures have their roots in the developments of the 1920s. The management of cities began to become a recognized profession under the leadership of A.E. Buck of the New York Bureau of Municipal Research and Professors C.E. Merriam and J.O. McKinsey of the University of Chicago.

The basic definition of a budget, given by Dr. F.A. Cleveland in 1915, was simple and to the point: a budget is a plan for financing a government during a definite period. The plan must be prepared and proposed to a properly authorized executive body and then in turn to a legislative body responsible for approving and supervising the plan as necessary.

From this static concept of accountability developed the modern concept of the budget as a plan and process of government. But the basic idea of accountability—that is, where the funds will be used and where they will come from—remains as the framework within which process and accomplishments must be fitted.

The primary function of the first modern budget was accountability. This was predictable, because the budget as a detailed and formal document arose directly out of accountability problems of the grossest type. The provision for appropriation of funds was so general that graft and inefficiency were the order of the day. The switch from the general or lump-sum appropriation to the itemized budget was a giant step toward curbing inefficiency and dishonesty. It, however, did nothing to reward the honest and economy-minded administration and, in fact, its rigidity handicapped the efficient and innovating administrator.

As the management abilities of municipalities increased, the budget became both a management and a financial plan. The items in the budget were grouped to provide for the performance of a service that the municipality was committed to carry out. This budget, which was organized to highlight functions, activities, and projects, was called a performance budget. Because of the service orientation of municipalities, they found the organization and aims of performance budgeting to be most appropriate.

The performance budget concept as well as the accountability budget remain an important part of the goals of municipal budgeting. However, we now see that they are to a degree only basic steps in making PPB possible. The great advance of PPB is that it comes to grips with the basic budgetary problem of setting priorities.

The accountability budget made certain that money went to purchase the goods and hire the people the budgetmaker wanted to purchase or hire. The performance budget organized these goods and personnel into groups to perform a specific purpose. The PPB does not neglect the fundamental accountability aspects of budgeting. They remain important, but they become only a portion of the budgetary operation.

PPB compares the productivity of various types of uses of government revenues. It even aims at determining whether funds are more productively used when they remain under private control or when they are publicly controlled. The PPB is aimed at providing line managers and division supervisors with information and analyses that can be used to decide resource allocation between a number of claimants. This requires budgeting for more than a year in advance and it makes careful marginal cost and marginal benefit analyses fundamental (See chapter 34.)

Budget Process

The budget process in a municipality must perform two roles. The first role is to determine a plan for organizing, controlling, and reporting revenues and expenditures. The second role is to determine how much of which service to provide. Basically, the budget process of a business concern must involve itself with only the first role. For a business, the second budgetary role of a municipality is performed in the marketplace. The customers by their purchasing decisions determine for the business firm how much of what to produce. Most of the services of a municipality are not sold. The how much of what is the big new responsibility taken over by PPB that was not included in accountability and performance budgeting.

The use of PPB in a city requires several steps. First, a group must be established to do in-depth analyses of the objectives of city government spending and how well these objectives are being met. Second, it is also necessary to carry out detailed multiyear planning. And third, a programming process is needed that presents data in a form that can be used in making major decisions by department heads, the city council and the mayor. Fourth, a continuing budgetary process is required to translate broad decisions into more refined decisions in a budgetary format for final council and mayor action.

The PPB approach requires a program and financial plan (PFP). Basically, the PFP provides information and controls the accountability and performance budget procedures. The big difference from the older approach is that both the services and the costs are projected as far into the future as is useful. Physical output data and financial data are presented together in tabular form. Objectives and performance are described in as specific terms as possible.

The PFP goes beyond annual performance budget procedures by considering future implications of current budget decisions. It should also help force choices among programs and to highlight where overlapping exists.

A second major document of a PPB system is the program memorandum (PM). PM should be developed to answer all legitimate questions of decision makers.

The PM performs this miracle in a very undramatic fashion. First, each of the programs recommended by a department is examined to see how it will meet the designated need during the period of years that it is projected to last. The total cost estimates are examined for how well it meets program goals and the types of needs perceived to exist.

Second, the program's objectives are described in quantities and in physical terms. This is done in the very most precise terms that is possible. It is *not* a simple essay of hopes. Third, the program is costed out over a period of a number of years. Again, great care is exercised to develop full expected costs over a number of years. Fourth, all the various alternative procedures of meeting similar objectives are examined in terms of costs and effectiveness. Assumptions and criteria appropriate for making choices are carefully spelled out.

Fifth, the PM spells out in great detail all the reasons for making the choice decided on. Sixth, all the uncertainties involved in the direction taken are brought out into the open. Each one is analyzed as to how these possibilities could change the expected results. The process demonstrates the sensitivity of the project to the uncertainties that have been considered.

The overall PPB approach is aimed at providing the direction of choices for government that the search for profits and the press of competition provides for the private sector. The PPB philosophy of analysis and detailed programming of resources required over a period of years to carry out a project does not eliminate the need for good judgment. But the PPB approach does require accepting the position that good judgment alone does not make for good decisions. Good decisions also require digesting and using detailed analyses of the programs being funded.

The PPB system is designed to give top management (such as the city manager, the council, and the voters) the information they want. It is information they can use in combination with good judgment in making the best use of the resources of the public sector. In doing this, the PPB system has six benefits:

1. It states concisely the goals of government activities.
2. It clearly presents to the decision makers alternative ways of meeting objectives.
3. It calculates the total costs of the project by budget period.
4. It permits marginal analysis and systems analysis of projected changes.

5. It develops a multiyear data base to permit reasonable estimates of future
    costs and benefits of the programs of the government unit.
6. It permits year-round review of programs instead of crowded schedules to
    meet budget deadlines.

Accountability

In the first section of this chapter we emphasized that municipal budgeting
cannot abandon its traditional function of accountability as it expands to
include PPB. In all cities, the line-item budget continues to be the core of the
control over the allocation of funds to operating units to make certain
expenditures are made in clearly defined ways. In addition, it is necessary to
assure funds use will be distributed appropriately to cover the entire budget
year. To do this, quarterly and monthly expenditure rate levels are set. These
expenditure rate schedules guide department budget officers and act as
controls to be enforced by the city's accounting office.

The personal services or the wage and salaries allocation is by far the
largest item in most city department budgets. It is likely to be broken down into
identifiable positions as illustrated in a typical personnel classification of a line
item budget of a fire department (table 7–1).

The accountability function of the budget is meaningless unless enforcement guidelines are established and adhered to throughout the budget period.
Each department must establish its own allotment schedule that becomes the
basis for expenditure control procedures established in the central accounting
office. (See chapter 41.) The schedule established is unavoidably based on
previous year experiences and normal seasonal responsibilities. Despite this
built-in inflexibility, the traditional accountability or control function allows
expenditure levels to be related more closely to expenditure goals.

For example, in addition to keeping streets in repair, a goal of expenditures
might be to alleviate local seasonal unemployment. The acceptance of this goal
in reality, instead of as a pious hope, could require a shift in expenditure
allocation distribution of considerable magnitude. It would also necessitate
changes in personnel priorities and more than likely negotiated understandings
with the appropriate employee organizations and federal, state, and county
governments.

Traditional control aspects of the budget do not remain constant. The
analyses of PPB that have been considered in a general way are certain to affect
the way traditional accountability functions are carried out.

Table 7–1
Line Item Budget, Fire Department

No. of Emp.	Personnel Classification	Range No.	1970–71 Budget		
			No. of Emp.	Proposed	Approved
1	Fire Chief		1	15,800	15,800
1	Assistant Fire Chief	26	1	14,100	14,100
1	Fire Marshall	25	1	14,098	14,098
4	Battalion Chief	25	4	53,723	53,723
3	Captain II	23	3	36,556	36,556
23	Captain I	22	23	266,969	266,969
1	Fire Equipment Mechanic	21	1	11,055	11,055
1	Assistant Fire Marshall	23	1	12,185	12,185
3	Inspector	22	3	39,059	39,059
9	Lieutenant	21	9	99,497	99,497
36	Engineman	20	36	376,308	376,308
3	Dispatcher	20	3	31,394	31,394
1	Radio Technician	22	1	11,607	11,607
47	Fireman	18	48	430,182	430,182
1	Secretary II	10	1	6,420	6,420
	Overtime and Callback			25,000	25,000
	Extra Help			5,900	5,900
	Volunteer Fireman			18,725	18,725
135	Totals		136	$1,468,578	$1,468,578

Source: "Budget Making," unpublished manuscript, Department of Finance, University of Oregon, 1974, p. 4.

Shifts in Traditional Practices

Before leaving this point of interaction between the new PPB functions and the municipal budgetary functions developed by Buck et al., it is worthwhile to identify some other impacts on traditional budgetary practices of moving toward PPB.

For example, the traditional budget calendar for a city with a fiscal year ending on June 30 would begin with a meeting of the budget people of all departments on about February 1. At this first session, instructions and work sheets for all budgetary divisions would be distributed. By March 15 the department budgets with all requests and substantiations will be submitted to general administration. This calendar means six weeks of departmental casting about for ways to preserve or increase the budget. Efforts would be made to learn the administration's attitude toward this program and that justification. The new budget would be slanted to take advantage of these attitudes.

Everyone who has been involved in this traditional process agrees this is no way to prepare the basic materials to determine next year's operations. A basic tenet of PPB is year-round budget analysis and preparation. PPB should eliminate the well-known sentence, "The budget season is here again."

Many cities must operate under state laws or city charters that do not always coordinate due dates for coordinating revenue collection and estimation and the formulation and approval of spending plans. All these legislated handicaps to sound city budgeting can, of course, be unlegislated. A year devoted to this type of tedious and frustrating activity must be the first step in clearing the deck for sensible allocation of city economic resources.

The review of departmental budget requests by the central administration and its finance staff traditionally takes place during the next month or six weeks, or from March 15 to April 15 or May 1. This should be the time when carefully developed analyses can be related to requests to make next year's resource use more efficient than last year's. Too often under the traditional approach it is the time when new programs suggested by departments are cut out. The pruning is done so that last year's programs can still be funded out of the limited resources allocated to the department by the central budget office. Here again, the introduction of PPB and the new approach can help to change such procedures.

When the review of department request comes under the influence of PPB, the question "What are we really trying to accomplish, and for whom?" becomes important. For example, using the previous street maintenance and employment goal, the question may require a very substantial turnaround in the organization of the street maintenance department for a year. This, in turn, requires the street department to make a commitment to do what had been previously largely a hope and aspiration. When this mandate is carried out by the street department, it affects old programs in a number of departments, including personnel, law enforcement, welfare, and transportation.

Adequate preparatory work is necessary to bring about this radical change.

Implementation

It is also true adequate means must be employed to ensure that decisions are actually carried out. The mere announcement of budgetary provision is not enough. This task has been frequently assigned to the accountability aspect of budgeting, but it really cannot be carried out under this heading.

The critical factor is the city council, the mayor, and the city manager. Without their full authority and support, department and division chiefs will stretch the new budget document to provide legal support for carrying out what they want rather than what had been intended. After all, again using the street maintenance and unemployment example, it is easier to have a permanent work force to repair streets, and to use welfare to support the unemployed, and to keep prisoners in their cells, which is why these activities are nearly always carried out in this fashion.

Presentation

The problem of implementation is closely associated with the next traditional budget step—placing the budget before the budget committee of the city and presenting the chief administrator's budget message. The budget message remains vital under PPB procedures. However, because of the expanded quantity of analytical information developed in PPB, general statements justifying changes and explaining impacts need no longer be given. Instead, using the street maintenance example again, exact information can be given on the impact of the change on all aspects of the budget, as well as on the general efficiency of the public and private economies of the city.

This type of presentation answers a large portion of the stated and unstated objections to the provisions of the budget document. It also acts to largely prevent the chief administrator from stating pious hopes. The analyses have been a portion of too many program shifts in their movement to the decision to reach the established goal to make abandonment very feasible at this stage.

The traditional budget time now has one to two months for consideration by the city council's budget committee, for airing by the communications media, and for presentations to citizen groups. In these days of inflation and high taxes, a major portion of telling the public about the budget amounts to an effort to gain voter support for the additional revenues needed to meet budgeted expenses.

Possibly, its innovative methods of explaining to the voters why additional funds are needed will achieve the acceptance of PPB that has been so illusive among city councils, county boards of commissioners, state legislatures, and Congress. The results in this area aren't in yet; however, we are in the first few years of some earnest efforts to change.

The voters do not have an important power of overseeing government administration actions that have to be given up with the initiation of PPB and the allocation of power concerned with end purposes—the big picture—rather than fiscal details. Voters have been increasingly feeling that they don't know what they are getting for their taxes that helps them, their families, their communities, the country, and the world. Budgets with their item-by-item control have never been attractive to voters. Also, only an insignificant portion of the voters care what brand of equipment is used, while an elected representative may rely heavily on campaign support from a particular company or union.

The partial introduction of PPB will lead to press releases, using the street repair example again, explaining how the program will help provide prisoners with good work habits, avoid acceptance of welfare assistance, and stabilize local purchasing power. Voters will find this information helpful in understanding the benefit-cost relationship of tax payments. It is also quite possible PPB analyses will demonstrate that services now supported out of general tax revenues could be better carried out with financing from service charges.

The referral of the budget to a city council that sees oversight of administration as a principal function will also require continued submission of a line-item control budget as illustrated above. If a two-track budget operation is underway, the city council should be presented with a budget that gives end purposes as well as the control budget. In this way, some progress can be made toward moving the council toward policy control while avoiding the difficulty of either PPB or the old procedures. It is also true that making voters familiar with the end purpose budget should help the political decisionmakers make up their minds.

Budget Acceptance

The budget with the changes required to gain council approval is presented as an appropriation measure that must be formally adopted in ordinance form or as a resolution. New legislation may have eliminated old laws that required very detailed appropriation action.

The appropriation act that provides considerable detail is a control instrument. When much of the budget detail is a part of the appropriation act, the city council has strengthened its power of control and weakened administrative discretion. All appropriations approved at the adoption of the budget should be available for expenditure at any time during the budget period. Also, the council should permit the administration to freely transfer funds between purposes and to spend less than the total amount approved.

At this point, the final budget document is approved as amended. Here again, the form will be affected by the influence of PPB thinking. PPB has three major impacts: (1) the statement of a goal, (2) a description of the actions necessary to reach the goal, and (3) a listing of the departments that will be involved in reaching the goal. Again for simplicity, we can go back to our original goal of using the street repair activity to reduce unemployment in the city. It has been shown that the public works department and the welfare department would be the primary actors.

The final budget document that is preferred should reflect this evolving situation as an appendix to the more conventional presentation. This would permit city employees and voters to begin to grasp what is involved in the move toward PPB. To prevent PPB from failing, as the performance budget reform introduced twenty years ago in the Hoover Report failed, requires the development of a system that transfers control and management to lower levels of government bureaucracy. If this is not done, routine crises will preempt planning time and planning evaluation. The result of this will undoubtedly be a return to the nonplanned or nonevaluated government sector, except as planning takes place at the lower operating level. At the start, this more than likely requires a two-track budget system.

This point is very important if the drafting of PPB is to become more than a structural façade added onto the old procedures. When cities initiate PPB, they must make certain the concept is more than agency justifications restyled to look like PMs. Also, the existing organizational frame cannot be accepted as appropriate for the new program goals. Their continued use must be understood to be only a temporary expedient to be followed only as long as required because of circumstances that are to be changed as soon as possible.

Summary

The city budget is a plan with dollar signs to carry out the activities the community needs. The activities are difficult if not impossible to provide on an individual basis or by a voluntary organization. This budgetary activity must be performed carefully and rationally if the required service levels and cost ceilings are to be met.

The PPB approach to city budgeting has the requisite procedures for a functioning budgetary system that sets priorities on a basis of thoughtful consideration of costs and benefits. The adoption of PPB procedures, however, has been slow and hesitant. The local government tax revolt in progress in the late 1970s will stimulate examination of PPB-type analyses. After all, PPB is the rational way to allocate city resources, whether abundant or scarce.

8 Budgeting Reduced Revenues

In these days of belt-tightening in city finances, a well-considered city budget must provide in advance for an orderly movement to expenditure and service levels below those previously established. The first decision requires deciding whether to eliminate low-priority functions to balance income and outgo, whether to starve selected services, or whether to reduce functions and departments by an overall flat percentage. A city moving toward, or desiring to move toward, a planning-programming-budgeting system (PPB) has an opportunity to relate costs to functions rather than departments, which allows it to move toward a greater realization of city government actions by all those involved in benefit-cost relationships.

Budget Cutting

The need to provide for a procedure to fit the city operations within a reduced level of budgeted revenues can be used to increase the use of fees and charges. For example, sewerage fees can be levied on the basis of full costs of providing the service. As a result, this service can be placed on a fully self-financing basis, and available federal funds can be more completely and more quickly utilized. (See chapter 40.)

Sometimes it is useful to develop a chart that extends relative priorities to both capital and operating expenditures for city function clusters. The chart can provide for reductions, for example, 2 percent, distributed over all activities on the basis of allocated priorities. The same chart would provide for allocation of larger cuts if they became necessary. This procedure can reduce old services that have lost some of their usefulness as well as reduce the speed with which new technical developments are introduced.

The knowledge PPB provides can become the basis for selecting the proper mix of programs to minimize harmful effects of underfunding. At the lowest level PPB should permit economic allocation of resources to maximize program delivery with the reduced financing. Without PPB type of detail, budget cuts are much more likely to fall on politically defenseless projects. The information of PPB cannot be expected to always prevail over political expediency, but it will provide a fairly substantial hurdle to be overcome by both the politically oriented and those wishing to settle for the flat percentage reduction.

Capital Budgeting

The separation of the capital budget from the operating budget arose when operating budgeting was only done annually. Under these conditions, only major capital decisions required planning over a number of years. The introduction of planning in the development of operating budgets for a five-year period eliminates much of the singularity of the capital budget. (See chapter 11.)

Today it is the method of financing that frequently distinguishes capital from operating budgeting. Capital spending for buildings and sewers, roads, and the like is apt to be financed with a serial bond issue. This requires a special election plus setting aside funds to meet annual interest and retirement costs. It is also true that funds from the state or from the federal government are frequently available to assist in the financing of a certain designated capital spending activity. This has sometimes caused critics to shift their resources in a way that is harmful to very useful ongoing programs. The shift takes place because the new capital improvement requires maintenance funds and may inadvertently and rather directly cause a related area to use additional funds to permit full use of the new facility. A good PPB system would be expected to prevent these situations arising as a surprise.

This problem and related difficulties with categorical grants to cities have resulted in renewed discussion of the desirability of only block grants or revenue sharing. If this development should take place, cities with well-developed PPB systems will be able much more effectively to use funds that might vary rather widely from year to year.

The capital budget requirements that developed after World War II encouraged city planning. To an important degree, these groups should provide a core around which a PPB system can be developed.

Departmental Incremental Budgeting

The budget prepared and submitted by a department budget officer is nearly always based on last year's figures. This practice of incremental budgeting is defended on the grounds that much complexity, uncertainty, and needless repetitive estimating is avoided. It also, of course, largely represents the activities necessary for continuing the operations considered necessary for orderly functioning of city services.

The departmental budget is only directly concerned with funds to meet costs when its services are provided on the basis of fees, fines, and service charges or special assessments. The departments are therefore largely expenditure budget-oriented and tend to look to the finance department, which is really the top administration, city council, and the voters, for funds. This lack of balance in departmental budget thinking tends to reduce constructive revenue collection suggestions at the service-providing (that is, the lowest) level of city government.

Budget Decision Centers and Making Choices

If the budget process were a simple, straightforward operation, largely mechanical procedures would be adequate. Because this is not the case, administration and elected official action is necessary to resolve differences as the budget is developed. The development of the PPB system may at the city level run into the same roadblocks that arose when PPB was attempted at the federal level. The federal opposition resulted in legislation requiring retention of traditional expenditure data, as well as the new information arising from the introduction of PPB. Under these circumstances, constant reference to PPB information will gradually make this approach understandable and familiar. Also, because elected officials are project- and service-oriented, they find PPB meets most of their needs much better than the old format. It is also true that department administration officers finds PPB fits in with their customary thinking and, therefore, they find it easier to discuss and present this type of budget.

Innovation

Although the experience and background of elected officials and voters are certain to influence their decision-making process, city government budget requests are apt to lose support gradually if proof of innovation in both revenue raising and service provision is lacking. Innovation with meaning should arise from the sublevels of government itself. The soundest budget provisions, and the ones most acceptable to elected officials and voters, are hammered out by government operating units. If these units are concerned only with spending and service provision, their contributions to revenue provision are largely lost. The budgetary information available to decision centers is badly unbalanced if benefits of the spending other than giving someone a job or an order to a local merchant are not carefully substantiated. Frequently, these benefits include reductions of various costs, and it is also frequently true that charges can be collected from those benefiting most directly. To neglect such information is to abort the logic of the budgetary process. The result is likely to be decisions that fail to make the city as useful and efficient a political and economic unit as is possible within the system.

Recently, attention has been directed to the full social costs of private and public actions, such as highway construction, steel production, or the disposal of solid wastes. These new dimensions of the benefit-cost calculation require a broader and inevitably less precise, but at the same time, more complicated estimation of net benefit. No longer, for example, can highway construction be justified by proof that individual user choice is optimized. At this time, techniques for evaluating the total impact of an action on social and physical environment are in their infancy. It is the next great frontier in resource allocation decision making. Nowhere will progress towards this improvement in resource use be more important than in city budget making. In city budget making, as in many other aspects of our economic and social life, we are truly entering the age of externalities. External diseconomies are costs that must be included in the benefit-cost calculations of the future. The challenge will not be easily met by the cities who in most instances are still on the threshold of a careful evaluation of the benefits and costs directly related to programs recommended and being carried out.

Summary

Since the days of the great depression in the 1930s, the nation has been continually turning to government to solve the difficulties created by our rapidly progressing and expanding society. The ability of private organizations to adapt to the needs of these new requirements was seriously doubted. Distrust of private institutional solutions has been so high that in most instances they were rejected out-of-hand.

As the years passed, government came to occupy the time of a larger portion of the population and to absorb a larger portion of the resources of the nation, states, and cities. This new environment has achieved less than desired and, in many cases, less than expected. Under the impacts of these disappointments, appropriate policies will be sought to reduce the public sector and increase private sector responsibilities. This, of course, must be done without fundamentally injuring citizen satisfactions.

9 Tax and Spending-Level Ceilings

Tax and spending ceilings at all government levels are attempts to provide public sector leaders with a basis for rejecting or reducing the limitless expenditure requests. The public sector's use of service charges and prices for services will always include only a limited portion of economic activity appropriately allocated to the public sector. A very substantial portion of public sector activities are not likely to use prices and, in a considerable area of activity, prices are not workable. The usefulness of price in both rationing and in covering cost of provision is not available in the public sector when prices cannot be used.

Property Tax Limits

The limitation of public sector activity in the past has been aimed largely on setting limits on property tax collections. Limits were often set by requiring various voting procedure hurdles to be overcome successfully before more taxes, or more than a limited additional amount, could be collected. Limitations on property tax collections have been used for years. In the 1970s there was an upsurge in the enactment of this type of legislation. The most frequently advanced reasons for the quickening activity has been dissatisfaction with the expenditure trends and to provide property tax relief for homeowners on fixed incomes.

Both these difficulties to be relieved by property tax limitations arise largely from inflation. State and local government employees have joined unions in rising numbers to protect themselves from inflation. The market value of residential property has risen rapidly, often resulting in an increased portion of the property tax being collected from this portion of its base.

Available data show that in states with property tax limits, local government spending increases along with increases in per capita income. On the other hand in states without limits, this relationship does not exist and per capita incomes tend to increase more rapidly than state and local government expenditures. Looked at from a simple cause-and-effect relationship, we can conclude that property tax limits do not hold down property taxes but actually may cause them to increase. More than likely the data relationship is not that straightforward. Rather, the states with property tax limits were experiencing rapid expenditure increases while those without them were not being pressed to spend more as incomes increased.

Another comparison of interest is whether local governments are more or less active in using own-source revenues to finance their activities when property tax limitation legislation exists. The possibility of this relationship cannot be dismissed completely. However, the degree of use of own-source revenues by local governments is probably more closely related to state legislation encouraging local governments to initiate income and retail sales taxes than to property tax limitation.

The bottom line, as developed out of experience in the 1970s, is that legislated property tax limits move taxes somewhat away from the property tax and cause some lag in expenditure growth. Instead of limiting property taxes, if legislation were adopted that increased state aid to local governments, a similar tax impact could be expected in those localities where local officials were spending at a preferred rate that was not affected by the source of financing.

There are a number of varieties of property tax limitations. The trend recently has been toward levy restriction that sets a definite percentage increase limit for each user of the property tax base. The allowed levy increase can be expanded through a vote of a designated group or a special general election.

The levy limitation is superior to the rate limitation because it avoids problems such as higher collections through assessment percentage increases and through rising values from inflation that occur under rate limitation. If "superior" refers to a property tax limitation that permits adjustment to inflation and to a growing need for services, then the rate limitation approach has some advantages.

The levy limit is inferior to the rate limit when the area is growing rapidly. Under these circumstances, additional revenues would be collected under the rate limitation to meet the rising government needs without carrying out procedures to exceed the limitation. The levy limit would not respond to meet this need and the limit would have to be breached. This process is often slow, annoying, and expensive.

Full disclosure is a procedure to change the manner in which tax decisions are discussed before the budget is set for the next operating period. This directs political responsibility for a tax increase, either because of higher assessed values or an increase in tax rates, or both, to the local government responsible for the level of expenditures. Public hearings on why the tax levy is being increased must be held, and approval must be voted by the board.

Expenditure Limits

Service levels may be in excess and therefore expenditure controls may be appropriate in several instances: first, when persons with a low level of demand are offered more services than they can use; second, when levels of service are too high because of imperfections in the political process; and third, when the relationship between costs and benefits is misjudged so that either benefits are overestimated, costs are underestimated, or both occur. Of these three factors, the influence on action aimed at expenditure control can be judged socially desirable only in the third case. Even here, however, action aimed at providing the voter with more information would be better than expenditure control.

A common rational for expenditure control during great inflation has been excessive cost increases. Public sector costs rise more than most private sector costs because productivity growth in the largely service provision public sector is slower than in the more capital-intensive private sector. Another element has been unionization and the political strength of labor, which have acted to speed up public sector wage adjustments to match private sector levels. The public sector has been able in some cases to exceed the pension provisions of private sector contracts.

An aspect of the excessive cost increases, and therefore the need for expenditure limits, continues to be the reliance on the property tax, which tends to cut into capital accumulated as residences after retirement of the owner. The circuit breaker, by reducing the taxes of low-income receivers with homestead wealth, has been effective in overcoming some of this difficulty.

The attractiveness of real estate as an investment of the middle class, combined with the fact that real estate is the only form of wealth subject to an annual tax, that is, the property tax, has created a strong antipathy to this approach to raising public sector revenues. The politically strong middle class find themselves in the same camp as owners of large estates. The result is effective political pressure to reduce substantially the taxes of the very rich, while assisting the middle class to meet their capital accumulation goals.

Expenditure controls are likely to decrease the relative well-being of the poor more than of the rich. It will be more difficult, for example, to maintain the level of welfare payments than to continue the level of police patrol activity in the suburbs. Also, basic services, such as education, are available only in the public sector to the lower-income receivers, while alternative private institutions can be used by the rich. Reductions in the level of public education services will not only affect the poor because of the reduced quality of the instruction, but also through loss of emulation when middle- and upper-income children are sent to other schools. Finally, expenditure limits are more likely to affect conditions in the large cities where expenditures are relatively high than in the smaller cities. Again the lower-income receivers are apt to experience the greater reduction of public services.

Ceiling Impacts and New Approaches

State aid to local governments, particularly to school districts, is frequently determined on the basis of dollar of assessed value per student. The lower the dollar of assessed value per student, the higher the state aid. During inflation, this practice can result in reduced state aid while the local government's position has not improved. In fact, the local government's revenue-raising ability has deteriorated under conditions of a property tax levy ceiling that has not been adjusted upward to compensate for the reduced purchasing power of the dollar. Under both these circumstances, financing ability has decreased.

Expenditure and tax limits will affect the operations of government differently, depending on the current inflation rate. Limits set with the inflation rate included as an annual adjustment—that is, indexing—would stabilize the general impact of limits. A price index for each type of local government would be needed to reach the goal of keeping the real general impact of tax and expenditure limits constant.

Property tax relief legislation, such as circuit-breakers, delays in taxing the property of the elderly, or reduced taxes to encourage commercial and industrial development, can through reductions of the property tax base prevent expenditure and levy ceilings from developing a downward pressure on property tax rates. Higher property tax rates, which result from exemptions and delays, develop pressures to reduce the portion of expenditures financed with property taxes. Revenues to make up for a decline in property tax collections must come from either additional state and federal aid or from the introduction of local sales or income taxes.

In this instance, and perhaps under most conditions, property tax levy or rate limitation reduces the independence of local government and stimulates the adoption of new tax sources. At the rate things are going, both federal and state grants—the two separately, not together—will soon be greater than property tax revenues from the nation's twenty-five largest cities, excluding New York. Property tax limits of all kinds and other fiscal shifts during the past thirty years have reduced by one-third the portion of local government revenues from all sources provided by the property tax.

The introduction of new taxes at the local government level is one of the likely results of property tax limitations. A property tax limitation plus an expenditure limitation is likely to encourage provision of public services by state or federal government and reduced local government independence.

Forcing the adoption of other taxes to pay for expenditures supported by the voters results in a reduction of the net satisfaction of the cost-benefit relationship. Placing a ceiling on expenditures tends to reduce the portion of activities included within the public sector. If this results in an elimination of public expenditures that can be carried out as efficiently in the private sector as in the public sector, but are in the public sector largely as an historical accident or tradition—that is, water and sewage spending—then a net benefit could arise from expenditure ceilings. Continuation of inflation makes all ceiling and limiting fiscal legislative more complicated and more apt to result in unnecessary reductions in the community's level of satisfaction.

The establishment of "caps" or limits on the amount of spending and/or tax collections set as a fixed percentage of gross personal income of the state has been accepted by such states as New Jersey, Colorado, Tennessee, and Michigan. This type of limiting legislation at the state level sets a growth rate of the tax-expenditure limit (TEL) equal to that of the gross personal income of the state.

Summary

The public sector needs some method to justify turning down the growing quantity of expenditure requests. The tax-expenditure limit (TEL) concept in a number of forms seems to have a potential for such assistance. The experience data available do not provide a definite answer. As to the usefulness of tax and spending limitation legislation, the growth of legislative action in this area, at both state and local government levels, appears to demonstrate that TEL could be somewhat useful to budget directors in their efforts to keep the public sector within traditional relative levels. If the movement only results in additional demands for funding at the state or federal level, the result will be additional centralization and reduced local option. This would be an unfortunate outcome.

The federal government may need to develop such caps—perhaps a constitutional amendment making a deficit budget unlawful except under extreme emergency conditions.

Figure 9-1 was prepared by the Advisory Council on Intergovernmental Relations (ACIR). It is a useful summary of much that has been discussed in this chapter.

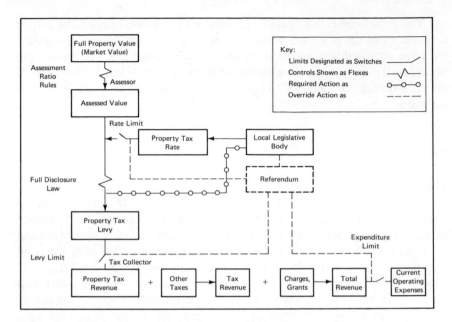

Source: Advisory Council on Intergovernmental Relations (ACIR) and University of Oregon Property Tax Seminars, 1978.

Figure 9–1. Limits and Controls in the Local Property Tax System.

Part III
Borrowing and
Capital Projects

10 Capital Project Evaluation

Outstanding local government debt is about twice the state total. The combined total of about $250 billion is nearly one-third the federal total. All government debt adds up to around $1 trillion. The federal government is a net payer of approximately $50 billion in interest, while state and local governments are net receivers of about $6.7 billion. The impact of government indebtedness on the efficient use of resources remains an area of difference of opinion.

The management of debt and debt policy is an important aspect of managing and financing state and local government. The insurance trust systems of state government hold some $100,073 million in cash and securities. The local governments hold about one-third this figure. State and local debt during the past several years has decreased as federal grants to state and local governments have been expanding along with the level of federal debt. (See chapter 40.)

Financing a Project

The extent to which public debt is different from private debt and federal debt different from state and local debt must be considered in setting state and local government borrowing and debt repayment decisions. One aspect of government debt different from private debt is that individuals and companies do not consider public debt to be a personal liability. Company X does not add to its private debt the portion of total public debt its GNP represents of total GNP. Federal debt is different from state and local government debt and private debt in that the central bank can be used to expand the credit supply to finance purchase of the debt.

All debt other than federal debt is a burden if the expenditures financed by the debt do not result in a benefit equal to the sacrifice the debt required in savings—that is, delay of consumption, repayment of debt, and taxes not available to finance current government activity. Whether a particular project should be undertaken is a decision separate from the decision to borrow. Any project that provides benefits in excess of sacrifices should be carried out. Interest payments mean the sacrifices are increased if the project is financed with borrowed funds rather than paid from current collections. These additional sacrifices of borrowing may not be as great as the disutilities of increasing taxes to cover costs as incurred. When this calculation is made, a rational decision to borrow or not to borrow or to abandon the project can be made.

A Borrowing Decision

The desirability of a state or local government entering into an agreement to borrow a quantity of funds to build a sewage system that reduces pollutants washed into a neighboring river seldom is considered when deciding whether a predetermined social rate of discount will be earned by the project. Sewage pollutes if it is not treated. It costs money both to finance the original investment and to cover operating expenses of a sewage disposal system. Action is required and the rate of return on the investment cannot usefully be measured.

A dollar value is never placed on the return enjoyed because of the investment in a sewage disposal system. To use this calculation to determine whether or not the system should be installed is not helpful. On occasion it can be decided whether a centralized or decentralized system of individual units should be used. When this is the case the investment and capital costs of the two systems should be compared. If the decentralized disposal approach did as good a job in all respects as the centralized system the relative price would become a prime element in making a decision.

If the original investment for the decentralized system would be less than for the centralized system, but operating costs would be higher, the price of borrowed funds would become an important element in the decision process. The market rate of interest varies from high to low by as much as 50 percent. This variation increases in importance as the portion of costs consisting of depreciation increases; that is, the greater the capital intensity and durability of the project.

The decision to borrow to improve the sewage system should be made on the basis of minimizing costs. If the money market is tight, interest rates are high, and at the same time federal sewage grants are available and the current system is causing a serious river pollution problem, several new considerations enter into the decisionmaking process.

First, unusually high interest rates—50 percent above the level of a few years ago—must be considered in deciding whether to borrow for the short term and refinance later when interest rates are back down to normal; finance for the long term and decide on the less capital intensive system; or delay, hoping federal grants will continue to be available. If the last choice is not really available because pollution abatement has become a political must, then the cost of funds will basically determine the action to be taken.

The political decision to install a modern, efficient sewage disposal system might become unglued if the cost of borrowed funds raises the price above the level originally expected. Under these circumstances, the method of financing the project must be reexamined.

The original financing might not have made any provision for assessing higher costs on those living beyond the average distance of users from the sewage plant. The assessment of the higher price on those at a distance would increase the general justice of the financing and provide the funds necessary to meet the interest cost and the repayment schedule of the borrowed funds. The new fee charges will meet depreciation and other operating costs of the capital intensive sewage disposal approach. Financing is in order and the government is ready to carry out the borrowing operation and to make the commitments necessary to solve the sewage pollution problem.

Borrowing

The advice of the state attorney general is helpful even though it is decided later to turn over all of the details of the loan to a firm or consultant specializing in servicing state and local governments making a debt obligation. Nine general aspects of a bond offering must be a part of the agreement: (1) maximum maturity, (2) debt service structure, (3) call provision, (4) maximum call price as percent of par, (5) manner of sale, (6) award basis, (7) minimum sale price as percent of par, (8) maximum interest rate, (9) computation of interest rate (whether net interest cost (NIC) or true interest cost (TIC) is to be used in evaluating bids and awarding of contracts). (See chapter 12.)

The borrowing of state and local government units is subsidized by the federal government. The subsidy is given by exempting interest paid on state and local debt from income taxable by the federal government. This subsidy benefits largely those subject to high personal income and corporate profits taxes. This reduced debt cost justifies state and local governments being more capital intensive than the federal government or private investors. In terms of deciding between the two sewage disposal systems, a city might minimize costs by using the capital-intensive system while the federal government would find the system requiring less capital less costly.

Justice of Borrowing

To a degree, justice to residents is highest if all capital goods are purchased with borrowed funds and paid off as the good wears out. When this is done everyone pays for the good as enjoyed. When a large capital expenditure is made from current tax revenues, intergeneration equity is destroyed. Future inhabitants benefit without paying. This would not exist if a large capital purchase of some kind was being made just about every year or month. Under these circumstances pay-as-you-go financing of capital goods enjoys intergenerational equity while also saving interest and debt management costs.

The desirability of borrowing to pay for a machine or building in the private sector can be determined on the basis of expected cost, productivity, and selling price of production. In the public sector, these tests are generally not available. To overcome this shortcoming and to provide a basis for judging whether an investment like a power dam should be made, the concept of the social rate of discount (mentioned above) has been developed.

Social Discount

If this social discount or interest rate is set at the correct level, and an investment in a government project is not made unless the calculated social discount to be expected is higher or equal to the market rate of interest, then the level of public investment is justified by its relative productivity. The social discount rate rests, in the case of dams, for example, on such factors as the sale price of electric power, value of fish catch, number of tourists, and boats that would navigate the water.

The earnings of all these uses vary through the years. Some, while being productive as measured at the project, cause an overall economic deficit impact. The fish sales reduce what farmers can get for their cattle. The river navigation reduces the business of railroads. The hydroelectric power delays efforts to use solar energy. Finally, the vacationists have been attracted away from other resorts. This, of course, is part and parcel of all investments. The difference here is that the government has attracted capital from the private sector to do damage to the private sector. Perhaps, if all costs were included, the social discount rate would not equal the opportunity cost of the capital used by the government. Recently many have said, for example, that the cost of environmental destruction is much higher than estimated because good natural environment has become much more valuable as its scarcity has increased.

Industrial Bonds

State and local governments have been given a free hand by the federal government to issue industry development bonds that are used to finance pollution abatement facilities. The effect of issuing these pollution abatement securities as well as small issues of less than $1 million for industrial development is to absorb the investment funds of those who benefit most from the federal income tax exemption of interest on state and local government securities.

A reduction of the reservoir of investment funds that find state and local securities attractive increases the interest rate on these securities. The use of funds from the state and local government security investment reservoir to fund pollution abatement and small industrial development issues reduces the ease with which regular state and local government debt can be funded.

Any relaxation in the limitation on the purpose for which securities with interest exempt from the federal income tax may be issued reduces the value of the exemption to established issuers. Outstanding tax-exempt securities will weaken in the market and new issues will have higher interest rates. To a degree, therefore, all taxpayers pay a portion of the benefit enjoyed by small industrial bonds and pollution abatement bonds because of their tax exemption feature.

The value of air pollution abatement equipment purchased was about $572 million in 1976. This total is nearly $100 million less than in 1974. In 1973, the first year for which data are available, purchases totaled $383 million. Water pollution abatement in 1976 is set at $76 million, slightly higher than in 1974, according to 1976 census figures. Over 93 percent of the funds came from industry. The federal government provides the remainder. State and local governments are providers of funds only indirectly, as described above.

Summary

Capital investment and related borrowing decisions of state and local governments possess many of the same characteristics and, therefore, difficulties existing in establishing levels of current expenses. One type of question related to this basic aspect of financing and managing state and local government is whether going into debt to finance a project that will provide sufficient earnings to meet the borrowing costs, and therefore one that can be financed with revenue bonds, is preferable to borrowing to finance a project not producing revenues and financed from general taxes.

The concept of a social rate of discount distinct from the rate established in the market has been developed for use in the public sector to evaluate the desirability of public borrowing. The value placed on the productivity of the public investment is capitalized with the use of this social rate of discount. The social rate of discount, which is basically set by government on the basis of social objectives, should be set below the market rate because the time preference of government investment is longer than that of companies or individuals.

Although the concept of the social rate of discount is helpful in understanding what is involved in setting public sector investment policy, it is not helpful in deciding most state and local government capital project priorities. These governments work with a number of conditions—such as categorical grants, political commitments, citizen safety—in making capital project evaluations and decisions. These are not appropriately decided by whether the productivity level is equal to some social rate of discount.

11 Capital Budgeting

The capital budget provides funds for the purchase or construction of a facility that, along with appropriate personnel and energy resources, will provide services or physical goods for a number of years. Typically, being included in the capital budget also means the acquisition is unusual and is likely to be one of a kind, which rules out regular replacement expenditures for typewriters, automobiles, and the like.

Capital budget requests require considerable prior background development of data and trends in many areas. Both land use studies and economic base studies should be completed in enough detail to permit a determination of likely intensity of use of the capital investment. Facility use level immediately on completion and through the life of the project are likely to require information on growth rate of industries within the project's service area, plus expected new industry, housing, and transportation developments. Each source of growth or reduction of use of the proposed facility must be researched in sufficient depth to develop useful figures.

Basic Considerations

Land use studies are particularly helpful when they provide a detailed inventory of land to be used for various purposes, as established in current zoning and environment maintenance requirements. A particular industry may have great growth potential and an abundance of suitable land, transportation, energy, and labor that can be acquired. Growth cannot proceed, however, if additional pollutants are produced and the new zoning needed cannot be expected to be acceptable.

Demographic and population characteristic studies can be most helpful in making a decision to construct, for example, either a swimming pool or center for the elderly in a new park. Data on existing population characteristics and action directions can also give capital budget builders helpful information for use in the preservation of the neighborhood before severe deterioration sets in.

Frequently, capital expenditures provide the capital basics of services such as transportation, education, recreation, sewage, and water. If these investments are made in a particular area, growth will be stimulated there and very likely retarded elsewhere. Many land use decisions are being made when basic service-related capital investments arc decided. Because capital investment to modernize an area originally developed under prior conditions

73

presents many difficulties, including high land costs and destruction of existing structures, capital expenditure decisions are always being nudged toward new outlying areas. An excellent way to make certain wise, long-term decisions are being made in these kinds of capital investment decisions is to develop a tax base and service cost comparison when an outlying and when a city basic service capital improvement is made.

Cash Flow

Local governments can always make additional beneficial capital improvements in many places. Also, there is always insufficient cash flow under existing taxes and other revenue sources. Under these circumstances, the temptation to favor capital investments that can directly generate a cash flow is strong. A swimming pool with its earnings estimates would get the nod over a public park with little or no direct revenues.

Cost-Benefit Analysis

The development of a cost-benefit study to determine the more efficient investment is very difficult (see chapter 10). Yet a study that realistically estimates costs and benefits is absolutely necessary in developing a capital expenditure program. Quantifying benefits is generally more difficult than quantifying costs. (Because of the progress that has been made in estimating externalities and spillover effects, this is less true today than previously.) An efficient sewage disposal facility provides substantial beneficial spillovers and externalities to those living down the river. Much of the benefit of a sewage facility is enjoyed by those not directly using the facility. Unless these "outside" benefits are compared with the cost, the capital invested in sewage disposal facilities, based on a use-benefit analysis, would be inadequate.

The relationship of cost to benefit can be rectified by enlarging the support area sufficiently to include a very large portion of total benefits—for example, benefits to those living down the river. This relationship is one of the cogent arguments favoring state, multistate, and national assistance in financing and planning capital investments with large externalities and spillovers.

Discounting Value of Benefit Flow

The benefit flow of a capital good continues during the life of the capital if the related service is helpful over this full period. An investment providing maximum services early in its life generates a greater benefit flow per unit of service than an investment with a relatively large productivity, but only after a number of years.

This relationship is based on the concept of the present value of a distant flow of services discounted by the time preference rate—that is, the going interest rate. Under this concept, the sum of all the present values expected to flow from the investment must equal or be greater than the total cost of the investment. This total is called the net present value (NPV) and looks, in theory at least, to be a very straightforward procedure for use in making decisions about preferred capital investments.

Actually, the concept is plagued with difficulties and is useless except as a means of developing a gross idea of the net benefits from an investment commitment. NPV requires, for example, an assumption of the market level of interest rates during the life of the project. This is only possible on the cost side if a borrowing operation has been completed. This known capital cost rate is not the proper one to use in arriving at present value of future benefits. (See chapter 12.) Also, NPV requires money value be placed on benefits as they are enjoyed through the life of the investment, another nearly impossible estimate to make, except in the grossest terms.

Voter Preference

Many capital projects are subject to voter approval. The voters look at how they and their section of the local government's area will be served by the proposed project. In these days of high taxes, the cost allocation and the increase that will be required in the property tax rate will often determine how the vote goes. It is always helpful in getting voter approval if the local government can point to resources that will be provided by other levels of government if the project is undertaken. In fact, this argument is apt to be so strong that it will stimulate projects with a low local NPV because the local out-of-pocket cost against which benefits are measured is so low. The justification for this state of affairs has to be that externalities and spillovers are very large for the projects, otherwise they would not be enjoying support from higher levels of government.

Records of voter acceptance and rejection of capital projects show that voters are rather sensitive to interest rate shifts—that is, when interest rates are unusually high, more projects are rejected. Voter acceptance is, however, higher during prosperity when interest rates tend to be higher than during recession. Also, particular types of projects are popular for a time and then they are replaced by another type. Apparently, recent tax increases to pay for general operations will reduce voter support for new capital projects.

Fiscal Capacity

Capital budget expenditures must rely on a cash flow in excess of that required to meet current expenses and the costs of carrying and retiring outstanding debt. A projection of the revenue flows and cash needs for five years into the future should always be made to provide an understanding of the possibility of the development of serious cash shortages. A government's fiscal capacity goes beyond the relationship between budgetary receipts and expenditures. Fiscal capacity rests fundamentally on the strength of the economic base subject to taxation in relation to current costs of government and the projected costs.

An expanded capital budget that will not require a local government levy of property taxes at a rate above the average prevailing in the area or that will not necessitate introduction of a new revenue source must be considered to be within the government's fiscal capacity. Another relationship related to fiscal capacity is voter confidence, as reflected by the support given to bond measures. Finally, confidence in the government may exist and current tax requirements may not be out of line, but a fiscal capacity that relies to a larger than average extent on grants and revenue sharing is in danger of proving to be inadequate some place down the road. Therefore, allowance must be made for revenue source in evaluating the fiscal capacity of an area to enter into new capital projects.

A convenient test of fiscal capacity used by municipal bond analysts is the percentage that debt service charges are of current revenues. The approach is sound only if the government unit is using average tax rates and if the own-source revenues are also typical. A better quick evaluation of the degree to which fiscal capacity is utilized is to compare total own-source revenue trends to debt service charge trends. Again, however, by not considering how typical the existing fiscal levels are, the measure fails to warn of an upcoming crunch.

Revenue Bonds

The issuance of revenue bonds can solve the problem of inadequate fiscal capacity of a government unit or the unwillingness of voters to commit themselves to additional taxes to support a new capital project. An auditorium or a hospital are capital projects that can be the source of considerable revenues and, therefore, can carry a large portion of the costs of finance and maintenance. These facilities can also add to the enjoyment and general life standards of the residents of a community. Therefore, the revenue bond procedure, which is outside the full faith and credit of the government's resources, can be used to cover debt and maintenance costs. Regular debt plus funds from other levels of government, usually the federal level, can finance the original construction and land acquisition costs.

Revenue bonds, because they entail some risk of repayment, bear a higher rate of interest and therefore increase the price that must be charged users of the facility. This shortcoming is rather frequently outweighed by the desirability of action before approval for regular financing is received. Revenue bonds of local governments to finance environment improvement facilities of local industries have been particularly popular. Industry likes the procedure because the exemption of the interest paid from the federal, personal and corporate income tax assures lower interest rates. Citizens acquiesce because the action helps to improve their environment.

Summary

The capital budget can become an opportunity for utilizing much basic data that are too seldom evaluated and used by state and local governments. The evaluation necessary to determine whether to build a capital project that may take years to complete and will be used by the residents of the area for a long time can have a useful secondary purpose. The evaluation, if properly done and widely discussed, will give the governments and citizens of the area an additional understanding of how their area is developing. This should improve overall and individual economic decision making.

The selection of capital projects cannot be a completely scientific process. The cost-benefit analysis in practice includes some heroic assumptions. Nevertheless, the approach forces asking the right questions; the results should help the voters who must vote on the bond issue needed to carry out the financing.

Capital budgeting is partially a procedure to take the lumpiness out of the regular operations budget. This process also provides some additional support for the use of debt to finance a portion of government expenditures. Although pay-as-you-go financing of capital as well as operating budgets has some support, pay-as-you-go budgeting of capital expenditures has much less support than such financing of the operating budget.

12 Debt Management

Government debt is basically a procedure for current taxpayers to allocate a portion of the capital cost and, in some instances, the cost of day-to-day operations onto the shoulders of future taxpayers. Many taxpayers of the future, however, will directly and indirectly pay taxes today. Therefore, the decision to borrow is also affected by whether existing taxpayers would rather cover all costs currently or whether they would prefer to stretch out the payment over a number of years.

Inflation Considerations

During periods of rising costs the early completion of a necessary project can result in considerable savings of future dollars. These savings may be eaten up in the added project cost arising from interest payments, which are usually considerably higher than normal during inflation periods. Nevertheless, the argument that early construction is desirable during inflation because of expected dollar savings has proved to be a considerable inducement to borrowing by state and local governments.

In the past, inflation and high interest rates have been characteristics of the economy found during economic prosperity and a high level of employment. Under these conditions, the speeding up of capital development encountered difficulties resulting from labor shortages and arguments of those who favored expenditure timing that worked toward stabilization of employment. When high unemployment is accompanied by inflation and high percentage interest rates, timing to stabilize employment does not coincide with low interest rates and a low level of inflation. The inducement provided by inflation counteracts the interest rate detraction as long as the yields required on new offerings stay within the parameters set by the inflation rate.

Arbitrage

Debt offerings of state and local governments enjoy an interest cost advantage over private and federal securities. The lower interest rate required by the money market arises from the fact the interest received by owners of municipals (that is, state and local government securities) is exempt from the federal income tax.

This lower interest rate on municipals has encouraged state and local governments to borrow funds prior to need. The difference in interest rates received when these funds are invested and cost of the borrowing is "arbitrage" to the state or local issuer. The U.S. Treasury does not favor this type of financial operation, with the result that it has been limiting arbitrage opportunities. The relationship, however, remains available and the earnings likely are high enough to encourage borrowing of all funds required for a project at its initiation and investing the original excess of funds. The amount invested is gradually reduced as required payouts are made.

Industrial Financing

The tax advantage enjoyed by the interest income of municipals has encouraged the use of municipal borrowed funds to finance industrial investment within the borrowing jurisdiction. The tax advantage available has been gradually limited by the U.S. Treasury, but it remains sufficient to provide tax-free financing of medium-sized investments and will apparently remain unrestricted on pollution control investments.

The temptation is strong to use the credit standing of a local or state government to issue debt to finance private investment undertakings that can be attracted by this assistance. When the fund-raising corporation is large, with a high ratio of equity to debt capital, the decision to induce development is not a high-risk undertaking for a city. When this is not the case, possible misuse of the city's borrowing power and actual monetary loss are high. On a broader perspective, industrial borrowing is undesirable because it increases the quantity of the exempt securities, which in turn acts to increase the relative interest rates on municipals generally. (See chapter 10.)

Market and Economic Influences

The finance officer facing the need to enter the capital markets for borrowed funds frequently has some timing leeway. This flexibility permits picking a borrowing time in which the market appears to be as receptive as it is going to be in the near future. *The Daily Bond Buyer* and *Barron's* provide the best current information in sufficient detail to permit understanding the present market for municipals. The impressions gained from the study and analysis of these publications should be checked with a reliable specialist in municipals. Finally, local issues can frequently be sold to local commercial banks and other local financial institutions and investors at a favorable relative cost. The exploration of the potential of the local market and the resulting direct placement can save a considerable portion of the usual fee charged by investor bankers and brokers.

The relationship existing in the market between long- and short-term interest rates and between municipals and other securities provides the key to the timing of a new security offering or other borrowing decision. When short-term interest rates approximate long-term rates—that is, when the yield curve is flat, it usually means the money market is tight and that this tightness will continue for only a brief time. It is a bad time to consolidate bank loans and other borrowing needs into a short- or medium-term security offering. Instead, the finance officer should renew his bank line of credit or enter the long-term market.

Obviously, when interest rates throughout the maturity period are unusually high, capital improvements requiring extensive use of borrowed funds should be delayed. Actually, state and local governments have practiced this degree of flexibility. During general high interest rate periods of the past some 40 percent of planned financing has been delayed or canceled.

State and local government reaction to high interest rates was formerly considered to be helpful in setting desirable economic stability policy for the nation. As we pointed out, high interest rates meant full employment and an overstretched economy. Under these conditions, a reduction of state and local government investment projects would assist in keeping the economy sound. Recently, high interest rates and underutilization of resources have existed side by side. Stagflation, as this relationship is sometimes called, makes it desirable economic policy for state and local governments to go forward with their projects even though interest rates are unusually high. Inflation, with little possibility of falling prices, also points toward the desirability of proceeding with any investment needs and plans.

Bond Elections

Although bond election procedures and timing are basically political decisions, the finance professional often becomes deeply involved. A good portion of educating the public to the desirability of borrowing now must be developed by the finance department of the borrowing government unit. The services that will be provided by the new facility and the related costs are also an important portion of this education.

The results of the bond election can also affect the interest rate set in the market. A bond issue that is not accepted enthusiastically by the voters is apt to get a similar reception by the market. Buyers of securities also see a record of bond rejections as indicating the government unit is reaching its taxpaying limit. On the other hand, readily approved bond offerings point to citizen willingness to meet new financial commitments. This favorable attitude can result in lower interest rates and therefore lower costs and lower taxes.

Call Provisions

A debt offering with a call provision generally permits payment by the borrower before maturity. The call price is usually at or close to the par price of the security. This provision permits the borrower to benefit from lower interest rates that may arise in the market during the life of the debt instrument.

Even though interest rates do not fall (that is, when the security was sold at par and remains at par), call provisions can be useful to the government unit borrowing. Sometimes unexpected revenues become available and early retirement of debt outstanding is judged to be the best use of the funds. A call provision is also useful when the original borrowing was accomplished only through the use of restrictive covenants. Since then, conditions have changed/ new loan arrangements can be completed without such covenants. These benefits of a call provision can apparently be enjoyed without any increase in contract interest cost.

Interest (Coupon) Structure

Municipalities have been beset with curious interest rate structures dreamed up by managers of buying syndicates to win competitive bids. All these devices actually result in inefficient bids because true interest cost, which takes into consideration the timing of interest payments, is not considered. That is, a dollar paid as interest ten years in the future is considered to have the same value today as a dollar of interest paid tomorrow.

Interest calculated in this fashion encourages high interest rates on early maturities and low interest on late maturities of a serial issue. This, of course, is the reverse of the typical situation existing in the money market, which basically follows the principles of annuity mathematics. The so-called interest structures developed by the complex bid offers of government bond houses result in a higher total borrowing cost if future money is worth less than current money, a basic assumption of annuity mathematics.

The best approach for managers of a new offering of state and local government serial bonds is to follow the interest rates as shown by the average yield curve on municipals. The yield curve, under relatively normal monetary conditions, reports lower interest rates on short-term maturities and gradually rising interest rates up to about fifteen-year maturity periods. From the fifteen-year maturity until the thirty-year maturity, the interest rate is very gradually rising. This information is available from *Moody's* and *The Daily Bond Buyer*.

The approach requires rather elaborate bond offer specifications, but it is quite possible.

For many years, the Canadians placed a true interest cost on serial securities through use of current value formulas. The Center for Capital Market Research at the Graduate School of Management and Business of the University of Oregon (Eugene) has developed a rule (algorithm) for solving this type of problem. Finally, the whole problem of setting suitable interest rates for the varying maturities of a serial bond can be thrown into the hands of the market. When this is done, the interest rate on all maturities is the same, and the market sets different prices for different maturities. Some issues will sell above par and some below. Under these conditions, the bidding of municipal dealers will result in an interest rate structure about the same as from the annuity approach.

Financial Reporting

Local governments in particular, but also state governments, must upgrade their financing reporting. Under existing practices, the investor cannot get a clear picture of the financial strength of the government unit offering the debt. Most annual reports do not provide a useful summary of local government finance conditions. And generally accepted accounting principles for municipalities just don't do what is needed to inform the investing public.

Some of the reforms in financial reporting that have been recommended by study groups include the following:

1. Provide sufficient pension and employee benefit data so their impact on operating and investing funds available can be judged.
2. Initiate disclosure requirements similar to those required of private companies by the SEC.
3. Disclose lease commitments on private property rented by governments and the conditions under which private users utilize government facilities.
4. Establish a balance sheet reflecting the local government's assets and liabilities on a full-accrual basis.
5. Present a single concise set of financial statements reflecting the fiscal condition of the government unit.

Summary

Borrowing funds by local governments and to a lesser extent states has been stimulated by the relative low interest rate the market sets on their debt instruments. This tax-exempt advantage has been transferred to the financing of business and housing through state and local governments entering into the private lending business.

The desirability of a borrowing decision by any state or local government is influenced by many factors. The rate of inflation acts on construction project timing. The relative tightness of the money market affects the level of interest rates that the securities will bear. Borrowing to finance businesses can be a way to meet competition for new employers and an additional tax base. The list goes on, but in most cases it is not a decision made by a trained executive on the advice of experts. Rather, the decision is made by the citizens in the voter booth. And they, plus others who become residents, must pay the interest and retire the debt.

13 City Financial Emergencies

Municipal economic conditions are affected by various types of external shifts. The examination of these externalities along with independent and related city management and finance decisions provide some insights into why cities experience financial emergencies. The seriousness of the crisis is related to survival measures as well as to the characteristics of the original situation.

Defaults

Mobile, Alabama, experienced the first recorded city default in 1838. The records show that before 1860, only nineteen cities encountered sufficiently serious financial problems to force default of indebtedness contracts. The external cause was apparently bank failures and some general tight money conditions that made loan renewal difficult.

After the Civil War the indebtedness of local governments grew rapidly, and so did defaults. During the 1873–79 period, about 25 percent of local indebtedness was in default. The expansion of local government debt had been particularly rapid in areas of the South operating with carpetbagger governments. The debts were often made to finance business undertakings, particularly railroads and real estate developments. About 65 percent of the defaults during the 1870s occurred in debt obligations issued to assist railroads in providing local services.

Another period of substantial municipal financial difficulty arose during the economic crisis of 1893. In the late 1880s and early 1890s, local governments borrowed extensively for general improvements and private development schemes. The general boom psychology of the period added to the acceptability of expanded local government indebtedness. The defaults in 1893 were large, but considerably less than in 1873, even though the level of local government debt at $1 billion was twice as large as in 1873.

From 1893 until 1917, local governments settled into a period of conservative financing. A few defaults, such as in Duluth, Minnesota, arose from overexuberant real estate development projects or from a disaster, such as that in Galveston, Texas; in addition, a few western irrigation districts went broke.

Those who thought local government defaults arose only during an economic crisis such as that of 1873 and 1893 were due for a surprise. The prosperous period of the 1920s proved to be local government debt default-prone. Many of the defaults and state assumption of local government debt obligations were special assessment bonds. The debt expansion of local governments to meet demands for services in excess of willingness to pay accelerated, despite an increase in municipal debt default.

The economic boom of the 1920s was not only in the stock market. A very active real estate boom also took place. To continue, it required local government commitment to invest in additional schools, streets, and sewers. In addition, there was an active demand for improved services and a lack of state controls over local government debt levels.

Then came the morning after. In 1932, debt service charges had risen to 19.7 percent of state and local government revenues. Ten years earlier, the percentage was 12.7. Property tax delinquency was already up to 19.9 percent and rose to a peak of 26.3 percent in 1933. The quantity of debt in default reached $2.6 billion, about 17.7 percent of the total outstanding debt.

Just as quickly as the local government credit crisis arose in the 1930s, state assistance and rising property assessment values restored the credit conditions to normalcy. Some 48 cities with populations of at least 25,000 that were in default in 1933 had corrected the problem by 1938.

The defaults of the 1930s deserve study to determine how that experience can be of assistance in meeting today's financial difficulties of local government and particularly city government. The actual defaults today are not, however, of cities, with Cleveland and New York possible exceptions, but are largely of turnpike, bridge, and tunnel commissions. The current amount of debt in actual default is really very small, around $500 million. About 80 percent of this total consists of the debt of commissions organized to establish highway toll facilities. However, some cities are in actual default today and many more could be in serious trouble if a sharp decline in economic activity comparable to that of 1873, 1893, or 1933 should arise. Even without a general economic decline, suburban development and central city budgets, already in a weakened position, are being struck a body blow as constitutional limits on use of the property tax are adopted and as the real estate boom matures.

The municipalities that have gone into default during the past twenty years have often experienced declining populations or growth realizations far below expectations. Another common element is a sharp decline of the economic base. Finally, as has been true throughout the history of the nation, financial difficulties follow when a complete lack of planning characterizes the management of municipal financing affairs.

Financial Condition Causes

City expenditures, as measured by the national income explicit price deflator for all state and local governments, have been consistently rising more rapidly than the Consumer Price Index (CPI). The higher wages paid the employees of city governments have equaled the inflation rate plus the increase in productivity of the private sector. In addition, cities have found it necessary to hire many relatively highly trained employees to teach the handicapped, to prevent air and water pollution, to reduce crime, to control traffic, and to collect and dispose of solid wastes and sewage. The costs of these new and better provided services add to the costs already arising from inflation and union rivalry aimed at keeping ahead of each other in the level of fringe benefits, including reduction of hours worked.

Local government expenditures measured on a per capita dollar basis are much higher in the central city (CC) than in outside central city (OCC) areas. A major cause of this differentiation is the higher noneducation expenditures in the CC than in the OCC. In the OCC, the emphasis on education, measured as a percentage of total local expenditures going for education, is 50 percent greater than in the CC. In the CC, about one-third of the budget is allocated to education.

Despite the pressures for higher noneducation expenditures in the CC, they frequently receive less per capita federal intergovernmental aid than the OCC. In addition, state aid for education is very likely to be higher in the suburbs than in the central city.

The relatively heavy emphasis on education expenditures in the OCC may be reaching the point of diminishing returns. On the other hand, the OCC is becoming contaminated with the expenditure pressures formerly isolated largely in the CC. This trend is requiring the OCC to develop an infrastructure that needs substantial tax support. The overall tax level effect of more federal aid to CC and the expansion of noneducation OCC expenditures is causing a trend of OCC tax collection that is rising more rapidly than collections in the CC.

State Control of Local Government Finances

Under the popular home rule concept, local governments are placed pretty much on their own. Home rule accepts the argument that conditions vary from city to city and county to county and that this difference can become a portion of the government procedures only if local government uniformity imposed by states is prevented through comprehensive state home rule legislation. To avoid the need for special assistance legislation to bail out local governments in serious financial difficulties, most home rule believers favor standby legislation that gives state government the power to step in when the best interests of all the citizens of the state are threatened.

Home rule gradually phases into a state and local government relationship that is best called a system of limited state administrative controls. The state under this procedure becomes intimately involved in the results of the fiscal policy of the local government. The state, for example, has the power to require a local government to bring current revenues into line with current expenditures.

State power of this sort leads to political interference by the state house into local politics. If the local political group is favored by the state power structure, an easygoing relationship can exist. Without such favor, constant interference and bad management practices can result. One area of state action with the potential for much good and little bad is in the provision of advisory services through a strong state agency operating in close cooperation with the state university and other colleges and universities of the state.

Complete state control of local government financial management is rather rare in the United States, and really only exists as a general practice in New Jersey and West Virginia. The depression of the 1930s stimulated legislation to broaden state control over financial matters of local governments.

Rather than having the state continually approving and disapproving most budget items, a formal state review of the local government financial activities at the end of each year might be appropriate. This review would include a carefully prepared recommendation for fiscal policy during the next year, as well as specific comments about proposals that are under consideration.

The right degree of local government financial freedom is important. One rule that can be used in all cases is to minimize the amount of routine paperwork. Regulation that consists of little more than papershuffling is costly and reduces local government responsibility without developing a worthwhile replacement.

There is no easy, obvious way of deciding who has ultimate responsibility for making sure the entire state is not harmed by unsound fiscal practices of one or a few local governments. A review board consisting of accounting and management specialists holds many advantages. But to give these specialists some political support and guarantee of competency, they would have to be nominated by the different state organizations of the different specialties and approved by the governor.

Summary

City financial crises have again become an important aspect of the operations of our federal system. This was also true during the great economic depressions of the 1870s, the 1890s and the 1930s. In these three periods, prices generally, and the value of land in particular, suffered sharp declines. The decline in real estate values cut sharply into tax collection levels.

The urban financial crises of today are generally not closely related to declining prices. Only some land values in a portion of some central cities have declined. Generally speaking, however, real estate prices have remained strong during the current difficulties. The financial weakness today comes from sources quite different from those of the past. The flight of urban capital from the city centers to the suburbs, with the city centers continuing to carry heavy expenditure loads in addition to education costs was not a part of earlier city financial emergencies.

Today, city taxpayers refuse to vote sufficient taxes, not because property values are falling, but because they don't wish to accept responsibility for costs arising from union contracts, state and federal legislation, and the like. In addition, the city can look to the federal government for revenue sharing; traditional expenditure responsibilities such as welfare, can be shifted to the state and federal levels.

Today we have a new type of city financial emergency. The old approaches of economy and good administration remain helpful, and will have to do until a new federalism is hammered out.

14 Cash Management

The management of cash by the state or local government finance officer has two fundamental goals, both of which work to minimize costs. The first aim is to minimize net transaction costs. These costs consist of money actually paid out less earnings during period funds held after transaction is completed. The second cost minimization goal is subjective and not actual. Here the cost is opportunity cost of interest earnings foregone to enjoy the convenience or satisfaction of a designated degree of liquidity.

Cost Control

Many transactions costs are approximately the same no matter whether a million or a thousand dollars is involved. Secretarial, office space, and often communication and decisions costs are examples of this type of cost. Other costs, such as brokerage fees and interest foregone during transaction and transfer period vary with the size of the transaction.

The cost of the size of the cash balance kept is an opportunity cost. The savings made because a payment can be completed directly and easily from this cash balance is a reduction of real costs. The cash balance management objective is, first of all, to value these two types of cost accurately and, second, to minimize the aggregate of the two types of cost.

One aspect of efficient cash management is the determination of the number of special funds and accounts to be kept. If it is accepted that the cost of managing each dollar of a fund or account decreases with the size of the fund, then cost-effective management would keep a tight rein on fund proliferation tendencies. In many instances the reduction of the number of special funds to a most efficient management level requires a repeal of legislation adopted years ago when a particular function was taken on.

Money Market

When examining the use of cash, the number of funds, and the average size of transfer to arrive at the most efficient and least cost operation, money market conditions cannot be assumed to be fixed. Interest rates on short-term money market instruments are constantly on the move. Along with these rate changes, there are delayed changes in vendor discounts offered for payment within ten days, interest charged on delayed payments, and the like. The length of the delay in adjusting vendor-delayed payment charges to shifts in money market rates provides an opportunity to decrease costs.

When money market rates are advancing rapidly, a most efficient handling of payments during a previous period may require adjustment in the direction of slower payment. When money market rates are falling rapidly, an adjustment toward more rapid payment could be advantageous. To avoid wasting costly manpower in making vendor and money market rate shift analyses that do not result in decisions adding to efficiency, a gross index of the average rate and rate of change of vendor and money market rates can be used to monitor developments.

The cash budget, when properly developed and adjusted to meet the impacts of changing situations, should give the cash need requirements on a daily, weekly, and monthly basis. The cash need quantities and dates of need established in the cash budget provide the basic data necessary for establishing the maturity distribution of the investment portfolio.

There are a number of alternative money market securities, such as debt instruments maturing in less than five years. The earnings available from each are affected by four or five elements that vary in importance with general monetary and economic conditions. Both *Moody's Investors Service* and *Standard & Poor's* grade securities according to likelihood of principal repayment and interest payment when due. The riskier the security relative to both these factors the higher the rate of interest. It is generally agreed the finance officer should not speculate with public funds; therefore, the grade of security legally purchasable is often defined.

Even though only the relatively highly rated securities are purchased, the danger of default exists unless only federal or federally guaranteed securities are held. Even federal government securities when the maturity is over a year can generate losses if purchased at an above par price or if early redemption becomes necessary. Actually, the finance officer should never purchase securities with a price partially determined by capital gains opportunities. This policy is sound because nontaxable state and local governments do not benefit from capital gains tax advantages. Therefore, a price partially determined by this possibility is too high for purchase by a state or local government.

Government finance officers have found the certificate of deposit (CD) offered by money market banks to be a convenient interest-earning resting place for cash until needed. CDs of over $100,000 denomination can pay as high an interest rate as the market requires, and need not keep within regulations of the Federal Reserve. The risk is limited to bank failure and, of course, higher interest rates in the market after purchase of a CD with a maturity of over a month. CDs offered by local banks are attractive because they assist in financing more local activities than do many other debt instruments.

The widely used money market securities include warrants (immediate call on the Treasurer of state and local governments), commercial paper of business enterprises, and bankers' acceptances, in addition to federal agency and U.S. Treasury borrowings. Because interest on state and local government debt is exempt from the federal income tax, the interest rate tends to be low and therefore they should not be purchased.

Cash Control

The cashier's record typically forms the basic control over receipts. The record should correspond with actual cash turned in at the end of each day and the individual stubs issued for all cash received.

Disbursement of cash must be supported by warrants drawn by the controller. All payments except minor routine amounts should be made through use of the "voucher-warrant-check," which identifies on its face the purpose and the fund providing payment. These transactions are recorded in the disbursement register.

The treasurer's daily record shows funds to which the monies received have been allocated. Certified deposit slips demonstrate the funds reported by the cashier are in safekeeping and can only be drawn on when established disbursement procedures are followed. Records must be maintained that show changes in cash available to each fund and the changes in the balances of the various bank accounts kept by the governmental unit.

Securities owned by the government unit should be kept in a single record. Securities controlled as collateral for deposits or contracts should be recorded separately. The collateral securities are typically left in custody of the treasurer for safekeeping, whereas other securities are left with the broker to ease sale and purchase transactions.

The minimum compensating balances required by commercial banks and the general policy of the government unit combine to set level of noninterest-paying deposits in commercial banks. The growth of NOW accounts and similar arrangements that offer interest and checking account service reduce the sharpness of line between checking and interest-earning accounts.

It is possible for local governments to slow disbursements through use of warrants in payment. When a warrant is presented to a bank by the recipient, it must be accepted by the government unit issuing it. This delays actual payment and tells the finance officer when cash will be needed. This payment procedure reduces need for demand deposit balances. The banks, however, may make an additional charge because of the extra time involved.

Summary

The efficient management of cash can add to earnings and reduce expenditures. Depository institutions are always pointing out the convenience of having a cash balance large enough to meet all possible demands. This siren call is often difficult to resist, because it alleviates the worry about some unexpected change in conditions that may cause a liquidity emergency.

The records kept of cash received and paid out should be simple but complete. Shortcuts of the established routine can be the harbinger of trouble.

Part IV
Land Use and
Property Taxation

15 Zoning

All governments are concerned with the use of land as a basic element of all production and the provider of space and location. In the case of local governments, this interest is more intense because the property tax is a major revenue source and because land use controls and decisions vitally affect economic and political soundness of the area included within its boundaries.

During the 1920s, the United States actively accepted zoning as a useful method for developing helpful procedures for establishing urban land use policies. Zoning legislation was seen as providing more security for the continued use of residential areas for exclusively, or nearly so, residential purposes. From this simple approach and purpose has grown the existing disarray in setting property values and land use practices found in the typical urban area. Undoubtedly, a considerable portion of the financing and policing problems of urban America can be legitimately tied to the way in which the concept of zonnig has evolved in the past fifty years.

The following brief discussion of zoning practices and their impacts provides additional understanding of such basic local government fiscal activities as administration of assessment for application of the property tax, the maintenance of separate government units, and spiraling city government costs.

Legal Basis

Zoning became a legal method for local government legislative bodies to protect the single-famiy suburb from the city when the United States Supreme Court in 1926 upheld zoning in the *Village of Euclid v. Ambler Realty Co.* (272 U.S. 365 1926). This decision effectively legalized all sorts of actions by local government units that establish how land can be used. The decision said that local government actions were proper to prevent the intrusion of industry and apartments into single-family zones. The Court held that intrusions of this type were first cousins of public nuisance and were therefore properly restricted through zoning legislation.

The use of zoning to protect the sanctity of single-family residential areas remains an important portion of its political support. Zoning itself, however, has gone far beyond this allocation of space for exclusive use by non-multifamily residences. To accomplish what city legislative bodies wanted required considerable expansion of zoning flexibility. This additional power of city governments to permit and deny continues to rest on the general concept supported in the *Village of Euclid* case. The Supreme Court has not seen fit to take additional jurisdiction over zoning because it continues to see zoning as regulations that affect only land use and not the rights of people. Discrimination through zoning restrictions has failed to attract the attention of the Court.

Flexibility and perhaps the phrase "opportunity for arbitrary action" has been extended and used under five basic procedures. Each procedure provides opportunities to make assessment of property values less precise and encourages sharp separation between residential areas and those in which commerce and industry is centered. Each is briefly described in the following list:

1. *Variance*—often called a safety valve. A particular property owner can appeal for a variance from the zoning legislation by demonstrating hardship or that conditions have changed substantially. Variance is most useful now in meeting relatively small shifts requested to permit a logical development.
2. *Special Permit*—often called conditional use or special exception. Under this approach the zoning law lists a few land uses that would be permitted at the discretion of local authority, but not as a right. Special permits have been used to postpone zoning decisions on unpopular activities.
3. *Floating Zone*—a particular land use is permitted, but the use is not tied to any particular area on the zone map. When a decision is made to carry forward a particular project it is located on the building zone map at a location determined by the authorities through amendment of the zoning ordinance.
4. *Contract Zoning*—a regular zoning law is adopted with appropriate maps allocating space to various land uses. However, the rules to be followed to change zoning are not given. When a developer wishes to change the use of land from residential to commercial, a contract or covenant setting down conditions as set by the current legislative group must be met. These requirements vary depending on the developer and the current composition of the legislative group.
5. *Planned Unit Development*—any type of land use in particular areas is permitted, but only if developers receive approval of their overall development plans. Usually considerable land must be assembled. After this is done, the existing zoning of the land is replaced with an approved planned unit development.

Zoning goals are frequently attached to zoning legislation. These goals have been abbreviated into slogans, which in turn have become titles that indicate a particular type of zoning. Some of these slogans or titles include impact zoning, performance zoning, incentive zoning, quality zoning, ecology zoning, and balanced community zoning. Each of these types of zoning assumes better city planning for efficient use of urban land by commercial, industrial, and residential users. Again, the current seriousness of urban economic and social problems seems to indicate the approach may be harmful rather than helpful.

The lack of apparent success, despite new names and goals, lies in the continued reliance of the programs on government action. The political pressures that affect government action press toward modification and special interest. The result is likely to be more graft and little useful action.

Efficiency Impacts

Zoning legislation has evolved toward administered actions based on political and personal relationships existing at the time of the decision. The result has been increased uncertainty of land values and therefore additional difficulties in administering the property tax.

An aspect of the preservation of residential areas from intrusion through zoning has been a reduction of the efficiency of urban areas as economic units. When industrial production is forced to locate around and beyond residentially zoned areas, its costs of operation have been increased. One aspect of these higher costs will be lower employment. Lower employment levels adversely affect attitudes of residents, resulting in more difficulty in maintaining decent and safe living conditions. Zoning, by preserving racial segregation, also stimulates conflict and reduces urban government efficiency.

The list of undesirable economic and political impacts of zoning is very long. Nevertheless, zoning remains very popular. The land use decisions arising out of zoning may not be acceptable to the professional tax administrator or planner, but they do meet the needs of the electorate in a variety of ways. Zoning provides a procedure to adjust somewhat the decisions of the market. Zoning also provides a means by which elected officials can assist their friends. In doing this, zoning becomes a procedure for the local officials to determine the manner in which land will be used in the area over which they have jurisdiction.

In the language of the economist, zoning is a useful procedure to handle spillover effects that the market does not adjust to sufficiently quickly. Also in the language of the economist, zoning reduces the economic efficiency of the urban unit and therefore the surpluses available to meet service needs of the residents. It is very difficult to measure the efficiency of an action, including zoning, of local government. However, one example of the impact of zoning legislation provides some understanding of its effect on efficiency.

Houston and Dallas are about 250 miles apart and are very similar in size and population composition. Houston, however, is unzoned and Dallas has been zoned for forty years. Another major difference is more than likely largely determined by the land use policies in effect in the two cities. In Houston, apartment rents are considerably lower than in Dallas. Houston also has a greater supply and variety of apartments available than Dallas. Lower rents create a greater ability to purchase other goods and services. The result is certain to be a stronger commercial economy and wage levels that businesses would find attractive.

Summary

If Houston's favorable housing situation relative to Dallas and other cities using zoning restrictions is actually the result of Houston's no-zoning position, then no or limited use of zoning can be a very desirable approach to the relief of urban problems. The greater investment in multiple-unit housing as a result of the elimination of zoning pushes down rents and increases the efficiency with which all city services can be provided.

16 Urban Single Housing: The Land Use Dream

The causes of the "great wasteland" or the ugly urban sprawl around our cities are being explored with some diligence by a number of people. Undoubtedly, the growth of the private automobile as a very popular and very common means of transportation was an important causal factor. This increase became possible through the provision at public expense of highways and parking places that permit millions of one-occupant cars to move bumper to bumper down one side of multilane highways and gathering together in huge parking lots in our cities. This situation symbolizes much of what is wrong with urban land use planning and American urban living.

The technical development of the modern automobile alone did not make its current dominance inevitable. It was also necessary to have expanded family incomes that could afford the machine and an aggressive automobile industry to convince them to use this income to purchase automobiles. Higher family incomes also permitted more and better housing, but this need not have been in suburbs. A considerable portion of the reason why suburban single-unit houses developed to meet housing needs was caused by governmental policy. The federal government encouraged single-family dwelling units, that is, low density housing, through subsidized mortgage insurance and low maximum interest rates on savings and loan deposits. Local and state government policies in such divergent areas as highway finance, school finance, and property tax administration have encouraged the urban area to spread out. To benefit from all of these government programs and subsidies, a family needed one or more automobiles and a single-unit home in the suburbs. A family renting an apartment close to work and schools and not engaged in land speculation was paying the piper but not benefiting particularly. In addition, other economic supports built on each other to create the unsatisfactory American urban development of the past thirty-five years.

Highways

The list starts with the use of public resources to build highways for use by owners of cars. The gasoline tax was introduced in Oregon in 1919. Later, gasoline excise taxes were collected by all the states and the federal government. Nearly all the revenues have been dedicated to financing highway development. For many years, dedicating a special revenue source to this purpose provided minimum funds. However, after the federal government also initiated the tax, and state plus county and municipal gallonage taxes were increased on the expanded truck and automobile fuel consumption, the revenues became a very major portion of all funds available for domestic government capital expansion programs.

If these very substantial funds had not been available to build highways, the automobile would have had much less usefulness and impact. The political willingness to destroy mass ground transportation by making the large public capital investments required by individual unit automobile transport facilities is very much an American phenomenon that has developed worldwide impacts. The automobile, the gasoline, and the highway construction industries found what they saw to be good and so did the people. What, after all, was fairer than a tax on fuel used to propel vehicles on the highway, with the collections spent to build more roads and bridges and places to park. As Stockfish writes about the gasoline tax, "The social costs of increasing traffic into already congested urban areas or of spoiling the national beauty of remote areas are ignored with a flair that can only be explained by arrogance or a fanatic dedication to pour concrete."

In the critical highway takeoff period of the 1930s, strong political support came because highway construction reduced unemployment, which was as high as 25 percent of the workforce. Employment expansion was an important element again during the Eisenhower Administration, when the federal gasoline tax and the giant freeway program was launched. Military arguments were also important in the late 1950s. The military generally considered the railroads too vulnerable and to possess too little capacity to meet wartime transportation requirements.

A natural question arises from this brief chronology. Why weren't the railroads and other mass transportation facilities improved and modernized instead of the highways? The basic answer must be that the railroads were privately owned and not government-operated as they were in Japan, for example. On the other hand, highways were built and maintained by governments from tax revenues. Also, American railroads did not aggressively seek government assistance because their managements had lost touch with a major portion of American social and economic development. The old public image of railroad wealth and monopoly also hurt.

Annual highway expenditures of state and local government are now about $24 billion a year. Most of these public resources might have been partially available year after year to improve the livability of urban areas if private automobile transportation hadn't so completely won the day. It is easy to conclude that subsidizing the automobile, from oil depletion allowances to lack of a legal requirement that the exhaust fumes be sharply reduced, was a mistake. However, it was an error in the good American and later worldwide tradition. To a degree each person with his or her own means of transportation, which could be used anytime, is an extension of the Jeffersonian ideal of self-reliance and the frontier goal of independence.

Housing

The federal government's encouragement of home ownership is, of course, also a relative of Jefferson's ideal society. The FHA- and later the GI-insured loans made individual homeownership possible, even though savings were very meager or even nonexistent. The mortgages were paid off along with interest and taxes like monthly rent payments. The housing conditions envisaged and encouraged were some kind of idyllic half urban–half rural residential area. If instead, renting had been subsidized, by being deductible from taxable income with interest and property taxes nondeductible, a tax pattern suitable for rental housing would have developed.

The American dream has actually frequently resulted in families living in high-cost, high-maintenance homes with inadequate sewage disposal facilities and in a neighborhood that meets few of the expectations outlined in the developer's brochure. Also, local finance and control of public services becomes next to impossible, as continuing school finance crises demonstrate. The rich or the middle-class or the industrial suburbs harden into political units and prevent the use of property wealth to support outside needs. The property base, and to some extent the income tax base, is separated from the service provision need.

The slowness and lateness of the condominium idea in America is partially traceable to early federal government stimulation of the single-unit set in the middle of a suburban lot. Also, expanding American incomes created a strong demand for land for housing and other purposes. The relatively large piece of land that went with each house managed to combine land speculation with housing. The relatively rapid upward movement of land prices, plus the ability of construction workers to push up their wages more rapidly than general prices, have combined to prevent a mortgaged single-family home from declining in value as it aged. Also, the economic inefficiency of family living in this manner was hidden by subsidies only now becoming apparent.

These subsidies were given by industry, the consumer, and the commuter. Industry reduced work hours, the consumer paid higher prices, and the commuter toiled behind the wheel of his automobile for an hour or two a day. The commuter's compensation was the building up of a capital asset out of housing payments. And the commuter also avoided high taxes, at least for a time.

Summary

The land policy impacts of highway construction financed with gasoline taxes plus central city subsidy of suburban development through conventional property tax finance of community services were central to urban sprawl and high-cost urban services. The reversal of these fiscal inducements to urban sprawl makes good sense, but progress in this direction requires abandoning a portion of the American dream of space and individual control of transportation.

17 Urban Growth and Treatment of Land

The plan of the American city, and to a considerable extent all of the United States east of the Atlantic seaboard, is based on the plan developed by James Oglethorpe for Savannah, Georgia, around 1733. The basic unit of the approach was a ward consisting of forty-eight lots. These lots provided a border for a public square in the center. The boundaries of the square included eight lots dedicated for use as public buildings. The city of Savannah was envisaged to grow by repeating these wards, a series of forty-eight lots surrounding public squares. This concept was followed in practice throughout the United States until about 1850.

The areas for possible urban expansion followed the orthogonal pattern. Planned urban development included provision for common land in each of the expansionary wards. Each ward consisted of forty-eight lots with a population of 400 to 500 people. The concept was pushed into the countryside and provided the model for the checkerboard pattern of land use plotting developed in 1785 when Congress set up the procedures for the settlement of the Northwest Territories.

As the western territories were settled and provision for land grants to private individuals were completed, the Oglethorpe idea of retaining public ownership of some land was adopted. The procedure established through federal legislation provided for towns of half a section (320 acres). The rectangular limits of the new towns strongly stimulated expansion beyond the original area by use of the grid plan. Throughout the nineteenth century, urban sprawl in the United States was effectively limited by the checkerboard pattern of development.

The crowding of the urban areas after the middle of the nineteenth century and the development of railroads and electric streetcars made attractive rural living possible for those employed in the city. Suburbs were born and traffic lines that violated the checkerboard pattern were laid out. The concept of the linear or string city development along the trolley or rail line was conceived. The garden city, and the suburb with a permanent green belt separating the center city where the jobs were from the residential areas also gained wide approval. In the garden city concept as developed by Ebenezer Howard, the urban area was expected to provide employment for most of the garden city residents.

The garden city concept failed to develop an economic base and the dormitory city of the 1920s based on the trolley car and center city jobs

105

demonstrated considerable adaptability. The radiant city with its separation of traffic based on speed was able to absorb the automobile and to meet the needs of separation of activities through the development of zoning.

Urban Renewal Program

Urban renewal was initiated through the Housing Act of 1949. The bill enjoyed broad support among both liberals and conservatives in Congress. The original legislation was substantially modified in 1954 and again in 1956. The program, through the twenty-five years of its existence, has not established new stable downtown neighborhoods and effective planning as envisaged by its backers.

The triumphs of urban renewal is found in tearing down old dirty slums and putting in their place new beautiful apartments and office buildings. The result has been to upgrade the mix of downtown buildings and occupants. Urban renewal has not provided better housing for the poor, but it has stimulated modernization of old downtown areas and provided more facilities for the storage of the automobiles of users and employees of downtown services.

Although most of the funds to finance urban renewal are federal, the local communities have provided over $1 billion. Most of the local funds arise from allocating the increased tax revenues resulting from the project to the financing of urban renewal activities. When the local government's commitment to urban renewal is paid off, the increased tax base becomes available to the local community. At this point, the local tax rate can be decreased or the city can use the additional funds to finance new projects and the like.

The projects actually undertaken by urban renewal must qualify under the general federal legislation. The first step to activate the federal legislation is adoption of a state enabling law that gives city governments the power to enter into urban renewal activities. Next, the city council must organize a local renewal agency. This same city council must approve an urban renewal project developed by their renewal agency. The decisions along the way must also benefit from citizen participation. Finally, acceptable provision of local funds to supplement federal appropriations is required.

The actual clearing of the land where urban renewal is to function and the entering into contracts for construction and rental or sale of the structure and/or land is carried out by the local level of government and private enterprise. Much has been accomplished. Central city pedestrian malls of many cities are a result of the program. The development of pedestrian downtown areas tied to business malls and new parking structures have also partially tamed the automobile.

New Towns

New town developments in England, France, Russia, Japan, and Sweden continue to grow and prosper. In each case, however, the program has been less than a complete success. The old difficulty of combining improved living conditions with work opportunities has not been eliminated. Even Russia, with its relatively complete control over the economy, has encountered this type of difficulty. In Sweden, about seven out of ten workers housed in their highly developed system of satellite towns go into Stockholm for employment. British experience proved that industry can be attracted to new towns, but it is difficult to induce sufficient office employment opportunities.

The European and Japanese experiments with decongestion arose out of ideological debate and new comprehensive legislation. For example, it was generally concluded that the ownership of the land should be in government hands so that profits from rising land values would be available to support government borrowing necessary to finance future projects. New town satellite developments in Europe and Japan have led to increased government regulation, finance, and land assembly activities.

In the United States, new town development grew something like Topsy as the result of individual private development efforts. The employment base arises from spending of incomes coming from other sources, including pensions, employment in the city, private wealth, and government contracts. Typically, the new town is oriented toward providing retail, scientific or leisure services. The developers often buy more land than they need so they can later profit from the sale of land adjacent to the new giant shopping and motel centers that are constructed. Decisions of location and type of development are largely made in the private sector, but they frequently require some zone changes and additional government services.

In 1968, the federal government through the Housing and Urban Development Act first became involved in new towns. Title IV created loan guarantee programs to developers of new towns and large central city residential projects. The maximum of $50 million guarantee was raised to $500 million in Title VII of 1970 legislation. The State of New York, through a specially formed Urban Development Corporation, borrowed $1 billion through issue of debt with interest exempt from the federal income tax to exploit the federal development incentives available.

The program has been partially successful. It has been accused, however, of sapping the vitality of center cities and of attracting their best citizens and industries. Title IV and VII programs are seen by some to be just another example of legislation touted to favor the poor and the old center city, but which turn out to be new subsidies to land speculators and the higher income receivers.

To reduce the land speculation opportunities, some observers have argued for local government ownership of land on which the new city is developed. If this were done, local governments would gain resources to carry out urban improvements without dependence on federal funds and therefore would be largely free of federal regulations.

Treatment of Land

When population and industrial activity of an area grows, the value of the land within the area increases. High-priced land means two things. First, the cost of living and doing business is increased. Second, someone has profited substantially from having been an early owner of land.

These two land-related results of the development of urban areas can be mitigated by adopting a program like that recommended in 1976 in the Land Policy Program Report prepared for the governor of Michigan. The report recommends the property tax be placed on the assessed value of land only. If this were done, better use of urban land and economic stimulation would follow.

In a study of Omaha, the Center for Applied Urban Research at the University of Nebraska recommended a substantial change in the property taxes as applied in urban areas. The current system was seen to subsidize obsolete structures and to penalize the new. Here the federal government's allowance of redepreciation of old structures at the sales price further increases the stimulus for retaining the old and dilapidated.

Sometimes those discussing the desirability of using land tax only identify valuation problems arising from separating the value of land from that of the entire real estate and its structures. More than likely, this argument is a red herring. Land only is given a value and taxed in a number of countries, including Australia. Many urban real estate properties have separated the value of the land from the structure and each part is owned by a different investor. The establishment of the value of land can also be calculated as a residual after establishing a depreciated value for the structure and subtracting that amount from the market price of the property.

The property tax combined with specialized districts, particularly the school district, have helped to bring about metropolitan disunity. The increase in the portion of property taxes resting on land values and the administration of this tax on a uniform statewide rate to finance basic school needs would place the property tax on the side of metropolitan unity.

The political attractiveness of the land tax has not been sufficient to overcome what some have called the trillion-dollar vested interest; that is, capitalization at the going rate of interest of the annual increase in the value of land. Another aspect of the support enjoyed by the land tax approach to urban growth has been the inability to develop the rather complex economic relationships into an appealing political slogan.

Summary

New town development, while reducing congestion, also adds to the influences leading to a downgrading of the central business district. This relationship supports the relative desirableness of expenditures for urban renewal.

Urban renewal has only recently begun to establish stable downtown neighborhoods. It has been learned after twenty-five years of experience that balanced neighborhoods and community involvement are necessary ingredients of success.

In Europe and Japan the necessary government regulation and ownership required for planned urban operations are more acceptable than in the United States. The new town developments in the United States are privately owned and directed and centered around giant shopping and motel centers.

The intensive use of the land tax possesses the potential of stimulating sound urban development while providing for the entire community a portion of the inescapable increase in land values as an urban area grows.

18 Using Planning with Property Tax for the Good City

The word *planning* means different things. Today, in the area of local government, planning means developing a consensus about what should be done and then establishing a procedure to do it.

Five steps are generally involved in consensus building. First, of course, those representing the major points of view must be brought together in an open meeting. Next, those involved need to learn how the positions of the different participants vary. Third, an understanding of existing data and how additional data might be generated is needed. Along with this technical availability must come an appreciation by all of the shortcomings of data that exist and that must be developed. Fourth, horsetrading gets underway to move contestant positions closer together. Offers of side payments and changes in emphasis and timing are offered and accepted after modifications. Finally, the consensus agreed on must be made a political instrument capable of causing decision makers to carry out the consensus developed.

The manner in which land is to be used and the way in which federal funds can be channeled are vital in keeping a community viable. Currently, these decisions include the older city as well as land for new subdivisions. Older city decisions, because of the variety of land uses encountered, are complex by their very nature. The land use decisions of new subdivisions have been made much more complex as the former uniform, rather low level development is being abandoned for planning to maximize residential densities and improve mass transit opportunities. Eliminating the uniformity of the use that can be made of lands owned by different parties lays the groundwork for dogfights.

Allocation of Economic Rent

Landowners that see damage from the plan to the point that they are not able to carry out a reasonable use of their land can attempt to abort the plan through the courts. Other landowners may see the government planning action as a taking act because a higher price was paid expecting a type of plan different from that put into force. There are always people who are damaged by a plan because they purchased land unaware that an existing plan restricted their use of the land.

All these problems arise because governments have not developed a "betterment tax" that would for all practical purposes take away the possibility

111

of profits through land speculation. The justification for the application of a substantial betterment tax on land values created through planning decisions is that land is basically a public resource, or at least values affected by consensus planning decisions are public values.

The planning efficiency of land use decisions must be compared to the decisions the market would make before one can be certain this is the best route to follow. It has been said that planning, zoning, and marketing result in waste, confusion, and inequity. The unnecessary costs the system requires are becoming insupportable. Urban renewal and its relating planning efforts have not been sufficiently attractive or efficient to command widespread belief that planning decisions are less wasteful than market decisions. A planning error that prevents best use of land is as wasteful as a market decision that leads to string development along a highway.

One type of plan consists of setting expansion boundaries. Government services of various sorts are not permitted outside an established boundary. The effect is to increase the demand for development opportunities within the limited service provision area. Another effect is to hasten development of small towns beyond the boundaries that possess some of the services required for housing and population expansion. The approach has two quite different effects on the efficiency of land and energy use. The filling up of the areas surrounded by the boundaries reduces use of energy in transportation and also in the provision of other services. The pushing of development to satellite villages increases energy use and maybe also service costs.

The net effect is perhaps greater efficiency, but less than it could be if much of the increase in land values within the boundary were taxed away to support urban government within this area. A betterment tax, say a higher tax rate applied to increases in land value since the initiation of the service boundaries, would decrease living costs within the service area. This reduction of living costs would remove an important cause of the rapid population growth of the satellite villages.

Federal Action

The scatteration of the cities and their related financial weakness has placed heavier burdens on counties, states, and the federal government. One impact of this financial pressure has been legislation at the federal level. This legislation sets down some basic planning requirements to become eligible for sewage and water development systems, for example. The federal government, however, has continued to operate as in the past and stimulates a farm-home finance program that encourages scatteration. Land using housing programs that stimulate the single-family home also continue to benefit from federal aid. The net effect of current federal intergovernment funding activities is to stimulate planning, restrict environment pollution, and to somewhat discourage high-energy cost urban sprawl.

The restriction of the geographical expansion of urban areas through planning enforced by federal grant requirements and the establishment of local service area boundaries produces a cornucopia effect. The demand for land is funneled into the restricted area of the base city. This inflow of demand for the land of the city gives the city an opportunity to meet its operating costs largely from the levy of taxes based on land values. The city, by focusing its revenue raising in this manner, is also assuring relatively low-cost housing and a tax climate attractive to industry. A substantial tax on land values reduces land prices because cost of ownership has been increased. The revenues from the tax reduces need to tax structures. The lower tax on structures and the lower price for land combine to reduce the cost of both residential and industrial development.

State and Local Government Policies

Several states, Hawaii and Oregon, for example, have initiated programs that require all government units to engage in a planning activity that meet state-administered standards. States generally have stimulated more efficient state and local government planning activities. A number of states have abolished small, high-cost, and overlapping local government levels and have introduced countywide land use plans. (See chapter 43.)

In many ways, county governments are the ideal level of government to become deeply involved in increasing the efficiency with which land is used. The new role of planning in developing economically sound local governments is rapidly giving county governments an expanded vision of their usefulness. The typical picture of a county as the collector of property taxes and the provider of a sheriff is changing rapidly. The county is becoming the source of basic economic data and the government responsible for developing and enforcing the planning function.

Old Structures and Blighted Areas

As these planning activities have progressed, the bad economics of the old approach to the property tax becomes apparent. The property tax encourages old buildings, while new buildings are discouraged by a tax rate levied on the new tax base arising from the high cost of new construction. The federal income tax, by allowing depreciation to continue on the basis of resale price rather than being limited to the original construction cost, also encourages continued use of old structures beyond their economic usefulness.

The continued use of old structures causes the development of urban blight, tax delinquency, and plans for urban renewal. Much of urban renewal has proven to be very expensive—with most of the funds provided by the federal government—and largely a failure in bringing about substantial additional land values as a base for property tax collections by the urban government.

In most instances, the ideas of many planners that a few new structures would act as a catalyst to new private activity did not work out. Instead, the uses to which the remaining buildings were put destroyed the value originally perceived in the new buildings.

Urban renewal destroyed entire functioning neighborhood social systems, and systems performing similar functions were not created when the new structures were completed. An additional weakness of the renewal efforts was a shortage of funds. In many instances the concepts of the plan were never completed. When this happened, taxable values frequently collapsed and property tax delinquency increased rapidly from the old rate which was already relatively high.

The loss of revenues from falling city land values that so frequently accompany urban renewal has resulted in greater emphasis being given to neighborhood rehabilitation and revitalization. It has been demonstrated that, under the right conditions, a neighborhood rapidly approaching large-scale property tax delinquency can be turned around to become a good source of revenues. The right conditions require strengthened social and economic institutions, as well as an improved infrastructure. One useful economic shift frequently advocated but seldom instituted is to remove the portion of the property tax resting on structures; by raising the rate on land, so that revenues are maintained.

One aspect of the preservation of property values is to reduce the quantity of property tax delinquency. Some cities have developed an outreach program that contacts owners of real estate in the inner city who are having difficulty in meeting their property tax liabilities. Programs that demonstrate a city's interest in preserving a neighborhood by working with owners of structures can in itself help to stimulate new investment. An outreach program can increase the confidence of existing and potential investors in the area; this will mean an increase in the property tax base.

Another aspect of maintaining the property tax base is the development of less costly and less time-consuming procedures for foreclosure and tax sales. If it takes four years, as is true in some communities, to take possession of a property for a tax sale, the time involved can cause further deterioration and loss of property tax base in neighboring properties. Also, the purchaser at a tax sale frequently does not pay taxes either, and drains the property further during the four years he has title.

Planners are now well aware that a few properties can destroy the value of many properties. The problem in most localities is to develop procedures to prevent the deterioration of a few properties so that generally lower values do not develop. One answer would be the development of an urban trust to take over these deteriorating properties and supervise their use, with return to private ownership provided when net costs of the stewardship are met.

Property Tax Delinquency

There are two basic types of urban property tax delinquency. One arises because the owner's cash flow is insufficient to meet operating costs and meet the tax bill. This "tax delinquency" is basically short term and will be resolved when the property is sold or the owner's economic position improves.

The second type of property tax delinquency is often called "tax-abandoned" real estate. This type of property is not marketable and does not generate enough income to pay taxes; its prospects for improvement are not good enough to justify "holding" speculation.

A popular solution to the tax-abandoned land problem in the late 1950s and early 1960s was urban renewal. The title to the property reverted to local government in the natural operation of the title process. The buildings could be razed and large-scale urban renewal could be initiated. What could be a better solution to the tax-abandoned property problem?

It was soon learned that large-scale urban renewal was really urban destruction. It destroyed neighborhoods and developed single-class living areas that were very unstable socially. In addition, tearing down the old structures, building new ones, and finding temporary housing for the dispossessed were very expensive. It was learned too, that social systems destroyed by renewal were not renewed when structure was completed.

Throughout all this expensive experimentation, begun on the assumption that new structures would turn blighted slums into new middle-class communities, the problem of tax-abandoned property continued. A new approach based on a new concept was needed. It came along and was called "neighborhood revitalization."

The theory suggests that a blighted slum developed out of individual decisions of occupants of the area and owners of property in the neighborhood. These individual decisions to abandon arise out of observed deterioration of the area and in turn caused further deterioration. If the cause-and-effect relationship could be slowed down, it was argued, the neighborhood would gradually become stabilized and property tax payments would be resumed.

The steps involved in this new process vary but generally follow this pattern: If owner disinvestment through lack of repairs and discontinuation of tax payments was underway but the property had not yet been abandoned, everything possible should be done to encourage rehabilitation and maintenance while holding off repossession because of property tax delinquency. If, on the other hand, the property had been abandoned, everything possible should be done by the local government to gain title to the property quickly. As soon as the legal hurdles in gaining title were overcome, the local government could move in immediately to rehabilitate the property. These actions by local government, it was hoped, would stimulate private owners to maintain and improve other properties in the neighborhood. The result would be an additional real estate tax base and a new stimulant to keeping inner city and older suburban areas as usable places to work and live.

Local government can gain title to property in several ways. The power of eminent domain is often available. Another approach, of course, is that of purchase from a willing seller. Both these procedures require budgetary support, which is often delayed because of controls over the outlay of public funds and also the problem of the budgetary drain. The unpaid tax acquisition approach can use existing administrative machinery and encourage the process to operate continuously day-after-day. By taking full advantage of bureaucratic momentum and of the selection process tax delinquency provides, the tax title procedure seems to be the best approach for devising revitalization strategies in most cases. If the theory is correct, this means that a sound municipal and urban-county economy is preserved.

A cooperative attitude by the banking and financial community toward new investments in areas on the verge of losing their economic viability can also be helpful. The very nearly automatic practice of "redlining" (arbitrarily ruling out financing in certain areas to certain racial groups) must be constantly fought by planners and others interested in making full use of the economic potential of an urban area. Again, planning plus political attention to neighborhood problems and a tax program encouraging development can be most helpful.

The new town development that many planners thought was the way to keep urban life livable and also to avoid the problems of bedroom suburbs has not lived up to expectations. (See chapter 17.) The development of the needed industrial base has proven to be more difficult than anticipated. Undoubtedly, one way to look at new town efforts is to view them as activities aimed at running away from the problems of urban existence in an industrial society. This was also a portion of the reason for the nearly uniform development of land within suburban areas.

Summary

An important portion of financing needed urban services and maintaining decent working and living conditions rests on the success of cooperative efforts between financial institutions, planners, city government, and cooperative state and federal governments. A city that provides the space and construction stimulants for good working and living conditions also preserves its revenue base and ability to finance additional, required services.

In short, the best way to keep property tax collections healthy is to keep neighborhoods of all kinds healthy.

19 Use and Development of the Property Tax

The property tax as established in the United States was quite a different creature from the local rates used in England for hundreds of years. The property tax in the United States has always been on capital value, not income generated. On the other hand, local rates in England are collected as a percentage of rent paid or enjoyed as an occupier of one's own property. Under the British procedure, land standing vacant or little utilized is taxed much lower than land developed and producing rents.

When the national government took over the monopoly of customs collections in 1789 with the adoption of the federal Constitution, the states lost their major source of revenues. They decided to remedy the situation by levying a tax on things owned and used. Gradually, the list became longer and all properties were brought together and taxed as a percentage of their market value rather than so much on an acre of wheat land, and so much on a buggy. By the 1820s a general property tax was evolving; during the 1840–60 period, these property tax concepts became the general ad valorem property tax and moved from local and state legislation to state constitutional provisions.

The Property Tax Reform

The general ad valorem property tax administered by local governments provided most of the revenue expansion required to finance free public education after the Civil War. These property tax laws were adopted by state legislatures but the states left the administration to local governments, frequently townships. The property tax prior to the 1890s was the chief source of revenues of the states as well as of school districts and other local governments.

A reform movement to make the property tax entirely a local government tax gained support as weaknesses in state use of the tax grew. It was argued that weaknesses in the administration of the property tax would be eliminated if use and administration were entirely at the same government level. This, of course, was nonsense; nevertheless, it gained strong political support and became the legislative trend. It also led to the statement by E.R.A. Seligman, a leading tax authority, in the 1920s that the property tax was "perhaps one of the worst taxes in the civilized world."

119

State Revenue Source

The property tax as a source of state revenues has gradually decreased through the years. The great depression of the 1930s caused real estate prices to fall, sharply accelerating state abandonment of the property tax. The need for additional local government revenues in the 1950s to meet costs related to the rapid population expansion caused the trend to continue. By the 1970s only a few states, such as Washington, Montana, Nevada, New Jersey, Arizona, and Wisconsin, made significant use of the property tax as a source of state revenues. The portion of state general revenues coming from the property tax does not go above 6 percent and is typically below 2 percent.

Local Use

The property tax is very largely a local government revenue source; about 50 percent of these local revenues support education. In the large cities, property taxes are needed to finance many expensive government activities not required in smaller communities. In smaller cities and rural areas, around 80 percent of property tax collections support schools. The heavy burden of the property tax in large cities is an important explanation for the introduction of both sales and income taxes by these cities and the urban fiscal crisis.

Coverage Shifts

The general ad valorem property tax as included in the constitutions of nearly all states provided for the inclusion of personal property, intangible property, and real estate in the tax base. This legal base has meant that special legislation and frequently constitutional amendments must be adopted to reduce the coverage of the tax. Nevertheless, the base of the property tax has been substantially eroded from its pristine condition when adopted.

Intangible property is one large area now generally exempt of the property tax. The introduction of state income taxes frequently justified cutting out stocks, bonds, mortgages, and accounts payable from the property tax base. Another procedure used has been classification, in which different tax rates are levied on different types of property. One popular classification has been to levy a very low rate on intangibles.

Personal property in the home is now generally excluded from the property tax base. This exclusion is often justified by the argument that assessment was difficult and involved violation of privacy. Inventories have been excluded more and more through the years. Here it has been pointed out that states eliminating inventories from the property tax base can attract wholesaling activity from the states taxing inventories. Business personal property, with rather generous exemptions given to agriculture, has generally remained taxable. However, some states, to attract industry, have taken business personal property out of the general ad valorem property tax base.

The inclusion of mineral resources and standing timber in the property tax base has always encountered serious valuation difficulties. These difficulties have led to some of these properties being exempted from the general ad valorem property tax. The revenues lost from such exemptions are regained by taxing the product when removed from the land. These taxes are called severance or yield taxes. (See chapter 22.)

Gradually, through exclusions and classification, which establishes lower assessment levels for selected properties, the general ad valorem property tax of the 1890s has become hardly recognizable. The property tax has become largely a real estate tax. The equal treatment of all property as envisaged by nineteenth century reforms was never really attained. In many cases, the property exclusion and classification legislation does not amount to much more than legal recognition of past bad practices of assessors. In other instances, such as the circuit breaker and inventory exemption legislation, property that was included in the tax base was removed through legislation. The property tax on the homes of low-income people had become politically unpopular as had the taxation of inventories.

The base for the unacceptability of the taxation of these two types of property was quite different. The circuit breaker reduces property taxes on the modest homes of elderly homeowners and in some states reduces rent paid. The inventory adjustment encourages the location of wholesaling and distribution business within the state and thus increases employment.

Uniqueness of Land

The base of the existing property tax, like Caesar's Gaul, is divided into three parts: land, structures, and personal property. Structures and personal property have the basic similar economic characteristics of having been produced by applying labor to materials to produce a good that would meet human needs. Therefore, the quantity and elaborateness of this kind of property varies depending on its cost and usefulness. When usefulness—that is, demand—decreases, the supply decreases and costs decline to compensate partially for the decline of need. As a result, quantity is adjusted to the new demand level by reducing supply and lowering prices.

Land, on the other hand, exists in a given quantity with a given location. It can only be moved or changed in usefulness in a relative sense, such as through improved transportation or use of fertilizers. Therefore, the supply of land does not increase substantially when the demand increases. The adjustment to balance demand with supply is made nearly entirely through higher prices. When the need declines, it is also through lower prices and not through reduced production that the adjustment is made. Market adjustment to a changed need for land takes place nearly entirely through price shifts. Supply is basically completely inelastic (constant).

The different supply and use characteristic of land in all of its applications, with the exception, to some extent, when consisting of an extractive resource, has given land a quite different historical treatment from that enjoyed by structures or personal property. The U.S. property tax reform in the nineteenth century abandoned this widely accepted difference of land from other wealth forms, and included all property under the same rubric.

The property tax base has been gradually reduced by excluding certain kinds of property and assessing others at a reduced value. This modification process has dealt with the unique characteristic of land by evaluating it for property tax purposes based on value if used for a particular purpose. Land is given a value if used for agricultural purposes, timber growth, or open space purposes, as examples. This value is less than the market value when it does not envisage the highest and best use of land. When the land is fully utilized, some portion of the tax savings previously enjoyed is often by law payable plus some interest on the tax savings enjoyed. (See chapter 23.)

A valuation of land that is based on value if the land is used for certain purposes results in an indirect subsidy to those who want to accumulate and hold an inventory of land. Here the special characteristics of land as a form of wealth become apparent. Land does not depreciate and can be used for a multitude of purposes. The same land that has considerable value when used to raise corn can have an even greater value when used to provide space for a shopping center. This expected higher value for land in the future is based on an expectation that the population and the productivity of society will expand. The value of structures and personal property, on the other hand, depreciates, resulting in lower values.

These characteristics of land mean that its market value is not related to any cost of production or length of the productivity period, as is the value of structures and personal property. Land has a value because it is in short supply, and therefore must be rationed. This rationing, in a capitalistic democracy, is largely performed by the price system, modified to some extent by zoning and tax policy. When ownership of land is transferred through payment of a price, the new buyer has decided the return on his investment in this use is greater than any other. The price of the land is bid up to a level where the return on land, every factor considered, is equal to other opportunities.

The price that bidders offer takes into account the taxes due annually on the land. As these taxes increase, and the spending of the money collected does not directly benefit the land, the price of the land declines. Higher property taxes on land tend to lower the price of land by the capitalized value of the tax payment. If the going interest rates on real estate loans is 10 percent, and it is assumed land retains its basic characteristics, an increase in taxes by $100 reduces the market price of the land by $1,000.

An investor in land can after the tax increase purchase the land for $1,000 less than before the tax increase. This saving is equal to $100 a year if the saving can be invested to earn the same return as available from an investment in land. The higher property tax of $100 just matches the earnings on funds saved because the price of land declined by $1,000. The collection of additional taxes on land permits government units to either offer a higher level of services or to reduce collections from property taxes on structures and personal property or to reduce sales and income taxes.

In a sense then, ad valorem taxation of land does not increase costs as does taxes levied on structures or personal property. Land is scarce, and therefore has value. The total price (interest and taxes) required to allocate land remains approximately the same whether the land taxes are heavy or light. There is some business advantage, in fact, to have higher taxes on land rather than lower taxes. Higher taxes reduce the capital needed to purchase land, which permits a more active market in land by making it easier for the person of limited means to buy land. Several other business advantages are that land taxes reduce the money tied up in land investment, and the collections would permit lowering other taxes that would stimulate purchases and might also result in somewhat lower taxes on profits.

Summary

The property tax as developed in the United States originally covered all forms of wealth. It taxed all of them by applying the same rate to market value. This ideal was never reached, and legislative modifications through the years have reduced coverage and sharply modified uniformity of valuation in setting the base to which the rate applied.

The property tax as envisaged by nineteenth-century reformers violated the need to differentiate treatment of wealth consisting of land and wealth of most other types. Because land does not have a cost of production, its market price is set by scarcity value and the role of price is to allocate ownership. Therefore, property taxes resting on land do not affect the quantity of land available nor do they increase costs because what is paid in taxes is saved in price (interest on funds to hold land) the market will set on the land.

**Part V
Valuation of Property**

20 Assessment of Real Estate and Personal Property

The basic question to be answered by assessment and appraisal of property is What is the market value? The answer is, of course, obvious—whatever it can be sold for in an open maket. But then there is another question: How can you determine what it could be sold for without actually selling it? A third basic question involves real estate consisting of more than just bare land: "How much of the market price arises from the land and how much from the improvements?"

The value of personal property and to a lesser degree of structures is also affected by the cost of replacement. The technical and economic problems associated with this concept of assessment are monumental, but the logic underlying the concept cannot be denied.

The market value of property can be approximated by sales consummated in other places, maybe next door. Every piece of property has certain unique characteristics that justify some value differentiation. These differences, some positive and some negative, must be taken into account to estimate their value impact. All these adjustments are only practical when related to a basic value that has been set by the competitive forces freely functioning in the market.

Importance of Assessment

The property tax is a tax on wealth represented by real estate, personal property, and still to a minor degree on representations of claims on income and wealth (such as money, stocks, bonds, mortgages, and other intangibles). The tax has become, however, largely a tax on wealth defined as real estate, but continues to be levied in many jurisdictions on such personal property as inventories, industrial and commercial equipment, and livestock.

The assessors are instructed to consider all elements that affect value and to then place a value that represents what a reasonably well-informed person could support. The courts are available to those who believe they have been unjustly taxed. Typically, these taxpayers own a large amount of property and feel that their property has been assigned a relatively higher value than other properties. Much less frequent are complaints that value has been set above the maximum legally permissible in the area. Of course, courts never hear cases in which the taxpayer claims his property has been underassessed.

127

Methods of Establishing Value

Market price must be used as the basic figure in setting value. Therefore the good assessor follows all leads that help in arriving at this amount. These leads vary among types of property and between different jurisdictions.

The first step involves identifying sales prices of similar properties within the general area. If these prices are generally 20 percent higher than the assessed values, the assessor has a *prima facie* justification for raising all properties, not just those that have recently been sold by 20 percent. The overall increase in value may not be justified if the sales fail to adequately meet the four tests frequently applied by the courts: recent, voluntary, bonafide, and the properties sold possess the same general characteristics as the properties having their values increased. Of course, the same approach should be followed if the sales are at prices below the assessed value.

Frequently, properties have such a character that sales within the general area that match them precisely do not exist. Under these conditions, sales of similar properties wherever they took place are appropriate bases to use in setting values. The sale of timber property in North Carolina can be helpful in setting the value of timber property in Oregon.

Value Construction

The value of all properties must be constructed to a degree—that is, sales data must be modified. In some cases, constructed valuation must carry the full burden. For example, land value in an older section of a city may be determined by the *land residual technique* of the income approach. The site is assumed to be used as the location of a modern apartment building. The estimated net return (above all costs, including depreciation and interest) from this newly improved site is allocated to the land. This income is then capitalized at the accepted interest rate when urban land is the security for a long-term loan. The earnings of the land in this approach are the final consideration.

To be certain the value at the highest and best use has been realized, the assessor should work out the earnings estimates from several types of improvements. The land value calculated by this approach on a few scattered properties can be generalized to improve land assessments of urban income-producing real estate holdings.

Another way to construct the value of land is appropriate when a broad valuation separation between land and structure is desired for properties consisting largely of owner-occupied houses. It is the *land value by abstraction method.* It relies basically on data gathered by the Bureau of the Census.

Census data are broken down into four national regions: south, west, north central, and northeast. These averages demonstrate, for example, that in the northeast and west lots form a higher portion of residential property value than in the rest of the country. These data also show that as the age of the improvement increases, the portion of total value consisting of land increases.

Another approach to the abstraction method is to determine the portion of the value of new homes consisting of the price of the lot. The average lot value arrived at by the application of this percentage is then applied to vacant lots within the area.

Ripening and Decaying Land

It is generally very difficult to assess land approaching a new and higher use and land located in decaying urban areas. The value of land within these categories has an unusually high level of speculative value. The ripening land has its value appreciated by speculation and the land in the decaying area has its value decreased by speculation.

The assessor is justified in spending a large amount of time on these two categories of urban land. The reputation of the assessor's office and the acceptance of the property tax as just by voters depends on how well these knotty assessment assignments are handled.

Rental Income

Setting the value of wealth is a difficult process. The British with their property tax have avoided it by using rent as the tax base. Of course, this does not avoid the difficulty when the property is owner-occupied. In that case the procedure just requires a different step—that is, the estimation of rent instead of market value. One method would not be typically any easier than the other.

In using the rent base, underutilized and vacant property pays little tax, even though the land may be very valuable. Some of the same encouragement to hold idle land exists in the common practice of placing a below-market valuation on vacant lots in the United States, because income is not being realized.

In the valuation of industrial and commercial property, rent paid and received should be included as one element in setting market value. Rental contracts are, after all, one evidence of the price at which real estate or personal property would sell if placed on the market. Using the rent-paid figure on rented property in setting a reasonable market value on owner-occupied property when capitalized at a given interest rate has three major weaknesses:

1. The appropriate rate of interest is nearly impossible to determine if the period of time is more than five years.

2. The rent payment does not give the payer the benefit of value increases in the future that are available to the owner.
3. Increases in value of real estate benefit from expensing costs and treating gains as capital gains that are subject to tax rates below that of the income to which expenses are applied.

Using income received by property owner or benefit from self-use of property as an element in setting value suffers to a varying degree from the three shortcomings of rent as a tax base. In addition, owner's income from property typically consists of two quite different income sources, the land and the improvements. Business owners are anxious to have as large a portion of the total valuation allocated to the structure so that their depreciation deduction is maximized. The assessor typically does not feel strongly about the allocation of the total value. The assessor's basic interest is in the total value. Therefore, undervaluation of land used for industrial and commercial purposes is common. This low valuation of land used at its highest and best use spills over into the valuation of unused land that will be used for industrial or commercial purposes when it is ripe.

Personal Property

At one time, furniture, clothes, rugs, and other property in the home were routinely assessed and included in the property tax base. Today, most states have exempted these properties. Nevertheless, the assessor still must enter the house to determine the number of bathrooms, fireplaces, flooring, and furnace to assess the value of the house.

Personal property consists to a considerable extent of the complicated machines used by modern industry. The placing of a value on these properties is complex and the assessor is well advised to employ expert assistance. Personal property used in a business that is not especially built for the company using it has a quoted market price. The historical cost reported by the owner in personal income tax returns should not be used without checking current sales prices.

The type of depreciation used by the owner for income tax purposes should only be accepted if it represents true depreciation based on average life of the equipment. If some type of accelerated depreciation is being used, the current valuation must be adjusted to bring value up to value after taking into account true depreciation.

Inventories make up the second largest aggregate included in the personal property total. This total is rather sharply divided between finished goods, raw materials, and agriculture livestock. Again, for establishing value, the approach must be that of an appraiser seeking market value. This goal is not satisfied by merely looking at the books of the organization. However, a careful examination of the books as an auditing function can be helpful in setting the value of inventories and other business personal property. The assessor must always keep in mind that the numbers in the books do not represent either market value or quantity—but they do provide useful information that should not be ignored.

Farm Appraisal

Every agricultural locality has a local farm real estate market. Even though farms may not have been sold recently, the farm real estate broker and bankers have a very good idea of what a farm would sell for. These general farm value levels arc useful, but during periods of sharp shifts in values they are likely to be out of line. This, of course, is also true of census figures, USDA market value indexes, and the various land value estimates published by state agricultural experiment stations.

Individual land value sales are affected by the terms of the sale and also by particular needs of the seller and the buyer. Raw sales data never represent true market value. Upward or downward adjustment must be made by the assessor before it is applied to similar properties to arrive at market value.

Two procedures are used in constructive farm market value based on capitalization of income produced by a farm operating at average efficiency. One is the "landlord estimate" and the other is the "owner-occupied method." Either procedure is acceptable for use by the appraiser, regardless of the plan being followed on the farm.

The landlord estimate is favored because of the serious problem of valuing family labor and the return on the owner's investment in equipment is avoided. A landlord estimate, on the other hand, only requires determining the rent being paid by the occupier of the farm and basic expenses such as taxes and depreciation, plus fertilizer and seed if their provision is included in the contract. The cost of the land or the interest on funds invested in the land should *never* be included as an expense in calculating net income from gross farm receipts.

Land costs need to be excluded because, in calculating income to be capitalized, the price of land has been determined by the net income from all sources included in setting the market price of land. Therefore circular reasoning is involved when land is considered a cost as well as possessing a price determined by net income.

Livestock, when included in the personal property total, requires the assessor to view the herd and to compare market prices being quoted. Basically the same procedure is required when grain in the granary or crops in the field are included in the personal property total of agriculture.

Rate and Assessment Levels

Considerable state legislation limits local government use of the property tax. One aspect of control over property tax revenue provision is the level of assessments and the level of rates. It is often claimed that higher assessment ratios do not result in equally lower rates. As a result, higher assessement levels result in higher property tax collections. The logic of this position leads to the conclusion that under rate flexibility, low assessments will result in lower property taxes.

If this were the way things worked out, a low assessment ratio policy would be a low property tax collection policy. This method of holding down property taxes is attractive because assessors can avoid the pressure arising from assessment increases. In a fashion, assessors are able to say "your high property taxes are not due to my action." The high tax blame belongs on the people who set the high rates. This is a much more diverse group than the assessor. Some blame will rest on the school board, some on the city council. Reducing or stabilizing property tax rates requires action to reduce expenditures, a bigger job.

In fact, research in areas with rate flexibility and low assessment valuations substantiates these expectations. Property tax collections prior to a reassessment of property to higher levels does not increase property tax collections, but results in reduced rates and some reallocation of the burden. Neither are property taxes generally lower where assessments are low. The low valuations are compensated for with higher rates.

The voters of a local government unit or a state can decide how they wish the property tax to be administered. If the voters are persuaded that high assessments do not mean higher taxes, a good deal of the public support for underassessment is eroded.

Summary

The assessment of property is the key step in the administration of the property tax. Values are soundest when set frequently by using market value.

All properties do not require the same care in assessment. Therefore, an assessment procedure that fails to vary time and effort on the basis of relative difficulty of problems encountered will be wasteful as well as inaccurate.

Although setting values on personal property is difficult, these properties do represent wealth, and local governments utilize revenues to provide them with police and fire protection. In these days, when payroll and income taxes are so popular, additional emphasis on wealth as a tax base may be desirable in developing a balanced tax system.

21 Taxation and Assessment of Rural and Fringe Area Lands

The application of the property tax to rural and fringe area properties is best considered from four different points of view: (1) environmental impacts; (2) efficiency; (3) tax justice; (4) elements that make taxing land different from taxing manmade capital and income.

Environment Effects

The taxation of fringe-area properties and vacant land within the built-up sections of a city is frequently carried out in such a manner that the tax relative to market value is lower than on land fully developed at its highest and best use. Fringe area market value in many states is established by its productivity at its current use. If the land is used for farming, grazing, or timber, the capitalized value of the income from this activity establishes the tax base valuation, and not the market value of the land which may be five to ten times greater. (This is called "use" value valuation.)

This practice has been included in the legislated property tax law of most states. Such legislation is often justified as a way of preserving a limited supply of agricultural land. In addition, the open spaces both at the fringe of the city and within the city proper are seen as making the city a better place to live and raise a family. Livability is improved if tax policy makes it easier to hold underutilized land, particularly if underutilized land is at the fringe of the city. Special tax provision is also often included for open space land.

Open space tax benefits are made available for a number of reasons. Golf courses frequently benefit from the provisions of valuations below market value because they provide open space and add to the value of neighboring properties. Other recreation land and open land that enhances scenic resources are included in open space lands eligible for valuations at lower than market value and therefore subject to reduced property taxes.

Holding Land and Efficiency

Two approaches characterize the property tax treatment of fringe areas and the general efficiency of an urban area. One group sees full property taxes on fringe areas as forcing urbanization of the land, with the effect causing the residential and business areas of the city to be spread out. That is, scatteration is encouraged.

In this approach, the intensity of land use within the existing city limits is assumed to be reduced by higher taxes on fringe area lands, otherwise high taxes would not result in development of additional acreage. During the past twenty years, nearly every city has experienced less intensive use of city center lands and more intensive use of outlying acreage. Whether this movement is caused by high taxes on fringe areas, high taxes on city center real estate or a number of other factors, including federal government subsidy of new houses and depreciation allowances on new structures, remains an open question. Nevertheless, political support for special tax favors to fringe area lands has developed out of this way of looking at a serious urban problem.

On the other hand, if fringe area lands in the ripening process are assessed at market value, the price prospective users would be willing to pay is decreased. The higher tax payments must be added to the cost of the funds required to make the purchase. The result, of course, is to require a reduction in funds bid for the land. In effect, the higher property taxes act as a loan to owners of the land on which they must make annual interest payments. The price for the use of the land paid to the government is increased and the price paid to the private owner is decreased.

This payment allocation, in contrast to that existing under conditions of tax favors, affects efficiency by increasing the people who can bid for the land. The higher taxes act as a loan to prospective buyers, making it possible for people with less wealth to bid seriously for land ownership. Also, the high annual tax payments requires a land use that develops a flow of funds. Passive investment in land awaiting the expansion of the city's limits becomes less attractive because of the annual higher tax payment and also because more competition for the land, as a result of reduced wealth requirements for bidding, will push up the price nearer to the break-even point. The net result will be more intensive use and greater efficiency in the use of land resources.

If the vacant land within the limits of the city is assessed at its full market value, along with the fringe land, another type of greater efficiency is achieved. By stimulating the full use of land within the city limits, the city reduces its need to expand its geographical territory. Two results that increase efficiency could be expected.

First, the energy needs for the transportation of people and goods would be lowered. This would reduce many per capita city costs from street maintenance to use of energy. Second, the demand for fringe area land would be reduced as more activities would occur within the existing city limits. Taking over lands with the potential for agriculture production for urban use will decrease the nearby supply of food. The result will be higher food costs and decreased efficiency in growing and distributing food.

Tax Justice

Rural and fringe area properties may be owned by families that have scratched for several generations to earn a living at farming. Also, the value of their land is determined by urban uses, not agricultural productivity; they have a chance to make a real profit by hanging on for a few more years. Assessment at market value will push up tax payments substantially and new indebtedness may be needed to meet the tax bill. Unfortunately, the owners are not usually capable of developing the land for urban use themselves. At this point, sales of the land to speculators and developers accelerates and a new breed of ownership takes over.

A land tax high enough to retard land price increases sharply as land use moves to a new higher level has elements of both tax justice and injustice. The levy of such taxes, in effect, means that the higher value was created by society; therefore, the gain belongs to society. The increase in the dollar value of the land beyond the inflation rate is not the result of management or technical skills, but the income is a windfall. The receipt of the windfall by the long-term owner is a happenstance; a short-term owner may gain a windfall because of available capital and knowing how city hall works. Both the long-term owner and the land developer view a relatively harsh tax treatment as unjust.

This feeling of being treated unfairly is substantially lessened when the rate and assessment procedures are the same on all land. Under these circumstances, the injustice arises when land wealth is taxed while as personal property or structures wealth is not taxed. For this tax treatment to be perceived as just, the tax must either be envisaged as a payment for special benefits accruing to the landowners or the land as a tax base must have important characteristics that outweigh an extra personal tax burden.

To an extent, land does benefit from a wide variety of government expenditures. In addition, because the quantity of land cannot be materially increased when price inducements are offered, the cost of land absorbs much of society's additional productivity; that is, higher land costs absorb the high productivity of desirably located land.

In reflecting the growth of productive activity because of its monopoly characteristics and because land ownership can be relatively easily determined, land has many desirable tax base qualities. Also, in a growing society, the special tax on land need not be so high as to take away value as determined in the market during prior transactions. These interrelationships then make up the complex web in which the justice of higher tax rates on land, than on other forms of wealth, rest.

Capital Creation

Capital, in the form of machines and structures, is produced by physical and mental labor, as well as producer goods built at an earlier period and natural resources. Labor and natural resources combine to provide goods that intensify the production process which has produced capital. Taxing this process retards the level of activity by increasing costs. This cost increase makes it too expensive for some capital goods to be produced and for some would-be capitalists to develop new enterprises that increase employment and the abundance of our lives.

When property taxes decrease construction and machine-producing activities, the tax has decreased the growth of productivity. Taxing rural and fringe area lands at their full market value at highest and best use, not at some value considerably below the market value, reduces the portion of total taxes that must be assessed on the incomes of investors in capital goods and the productivity of mental and physical labor. The primary effect is to stimulate capital creation. A secondary impact is to reduce the price of land at the fringe, making it possible for persons of less financial strength to compete actively for control of these lands. Economic stimulation is the general result of a higher per-acre tax on lands at the fringe of urban development and reduced taxes on machines and structures. The stimulation, of course, arises from the lower cost of both capital and fringe area land.

The higher tax on land, whether at the urban fringe or in the center of a city, does not materially affect the overall quantity of land. The effect of the higher land tax on land actively offered on the market, however, is obviously to increase the quantity and decrease the selling price. On the other hand, higher taxes on wealth other than land and natural resources decreases quantity produced and therefore quantity available. If demand remains relatively stable, the result is higher prices up to the point where a new equilibrium market price is reached; that is, the amount produced under the new higher cost can also be sold at the new higher price. The overall effect of higher taxes on manmade goods is higher costs and higher prices. The impact of higher taxes on lands, basically because aggregate quantity is fixed and quantity offered from underutilized acreage may increase, avoids much of the price increase and productivity reduction problem of taxes using another base.

Summary

The price of land is very largely a method of allocating control over land; that is, price is a rationing device. The price of manmade products includes the costs of production, which also includes the rationing price that must be paid for the use of land and taxes. Agriculture and fringe area taxation policy can be used both to encourage full use of land and space and to promote economic growth. The lower price that fringe area land demands, after taxes have been equalized by using market value as the tax base, frees savings formerly needed to hold land and makes them available to finance capital goods.

22 Taxation of Timber and Natural Resources

Wealth data in the United States is very incomplete. For example, there is no procedure for gathering information about the distribution of ownership of natural resources. The data gathered regularly from individual and corporate income tax returns do not, at this time, regularly distinguish the income or profits arising from operating a department store from those arising from control over natural resources, if both were controlled by the same firm. The rent figure used in national income data excludes rents earned by real estate management firms. The rent data reported in the Statistics of Income is limited to taxpayer designation as rents and royalties and rights to natural resources. The portion of personal income consisting of rents also includes imputed net rental income of owner occupants of non-farm dwellings. Rents amount to only about 2 percent of all personal income.

The manner in which natural resources are controlled and the way in which incomes arising from these sources are distributed results in a vague feeling of inequity. Although too deep a concern with tax equity causes rules and regulations to violate the good-tax canons of certainty, simplicity, and economy, the causes of observed differences should always be under scrutiny—for example, to determine if the existing procedure encourages efficiency and if the efficiency gains are sufficient to outweigh observed inequities to justify retention. A basic fiscal principle is violated only at great risk by public sector policymakers—the geometric relationship in the increase in anger over injustice as the burden of taxes increases.

The typical citizen feels comfortable with political power used to grant favors to activities considered necessary in carrying out basic and needed functions. Resentment builds up, often erupting during economic hardship, if political power results in unmerited advantage. Economic rent arises from the utilization of natural resources under conditions where the sale price is greater than all costs, but excludes those arising from purchase or rent of the land or other natural resources. All economic rent must be carefully monitored and put aside so that it does not become the basis of nonfunctional receipt of income and political power.

Economic rent arises as resources become scarce when the needs of society expand. Economic rent cannot be destroyed, but it can be absorbed in various ways. The countries with legal systems within the Spanish tradition of *utilidad publica* keep ownership of all resources beneath the surface under government ownership. The economic rent becomes available to the people as represented by the government to be used as decided. All the economic rent either can be absorbed in unproductive supervision and work rules that sharply increase costs or can be used to finance an efficient system of free public education.

Natural resources in areas allowing private ownership are often subjected to a special severance tax based on current production. This special tax can be nominal or very substantial, and can be based on either the quantity or the value of the resource extracted and sold. The tax would not be levied on manufacturing or retail activities. The U.S. Census Bureau reports severance tax collections in thirty states, particularly in such oil- and gas-rich states as Texas and Louisiana.

The Census Bureau's definition of a severance tax is "taxes imposed distinctively on removal of natural resources—e.g., oil, gas, other minerals, timber, fish, etc.—from land or water measured by value or quantity of products removed or sold." Obviously, the economic activity that would develop a severance tax liability could also develop a liability to both individual and corporate income taxes, and most surely to payroll taxes and unless specifically exempted, to the general property tax.

The levy of a severance tax is somewhat justified by the belief that gifts of nature—such as water, air, sunshine, land, natural resources, and the like—are distinguishable from conditions and properties that are largely the result of human effort. Oil, gas, minerals, timber—in fact, all land—can be legitimately taxed more than wealth more closely associated with human effort, because value arises due to a limited reserve that, generally speaking, cannot be eliminated through additional human effort.

States, and local governments to a much more limited degree, have several ways of applying special taxes or different tax procedures to timber and natural resources.

Timber

The special taxation of timber developed by Fred R. Fairchild sets a value based on the current discounted value of timber that was to be harvested at some future date of maturity. Standing timber ready for harvesting was given a value based on current market price, less the property tax and other taxes. The procedure minimizes capital values subject to the property tax. The reduced property taxes on timber arising from this procedure encourages higher asking prices that will tend to increase the tax base of the property tax. To a degree, therefore, the low value arising from the Fairchild approach has a partial built-in correction, if modern assessment procedures are used.

Placing a market value on trees for use in the application of the property tax has proven to be difficult, at least politically. Therefore, severance and yield taxes have been advocated and adopted. The yield tax is a levy on the market value of the log after being cut and prepared for transportation out of the logging area. This yield tax is a replacement for an *ad valorem* property tax on the standing timber. The land, however, is real estate subject to the prevailing state and local property tax rates.

A severance tax differs from a yield tax in that land is taken off the property tax rolls. Under a yield tax, on the other hand, a local government continues to have the value of bare land in timber areas as a base to apply the property tax rate. This would assume some revenues from timber areas even though logs were not being cut. The severance tax replaces all property taxes and, therefore, revenues from timber areas would be zero if harvesting was zero.

The custom of financing most school costs from real estate taxes levied on the assessed value of property within the school district substantially cuts the support given by these valuable forest properties to the financing of education. School districts made up largely of timber-growing areas are sparsely populated. Therefore, the number of children to be educated per $1 million of value is small, which also tends to be true for valuable oil and gas properties.

The severance or yield tax levied by the state or county makes the income and wealth related to timber, as well as natural resources generally, available to a larger number of persons. The state or county could instead, or in addition, levy a general property tax, perhaps on only the assessed value of land, which would also act to spread more broadly the tax base provided by natural resources.

Taxing Wood Fiber Production

A very different way to tax standing timber is to treat the tree not as a natural resource or as an agricultural crop, but rather as a factory engaged in the production of wood fiber. Then wood fiber produced each year would be assigned the existing market value. The value of wood fiber produced would be treated as gross receipts and taxed annually as value is added. If the tax base is net income, rather than the receipts or value added, the expenses incurred in producing the wood fiber would be deducted in arriving at the base to which the tax rate would be applied.

The wood fiber production approach, combined with a 2 or 3 percent uniform land tax, would encourage efficient use of timber lands. The production approach would largely eliminate the problem of the tax causing a delay in harvesting due to creation of tax liability that exists under the severance and yield taxes. Speculation in rising wood fiber prices on standing timber that is past its rapid growth life, however, would increase, but the uniform 2 to 3 percent land tax would act as a substantial retardant. This weakness of speculation in old growth must be weighted along with the advantage of relatively stable annual wood fiber tax base and avoidance of the problem of setting an accurate value on standing timber.

A state-wide administered tax based on capital value of timber land and standing timber still can provide a well-aligned tax policy. In addition, such taxes encourage efficient use of resources. Also, the approach provides a relatively stable tax base from which to finance public sector activities. Political difficulties and very real timber valuation problems cause wide abandonment of the standing timber as well as the land value base.

Under the federal government's corporate and personal income tax policy, gains from the sale of timber are treated as capital gains, while timber management costs are expensed as incurred. This tax treatment encourages forest management techniques and the establishment of separate timber-producing companies by the large wood products groups.

Oil and Gas

Oil and gas properties are generally taxed by applying the local property tax rate on a base that the law usually states to be the current value of the recoverable oil and gas. In addition to the application of the general property tax rate on the assessed value of oil and gas reserves, several states collect a severance tax. The severance tax is sometimes like a gross receipts tax of a given percentage and sometimes it is a given amount per barrel of oil of varying qualities. In some states, this severance tax has replaced the property tax. Louisiana, for example, bases its severance tax on income per barrel and exempts oil and gas reserves from the property tax. Texas, on the other hand, uses a percentage of gross receipts as its severance tax and levies the existing local property tax rate on the assessed value of oil and gas reserves. In both of these states, and in a number of others, with Alaska making the greatest use, oil- and gas-related revenues provide a very substantial portion of total state and local government own-source revenues.

The local application of the property tax to oil and gas properties sometimes results in a production or gross receipts tax. The assessed valuation of oil and gas properties in these tax jurisdictions closely approximates the gross value of production. The property tax in practice becomes a production or severance tax. A few years ago, both Colorado and New Mexico developed instructions for assessing oil and gas properties that are based directly on the value of production.

The difficulty of setting the value of reserves of oil and gas properties and the continued pressure of producers to have tax liabilities arise when income is received results in severance-type taxes. The application of true *ad valorem* taxes on the capital value of oil and gas properties requires estimating the present worth of future income in excess of costs other than royalties or capital outlay. Although these estimations are useful, it is also necessary to adjust the value arrived at by the price at which similar properties are being sold and purchased.

A severance or production tax tends to retard production and stimulate speculation in oil and gas properties. The levy of true *ad valorem* property tax stimulates production and reduces speculation. An oil and gas field contains a finite quantity of reserves. As production continues, the quantity of reserves decrease and the cost of bringing a given quantity of oil and gas to the surface increases. Both these developments are reflected in the market value of a field and in formulas aimed at calculating capital value. As a result, as a field becomes exhausted, the assessed value of the field declines. When a severance tax is used, the tax paid per unit of output is not affected by rising production costs and reduced reserves—a rather important weakness.

Profits from oil and gas properties are reduced by applying a depletion rate. Using up reserves is seen to be like the reduction of inventories, which is about the same as using up capital. Adequate allowance should be made so that, after paying all taxes and other expenses, enough remains after normal profits on an investment in oil and gas properties to replace the original invested capital in real terms. The depletion rate needed to provide this protection of capital must be high enough to purchase a new field similar to the now exhausted field. With general scarcity developing, this degree of protection will be difficult to provide.

A tax on the value of the estimated capacity (that is, a property tax) stimulates production; as the reserves are used, the tax payments required are decreased. Stimulating production will assist in maintaining orderly markets. This self-adjusting tax will bear more heavily, when looked at as a burden on production, on the new properties than the old fields. Again, as in the case of timber and timber land taxation, the property tax has some rather desirable features.

Minerals

Valuable deposits of iron and copper ores are limited to a few areas of the United States. Mineral taxes have been affected by the feeling that these deposits should bear more taxes than ordinary business enterprises. The aim, particularly in Minnesota, with regard to iron ore deposits, has been to induce development while taxing away much of the economic rent. The discussions in Minnesota have used the term "technical surplus" or "franchise payments." Whatever the name, the aim has been to establish the value of the iron ore deposits in place. Again, the effort requires estimating the annual flows of income that can be expected. Next, these amounts must be given a present value calculated by discounting future income by an acceptable interest rate. After this is done, a franchise tax must be assessed to reduce the annual earnings to a level that would be just adequate for a prudent investor to continue operating the iron mines.

Under this procedure, the state collects royalties. The people of Minnesota have benefited from the economic rents of a natural resource of their state. They receive public sector benefits through a higher level of services or a lower level of taxes. Indirectly, their incomes are increased beyond the level of stimulation the additional jobs provided.

When the iron ore began to run out, and competition from iron ore deposits in other nations began to develop, a new approach to iron ore mining was adopted in Minnesota. A production tax was introduced to replace the franchise tax. New legislation also removed control over tax rates from local hands and gave it to the state legislature.

Return and Capital Value

In a given situation, the lower the rental income (rent payment), the higher the tax payment must be for the right of ownership. If earnings from exploitation are above the rate of return required to support the existing capital value, the capital value will increase until the given earnings are only equal to the market rate of return on the capital. The movement in capital values keeps the rate of return equal to the market rate. If the tax rate is increased, the return from ownership is reduced. This rate increase causes a reduction in the capital value of the resource until the new return from ownership provides a rate of return equal to that prevailing in the market.

The market value of land and natural resources has a constant relationship to earnings. As the price of corn or the price of copper increases, the cost of ownership of the farm land or the mineral property increases to absorb the additional income arising from the higher prices. Under these new conditions, the profitability of ownership is back to the previous levels. Again, there isn't any money in farming or in copper mining. But the previous owner reaped a substantial capital gain when land prices went up in response to the higher corn prices and copper mining land went up to meet the higher earnings from copper mining.

Alaska recently enacted a very substantial income tax that applies only to petroleum companies. Operating companies feel this approach to natural resource taxation penalizes their success. It also, of course, induces a reduction in production as well as exploration activity.

Summary

The natural resources of the world are the source of surpluses that can be allocated for use by the public sector without increasing costs. The world's resources are limited, and price above cost outlays that make the resource available for use perform a rationing function and are not payments to meet necessary production and distribution costs. Therefore, property taxes can be levied at normal rates and based on assessed value without much of an increase in costs because the payment reduces economic rent paid as royalties to owners by about the same amount as the property tax payment.

For the general citizenry to benefit fully from the bounty of nature, taxes must be introduced that capture as public receipts amounts that would otherwise be paid to a few private owners in carrying out the necessary rationing process. The private enterprise market system keeps use equal to supply by charging a price. This price usually consists largely of labor costs and necessary capital costs. In the case of primary goods that are natural-resource dominated, price to perform its function of equating use and supply also includes economic rent. Economic rent is not used to pay for labor or capital; nor is it a payment required to carry out the economic process. Therefore economic rent can be reduced and replaced by tax payment without disturbing the efficiency of the price system in allocating scarce goods and services. Neither does the substitution of a tax payment for the rent payment reduce profits below the level needed to attract capital on a basis equal to that enjoyed by other industries.

23 Environment and Natural Resource Control

Local governments and states have enacted a variety of laws and ordinances concerned with the improvement and preservation of good physical environment. The impact of this legislative action, on the quality of the air, opportunities to engage in desirable recreation activities, and the like, is difficult to measure. It is even more difficult to develop any way to calculate additional costs of all kinds required by the new legislation.

Improvement of the environment, for example, might include action to provide more open space for parks and playgrounds. One cost-increasing result of this decision would surely be greater travel distance between home and work, additional miles of utility wires and pipes, and more space to be covered by mailmen, policemen, and firemen. All these costs decrease the surplus potential of action aimed at more parks and open space.

Individuals or companies in search of an environment appropriate for their activities that minimizes their costs can cause the total efficiency of the area to deteriorate. Taxation policy adopted and carried out by the national government and by the lowest level of local government will affect the choices made by all members of a community. If the taxation policy, for example, encourages full use of land, the pressure exerted to reduce scatteration could compensate for the less intensive use of land brought about by the provision of additional space for parks and recreation.

The types of taxes used and the method of application and, of course, the emphasis given to different varieties of expenditures affect the working and recreation environment and the efficiency with which natural resources are used. The allocation of considerable municipal funds for bicycle paths and sidewalks nudges the community toward quite a different environment than would the provision of additional parking facilities.

Image Projected

The construction of parking facilities would quite likely lead to collecting charges that might pay a considerable portion of construction costs plus the direct loss of taxable real estate. Bicycle paths might become a base for some additional license fees, but the direct recovery of funds spent would be much less than for the parking facility.

There is little doubt but that a decision process within the public sector that relied upon direct earnings and capital recovery would go further toward provision of parking facilities than would one dependent on environment. If the decision process included indirect and related benefits, a rather large group of fuzzy interrelationships would have to be considered—for example, the overall effect on property values of the provision of bicycle paths and the provision of parking facilities. When the analysis is given this sort of breadth, the gate is opened to a variety of considerations that are much more difficult to quantify than the original simple revenue model.

Nevertheless, some comparisons, with a wide range of reliability and usefulness, can be made. One obvious approach is to compare real estate value trends in cities that have built new bicycle paths during the past ten years with those providing additional parking facilities. This crude and relatively inexpensive approach and all the attendant shortcomings possess one overriding strength that makes it or some similar comparison an absolute must. This strength rests on a widely held belief that real estate market value trends provide an excellent gauge or index of expectations arising from psychological attitudes to choosing the area for a new electronics plant or another type of modern clean industry with well-paid and educated employees.

Bicycle paths, as opposed to parking space, provide a visual expression of the likely livableness of an area and of the progressiveness of its business community. Along with more bicycle paths and no increase in parking comes improved public transportation and more compact industrial and commercial areas. All these expectations are reflected in improved real estate market values through reduced need for additional municipal service expenditures and therefore a reduced property tax burden on real estate values.

This process outlined can be strengthened by the introduction of a property tax that emphasizes land in the base. This emphasis can be inserted by exempting buildings from the tax base or by reducing the portion of the full value of structures that are included. This encourages property owners to utilize more completely the full potential of their land site.

Nonfiscal Land Use Controls

The approach discussed briefly above relies on fiscal activities—taxes and spending—to accomplish environment improvement and resource conservation. Government policies controlling land use at all government levels can cooperate with and substitute for fiscal efforts. Legislated land use policy makes land much more a public good and establishes detailed legal boundaries within which all private land control actions must fit.

Federal Legislation

The national legislation required for this approach would resemble the Clean Air Act and the Federal Water Pollution Control Act, as well as the National

Land Use Bill. Such an act would set down procedures for introducing state and local controls that would meet the standards of the national legislation in a manner similar to that now followed under the Clean Air Act.

Air and water pollution control received favorable public reception as the spaceship earth concept gained popular acceptance. The realization that air and water pollutants could kill and could be widely spread beyond their source made control legislation possible.

In the case of air and water, private ownership was limited and, therefore, public control was not a "giant step." On the other hand, land control and ownership, and the concomitant control over land speculation, is "mother lode" of the American dream and will not be changed easily.

In a way, all decisions of individuals and businesses are land use decisions. For example, a decision to have cheap energy is also a decision to have low density, scattered development, wasted prime farm land, and social isolation. A national land use law would require high density, reduced scatteration, and integrated neighborhoods. Such legislation would prevent the undesirable impacts of cheap energy, while retaining the desirable impacts such as higher levels of technology in the home and industry.

State and Local Action

What has been accomplished without national land use legislation varies widely from city to city, state to state. All the varieties of land use controls have one aspect in common: they reduce individual control and increase community oversight of the individual plot. These actions taken in the past at the local government level are now being affected by state legislation. When land use actions were embodied in local ordinances the courts determined what was proper and what violated state legislation and the state constitution.

Currently, the courts are requesting state legislatures to adopt statutes to provide goals and standards of how land should be used. For example, the definition of what amounts to a fair share of land space for particular uses is being recognized as essentially a legislative and not a judicial function. In a society that relies on supply and demand, as represented in the competitive market, to determine who uses what, the whole concept of government control and allocation, whether by the courts or the legislature, is unacceptable.

Public and Private Rights

It is our historic heritage that has caused the conflict between public and private right to control land use to be more vitriolic in the United States than in Europe. From independence until the late nineteenth century, the basic aim of U.S. land policy was to transfer land ownership and control from the public to the private sector. In the Massachusetts Bill of Rights, for example, John Adams wrote that "all men . . . have certain natural, essential and unalienable rights, among which is that of acquiring, possessing and protecting property." For all practical purposes, this became the guiding principle of the relation of land to government and its citizens, even though the Fifth Amendment limits the protection of property rights to those who possess them.

The root cause of the profound U.S. emotional attachment to preserving very nearly complete private control of the use of land rests in the frontier ethos and the property rights portion of the American Revolution. These feelings are so deeply embedded that they have acquired the same emotional strength as gun control or abortion. The result has been considerable political support for the retention of private control over land use decisions.

Under these conditions, overall federal umbrella legislation cannot be expected to ensure general enjoyment of land, as provided in the Clean Air Act and in the Federal Water Pollution Control Act. Instead, progress must rely on some state legislative action plus court support based on government interest independent of, and in addition to, the titles of its citizens to all the earth and air within the domain of the particular government. (See *Georgia v. Tennessee Copper Co.* 206 U.S. 230 (1907).)

Federal Environmental Protection Support

The Environmental Protection Agency (EPA) operates somewhat differently under the Clean Air Act than under the Federal Water Pollution Control Act. The goals of the two acts as stated in the legislation vary somewhat. Under the Clean Air Act, EPA is charged with protecting people's health and within a reasonable period of time of determining which air components have an adverse impact on public health and therefore public welfare (42 U.S.C. ¶ ¶ 1857 et seq). Under the Federal Water Pollution Control Act, the EPA must restore and maintain the chemical, physical, and biological integrity of surface water throughout the country. (See 33 U.S.C. ¶ 1251 et seq.)

In carrying out its clean water responsibilities, EPA places considerable responsibility on the states. The states must develop water quality standards and plans to implement them. The EPA retains the right of review and approval. The EPA sets clean air standards and goals and the states are responsible for developing procedures to meet these standards.

Obviously, state level activity is encouraged by federal clean water and air legislation. The local government, however, in many instances, remains involved in the costs of meeting the standards and enforcing continued compliance. An uncooperative local government is certain to affect adversely the ability of federal legislation to meet its goals.

It is becoming clear that setting water and air pollution standards affects the location of economic development. An area with air considerably above acceptable pollution levels cannot attract additional industrial development. When this is recognized, the basic question becomes: Is it less desirable to have the air of an area already dirty to become somewhat dirtier than to destroy pristine air quality of another region?

Impact Spillovers

Undoubtedly, water and air quality requirements will prevent use of certain fertilizers and production methods and industry location decisions. These will have spillover production cost effects that will decrease the international competitiveness of U.S. industry. Some regions will experience a declining employment base. Local government must be concerned with these impacts, which may result in a reduced property tax base and higher welfare and crime control costs. International agencies must also be concerned as pressures develop to prohibit international trading in goods produced under conditions that pollute the air and water to a degree that violates standards set by some nations.

Action Stimulants

The clean water and air approach to establishing land use standards through spillover impacts often operates on a very gross basis. Therefore, it becomes necessary to grant exceptions when the date for meeting the standard is reached. An approach that needs more development rests on the assessment of fines on the polluters that are not so high as to make production impossible but would make pollution less profitable. The fines can be gradually increased on a regular schedule.

The use of tax exemptions to encourage installation of pollution equipment can be helpful. The burden it places on the budget is really unjustified, because it establishes a subsidy of a few financed by the general community. The federal government exempts investments in pollution-retarding equipment from the restrictions placed on issuing securities by state and local governments to finance private industrial investment. This financing procedure reduces interest costs because the interest on these securities is exempt from the federal income tax.

Summary

The protection of the environment has become a recognized responsibility of government. Such activity affects both costs and revenues and disturbs the degree of private control over how land is to be used.

Land use control by the private owner is so deeply embedded in the United States that progress cannot be expected to be as rapid and complete as in Western Europe. After all, many of our ancestors came here to avoid government control over land and to own property that would provide economic independence. Therefore, the common good in this area is sometimes achieved only slowly and indirectly. Sometimes more competition in the market where land is purchased and using land more intensively as a tax base can be helpful.

Part VI
State and Local Taxes
Other Than
Property Taxes

24 Retail Sales Taxes

The first state sales tax was enacted in West Virginia in 1921. This innovation did not attract followers until the great depression of the 1930s. Mississippi followed with a retail sales tax in 1932. Before the end of the 1930s some twenty-four states were using a general retail sales tax; today the retail sales tax is used in forty-seven states.

Retail sales taxes levied by many local governments were initiated about the same time as states began to legislate similar taxes. The revenue growth rate of local sales taxes has been much slower than that of state sales taxes. About twenty-seven states use a general retail sales tax by local governments, however. In these states the general sales tax as a local government revenue raiser is mostly limited to the larger cities.

General Retail Sales Tax

Retail sales taxes date back as far as written documents speak of taxation. Historical records show that the sales tax was a portion of the tax system introduced by the rulers of ancient Rome when the booty of war became insufficient to cover expenditures. The sales tax came along with the development of commerce in medieval Europe. At that time, it was a tax on the rich because the worker and the serf purchased little. The land the serf tilled met most of his consumption requirements, and the worker earned little more than board and room for himself and his family.

Economics of Use

The eighteenth- and nineteenth-century British economists frowned on introduction of the sales tax because the *alcabala*, a Spanish sales tax, was seen to have been a major cause of the decline of the Spanish empire. Also, the economic theory developed by the Scotch and British philosophers concluded that any tax increasing prices or reducing savings decreased the growth of the wealth of nations. These analyses resulted in a reduction in the public sector generally and particularly in a reduced use of sales taxes.

Legal Allocation

The federal Constitution gives Congress the power to levy excises without restraint, as long as they are uniform throughout the nation. These sales taxes may be selective or general and they could be levied on sales at wholesale or by the producer as well as on retail transactions.

Through the years Congress had failed to use its indirect (sales and excise) taxation powers. Legislation to enact a national sales tax failed to pass during World War I and again in 1931, just before the wave of state general sales tax legislation. Again, during World War II, a national sales tax was suggested but failed to receive needed congressional support. Finally, in recent years, a national value-added tax (a tax based on marketed production) has been discussed (see chapter 28).

Sales Tax Concept

The sales tax in the United States is largely a retail sales tax that is typically paid as an add-on to the quoted selling price. This type of tax had a twofold purpose: first, the voter would be aware a tax was being paid; second, the tax would be on the purchaser and not the retailer. Also, the small payment by the voter at any one time, for example, made the tax more acceptable. And the sales tax was largely a replacement for the property tax, which in turn was paid 60 percent or so by business and was less easily shifted to buyers.

The qualities a sales tax needs to be a basic and stable revenue raiser are now fairly well understood. However, legislative activity has not always moved toward the ideal qualities that a sales tax should possess.

One desirable characteristic is a distribution formula of tax collections to local governments that meets certain qualifications. The government unit, for example, must levy property taxes at the average state rate and the government must be multipurpose. An ideal sales tax should also apply to sales outside the jurisdiction of the taxing unit to the same extent as to sales within the area collecting the sales tax. The destination principle, in other words, would be abandoned. As a portion of this approach, use taxes would be repealed. A tax that can't be enforced is always a bad tax, and use taxes can't be enforced.

A sales tax that has its base narrowed by eliminating food, medicine, and the like increases enforcement problems while violating a major premise of the tax. One result is, of course, to lay the base for other exemptions. What about clothes, automobiles, and furniture? They are all needed to survive in our society. People buy different kinds of food and other goods depending on wealth and income level. Luxury spending is not limited to jewels and fancy vacations.

A good sales tax should cover sales of services as well as sales of goods. The sales tax is not suited to bring about a redistribution of income and wealth. Efforts to develop a sales tax that corresponds to the ability to pay are bound to increase administration costs and sharply decrease revenue stability. If, however, it becomes a political necessity to make a sales tax progressive, then either a credit against income taxes for those reporting incomes below $10,000 or some similar procedure is preferable to an exemption program. Real progress toward making a sales tax progressive requires introduction of an expenditures tax.

Rate Differences

The central city is very limited in the adjustments it can make to reduce the impact on commercial activity of higher sales tax rates than in neighboring areas. One possible approach is to issue cards to residents living close to or in border population and retail centers. Adoption of the procedure, however, increases fraud opportunities.

The only sensible approach for central city governments is to keep their sales tax rate at a level approximating that existing in the area. The income tax is a better commuter tax than the sales tax. The property tax, particularly the portion levied on land, is the best way for a center city to use a tax rate higher than that used by its neighbors and competing metropolitan areas.

One more aspect of the sales tax should be considered in analyzing its usefulness. The administration of the tax as applied to small retailers and providers of taxable services is weak. The sales tax provides these businesses with the equivalent of a modest subsidy. Louisiana has sharply reduced avoidance by levying the sales tax at the wholesale level. The purchase tax (now replaced by VAT) in the United Kingdom was also administered at the wholesale level. Although the political opposition of many small merchants can be expected if the retail sales tax becomes a tax administered at the wholesale level, it is a reform worth trying.

The concept of "nexus" has been important in court decisions relative to the collection of sales and use taxes on interstate transactions. Nexus is the requirement that some minimum relationship (or nexus) exists between the government attempting to levy a tax and the person, transaction, or property being taxed. If the minimum nexus, such as a facility for storing goods or a collection and sales office exists, then a reasonable tax at the same rate as levied on intrastate sales may be legally collected by the states. That is, the federal Constitution's requirement of due process and not a burden on interstate commerce has been met.

Philosophy

Favoring the sale of inexpensive services over high-cost products is somewhat combined with an effort to make the retail sales tax burden allocation less regressive and to encourage employment. Because exemptions and low rates must be generalized, tax reduction benefits are not limited to low-income receivers and the holders of little wealth. By giving credit on income taxes due for assumed sales taxes paid, and by providing for negative income taxes, a few states have tied sales tax liability to the economic condition of purchasers. However, the procedure has proven to be less effective than expected when introduced in Indiana in 1963.

A point of view relative to the public economy that ties revenues to services provided by government and enjoyed by both high- and low-income citizens requires a joint examination of taxes and expenditures. The retail sales tax finances such services as education and police and fire protection that are needed and utilized by low-income receivers. The dollar the average worker spends on taxes provides perhaps even more useful services than many dollars spent at private businesses.

In this approach, public sector services are appropriately financed with general sales taxes, just as bread is appropriately financed through payment of a price. The relatively small groups living in poverty are best assisted through special programs and not through a tax that attempts to provide government services free to some groups while collecting large payments from others.

Special Provisions

State sales tax legislation frequently provides for local sales taxes and sets down conditions for their use. About 50 percent of the largest cities of the nation use a general sales tax; they rely on the tax to provide around 25 percent of total city tax collections. The general retail sales tax provides about 14 percent of total state and local government revenues from own sources.

To avoid endless confusion and high collection costs, these city sales taxes must conform with state sales tax provisions, particularly as to vendor payment and the use of a uniform base.

The state and local collections of sales taxes continues to grow through rate, price, and economic growth impacts. The tax is used in nearly all states; therefore, any new sales taxes will be adopted at the local government level. New sales tax legislation will concern itself mostly with coverage and equity. The theoretically ideal retail sales tax has not yet been enacted.

The general sales tax of all states except Hawaii, Louisiana, and Mississippi is levied on the retail transaction. In Hawaii and Mississippi, a multiple-stage sales tax is used. That is, a tax is levied on wholesale transactions and on producer sales as well as retail sales.

Rather frequently, sales of such utility services as transportation, electricity, telephone, gas, and water, are not subject to the regular general retail sales tax. A separate utility tax is levied on these service sales. Frequently, these services are subject to a tax similar to a retail sales tax when purchased by consumers and exempted or taxed at a lower rate when purchased by production and transportation companies.

Sports and entertainment events, restaurant meals, and transient lodging are frequently taxed differently from general retail sales. The tax on meals is often not applicable on meals below a set price, usually around $1. Sports and entertainment events are sometimes taxed on gross receipts, or the rate varies between different types of offerings. Also, participation sports are sometimes tax-exempt.

Transient lodging has become a widely used base for the assessment of regular and also of special retail sales taxes. Rents paid for lodging are usually exempted after occupancy of 30 to 90 days. Rents paid for all permanent quarters are always excluded from the retail sales tax base.

Summary

As used by states and local governments, the general retail sales tax is not really general or a tax on a retail sale only. The tax also carries its share of administrative difficulties that have multiplied as rates have increased and the number and complexity of special provisions have expanded.

The retail sales tax has become a major source of state and local government revenues through default. Actually, a national system of production or business marketing taxes would possess many advantages over the state framework that has developed. These advantages approximate those now enjoyed through use of a national level income tax.

A few basic reforms, particularly the concept of taxing all sales wherever made by the vendor—that is, tax at the source—would sharply reduce evasion and administrative costs.

25 Corporation Income Tax

In some form, the corporation income tax (CIT), is used by all states and by a few local governments. A few states use the CIT instead of the income tax. Total state CIT collections during the past ten years have tended to decline relative to income tax collections. In the 1960s, state corporate income taxes were about one-half as great as state income tax collections. The ratio has declined to about one-third. The relative decrease in the importance of corporate income taxes has two basic causes: (1) the failure of corporate profit levels to keep up with the growth of personal income, and (2) the more numerous legislative provisions that increase effective income tax rates rather than increase effective corporate income tax rates.

In 1911, Wisconsin initiated the first modern CIT. Since then, most states have established a CIT to go along with the income tax. Over two-thirds of the states have flat CIT rates that vary from 4 to 12 percent. About two-thirds of the states apply their CIT rates to a definition of taxable corporate income that corresponds with the concept developed by the federal government.

Multistate Corporations

The administration of CIT by states and local governments is complicated when taxable income is earned by a corporation operating in several states. Basically, it is not always obvious where profits should be sourced. For example, do profits arise where production takes place? Or where the sale is made? Also, do the states through which the product is transported and perhaps stored have a claim to a portion of the taxable corporate income base?

These are persistent and serious questions that have not been satisfactorily answered in either law or practice. The conflict must be carried out within limits set by the federal government under the constitutional provision prohibiting restriction of interstate commerce. With requirements of the federal Constitution in mind, general rules for dividing a corporation's taxable income among the several states has been worked out.

The three elements included in apportionment formulas are property, sales, and payroll. The so-called Massachusetts formula gives equal weight to each element. Under this formula, which is the most widely used of all similar state formulas, a firm with 10 percent of its property, 30 percent of its sales, and 2 percent of its payroll in state X would be subject to the CIT of state X on 14 percent of its total taxable income. The simple and generalized calculation is:

$$\frac{10 + 30 + 2}{3} = \frac{42}{3} = 14.$$

If all states used the same formula and all states used the same tax rate and the same definition of taxable income, the application of the taxable income allocation formula would result in the same total tax being collected as would be true from a national tax of the same rate. Because states apply a number of formulas and because the definitions of taxable income varies somewhat between states, the multistate corporation often pays state CIT on a base that is considerably less than the national total as established by the federal government.

Since at least 1956, Congress has been actively engaged in the development of legislation that would fairly allocate corporate income to the different states while avoiding taxes that would restrict interstate commerce. At the same time, the courts have been concerned with defining exactly when the federal Constitutional provision guaranteeing freedom of interstate commerce is violated.

Allocation Conflict

The pot came to a boil in 1959 when Congress restricted the states from collecting taxes from a corporation that only solicited orders within a state. A year later the Supreme Court, in *Scripto, Inc. v. Carson* (362 U.S. 207 (1960)), restored the states' ability to declare a corporation to be doing business within a state that was based on sales only.

A massive study, titled *State Taxation of Interstate Commerce*, was completed in 1964. One result of the study was active development and presentation of federal legislation requiring use of a uniform two-component (payroll and property) profit allocation formula. This legislation was actively fought by states that provided large markets for sales of goods produced in other states. The legislation was not adopted and died in the U.S. Senate in 1968. While this legislation (the Willis Bill) was pending, a group of professionals in state and local taxation under the auspices of the Council of State Governments drafted "The Multistate Tax Compact." The Multistate Tax Commission (MTC) operates under the provisions of this compact.

The use of the sales factor in the allocation of corporate income between states usually results in undertaxation. This arises because the corporation deducts full out-of-state sales from its home state tax base but does not report fully those sales as made in other states. The Multistate Tax Commission has made some progress in overcoming state CIT enforcement administrative difficulties; for example, expansion of joint audits of the books of corporations doing a multistate business. Growth in this direction seems much more likely, and perhaps desirable, than either a federal CIT slice made available to the states on an agreed-on uniform basis, or a continuation of the existing expensive and inaccurate administrative machinery.

State activity toward joint audit and administration of CIT is organized under the MTC. It includes over 15 full member states (mostly in the West) and another 15 associate members. Progress continues, but slowly. Recently, legality of MTC actions were upheld by both state and federal courts.

The legitimate principal goal of a corporation is making a profit. Yet profit is used as the base of the CIT. Efforts to avoid the full impact of the CIT have developed extremely complicated legislation and regulations. Such a wealth of special deals and pitfalls have been created that the oracles of the Internal Revenue Code must be consulted at each business decision and personal investment choice.

The selection of one particular accounting concept as the base to which a high tax rate is applied has resulted in continued pleas to Congress for places to locate earnings so that they won't be counted in taxable income. The high combined state and federal CIT rates make efforts to reduce taxable corporate profits eminently worthwhile. Possible savings justify allocation of the very best corporate brainpower to this activity.

As someone has said, "If a mad genius were to sit down to develop a method of taxing business that would maximize uneconomic behavior—the outcome would be the American CIT." But if this same genius were asked to devise a tax that would do most to facilitate monopoly he would come up with something like CIT, and he would not be considered mad.

Incidence

The popularity of the CIT with economists and the unsanctified arose from its supposed incidence—that is, the location of economic burden. The incidence was believed to rest on profits—that is, the return to equity capital—and not on wages. It was further believed that providers of equity capital, owners of common stock, could not recover the tax payment with higher prices and profits. The whole house of cards was built on a belief the marginal firm—the no-profit, and therefore the non-CIT paying firm—set prices. This may have been true in the days before the corporate giants. It is no longer the case.

In considering the incidence of CIT, several questions come to mind. How have profits as a percentage of national income been affected? How has the return on investment been affected? How have profits as a percentage of business sales changed?

The rate of return has not fallen as the CIT rates have increased. Based on this fact, we must conclude that the corporate income tax does not reduce profits. Profits as a percentage of national income, however, have decreased as CIT rates have risen. Also, profits as a portion of business sales have decreased as corporate income taxes have risen. Does this mean CIT has reduced profits after all?

A reliable study shows that the increase in the after-CIT earnings per dollar of investment has been due to the added efficiency per dollar of capital in terms of dollars of sales. This same effect could have arisen by setting prices to meet a profit goal.

The net rate of return on the total capital base of all manufacturing corporations is calculated to have been 7.6 percent during the 1927–1929 period when the statutory rate of the federal CIT was 11 to 13.5 percent; the net return was 6.3 percent during the 1936–1939 period when federal corporate statutory rates were 13 to 19 percent. In the 1955–1957 period when CIT federal rates were 52 percent, the profit rate was 8.5 percent. The highest after-tax profit rates arose when federal CIT rates were the highest.

Another study, covering the 1923–1941 and 1946–1959 periods, concluded effective tax rates were statistically insignificant in determining corporate profits before taxes and before depreciation. The study showed that corporate profits taxes had their incidence on corporate profits and that the expanding rate of return after taxes resulted from a shortage of capital.

Obviously, all the studies are unsatisfactory. Many elements, such as inflation rate, union strength, international competition, changes in definition of profits, and the like, affected their findings. The impact of CIT cannot be isolated satisfactorily.

Perhaps the most thorough and also the most unsatisfactory study concluded that after-tax corporate profits were increased by higher corporate profit taxes (see Krzyaniak and Musgrave).

Marginal Firm

Theoretical developments built on the research findings have demonstrated the CIT is not absorbed, at least in the long run, by the stockholders. It has also been demonstrated that prices are set by the most profitable and powerful firms, not by the usually economically weak no-profit operation. The dominant firms of an industry set prices to reach appropriate profit margins. The profit goal is income after CIT has been paid or estimated, and not before.

The marginal firm under this set of circumstances is a very different creature. It is not the hardy pricesetter. It becomes the firm being protected by an umbrella erected by the high CIT payer. In the long run, the high CIT payments of the stronger and more efficient firms cause prices to be set higher than would be the case without the tax. This takes place during the normal business of setting profit targets. The gradual adjustment to a new CIT level permits weak firms to charge higher prices than they could if the efficient and high profit firms were not subject to CIT. They are able to survive, at least for a while.

Another source of early CIT support was a belief it reduced savings. This was associated with the idea that its incidence was on equity capital providers—the last of the big savers. Lower savings was an economic change to be desired in the 1930s, with its 2 percent interest rates and 10 to 25 percent unemployment levels.

Excess savings may again become a problem, but this is not the current expectation. The rebuilding of many cities and the need for investment in environment preservation and urban transportation are a few among the many expected savings absorbers. This year, and for many years ahead, it looks as if all the potential savings will be needed that can be generated in a society bombarded continuously by consumption appeals and continually improving its protection from loss of income and poverty through sickness or old age. One development decreases ability to save and the other the need to save: a one-two punch that could quite effectively keep savings in short supply.

Savings Shortage

CIT as a separate and double tax on profits paid out as dividends has lost favor because (1) national savings levels are not in excess, (2) the incidence of CIT is not certain, and (3) its revenue-providing instability is now seen to have economically destabilizing elements that may outweigh cyclical benefits attributed to CIT because it sharply decreased government deficits during prosperity and increased deficits sharply during recession periods. Another shortcoming of CIT arises from the favors it gives to business debt financing relative to use of equity. The individual income tax is applied to corporate profits distributed as dividends at the same rate as corporate payments of interest. These same dividends, as corporate profits, have often been already taxed at the high CIT tax rate. Interest payments, on the other hand, are deductible from corporate profits before the CIT rate is applied. The effect is to encourage financing with debt capital and to discourage use of equity capital. As a result, businesses must maintain stable cash flows, a situation unsuited to aggressive entrepreneurship and an economy possessing substantial discretionary purchasing power that shifts rather quickly between various offered products and services. Finally, the taxation of capital gains from ownership and sale of corporate common stock is a third tax on corporate profits.

Summary

The United States pioneered in the development of CIT. Its original popularity arose from a belief that it was a tax based on ability to pay. Later, after the Keynesian economic policy was accepted, CIT was favored because it helped to prevent an excess of savings. Finally, the tax found favor because the sharp variation in the level of collections between prosperity and recession provided a built-in countercyclical fiscal impact. These aspects of CIT, which were accepted without doubt, are now being questioned.

The use of CIT by the states raises allocation of profit problems that are more serious than the allocation difficulties encountered in the administration of retail sales taxes. The unitary or formula approach to the taxation of profits largely prevents loss of a portion of the profits base by state governments. This approach is being developed by the Multistate Tax Commission.

26 Personal Income Taxes

State use of the income tax was initiated when Wisconsin adopted an income tax in 1911. The spread of the tax to other states was slow but relatively steady; by 1930, thirty states had an income tax. The tax is now used by over 90 percent of the states, but in several of these user states collections are nominal. State collections have been expanding rapidly; they now nearly equal state sales tax collections.

Local income taxes are levied in about a dozen states. Most of the use exists in states without an income tax or that make very nominal use of the income tax at the state level. These states are clustered in the Midwestern industrial portion of the nation. The local government income tax collections are about one-tenth as great as state collections. The rate of growth of local government income tax collections has also been somewhat slower than that of state income tax collections.

National Progressive Rate Tax

The federal government actively entered the income tax arena by adopting the Sixteenth Amendment to the federal Constitution in 1913. The substantial use of the income tax by the federal government has restrained state use of this type of taxation that was originally the prerogative of the states. Roy G. and Gladys C. Blakey, in their 1940 history of the U.S. personal income tax, conclude that the Sixteenth Amendment and the 1913 establishing legislation were "really the result of a great equalitarian movement generated by two prolonged post-war depressions of great severity." Twenty-five years later, Goode quotes with approval the *Internal Revenue Bulletin* and sees the 1913 income tax to be a response to "the general demand for justice in taxation, and to the long-standing need of an elastic and productive system of revenue."

To the ordinary voters, as the Blakeys saw it, income meant money to spend, and most were short of spending money. However, some—the big income earners—had lots of spending money; so taxing incomes was fine—but only the big incomes—then those with a shortage of spending money wouldn't have to pay taxes. Goode seems to believe the voter was considerably more sophisticated. More than likely he is wrong, as was the *Internal Revenue Cumulative Bulletin* of 1959, when they reprinted a portion of the House Report of April 22, 1913.

The Blakeys' argument is more persuasive. Most voters probably favored the income tax in 1913 because they wouldn't have to pay it. Also, they didn't believe the tax would be harmful to the country and therefore indirectly to them. This tax, restored after use during the Civil War, was to be paid by those relatively few defined by the law to be subject to the tax.

The 1913 Income Tax Act collected taxes from less than 1 percent of the population. Even as recently as just before World War Two, less than 5 percent of the population made out federal income tax returns or were dependents of those who did.

However, most purchasers of tobacco and alcoholic beverage products paid a federal tax, and they knew it. Also, tariff duties, that on sugar, for example, looked as though they increased prices; prices paid by everyone out of incomes that were too small to meet all of the needs of the family.

It has always been difficult to definitely determine how a tax basically affects prices of goods sold for consumption, or prices of goods or labor used in production. The voter to whom the politician was appealing in 1913 was convinced that the things he purchased would not increase in price if 1 percent of the population began to pay an income tax, nor would it cause his personal income to decrease. The problems of defining what income was or how income from one source differed in ability to bear taxes from income from another source was an academic question for the 99 percent of the population exempt from the tax in 1913.

The question is no longer academic today. Over 75 percent of the population pay an income tax or are dependents of those who do. Despite the vast increase during the past thirty years in the portion of the population required to pay the tax due on this quantity called taxable income, really, relatively few questions were asked before 1968, when Joseph W. Barr, the outgoing secretary of the Treasury, talked of a taxpayer's revolt. But then revolt was in the air in 1968 as it is again in 1979.

When the voter of 1913 stopped to contemplate why 1 percent of the population should pay the new income tax, he more than likely concluded it was because those with a taxable income that high possessed an unusual capacity to pay. If the voters of the 1970s thought about why they considered the income tax desirable, they would probably say because the tax was based on ability to pay, but that they, as individual payers, didn't have the ability. Actually, the question of whether an income tax is a good tax is not being asked in any concerted fashion. Although U.S. economists have been raising the question, but in the United Kingdom not even this group seems to have bothered. The reasons for the general lack of concern of economists and average voters, as the income tax became a substantial tax paid by about everyone, must be related to too many things happening too quickly—the initiation of tax withholding, the need to finance a big war, inflation, and the introduction of social security—all took place within a short seven-year period.

In addition, U.S. private enterprise in the 1940s found protest action difficult because business was still suffering from the scandals and failures that had been securely tied to it during the political campaigns of the 1930s.

The failure of the British economists to even consider whether income as defined for setting the base of the income tax also represented taxpaying capacity seems to be the result of complete mesmerization. Over 100 years of British tradition have made income and taxpaying capacity synonymous— even to economists. So in the United States and the United Kingdom the income tax grew—hardly with a challenge—and the efforts to define a basically undefinable concept became even more frantic, and exemptions and adjustments and special provisions became ever more complicated.

Actually, as Gunner Myrdal, the 1974 Nobel prize winner in economics, has pointed out, the entire theoretical framework of justice used to support the progressive income tax is faulty, without arguing the merits or demerits of utility and individual satisfactions.

The aim of equating satisfactions from spending or receiving the last dollar works at the margin and does not consider total satisfactions. Actually, any value judgments must be concerned with total utilities. Myrdal concludes that "even if subjective value theory could evolve a political rule, this would have to aim at a maximization or a just distribution of *total* utilities and not of marginal utilities."

How can the effect on total satisfaction of a tax-created income equalization or disequalization be measured even subjectively? The heart of the artichoke is that the plausible justification of the progressive income tax provided by marginal utility analysis fails even if all assumptions are accepted. (*Marginal utility* is a measurement of the satisfaction of the last unit and this is not the appropriate concept to use in measuring total satisfaction. Rather it is the concept of total utility that is needed, and the conceptual job of dealing with total utility is unresolved.)

Horizontal Equality of Treatment

To the average voter and taxpayer, the personal income tax is just because the amount paid corresponds with the individual's ability to pay. The meaning of this abstraction is that those with larger incomes, however measured or defined, can pay a bigger portion of these incomes in taxes without giving up expenditures for goods and services included within the good life, which is the way it happens under the progressive personal income tax. It was not until 1968 that studies were publicized that demonstrated how many wealthy receivers of large incomes paid very little income taxes.

More than likely, the average voter will always give little consideration to the way the high and progressive rates goad "the capitalist into irrational and anti-social behavior in order to escape taxes." The effect of taxes on society's well-being, arising from the uneconomic decisions stimulated by the progressive income tax, is not yet a portion of the voter picture of the tax.

The social cost or impact on the efficiency of a basically market economy of high income receivers acting in a tax-determined fashion is indeterminant. There may be a social benefit—for example, tax-deductibility has apparent considerable expansionary impact on charitable and other gifts. There may also be a social benefit arising from the pressure toward homeownership arising from the exclusion of imputed rent from occupancy of an owner-occupied home.

These social benefits, if they exist, must be weighed against the locked-in effect high income taxes have on successful investments, the pressure they provide for business consumption spending, the reduction of corporate profit distributions, and the like.

The social benefit of some income-use redistribution must also be weighed against the horizontal inequality arising from the deductibility provisions allowed in arriving at taxable income. Persons in the same economic position, but one renting and one owning his own heavily mortgaged home, have, as a result of the law, quite different income tax liabilities. Also, one taxpayer married and another unmarried, with identical incomes, have quite different tax liabilities. None of the benefits provided by the wife are taxable income, while the purchase of these services when there isn't a housewife to perform them is not deductible.

State Provisions

Only about five states have income tax laws that follow the provisions of the federal income tax nearly exactly. The federal income tax law provisions, nevertheless, extend considerable uniformity to state income tax legislation by providing a model that is not available to those responsible for state sales tax legislation. In fact, several states now apply their income tax by merely collecting a percentage of the federal tax liability. This approach would spread more rapidly if the federal government could once and for all complete its tax reform legislation.

State collections from their income taxes are now nearly equal to the size of sales tax revenues. The growth rate continues to be somewhat more rapid than that of sales taxes. The degree of progressivity existing in state income tax rates has been increasing. Because the states don't generally index to avoid higher rates due to inflation, higher real tax payments result. Greater progressivity, inflation, and failure to index account for a considerable portion of the rapid expansion of state income tax collections.

The median state income tax rate is a little over 3 percent on highest incomes. The top rates are in the 10 percent range. A major determinant of the progressivity of state income taxes is the degree to which federal income taxes are deductible from the tax base. Ten states provide for complete or nearly complete deduction, a growing number limit the deduction, and most states don't permit the deduction. The federal government continues to allow deduction of state and local income taxes from taxable income.

It has been suggested that the federal government give the same treatment to state and local government income tax payments that are now given to income tax payments to foreign governments. Under this procedure, the income tax paid to a state or local government becomes a tax credit and deductible dollar for dollar from income taxes owed the federal government. The income base to which the federal government's income tax rate is applied becomes the gross income total after adding back income taxes paid to state and local governments.

Nearly all states using the income tax have a tax withholding procedure that applies to wage and salary income. Oregon was the first state to introduce withholding. California was the famous laggard and did not act until 1971.

All states with income taxes operate under a federal agreement providing for state cooperative use of returns. One of the amazing aspects of state and local government tax administration is the failure to enact legislation to make income tax returns available to property tax administrators. This information would be very helpful in setting property sales values and therefore the market value of taxable real estate.

The income tax is typically payable to the jurisdiction where the earning activity is sited. A person living in Vancouver, Washington (a nonincome tax state), and working in Portland, Oregon, pays income taxes on salary earned in Oregon (an income tax state). The Oregon rate applies, however, only to earnings in Oregon, and other income sources are not included. If both states have an income tax, the person working in another state can credit against income tax due in his home state the tax on income earned outside the state. There are only one or two states where some difficulty exists in getting credit for income taxes paid on income earned in other states.

Local Government Provisions

Local governments make much less use of the income tax than of the sales tax. The local income tax has not spread across the nation; rather, it is concentrated in a few states and provides only about 2.7 percent of total own-source revenues of local governments. Recently, local income taxes, used as an add-on to all or a portion of the state income tax base, has become popular for financing of transit districts. The tax, when used in this fashion, is entirely withheld by the employer and does not include income other than that included in payroll.

The traditional local income tax does not attempt to go beyond earned income. Earned income is made up largely of salaries, wages, and commissions. Several states make the state income tax base available to local governments. This procedure widens the base of local income taxes while it eliminates the administrative problems associated with a variety of tax bases. Close cooperation of administrators of state income taxes and local tax officials is widely enjoyed where a state income tax exists. Of course, if the state does not have a well-developed income tax administration department, state assistance is not available.

Local income taxes that don't benefit from being coordinated with a state income tax are typically largely payroll taxes, and a flat rate is used. In other instances, such as in New York, the taxable base includes all income included in the federal income tax base. Recent local income tax legislation has tended to exempt low-income earners; rates also tend to be somewhat graduated. The top rates of local income taxes are often below 1 percent and seldom go above 3 percent; therefore graduated rates don't have much income redistribution impact. Where local taxes are a percentage of state taxes, some income redistribution is provided by local income taxes.

Commuter Tax

Frequently the local income tax is seen as a commuter tax. The central city, where most of the high-salary office jobs are located, taxes the people holding these positions; they in turn often live in outlying suburban areas organized as independent governmental units.

A convenient procedure that works toward equity is to have the revenues of local income taxes divided equally between job site and residence site. Living and working in the same community would be encouraged slightly. This could result in some tendency to work closer to one's residence. A result might be retarded scatteration and reduced energy consumption. Location decisions for both jobs and living quarters are affected by many elements. These range from being near friends to making use of land already owned. The impact provided by differences in a low tax rate on income is not likely to control the location decision, but it would be an element in the decision process.

Administration

The costs and efficiency of administration vary, depending on the complexity of the law, the degree to which local enforcement powers are used, and the cooperation received from state and federal governments. In medium-sized cities, the cost of acquiring information on income other than wages and salaries is likely to be greater than the additional revenues. Therefore, if a city or school district is unable to benefit from state administrative support, the actual tax base—no matter what the legislated base is—will be wages, salaries, commissions, and some local business profits.

The local income tax must be withheld by the employer. The right to withhold is somewhat more limited than the right to tax, and legal difficulties sometimes arise when the administrative office is outside the boundaries of the city, but the income is earned within the city. Withholding on the wages received by state and federal employees has been difficult, but legislation increasing local government's power in this respect has been adopted. All these difficulties should be resolved where state and federal employees are taxed on the same base as private sector workers.

The costs of administration of local income taxes tends to be higher than for good property tax administration. The relatively higher administrative costs of the income tax increases when the property tax is limited to land. No local government tax has lower administrative cost than the land tax. The local income tax, if complexity is kept in line and good administrative procedures are used, can be a productive tax with low rates. The administrative costs and the equity of the tax under these conditions will be acceptable.

Summary

The use of general revenue sources such as income taxes has evolved as the state and local government sectors have grown. The administration of income taxes can benefit from close coordination with national information sources. Also, the taxpayers of the nation can benefit from uniformity of approach and a minimum of devices aimed at reducing the relative portion of the tax paid by local residents.

For a time it looked as though the property tax would be largely replaced with income taxes. At least for the time being, this trend has abated. The relative acceptance of the property tax improved with the strong market for land. At the same time, inflation has worked to reduce the desirability of a tax directly deducted from wages that seem to fall behind price increases. The rising social security taxes and the failure of the federal government to index its individual income tax have combined to cause hesitancy in making further use of state and local income taxes.

27 Local Business Taxes

Several business taxes are of growing importance: franchise levies, licenses, and special business taxes using payroll, number of employees, gross receipts, and allocated profits as the base. One stimulant of recent years has grown out of the need for revenues to finance transit district deficits and to encourage pollution control.

The typical city business tax is related to a license or a franchise of some sort. These are usually flat rate taxes and in many cases do not provide revenues in excess of related regulatory costs. In granting the right to operate a business within a city, the city is also assuming responsibility for protecting its citizens from being harmed by the activity.

Franchises granted to utilities, on the other hand, are frequently taxed as a percentage of gross revenues. The rates are typically around 2 or 3 percent, with the rates on telephone receipts somewhat higher than on electricity or gas.

Legal Position

The power of municipalities to collect revenues from those engaged in business within its boundaries is not absolute. Both city and state legislation and constitutional provisions limit city ability to tax businesses. In general, the grant by the state to an incorporated city of the power to do what is needed to carry out its local affairs includes the right to levy business license fees, special taxes, and the like.

Business taxes need not be general but can allow exemptions and special treatment. Wholesale businesses, for example, can be taxed differently than retail businesses. Different services, crafts, and different-sized establishments may be subject to various rates. These variations need not be justified by a variation in ability or in the cost of control or protection. The tax differences, however, must be reasonable and not confiscatory. The tax or fee assessed must also be based on the same measurable base for all businesses included in a classification. The classification system must be capable of general application and not established to place an economic burden on a particular establishment.

Different tax rates are sometimes used to make special business and professional taxes applied to gross receipts correspond more closely to economic information as to the portion of income that is above costs. The rate variations can be set on the basis of federal information on mark-up and profitability of different business and professional activities. The procedure is an effort to make special business and professional taxes correspond more closely to a widely accepted concept of fairness. The resulting classes of taxpayers are sufficiently general to meet legal requirements of generality.

Actually, these rate variations for different businesses and professions result in a tax burden that roughly corresponds to a value-added tax (VAT) (see chapter 28). The tax paid depends on the addition to costs in the establishment in arriving at price. Most likely, municipalities have selected rate differences rather than base differences because of familiarity and because records of business costs are not required. When different rates are applied to gross receipts, only sales data are required.

Local business levies are somewhat limited by Article 1, Section 8 of the federal Constitution; that is, the commerce clause. This provision prohibits the payment of a license tax as a condition on carrying on interstate commerce. The interpretation of this prohibition permits the levy of taxes that are not greater than a fair share of the costs of government. Even interstate commerce must pay its way, but taxes or license fees of a state or locality may not discriminate in favor of local firms at the expense of interstate trade.

The Supreme Court decision in *Michigan-Wisconsin Pipe Line Co. v. Calvert*, 347 U.S. 157 at 166(1954) remains the best statement of what can and cannot be done in taxing interstate commerce. The Court stated:

> a tax imposed on a local activity related to interstate commerce is valid if, and only if, the local activity is not such an integral part of the interstate process, the flow of commerce, that it cannot realistically be separated from it.

Municipal governments typically run afoul the commerce clause of the federal Constitution when an attempt is made to levy too heavy a tax only on business done in the city by those without a local establishment or office of any sort. The Court has said that local business taxes must be of such a type that interstate business can be conducted on a plane of equality with local businesses.

Business Tax Allocation

The Multistate Tax Commission (MTC) and the revenue departments of different states and cities are refining the concept of taxable business income sales, particularly the allocation problem associated with determining where a sale takes place and where income is earned. Although the concepts of the destination and origin principles are loosely followed, they have not been adequate to carry the full burden of the allocation assignment. (*Destination principle* is defined as sales taxes levied where the ultimate consumption takes place; the *origin principle* as income allocated to the area where the production took place.)

The three-factor formula for allocating all business income, and treatment of income of the business firm that arises from non-business activity are two areas of considerable hassle between different users of business income as a tax base. That is, wages, property and sales taking place in the jurisdiction as a percentage of the total are added and divided by three. The resulting percentage is applied to income.

Another area of difficulty has been whether the property percentage allocated to a state under the three-factor formula should be calculated on a property base that includes property located in a state not taxing the income of this business firm. The same adjustment in the sales and wages total would be carried out. The term *throwback* is used to refer to out-of-state sales made in an area that has no jurisdiction to tax them. These sales then become taxable in the originating state.

Property, wages, and sales not allocated to nonbusiness taxing states increases the base to which the calculated percentage based on actual activity are applied.

The unitary rule, which is being actively developed by the Multistate Tax Commission and its member states, has gone beyond advocacy as a domestic policy. The proposed tax treaty between the United States and the United Kingdom was modified by the U.S. Senate to provide for the application of the unitary rule.

The unitary rule provides that all the income of the businesses within the control group—wherever earned—would become a portion of the base to which an allocation percentage would be applied. Businesses operating only domestically and those operating on a worldwide basis like to play the shell game. The game is to transfer income between different corporations to minimize the base allocated to the jurisdiction using substantial tax rates. The application of the unitary rule largely closes down the game.

Several counterpoints bear consideration in evaluating the unitary approach to business taxation and the work of the MTC. The treatment of corporations on a unitary basis is said to justify the allowance for income taxes paid in other states. If this were done, all states would be treated as a combined tax collection unit, just as all the corporate members of a group are combined to become a single taxpayer under the unitary approach.

Another shortcoming of the MTC and the compact developed by member states arises because only about one-half the states are full members and they represent less than one-half of American corporate activity. Therefore, the compact approach largely results in just another variety of corporate taxation. The voluntary nature of MTC means the likelihood of full state representation is small. The states have used corporate tax legislation as a policy tool to attract industry and to reduce taxes paid by voters. They are not likely to abandon this aspect of tax legislation. As a result, membership in MTC will fluctuate and the trend to date demonstrates that membership is as likely to decline as increase. This will continue to be true unless federal legislation makes membership very attractive to the states, or corporations push actively for the adoption of the compact.

Uniform auditing procedures permit one group of accountants from MTC to go to corporate headquarters and complete the audit for all the states in which the corporate group operates, thus reducing auditing cost to the revenue departments of both the states and the corporation. If the tax laws of the states vary, correction for this variation can be accomplished by the individual state after the MTC audit is completed.

One aspect of the growth of the MTC efforts to develop uniform corporate tax administration by the states has been a realization of the importance of the problem of enforcing state corporate income tax laws and also sales taxes. The declaration of the legality of the compact and the additional revenues state membership has provided means the concept is here to stay. Tax uniformity will not be complete, but state administration of taxes under modern conditions will be improved. This in turn will help to relieve the federal government from some revenue-raising responsibility.

Gross Receipts Tax

Special gross receipt business taxes, whether at one rate or a variety of rates, have proved to be relatively easy to administer. The gross receipts tax problem of inequity if only one rate is used and difficulty in setting appropriate rates for each business if a variety of rates are used can be reduced by giving each firm a choice of paying on the gross receipts base or the net profit base, with an appropriate rate for each base. The gross receipts or net income choice solves a number of difficult administrative and justice problems. The choice also tends to increase the decline in revenues during a recession and to dampen the increase in revenues during a boom. The impact of these two forces may somewhat stabilize receipts, but does so at the expense of lower average revenues.

The use of a choice of tax bases would generally result in the use of the base which at the existing rate would produce the lowest tax liability. A firm producing products largely sold outside the city of production would treat the tax, whether on profits or receipts, as an expense to be allocated among products sold or recovered in lower payments for labor, land, and capital. If the business tax, added to property taxes and all other costs including land costs, turns out to produce a higher cost than would exist at an alternative location, then, of course, the firm would bargain for an adjustment and make plans to expand at other locations. Business taxation costs, other than payroll taxes, often become a marginal consideration when two possible locations are about equally attractive.

The taxation of businesses producing for an export market is restricted by relative costs. Taxes cannot be so high that the advantages of the location are more than eaten up by tax liabilities in excess of those existing elsewhere. Taxation of businesses servicing local businesses and meeting consumer demands are restricted to limits set by cost and convenience of alternatives. Both these limits to local and state taxation of business vary between types of activity and because of special circumstances; for example, quantity of sunk investment and variation in market strength.

In setting business taxation policy, general guidelines such as those mentioned can be helpful. One does not wish to kill the goose that lays the golden eggs, but local government wants to gather in its share of the bounty.

License Fees and Taxes

The use of business licenses with low flat rates can be defended as needed to provide some control over business operation procedures. The removal of license or failure to grant a license can be very helpful in causing a business firm to operate as established by municipal and state legislation. The charge made is a cost of doing business and a payment for certain inspection services that can be helpful to both the business and the customers. The use of a flat fee favors the larger businesses. This favoritism is often modified by adding on to the basic fee an amount for each employee, and in some cases making the square feet of floor space an element in setting the license charge.

Making adjustments to the flat license charge can become extremely complex. The defenders of a simple, flat rate point to the advantages of administrative simplicity and ease of compliance of the flat rate. They think that only if a *patente* business tax system (that is, major local French tax of business based on physical evidence of level of business activity) is introduced, the level of business activity indications should become an element in setting the license charge.

A city license fee system that tacks on an additional $5 for each employee provides additional revenues at a low compliance cost for employers. Receipts will expand as employment grows. The number of employees, of course, does not reflect the profit margin and therefore is unacceptable to those believing all business taxes should be based on ability to pay as measured by profits. Actually, many government costs related to business are closely related to size. The expenditures demanded for police, fire protection, education, streets, and the like are more closely related to number of employees than to profits.

General Points

There certainly are many justifications for using profits as the basis for taxing business. Taxing profits is a method for the general society to share in the good fortune of profitable enterprises. When only profits are used as a business tax base, those businesses not earning a profit, in a fashion, are not carrying their fair share of the costs of government. Government costs are not limited to meeting the needs of profitable businesses. Government service needs are likely not to vary because of the profitability or unprofitability of business firms.

In practice, no general principles seem to be followed in setting rates of flat fee business taxes. They, however, usually vary by type of business, such as retail, manufacturing, or storage. The rates tend to be higher for licensees who don't have a fixed place of business and therefore do not contribute directly or indirectly to the city's property tax collections. These businesses, in addition, do not contribute to the citizen government activities of the community.

Also, in practice, almost no aspect of business has not been used as a base for a tax on business. The variety of classifications go from pinball machines to multiple-unit apartments. Many of these tax classifications have gained additional justification as personal property assessments have failed to keep the business property tax rolls current.

Pollution Control

The National Environmental Policy Act of 1970 committed the federal government to limiting the pollution of air and water of the nation. All states have enacted legislation of various types and with various degrees of effectiveness aimed at reaching similar goals. An important portion of this overall national effort to control pollution is the use of state and local government taxes to induce businesses to cut back to federal standards before the deadline; and in many cases to meet even stiffer state and local pollution standards.

Basically, two procedures speed up introduction of pollution control equipment. One is to give subsidies such as rapid depreciation or tax credits if polluters clean up their operations. The other is to assess fees or levy taxes on all pollutants in excess of an allowable limit; in other words, you pay to pollute. Under the first procedure, the polluting industry is likely to stay. Under the second approach, threats to leave or close down can be expected. However, under the first procedure all nonpolluting industries will become restive, for in a way they are paying the pollution control costs of the polluting firms.

Another approach to pollution control is to levy a special tax on products that are produced by pollution creation processes. The higher price would induce people to reduce their purchases, which might cause the producers to abandon the product or to introduce nonpolluting production methods. The special excises collected by the state and local governments could be used to help pay for improvements in local sewage disposal systems.

Summary

The major nonproperty business taxes used by cities are included in the following three classifications:

1. Taxes imposed on franchises granted to public utilities for the privilege of doing business within the city. These collections are partially a procedure for sharing with the people a portion of the monopoly profits arising from the exercise of the franchise. The payments, in addition, amount to compensation for the inconvenience and expense caused by the operations of the utility.
2. Fees and payments required of businesses to pay costs of required regulatory activities so the people of the city will be protected and the city will know the types of activities being carried out by businesses within its limits. The use of taxes to control pollution of air and water is a new area for use of traditional local government regulatory and fee assessment traditions.
3. Business taxes based on a number of measures and classifications where the collections are considerably in excess of any regulatory cost.

28 Reform and Experimental Taxes

State and local government own-source revenues and the federal government's grants and aid programs rely for funds on the same three-legged tax stool—sales, property, and income. To a considerable degree, however, the revenue sources used by each level of government are separated. This traditional separation of tax revenue sources allocates income and profit taxes to the federal government, sales taxes to state government, and property taxes to local governments and special districts. It provides a rough approximation of taxes basic to financing the three divisions of government. Revenue separation was never wholly achieved; in fact, today there is considerable doubt that the goal is really desirable. Weaknesses of sales, income, and property taxes have also become apparent as rates have been increased and exemptions expanded.

Expenditure Tax

The taxation of expenditures after allocating them to individual spenders, with the tax rate increasing with the annual total expenditure level of individuals or families, has been advocated since Thomas Hobbes favored it in the seventeenth century. The expenditure tax has always been considered a practical approach to the levy of a tax with progressive rates on the amount people withdraw from the common pool of consumer goods and services produced with available labor, natural resources, and capital.

Nearly always, the expenditure tax has raised discussions about whether it is a better way to raise revenues than the personal income tax with progressive rates. Also, analyses have looked at the tax as a national levy, not as a local tax. More than likely, both these emphases have reduced experimentation with the tax.

State and Local Government Use

The expenditure tax has two faces—conservative and liberal. The tax, by applying a progressive tax rate on spending and exempting a basic spending to support life, can be a tax on the big spenders and those who have demonstrated an ability to pay by their spending decisions. This is the liberal face.

By exempting income not spent (that is, saved), the tax favors high-income receivers. Those able to save a large proportion of their income are generally the high-income receivers. Therefore, the expenditure tax levies a low level of taxes on the high-income receivers that are careful spenders. This is its conservative face.

The tax would probably be as easy to levy by local governments as the retail sales tax or the personal income tax. The expenditure tax at the local and state levels would not benefit from federal enforcement as does the personal income tax. But, because the federal government does not levy a general transactions tax, state and local governments are largely on their own in the administration of the retail sales tax—as would be the case if an expenditure tax were used. For both the expenditure tax and the retail sales tax to some extent, however, personal and business income tax data can help to identify at least the general limits within which the tax base of individuals and families should fall.

The expenditure base on which the tax rate is applied can be calculated most easily by requiring a listing of all financial assets sold and subtracting all financial assets purchased. The resulting net figure is added or subtracted from total income to arrive at an expenditure base. This base then can be adjusted in the same way as gross income in arriving at taxable income under the income tax. The administration of the tax is not simple, but neither is any tax once the special interest groups modify the basic concept to make it "fair."

The advantage of using the expenditure tax for a local or state government is its attractiveness compared to the basically regressive retail sales tax and the higher taxation of wage income and profits, which are already being subjected to a number of taxes. So far, no state or local government has tried the tax. It was used in India and Sri-lanka, but dropped in 1966. The federal government talked about it in 1942 to assist with the financing of World War II, but the Senate Finance Committee rejected the proposal. The expenditure tax is a viable alternative to the traditional personal income and retail sales taxes as a revenue source for state and local governments.

Treatment of Savings

Advocates have found calculating the level of expenditures an administrative difficulty. For most people, however, the level of expenditures can be calculated by subtracting or adding changes in savings to the income received. An increase in savings would demonstrate an expenditures total less than income received.

A decrease in savings shows an expenditure level in excess of income by the amount of the dissaving. The tax rates would be progressive based on total income, minus or plus changes in savings.

Advocates see the tax to be particularly desirable in developing countries

,because savings go tax-free whereas expenditures are taxed at progressive rates. The relative weakness of the tax administration services of low-income nations has made the expenditure tax impractical in the very areas where it would be most useful.

It may be impractical in a modern society, with savings and wealth in many forms, to determine the level of dissaving or additional saving to arrive at the expenditure total of those with considerable wealth. If this is the case, as seems quite likely, the base of the expenditure tax would have to be calculated directly from information about purchases. Fair enforcement, in either case, would require considerable investigation into the private lives of citizens.

Site Value Tax

The general property tax at one time was seen to be a tax that included all wealth. The Kelley Act of 1846 in Ohio brought this concept to fruition in the uniform rule of taxation according to value of all property not exempted by the legislature. Since then, exemptions have increased; recently, the application of different rates on property of different types or uniform rates to values below market value if the land were used for certain purposes has been provided for in state property tax legislation. These developments, plus some basic economic concepts relative to land that go back to the beginnings of agriculture societies, have resulted in proposals of the site value tax (SVT) concept. SVT is also called Land Value Tax (LVT); see chapter 18.

SVT, which is levied on the full market value of land, envisages that taxes on structures would be repealed. The loss of structures and personal property as a portion of the property tax base reduces the base to around one-third of the existing level. Under the SVT concept, a large portion of the revenue that would be lost if the same rate applied to a much smaller base is made up by applying a higher rate to the base now consisting only of land. In addition, it is envisaged that greater use will be made of charges for government services that may be required. The services can be quantified by use, so that charges can be assessed.

The SVT approach to property taxation is used abroad more than in the United States. It is predominant in Australia, New Zealand, Dénmark, South Africa, and Jamaica. It is used in Western Canada and in localities of Michigan, Alabama, California, New Jersey, and Pennsylvania. Hawaii has experimented with SVT at the state level and every year SVT legislation is introduced in a number of state legislatures.

The big advantage of SVT is that it rests on a factor—that is, land—which is not produced; therefore, the quantity will not decline if the profitability of ownership is reduced. An important aspect of the movement away from taxing capital value of houses and other structures is that the cost of ownership may be reduced and certainly does not increase as additions and improvements are made. This cost reduction stimulates construction, which is seen to be a step toward reduced prices for housing and commercial and industrial buildings. The price reduction of structures is seen to be the result of the free market adapting to an increase of supply. In addition, the service charges plus the SVT at the new high rates will be lower as a percent of total value on well-developed properties than under the traditional property tax.

SVT encounters all the difficulties inherent in introducing change which makes some people worse off, at least in the short-run. The use of SVT increases the taxes on land that is not developed up to its full potential, such as vacant lots. The owners of such land can prevent an increase in taxes as a percentage of capital value by bringing the improvements up to the average level in the tax district. It takes time to do this, and perhaps several sales of the land will be required before a person capable and willing to make full use of the land becomes its owner. During this period, the land will decline in value because of larger carrying costs arising out of the higher SVT tax rate.

The advantage to a local or state government in using SVT, at least in a modified form, to raise additional state revenues to pay the costs of education, for example, is that the higher tax encourages business and avoids higher tax deductions from payroll checks and higher costs of living. SVT is the only tax approach with both these strengths. The complete adoption of SVT would also reduce the administrative costs and difficulties of the traditional property tax.

Value-Added Tax

Since Michigan adopted a value-added tax (VAT) in 1953, repealed it in 1967 and then readopted it in 1975, this tax has been considered at one time or another by most of the states of the nation and some cities. The tax has been used less in the United States, however, than in Western Europe and in several of the new industrialized nations.

VAT goes under a number of names. Michigan, for example, used "Business Activity Tax" (BAT) between 1953 and 1967, and "Single Business Tax" (SBT) in 1975 legislation. The term "commercial transaction tax" has been considered by many to be the most accurate title. However, whatever title is used, the base of VAT is the portion of the selling price that represents value added by the firm making the sale.

For example, the base of VAT can be considered as the selling price of the good. The VAT paid in the purchase of goods and services used by the firm is deductible from the VAT collected on sales. This difference sets the size of the check the firm sends to the tax collector. Each taxpaying firm collects the VAT it has paid on its purchases from those purchasing from it, until the service or product finds its final destination—that is, when it is used by someone not involved directly in commercial production or commercial sales.

This example illustrates two major points often made. First, VAT is a tax with a widely distributed burden. Second, VAT is only a complicated sales tax and its burden rests on consumers. Both of these statements are partially true, but because VAT does include sales made by business to business, and its base is built up by production activity as iron ore, for example, moves from an iron mine in northern Minnesota to an automobile sold, it is more accurate to say that VAT is a tax on GNP and even on that portion of GNP used and produced by governmen

VAT is a tax on production that enters the market, plus some in-firm capital goods production activity. Therefore, VAT is a tax on production, but the tax is not payable generally until the sale is consummated or in some cases the price is paid. Therefore, VAT is a production tax administered through the marketing mechanism.

The advantage of VAT over a retail sales tax, for example, is that sales other than retail are included in the base. For example, goods manufactured and sold abroad or in other states or in case of a local VAT in another city, are taxable and in the base to which the rate is applied. Also, if a government wishes, export sales can be encouraged by refunding VAT on these sales.

Michigan's experience in administering and paying a VAT generally indicates that as long as taxes must be collected, a portion of the revenues, and perhaps a relatively large portion, should be collected from the application of VAT. If more revenues are needed, and the retail sales tax rate appears to be at its upper limit, VAT is a very workable alternative. If this were done, larger revenues could be collected at lower rates.

Summary

Three major tax concepts—the expenditure tax, the site value tax and the value-added tax—have many strengths, but have not found favor in the United States. The record of taxation change demonstrates that new forms of taxation are only introduced when political and economic pressures are particularly strong. On occasion, it appears that such levels of dissatisfaction have been reached in the United States, but significant tax changes have not yet resulted.

There is an old saying that a "good tax is an old tax." The truth of this adage lies in the price and income adjustments that have been completed under the old tax. The introduction of a new tax and the abandonment of an old tax requires a whole new set of price and income interrelationships. In the process, the economic position of some will worsen. Those harmed will see the new tax as a bad tax.

Part VII
Relating Service
Levels
to Revenues

29 Public Prices and Government Services

When a business or an individual consumes or uses a commodity or service, a price must be paid. The price asked by the seller is paid by the buyer, and the buyer uses and enjoys the purchase. The buyer will reject the product when it is not an absolute necessity and the price is seen to be much too high. The product or service, no matter how useful it would be, cannot be purchased, of course, if the potential user does not have the funds needed for payment and cannot borrow them. Both the public and private sectors can operate in this fashion. In addition, the public sector, through use of tax revenues, can purchase the needed product or service and provide it freely to the user.

Tax-Financed Use and Income

If the government producer, instead of selling for a price, made the goods and services available free with costs covered with a tax, then goods are provided through the public sector under conditions quite different from those existing in the private sector. Extent of use is not set by willingness to pay a price that covers costs set under conditions described. Instead, use is determined by quantities available, and ability, because of certain conditions, to utilize the service or good. The phrase "use according to need" is the shorthand statement of the conditions existing under tax financing of the provision of a good or service that is consumed and directly used by people in carrying out their daily activities.

A large portion of the expenditures made by government from taxes collected do not directly finance the provision of designated goods and services used and enjoyed by the people. This use of tax funds is much more important at the federal or national level than at the state and local level.

The three largest federal uses of taxes collected are national defense, income security, and interest on the federal debt. Expenditures on housing, education, health, and natural resources and environment are of growing importance at the federal level. The federal government's activity in the actual provision of goods and services is often a portion of intergovernment revenue provision, and therefore actual provision, or "use according to need," is muted as a federal act and expanded as a state and local government act.

Tax financing of substantial income maintenance or security is called "transfer payments." The word "transfer" distinguishes them from salary and goods purchases payments. The same relationship and the same terminology are used for private pension payments.) These payments absorb a portion of GNP when they are spent for goods and services chosen by the recipient. How much and what is purchased and what is saved is determined within the limits set by the total amount received by the individual receiving the transfer payment. These purchases in an economy like that of the United States are largely made in the private sector. A portion of these payments received by the private sector will be used to pay taxes. A portion of these tax payments will finance transfer payments of the future and further purchases of goods and services, again largely from the private sector. Both the financing tax payment and the reduction of the stock of goods and services through current consumption without current production push up private and public sector prices based on costs.

The manner in which an income earner or a transfer payment recipient spends disposable income varies according to family circumstances and many other factors. The fact a receiver makes the greatest expenditures for basic necessities like board and room may not change the portion going to tax payments. The portion of these payments going into taxes depends on the profitability of the businesses providing the services, the portion of cost made up of wages, and the assessed value of premises used for sale and production.

The payment of taxes out of expenditures is not particularly related to the economic well-being of the spender. In other words, taxes as included in prices are not increased or decreased on the basis of the economic and social characteristics of the person making the purchase.

After an impact-burden-location theory is declared, modifications are usually inserted. Sometimes the diffusion doctrine is accepted. This position, according to Nicholas Francois Canard, is that taxes are distributed around so that the relative position of participants in the economy return to where they were before the new tax. The increase in the price of a product like bread sometimes results in a subsidy or a rollback of its price so that the poor will not suffer as much through a general price rise caused by the diffusion of the new tax. In a manner of speaking, the government is saying that because a good is purchased in large quantities by the poor, the price should not cover normal costs. On occasion, monopoly pricing is seen to exist and government establishes a production unit to set a price yardstick. The decision to construct TVA and its electric distribution system was partially a result of this approach to the pricing of a basic service—electricity.

Prices of Government Goods and Services

At other times the subsidy or price control approach is considered inadequate to remedy increases in prices because consumer subsidies and price controls stimulate consumption without supporting increased production. Under these circumstances, the government might decide to meet supply shortages by entering into production and sale with price set below costs. A policy of this sort soon makes the government the only provider of the service. The provision of urban mass transportation in most areas of the world arose through this sort of process.

The government's losses from selling urban bus and train services below cost must be met generally from taxes collected at some government level. The direct benefactors are those who use mass transportation facilities. Indirect benefactors include those owning businesses and real estate, largely at the extremities of the system, and those using the roads that now may become less crowded. The gains and losses of different income level groups from the subsidy of mass transportation is more complex than only looking at the user of the service and the size of the tax contribution made by different groups.

Cost-Price Relationship

Government provision of such services as urban transportation or hospital beds tend to have one thing in common—they need government revenues from taxes to keep them in operation. Continued inflation requires continued price increases to keep up with costs. Because government finds it difficult to increase the prices it charges, adjustment to the new costs is slow. When prices and costs are declining, or relatively stable, government service prices do a much better job of covering costs.

Another aspect of the price-cost problem faced by government as producer is that health, old age, unemployment, and injury insurance level and coverage is not adequate or complete in the United States. In most industrial nations, the levels of insurance payments and the breadth of coverage permit payment of normal medical-social costs out of these receipts.

Retardants to Development

The relative slowness of U.S. action in this field arises, at least partially, from the basic allocation of these responsibilities to state and local governments. This is not true, at least to this degree, in other countries. Added to this is the American philosophical position favoring private charity and individual responsibility.

There is another wide area of user charges whose failure to cover costs appears to be largely the result of lethargy and outright bad administration. Parking meter charges can be moved up to make the real returns equal to rates originally set, without placing a heavy burden on the poor or on industry. Water meters can be installed to reduce waste and cover the costs of providing water used.

Tax Treatment

A legal hurdle of user charge development has been the difference in treatment under state and federal income tax legislation of user charges and property taxes. Income tax legislation permits a householder to deduct property taxes from taxable income. The householder, however, is not permitted to deduct other occupancy and ownership costs. For example, insurance and repairs cannot be deducted by households in arriving at taxable income. Householders cannot deduct user charges from taxable income, even though the funds are used to finance the same householder services as property taxes. For example, a user charge to pay for the removal of garbage is not deductible from taxable income, whereas a property tax to pay for this service is deductible. Expenses, including user charges, are always deductible from business income in arriving at the income tax base.

The income tax treatment of user charges is becoming of reduced importance as the federal personal income tax shifts away from the use of itemized deductions. Nevertheless, the problem continues and should be completely removed by allowing households under the personal income tax law the same treatment on real estate–related expenses and city services that are enjoyed by landlords and other businesses.

The limitation of use to those paying a price covering cost that is followed in the private sector can also be useful in the public sector. However, for the system to efficiently stimulate production and to limit consumption to those deciding this is the best use of scarce resources, such characteristics of the private sector as competition, rewards for efficiency, and individual choice must be introduced, which removes a considerable portion of the reason for public sector production, financing, and selling.

General services of government, such as pure water, cannot be closely associated with a particular user, which makes government the only feasible provider. Where a service such as transportation is being offered, the government becomes involved because a public choice to subsidize this type of service has been made. When the price charged by government covers costs, government involvement must be justified to avoid private monopoly or because the private sector misjudges the risk or has to pay more for capital than does local government.

Summary

The public sector, by collecting for services when used, is taking advantage of the usefulness of price in determining the strength of the desire for a product or service. When service charges are substantially less than cost, or the good or service is offered free, several conditions develop that are not entirely desirable.

The good or service may be wanted because it is free. Crowding will develop so the facility or service cannot be enjoyed by anyone. Large specialized users of the good or service arise and the government subsidizes a particular activity.

Efforts to use service charges to take advantage of a monopoly position and to assess a charge substantially above normal cost results in inefficient use of resources in the public sector, just as it does in the private sector. A local government should also avoid the use of service charges when administration of collection is very high. Following these general guidelines leaves a substantial opportunity to finance local government services with user charges.

30 Service Fees and Earmarked Revenues

One aspect of voter mistrust of the wisdom with which tax payments are used has been a desire to relate government benefits to cost. Benefit-cost analyses inevitably lead to consideration of charging those who use the service or facility. The price system of the private sector is examined to see if it cannot be used to a greater extent in the public sector. This examination is worthwhile and is best carried out if coordination and direction is provided through the city's budgetary personnel.

Charging for the cost of a city service or facility as businesses charge for their services is only possible where exclusion can be practiced. The key to exclusion from enjoying government services is the possibility of physical divisibility of the service. Voluntary purchase is not a requirement of government sales, as in the case of most business sales. Government can charge prices and fees for services that citizens are very largely required to buy (see chapter 29).

The essence of the situation is that the externalities of a purchase that must be compelled are relativey high. The resident is willing to pay the cost only if everyone else is also willing or actually does pay. The resident will buy if others do.

For the median taxpayer, the choice is between high prices or high taxes. Unless there is some very strong social argument, the greater resource allocation efficiency through use of the high service price makes it preferable. The price or service charge collected need not cover the full cost. It could, for example, be at a level corresponding with payer's benefit, with the remaining cost a justifiable expenditure from general revenues because of the beneficial externalities. The provision of hospital and bus service is, for example, appropriately financed in this manner.

General Principles of Use of Fees

Fees are appropriate when there is great likelihood of waste under a finance system not closely associated with cost, the satisfaction and assistance provided by the service can be relatively closely associated with an individual or family, the collection and general administration cost is not excessive and does not require the giving up of civil rights, and facilities are exempt from the property tax but enjoy municipal services.

The cost of paying for government provided necessities should be as much a part of cost-of-living budgets as the price of food or medical services. The payment levels to welfare recipients and pension levels to the aged must be high enough to pay for these necessary expenses. Church, lodge, school, and eleemosynary facilities generally must be budgeted to cover costs of municipal services, just as they are budgeted to cover fuel costs and other necessary services.

The compelled purchase is commonly used to finance a substantial portion of the cost of sewage disposal. The city budget officer is well advised to inform superiors of the possibility of expanding the required purchase financial approach. For example, a little rethinking could develop a program to finance much of police and fire protection costs in this manner. The great advantage of the compelled purchase is its ability to provide a financing procedure half-way between a market price allocation and a costless provision out of tax revenues. It makes possible the expansion of service charge financing into areas where the divisibility of some portion of the benefits is possible and where externalities are large and beneficial. The city is well advised to charge a price for a service, even though the exclusion principle operates much less effectively than in the distribution of bread, for example.

The use of price to allocate city services provides a beneficial externality useful in managing the timing, quantity, and location of city services. For example, a swimming pool in a poor neighborhood could use prices in combination with a program of free token distribution. The tokens would be given away by welfare agencies as well as being offered as prizes to those participating in clean-up campaigns or winning competitions. In a wealthy neighborhood, the amount collected would be helpful in determining such factors as hours of operation, need for expansion, and desirability of an inside pool.

The governments of all cities have an interest in a city that functions as an efficient economic unit—that is, one able to provide good services at a low cost. The use of fees can help to realize this aim. For example, flat fees penalize the efficient crowded areas of the city and subsidize the suburban and spread-out areas. Under a good fee system, the costs of refuse collection should be reflected in the charges. The result would be lower fees in crowded areas and higher charges in spread-out areas. Also, the cost per family for police protection and fire protection is higher in the scattered areas than in the crowded inner city. These cost differences should be fully reflected in the fee schedule applied in collecting for these compulsory purchases.

Currently, the use of the general property tax to cover city service provision costs is subsidized by the federal government and the states using the income taxes. This situation arises because property taxes are deductible from household taxable income, whereas license payments and fees are non-deductible. This is an area in which federal and state legislative action could be helpful in bringing about more efficient city financing and managing (see chapter 29).

The first step in an orderly city program toward a wiser use of service charges is a careful review of the existing structure. The current city revenue shortages and the urban renewal programs make the present a good time to initiate a careful review of the service charges. This portion of the revenue side of the budget must be closely associated with city spending benefits. It is an area where Planning-Programming Budgeting (PPB) techniques can be used to make the city provided benefits more closely related to benefit costs.

Automobile Costs

A great portion of the police, street maintenance, parking, and environmental deterioration in U.S. cities is directly related to the automobile and other internal combustion engine vehicles. It has been assumed in the past that rather nominal automobile licenses, parking charges, and gasoline gallonage taxes have met the costs of the automobile to society.

This assumption is false. In addition to the land use costs of the automobile outlined in this section, other costs can be attributed to the automobile, such as the decline of friendly neighborhoods and sidewalk life and the pollution of the air with noise and poisonous gasses.

The charging of total cost to the movers of people and goods has, in the past, meant meeting the costs of land required for highways or rail construction, maintenance costs, and policing and snow removal. When these costs were covered from general collections of gasoline and vehicle license fees, it has been concluded an economic highway transport operation existed. A more careful rationalization of automobile transportation pricing to include the many costs excluded in the above listing dramatically increases the direct costs of automobile transportation. Full costing of automobile transportation would also affect the price and utilization of complimentary goods. Also, rationalization of motor transport prices would affect incomes of other, competitive bidders for a share of a society's personal income.

One significant cost of the use of the automobile in the urban area is the land used for local crosstown, arterial, and throughways. Because roads are not a portion of the tax base, land used for this purpose is taken off the tax rolls. Even more important, land used for roads is not available for other uses, such as parks or playgrounds.

Land used for roads amounts to about 30 percent of all the land in an urban area. Much of the land dedicated to roads is grossly underutilized. Often, a road's only economic function is to provide access to thinly populated, exclusively residential areas. Where the access roads serve active commercial and industrial areas, they are used much more completely and their use is also much more complete when they serve residential areas that are much less spread out than is typical in suburban America.

A typical U.S. city of 100,000 population or over uses up about 1,227 acres for each 10,000 of residents. This total is divided up between five selected categories of use:

Public streets	218 acres
Other public and semipublic uses	158 acres
Private residential property	443 acres
Commercial, industrial, and railroads	139 acres
Undeveloped private land	269 acres

This use, of course, does not correspond with the SMSA concept, which typically has a less concentrated population and includes much more land relative to population.

Taxes foregone, efficient production of agricultural crops close to markets and labor supply foregone, and recreational areas and residential and commercial space used for roads are a portion of the cost of highway transportation. Suburbia and its unintensive use of land space is subsidized by parking facilities at both the residential and commercial ends of the automobile use. This reduces the availability of land sites for other purposes such as mentioned.

The need for parking space is an important element in reducing the efficiency of the urban complex, in the spreading out of houses, and in using space that could be enjoyed as parks and playgrounds. Parking need is a force pushing sites further apart and therefore increasing service costs of all types, including disposition of sewage and delivery of materials.

The costs of the provision of services for automobile transportation not included in pricing do not stop with the costs of land in roadways that are underutilized. The costs of the provision of all government services are increased by the geographic sprawl and by the economic and political isolation stimulated by the subsidization of urban automobile travel. These higher costs and how they should be dealt with in a system of rationalized pricing of government services are considered next.

The substantial costs required to provide for the automobile are being covered in a great variety of ways. For example, vegetables cost more because agricultural land close to the city is covered with roads and housing sprawl. The land available to bear taxes is reduced by an elaborate network of roads occupying tax-exempt land. Government service and private utility costs of all kinds from police to waste disposal to telephone service are increased.

How can the automobile be made to cover the total costs of its use? The answer, of course, is to develop an appropriate series of service charges. Service charges will also help to reverse the disastrous impacts on urban living conditions resulting from the dominance of the automobile.

It is very expensive to subsidize an entire major activity such as automobile transportation. The better approach is to subsidize particular users. It would be good policy to subsidize where the payment of the full cost creates individual hardship or when undesirable externalities arise from underuse of the automobile, or because incomes remaining after paying for the necessary service are insufficient to purchase other basic needs.

Full Cost Pricing

Collecting full cost for services that benefit the automobile would start with the payment of a city license to use the street by all residents of the county, and a more expensive license by all residents of the city. All registered automobiles not paying a city or county license fee would be required to purchase a state license that would be priced to equal the average charge made by counties and cities. The funds collected by the state would be distributed to all counties on the basis of automobile population estimates. When entering the state, all out-of-state automobiles would be required to pay a fee to obtain a proper identification good for one month of driving in the state. Each month a different kind of decal would be used. Out-of-state automobile owners could also purchase the regular annual state license.

These licenses would be in addition to the current state license and would be uniform for all vehicles. The next step would be to substantially increase the tax on all gasoline or other automotive fuels. This tax could be set at 100 percent of the before-tax price of the fuel.

The final step of the program would require metropolitan areas to issue special permits to use certain streets and throughways during certain hours. These permits would be sold only on the basis of the portion of the calendar year remaining when purchased. To induce car pools, they would not be tied to a particular vehicle but would be issued to individuals. Out-of-state licensed vehicles, except when traveling to work involves two states, would be exempt.

The charges placed on automobile users would provide funds to be paid to cities in lieu of taxes on the land occupied by roads. Such funds accomplish two very worthwhile economic goals. They make the private car transportation system a full cost pricing system. As a result, resource allocation within the transportation industry is improved. They remove the subsidy from transportation, which reduces the attractiveness of urban sprawl and increases the efficiency of the city as a service producer.

Price Justice versus Tax Justice

The prices of the market system are never considered in the light of their income regressivity or progressivity. Sometimes, however, market set prices are considered in terms of being fair or just. When this is done, the consideration is in terms of economically more powerful or better educated people taking advantage of their position.

The price of bread is not called regressive because low-income receivers with large families spend more income on bread. But the price of bread may be considered too high because the monopoly power of bakers is not sufficiently controlled.

A recent analysis of sewer user charges considers the degree of progressivity or regressivity of various procedures. The charge is not being considered as a price for a service. Rather, the user charge is being treated as a conventional tax. This approach prevents the user or fee charge system from carrying out the distinct role it is capable of performing in financing services best allocated to government.

Sewage Charges

Sewer services are a necessity, like electricity or telephone services or even bread. The cost of sewer services can be rather accurately set. Every user of these services, just as every purchaser of bread, should pay a price that covers the full cost. The person with a relatively low income, in most instances, will then pay a larger portion of income for sewer services than the high-income person. It also will result in a no-profit corporation making as large a payment for the service as a similar profit-making corporation.

A sewer charge system can be set up to cover full costs and each user of the sewer services can be billed rather accurately for the cost of service used. The biggest industrial users of sewer services are the food and the chemical industry.[1] The cost of providing sewer services should include measurements of water, the bio-chemical oxygen demand, and collection and transmission costs.

A careful study of sewer charges concluded, in general, that equity is best served by using a formula that equates the total charge with cost caused by each user. The formula used should include a flat fee and a variable charge based on both the volume and strength of sewage.

In charging full sewage cost caused by each user, a city also exerts some economic pressure to speed up development of properties nearer the center of the urban area, which, in turn, makes the city a little more efficient in providing its services.

Sewage charges in 1967 were about equal to current expenditures for this purpose by all American cities. There is no reason why they should not be set at a level that will cover capital expenditures as well. Although this revenue record is inadequate, it is much better than the situation in the 43 largest U.S. cities. The sewage charges of these metropolitan areas, which also have such serious continuous fiscal problems, were only 35 percent of current sewage outlays.

The subsidy apparently is going largely to industrial users and to those in outlying areas. And the subsidy, to the extent it is provided by property taxes, comes from a tax that, at least on the portion of its base consisting of structures, retards economic development.

Garbage

Although the municipal record in collecting sewage is quite unacceptable, the record in charging enough to cover costs of garbage removal is much worse. Data for all municipalities show they are collecting only 21 percent of their garbage costs; the 43 largest cities collect only 8 percent. Typically, the suburban high-income residential areas and hotels and restaurants are the greatest deficit users of municipal garbage collection services.

Water

Most cities no longer provide water on the basis of a flat charge. Setting of water charges on the basis of metered use has just about made the characteristics of the utility industry apply to this municipal service. Water service charges were first introduced in New York City in the early 1840s. The transformation of the provision of water from a tax-financed service to a purchased service on the basis of cost of quantity used also illustrates the potential of transformation to a regularly charged-for utility from a government tax-financed activity. The introduction and development of service charges in new areas would tend to stimulate a similar development.

The utility companies are just beginning to seriously consider setting prices on the basis of extra costs involved in providing services to outlying urban areas. The cities, in charging for their services, should be leaders in the setting of prices that cover full incremental costs. In many cases, this would mean considerably higher charges to new suburban areas than to central city users, particularly if charges were set high enough to cover all capital costs as well as current expenses.

Fire Protection

The establishment of fire protection charges is just in its infancy. It, however, is a service that lends itself particularly well to finance through the payments of fees. Elaborate data, based on fire insurance premium charges for different types of structures and on structures located at different distances from the fire station and from known fire hazards, can be used to set charges to cover cost of fire protection that would become a part of the fire insurance payment. When the structure is not insured, the city could collect the charge directly. In fact, firefighting can be moved into the private economy. If this were done, it is very likely economic pressures would develop to press for a considerable increase in efficiency.

Police Protection

A study of Eugene, Oregon, a city of 75,000 people, showed that about 75 percent of all police activity was directly associated with the automobile.[2] Therefore, a portion of the municipal automobile license fee mentioned previously would be sufficient to cover 75 percent of municipal police costs. The other costs could be readily allocated to structures by using a formula that includes costs of attention required. For example, in Eugene, the outlying areas consumed much more police time per structure than did downtown areas. This attention, related largely to burglaries and animal control, would be included as a portion of the charge. The Eugene study concluded that reasonable charges would provide sufficient revenues to meet police costs.

Earmarked Revenues

In a sense, all revenues of state and local government are earmarked. If the revenues of a particular tax are allocated by legislative action or by the constitution to financing a particular activity, the extent to which the tax is used affects the level of government expenditures for the identified purpose. This relationship to the revenues from a particular tax are less direct when the expenditure is a commitment made in the budget.

The two great earmarked taxes at the state and local levels of government are often called the gasoline tax and the unemployment compensation payroll tax. However, in about half the states, the allocation of a certain percentage of selected taxes, such as sales, tobacco, and alcoholic beverages, are made available to certain local governments as earmarked taxes. If the concept of earmarking is expanded this far, why not also include as earmarked taxes the different expenditure purposes of the millage rates that make up the property tax rate applied to assessed value of taxable property?

Earmarking could be expanded to meet the current desire of voters to prune state and local government budgets. The setting of maximum property tax rates considerably below existing levels and making new revenue sources next to impossible to adopt has been called the meat-ax approach to government economy. The voters could decide for or against a series of millages, each one assigned to a particular purpose, from the property tax revenues. This could be called the fine-tuning approach to economy in local government. The same idea could be expanded to include state income and sales tax rates.

The confusion and uncertainty this citizen-oriented fiscal program may engender cannot be really envisaged. Yet, to an extent, its adoption would be nothing more than an extension of the earmarked revenue programs in existence. It could eliminate the earmarking of a portion of general revenue sources to carry out certain activities.

It has been pointed out by analysts that general revenue financing allocates more funds to expenditures with an elastic demand. Earmarked financing increases the revenues for services with an inelastic demand. A procedure to earmark general revenues would tend to increase government activity of the type Adam Smith favored.

In a way, federal grants requiring state or local government matching funds earmark portions of general revenue for purposes favored by the federal government as evidenced by its grants. Debt carrying charges are another expenditure that acts along with trust fund provisions to earmark general revenues.

Another aspect of revenue earmarking is the custom of borrowing for a particular purpose. For example, the revenues of a bond issue are dedicated to build a school or to install a new sewage disposal plant, or special assessments levied on properties to pay for improvements that benefit particular areas.

The impact and desirability of earmarked revenues are not entirely clear. Analysts disagree about whether earmarking expands or contracts the availability of funds for services allocated by earmarked revenues. Diversion of gasoline tax money from expenditure for highway purchases has always been an attractive way to finance an activity without reducing general revenue funds available to finance established expenditures.

In a way, earmarking is an approach to meeting citizen distrust of the wisdom of government in its selection of spending priorities. Service charges are equated by citizens as "let those who use pay." In the use of earmarked revenues, citizens are saying "we will pay taxes if the money is spent as we want it spent." The two approaches arise from a single psychological relationship between voters and government—that is, distrust of the political power of those not willing to foot the bill. Both approaches reduce the need for government budgetary decisions and reduce the ability of government to make independent decisions.

Special Assessments

The special assessment had one principal purpose: to finance public improvements that largely benefit properties located adjacent to or in the proximity of the development. The total cost is usually not allocated to those receiving special benefit when the general community enjoys considerable benefit from the project. The portion of the cost picked up by the general government is usually negotiable, but is based largely on prior practice under similar circumstances.

The benefits enjoyed by different properties vary and therefore the assessment per front foot or square foot will vary. Usually the strip procedure is used to establish zones with varying assessments depending on benefit. The strips are laid out parallel to the street or sewer improvement. This procedure accepts the assumption that abutting property benefits more than properties farther away.

Underlying the whole idea of special assessment is the assumption the improvement provides an economic gain that exceeds cost. An economic benefit surplus, however, does not necessarily result from a wider street or separate storm and sanitary sewers. The economic benefit makes itself observable in property values, which may be reduced rather than increased when the annual special assessment is added on to the payments for the property itself.

Usually, the city contracts for the improvement after 50 percent of the property area or linear footage request the improvement and the special assessment. Next, plans are drawn up and presented to the general governing body. The final decision rests with the city council, county commissioners, or some other appropriate local government with the powers to tax and incur debt.

Financing is usually accomplished with special assessment bonds issued in serial form. In this way, bonds are retired annually as the special assessment installment payments are made. If the bonds are general obligation bonds in addition to being based on special assessment, a default in payment would result in a debt to be met by the general government from revenues collected from the community. The use of special assessments to finance improvements needed in a new development are most likely to go unpaid, causing the bonds to become an obligation of the community.

The use of special assessments varies widely from state to state and between different cities within the same state. In Minnesota, for example, special assessments provide a very substantial portion of total municipal revenues.

The new procedures under Federal Housing Authority regulations require developers to provide basic road, sewer, and sidewalks. These costs are added to the selling price of the lot. The result is a sharp reduction of special assessments to finance basic requirements for development of new properties.

Another cause of decline in special assessments has been increased complications involved in separating private from public benefits of an improvement of public facilities. Another factor has been the greater availability of gasoline tax money to finance road improvements. Also, special assessments are considered by the federal government to be expenditures that increase the value of property by the amount of the outlay. Therefore, special assessment payments cannot be deducted from taxable income as are property tax payments. In fact, special assessment–financed public improvements may cause property tax assessments to increase, based on the assumption that the value of the property must have increased by the amount of the public investment financed with the special assessments.

Summary

A substantial portion of the services financed with city tax collections could also be largely financed through use of fees, service charges, and earmarked taxes. The desirability of moving in this direction has been expanded with the increases in both the level of minimum wages and income maintenance payments from a variety of sources.

Freely provided services and opportunities may not be as fully appreciated in our culture because payment and choice cannot be exercised by the user or potential user. The costs of the various services provided through the public sector are hidden to a degree when cost is met through general taxes. It is often forgotten that government services financed through tax payments largely means that all purchases are joint purchases. Private and public good costs are included in the price charged at the store for a shirt, for example. Consumer purchasing power selectivity could be improved if the cost of private goods purchased did not include through a general tax levy the financing of the cost of unwanted public goods. The use of service fees and earmarked revenues does to some extent increase the closeness of the cost-benefit relationship between payments to the public sector and benefits received.

31 Taxation and Encouragement of Business

Attracting and holding industry have been the goals of state and local government policy since the secrets of the textile industry were brought from England and France to New England. More recently, nearly all industrial nations have initiated programs to improve regional economic conditions within their countries. These regional programs are largely administered and financed by the national government, with local governments playing a minor role. Uniformly, however, they have largely failed.

Italy, Sweden, Belgium and England have all used tax incentives to induce industry to locate where wages are low and unemployment is high. U.S. firms seeking location within the Common Market and generally without strong ties to a particular region have found the tax advantages plus financing assistance to be sufficiently attractive for them to decide to locate in the less desirable sections of these countries. In Ireland, the entire nation has offered very attractive tax inducements to foreign investors producing products that will enjoy a substantial export market as well as advantageous wages to Irish workers.

Attracting Industry

The active bidding for foreign investment and inducements to locate in particular regions is a game the United States is also playing. In federations like Canada and the United States, the provinces and states actively seek out and then offer favors to foreign corporations to induce them to invest and produce within their boundaries. The United States as a national government has not attempted to attract investments of foreign firms through tax advantages or favorable funding.

State and local governments, however, have been so active in bidding for investment that their competition has become an important reason for national legislation aimed at uniformity in social security and pollution control, for example. The states retain some control over how unemployment benefits are distributed and their level, but the legislation enacted by the state legislature must meet federal guidelines. If it does not, the federal tax of 2.7 percent is activated as a separate revenue source and no longer counts as a portion of the state tax rate.

In pollution control, state fights state and local community fights local community. The reason for this rather heated response is clear. The area

207

benefitting from the income of the polluter is often not the area that suffers. Therefore, national legislation is adopted and constant pressures for more national action exist.

Both unemployment insurance and pollution control have international aspects, also. The pollution of the Great Lakes affects both Canada and the United States; garbage thrown overboard by ships in midocean floats ashore on the distant sandy beaches of vacation resorts. The unemployed Turkish worker in Germany draws unemployment benefits in German marks, which, when used to purchase Turkish lira, adds to the foreign exchange earnings of Turkey and helps to stabilize the international value of the Turkish lira.

The international effects of business activity have been growing as industrialization spreads around the world and as the total output of goods through chemical and mechanical means expands. Companies in the most highly industrialized countries, such as the United States, Japan, and Western Europe, after developing a product or process, usually wish to take full advantage of the potential for profit by establishing plants in the main market centers of the world. The same basic situation exists when a U.S. company is engaged in producing a product with a nationwide market.

After a period of growth and expansion of the home plant, it becomes profitable to decentralize production and invest in new facilities. Selecting a location for this new plant in the United States will be largely determined by four basic factors: closeness to market, and available raw materials, power, and labor, as well as the regional variation in the tax liability.

Established Industry Needs

Many groups from the state and county of the original development would like to keep the expansion in that area. Their competitive effort to attract the new investment is handicapped because of transportation costs or perhaps because their area has fully utilized the available air and water under existing national pollution limits. They are also handicapped in making special tax offers because the revenues arising from taxation of the original operation are usually being fully utilized; therefore, a tax favor cannot be extended to all the company's activities within the area.

When the expansion at a new location has been completed, the company's planners are likely to find the new location better suited for their activities than the original location. This situation typically occurs because the original location was not as carefully selected as the new site. When the advantages of the new location become so great that the head office has been moved, the company has basically left the area of original development. Falling employment and land values are likely to follow, as illustrated by the movement from the Northeast and Central United States to the so-called Sun Belt areas. What can a city do about company relocations? What should the city do about them?

Both questions are difficult, if not impossible, to answer. Federal tax and subsidy assistance have been spotty. Another federal and political approach is to press the federal government to locate some of its new facilities in the area and to withhold closing those in the area.

An approach that accepts the new circumstances should assist the unemployed to find jobs elsewhere while developing new industrial parks and increasing the efficiency of the urban area as an economic operating unit providing needed services to business and families. Taxation reform, not aimed at special privilege for the remaining private sector activity but rather toward providing an evenhanded approach to revenue raising, can be helpful. New general revenue provision and expenditure priorities need to be established on the format found to be attractive in other sections of the country.

Tax Load Considerations

Studies over the years have demonstrated the tax load industry carries in various states. These studies have several basic weaknesses. First, they either assume that public services enjoyed and used by industry do not change as a result of the level of taxes or that the relationship between taxes and expenditures is too tentative to be useful. Recently, for example, quality of education services have been shown by some researchers to be unrelated to level of expenditures. Second, the studies assume that all types of taxes are seen by industry to be the same, and the only important fact is the amount of taxes paid. This is obviously not true, either between taxes or the same tax in different economic environments. Third, it is necessary to group all personal and business taxes together in arriving at a burden, or to attempt to draw some sort of rather arbitrary line between business and personal taxes, and in addition make some kind of assumption as to the difference in business decision-making of a high personal income tax and a high corporate income tax. Finally, the level of existing taxes can be changed. The political climate that created the political acceptance of a given level of state and local government expenditures and taxes can be shifted to meet the new set of circumstances.

One aspect of the tax environment that state and local governments can change to everyone's benefit is the complication existing in regulations and provisions of the tax legislation. Minimization of compliance problems under state or local income and retail sales taxes can, however, only result after careful study of the niceties of business operations as they are affected by the myriad of features under the tax law. Elimination of unproductive taxes is another area of taxation that would be universally helpful. In all cases, state and local taxes that can become just another aspect of carrying out federal tax requirements can make everyone's job easier.

Both simplification and revenue collection that would encourage further business investment could be stimulated by moving the property tax away from the taxation of personal property (machines and inventories) and structures and using only land as the base. Undoubtedly, many features of the property tax have a variety of effects on industrialization. However, what they are and how they should be taken advantage of is just about impossible to establish. The restriction of the property tax to land would largely neutralize these effects by limiting the coverage of the tax and would make it easier to evaluate different proposals to strengthen the economy of an area through taxation policy.

Industrial or Development Aid Bonds

The assistance of local governments in meeting financial needs of business has been rather too successfully provided through industrial aid bonds. In some instances, these bonds are backed by the local government issuing them. In most cases, however, they are revenue bonds, with the backing consisting only of the business firm's ability to meet the interest when due and to repay at maturity. The local government, in these instances, acts merely as a conduit that changes private industrial debt into local government obligations. The acceptance of the security by the investment community is determined very nearly entirely by the judgement of the financial soundness of the industrial firm borrowing and investing the funds.

The attractiveness of industrial aid bonds rests largely on the exemption from the federal income tax of the interest owners of the securities receive. The interest of these bonds benefit from the same favorable treatment relative to the federal income tax as do other debt securities issued by state and local governments. The interest rates on the securities having these tax advantages are about one-third lower than that carried by taxable bonds of equal quality. This results in a substantial reduction in the cost of capital, and can provide a worthwhile inducement to even the richest corporation.

For a number of years, arguments opposed to this type of activity by local governments have been abundant and have gained some political support. One result was limiting legislation that reduced the permissible size of these offerings. However, the device had proved to be so practical in working out cooperative investment arrangements with local government and business that the size of offerings was not restricted when the funds went to finance pollution control investments.

Summary

Industry is a source of local and state government expenditures and tax revenues. The addition of revenues is often at maximum shortly after the investment is made, while the expenditure maximum is reached when schools and public services must be provided.

Local commercial groups see new industry as additional customers for their products and services. Landowners and real estate developers look at new industry as demanders of land and space. Such new demands results in activities to attract and hold industry.

Many undesirable features of economic growth have been surfacing as social and physical environment problems require more attention. The ability of economic growth to increase the size of the economic pie to be divided continues to be attractive, and stimulation through tax breaks and capital provision continues.

32 Meeting Growing Fiscal Stress

The United States is a federal government established under a constitution that limits the powers of the central government and envisages states with adequate powers to provide for the social needs of its citizens. A portion of this state power is the power to establish local governments to assist the states in carrying out their responsibilities.

What happened in the United States and in many other countries, some with an economic base comparable with that of the United States, and others with a much lower income, was a multifold expansion of the social responsibilities delegated to government. Local governments were generally not seen to be appropriately organized and administered to carry this greatly expanded government load.

Social Program Background

This attitude toward the government level to be used in meeting social expenditures was a complete switch from the pattern during the first 190 years of the history of the United States. When the very important social good—public education—was being developed in the middle of the nineteenth century, local governments and their property taxes financed this very revolutionary social program. Later, in the first quarter of the twentieth century, state governments and their newly initiated gasoline and automobile license taxes financed the new highways needed by the automobile.

The provision of free basic education, the development of the highway for the automobile, and the federal program of distribution of public lands were the three great government internal economic and social development programs prior to the great depression of the 1930s. In the 1930s, the huge problem of raising the prices of farm products, finding jobs for the 25 percent of the labor force unemployed, and taking care of the aged and meeting other welfare goals seemed to be too large for the previous state and local procedures. It was believed, however, that they could be carried by the federal government.

The federal income tax, which had become the principal revenue source of the federal government during the 1920s, provided $2.4 billion of revenue in 1930 and less than a third that amount in 1933, the worst year of the depression. Certainly this kind of tax could not meet the revenue requirements of the new social programs. A portion of the obvious revenue shortcoming was relieved by new unemployment and social security taxes levied after 1937 on wage income up to $3,000 in a single year at rates of 1 percent. The unemployment tax was paid only by employers; under the new social security tax, both the employee and the employer paid a 1 percent tax. These new taxes were limited to basic wage income.

In the 1930s, the federal government for the first time, except during wars, entered into deficit financing. The procedure was supported by some advanced economic thinkers who had been advocating countercyclical federal government fiscal action. State and local borrowing required to finance the new programs could only be completed if revenues expected were sufficient to pay debt and retirement costs; on the other hand, the federal government could meet these costs by expanding central bank credit as long as monetary reserves permitted. The die was cast, but the ability of the new approach to meet the government's social goals of a suitable level of prices, employment, and assistance to the aged and the needy was not tested at that time. World War Two began in 1939 and United States directly participated in 1941. Perhaps the testing is finally taking place today, or perhaps it has been completed and found wanting.

Social Program Financing

The United States federal government as well as the central governments of other countries have through years of experience learned that the financial burden of the new social programs is very heavy indeed. Some also question whether the advantage of national level financing outweighs the inefficiency of uniform programs and the political pressures of spending demands at the central government level.

An apparent result of the political and economic characteristics of central government social program activity is more and more projects with greater and greater administrative complications. In the United States, this has resulted in what is frequently called the chaos of federal programs aimed at state and local government cooperation in meeting federally identified social goals. The use designated for the funds from the federal government, if they are to become available, frequently violates expenditure priorities of the states and of local governments. They would never spend their own money in this fashion if some allocation were not required to qualify for the free federal money, and an expensive countywide planning agency would not be created.

The expansion of national government social programs has continued even though efficiency has, in most cases, decreased. Generally, national governments have, in addition, devalued their currencies through money supply expansion that was required to finance deficits caused largely by social programs and employment expansion projects.

As time has passed, the straightforward justification of federal government social program expansion based on generally accepted need and state and local government fiscal weakness has been expanded substantially. The most pervasive rationale relies on an analysis based on the concepts of spillovers or externalities—that is, the location of the final benefits of government programs. When many of the gains produced are enjoyed by those living outside the spending government's territory, the level of the service provided will be below that needed to meet the goals—the spillover or externality is large—of the government with the larger territory.

The concept has proven helpful in understanding why voters act generously when deciding expenditure levels to improve safety and fire protection outlays. It is more than useless, in fact it is harmful, in understanding why some areas are more generous in supporting the needy.

Maximum Tax Level

Through the years of expanding social and economic responsibilities of government, analysts have considered the optimal level and also the maximum safe level of assumption of these obligations by government. At one time the maximum level was generally agreed to be taxes of 25 percent of national income. Now that countries like Sweden and Great Britain are approaching the 50 percent level, new and higher levels appear to be workable. Nevertheless, the high inflation rates in Great Britain and, to a lesser degree, in most of Western Europe and the United States lend some support to the position that too large a portion of total spending is being done by government. However, before inflation is taken as an indicator of too high a relative level of government spending, nations with low inflation and high government spending (such as OPEC countries) and high inflation and low government spending (such as most underdeveloped countries) provide an appropriate comparison.

In the United States, the growing demand for government action, and at the same time for reduced taxes, has resulted in huge federal government deficits year after year. At the same time the inflation rate, based on historical standards, has been three to four times as high as it should be. These three realities have caused state and local governments to increase their self-financed spending levels.

The economic resources of states and local communities vary greatly, but the expectations of the residents of all areas tend to be similar. The result is great variation among states and local communities in fiscal pressure, which is measured as taxes being collected as a portion of resident personal income and the annual rate of change in tax effort. The states with a high and rising fiscal pressure tend to be the states with large urban areas, but there are exceptions. The fiscal pressure of Ohio and Kentucky, for example, is not high yet, but it is rising. The states with a balanced economy and few large cities are enjoying a low fiscal pressure; indications are that, relatively speaking, it is going to get even lower.

These comparisons are sometimes used to justify additional aid to states in the North and far West, which is not really an appropriate position. In fact, the states with these characteristics enjoy a considerably higher per capita income and higher per capita level of government services than most in the South and Southwest. The lower fiscal pressure of many southern and southwestern states is the result of prudent state and local government spending levels, not to a strong economic position. Also, in the United States, higher incomes mean a higher marginal rate of federal income tax and therefore an ability to write off a larger portion of the heavier state and local taxes.

Embarrassing State Surpluses

The surpluses of state and local governments and the deficits of the federal government are relative to the federal revenue sharing and grants program. In defending federal revenue sharing and grants even after the idea of the reality of the fiscal dividend began to fade, Walter Heller wrote in 1968:

> One might add, in answering the critics that it is precisely to enable states to overcome some of their weaknesses that broadgauged grants are so badly needed. Denying the state such assistance would perpetuate those evils that are not simply in the eyes of the beholders.[1]

Clearly, financial assistance was not the chief goal of revenue sharing and grants. The main goal of revenue sharing was, and is, to expand spending in designated social and environmental areas. Failure to adequately control the manner in which aid funds are spent is lamented by the advocates. The fact that federal fiscal system failed to develop a fiscal dividend that justified the revenue sharing program is seldom mentioned.

Fiscal Strength

The state budgetary surpluses and the need to distribute surpluses and initiate tax reductions is also embarrassing to state governments. The "to complicate" aspect of the meaning of the word "embarrass" is paramount. It is more difficult for New York State to back up the City of New York in its request for federal aid when the state has a $360 million surplus and the governor has called for a $755 million reduction in personal and business taxes.

California's surplus involves the type of embarrassment that relates to its "causing financial difficulties" meaning. A conservative policy of holding back excess funds to meet switches in available federal funds or sharp declines in economic activity appears to lead to difficulties for the political decisionmaker.

A general embarrassment has arisen from experience with state and local government surpluses at the same time as the federal government carries out a large revenue sharing and grant program with a budget in substantial and chronic deficit. Obviously, nationwide uniform social and environmental programs are needed. The present procedure, however, cannot be justified on the basis of a weak state and local fiscal base and a strong federal fiscal base. Also, for the federal government to reach certain serious poverty and high cost pollution control areas, it must provide equal support to a large portion of the United Sttes that does not need federal assistance.

A better approach is needed than this costly, wasteful, and inflationary method. Perhaps a tax-threat penalty system like that in the unemployment insurance legislation would be appropriate. The procedure would set up a variety of appropriate tax schemes that would be activated if federally established levels of program activity were not met by state and local governments. The revenues collected from the special statewide tax would be used by the federal government to finance activity levels legislated by Congress.

Summary

The traditional measurement of fiscal pressure has been the ratio of taxes collected by state and local government to the annual personal income of residents. While this is a useful measurement, it largely fails to account for taxpaying ability of areas with valuable mineral resources, favorable climate, and rich farmlands. These natural resources can bear relatively heavy taxes without reduction of activity. In fact, heavy taxes tend to stimulate the level of activity.

The movement toward federal financing of social support initiated over forty-five years ago found favor because it was seen to provide national uniformity and federal financial support, both of which were considered to be fundamental. Today, conditions have changed. The federal government is finding the financing demands of social programs to be endless and its financing ability finite. The types of social programs favored and appropriate for different sections of the nation are varied and attempts to make them uniform are wasteful.

Part VIII
Simulation
and Efficiency

33 Models as Policy Instruments

Macroeconomic models are developed to capture formally the basic characteristics of an economic relationship. A formal representation, either by using a simple functional relationship or by employing a simultaneous system of equations, is very dependent on economic theory and our knowledge of institutional responses. All models consist of two parts: first, the scientific or systematic part, which tests the validity of economic relationships, and second, a judgmental part which relies on our subjective knowledge about how a specific institutional environment functions.

Macroeconomic models are grouped by their major orientation. A fiscal model, for example, focuses on the impacts of fiscal action (for example, changes in social security taxes, the impacts of personal income tax reductions on economic aggregates). A monetarist model analyzes the impacts of changes in monetary variables (such as changes in reserve requirement, changes in discount rates). An employment model emphasizes the aggregate impacts in the labor market (such as unemployment rates, employment level). A demographic model pays specific attention to the structural changes in population (for example, birth rates, death rates, and age composition).

Models also come in all sizes. Size depends largely on the number of endogenous, exogenous, and stochastic variables. Brief technical descriptions of these components of macroeconomic models are presented in this chapter.

Basic Modeling

The various types of macroeconomic models partly reflect various assumptions made in economic theory. Models are also influenced by different subjective interpretations of specific economic relationship. Models are also constructed to respond to the development of major economic events, such as 1973 oil embargo.

There are three generations in the history of macroeconomic models. The first generation of model-building was introduced into the United States by L.R. Klein in the 1940s. Klein, influenced by Keynesian tradition, used the Keynesian analytical framework, which is basically a circular flow of income and expenditure as used in the national income accounts.

Klein's principal equations described the main components of aggregate demand—personal consumption expenditures, business fixed investment, business inventories, and housing. The model excludes government purchases of goods and services and exports. These excluded variables are called *exogenous variables*, in contrast to *endogenous variables*, which have numerical values internally determined in the model.

The second generation of models began with the large-scale econometric model of the Brookings Institution in the early 1960s. One of the five advancements in the second generations is the inclusion of state and local government taxes and expenditures. At that time, the efforts to disaggregate the revenues and expenditures of every state's or every government's units were incomplete because of both time and data limitations.

There were several other advancements in the second generation of modeling.

1. The applications of input-output analysis developed by Simon Kuznets during World War Two provides a basically static framework to calculate production of changing technology in a time series framework.

2. The introduction of seven U.S. financial markets (markets for bank reserves, currency, demand deposits, U.S. securities, savings and insurance, and private securities.

3. The use of demographic elements; for example, the demand for the automobile was associated with the growth of the driving age population, the expansion of health-related services was linked to growth in number of aged in the population.

4. Social indicators were introduced, for example, by using quarterly data on public opinion toward inflation and unemployment collected by the University of Michigan's Institute for Social Research (a consumer sentiment index), and by using unemployment rates of different age groups.

The third generation of models resulted from the oil crisis of 1973–1975. The old macroeconomic models failed to predict the turning points and the full disruption of the cyclical events in those years. Substantial changes developed in the economic impact of various disaggregations including, among others, asset and debt positions of household, linkage between monetary policy and mortgage markets, and modeling expectations and consumer confidence. The current emphasis toward disaggregated and microeconomic analysis became the theme of macroeconomic modeling development.

The macroeconomic models developed up to 1973 emphasized demand. Model builders have since changed many equations so that they are sensitive to stochastic disturbances (disturbances subject to random shocks) from the supply side, in addition to those from the demand side. Despite these largely microeconomic improvements on the supply side, macroeconomic models should be used with great caution.

Scientific and Theoretical Aspects of Modeling

Model construction involves the use of economic theory, mathematics, institutional knowledge, and consideration of practical limitations, including the degree to which existing economic theory can be translated into equations and the availability of adequate institutional information and data. In addition, a choice must be made from the various estimation models available.

To test whether a macroeconomic model has ability to simulate or to track the historical observations, a model construction simulates or replicates a real situation. Ideally, simulated values are not much different from historical values (see the section on model evaluation). Again, there is a choice of procedures.

Analytic and numerical simulation consists of algebraic manipulations of the whole set of equations. The result is a formula called the *fiscal multiplier formula*. The Congressional Budget Office (CBO) has analyzed macroeconomic models involving the federal budget by comparing econometric model estimates of the impact of changes in fiscal policies in *The CBO Multipliers Project*. The *CBO Multipliers Project* also yields quarterly results of numerical simulation from such major macroeconomic models as Data Resources, Inc. (DRI), Wharton Econometric Forecasting Associates, Inc., (Wharton), MIT–University of Pennsylvania–Social Services Research Council (MPS), and Fair Model (Yale).

Deterministic and stochastic simulations make up another type of simulation. Deterministic simulation provides an "if" clause with the exogenous variables solely determining the values of endogenous variables. Stochastic simulation provides an "if" clause that specifies the errors associated with exogenous variables, in addition to specifying exogenous variables as main factors determining endogenous variables.

Empirical Estimates and Results

With the advancement of computer technology and the increasing data availability at the disaggregate level from various surveys, it is possible to derive empirical estimates of the net result of basic economic forces at work. Most macroeconomic models agree that changes in fiscal policy have important effects on aggregate private economic activities, although the specific magnitude (such as the economic impact per dollar of budgetary change) and time pattern (for example, the time lags) of these effects differ. Furthermore fiscal policies have a feedback effect on the federal government as well as on the state and local government budgets.

Specific and simplified illustration on the aggregate economic impacts (that is, GNP, real GNP, employment, and price level) of a $10 billion step increase in federal nondefense spending as of mid-1977, is presented in figure 33–1.

Figure 33–1 illustrates different magnitude and time lag aggregate economic impacts from four major macroeconomic models (DRI, Wharton, MPS, and Chase). All macroeconomic models agree that the forces leading to

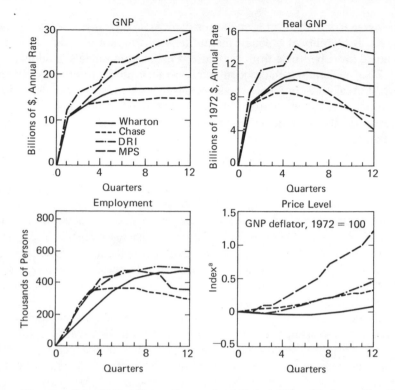

Source: Congress of the United States, Congressional Budget Office, *Understanding Fiscal Policy*, background paper (Washington, D.C.: U.S. Government Printing Office, April 1978), figure 1, page 14.
Note: Step changes begin in first quarter.
[a]Records number of point changes in the index.

Figure 33–1. Impact of a $10 Billion Step Increase in Federal Nondefense Purchases, 1977 Economic Conditions.

a positive impact on GNP outweigh factors leading to a negative impact. DRI models, which are close to MPS, seem more optimistic than the others. All models agree that the initial impact of this fiscal policy change is mostly on output, rather than on prices. The peak effect on current dollar GNP ranges from a low of $14 billion in the ninth quarter (Chase) to a high of $29 billion in the twelfth quarter (DRI). The range of peak multipliers (computed from direct spending of $10 billion) from 1.4 (Chase) to 2.9 (DRI).

The *direct* budget cost of these policies is $10 billion per year. However, the net effect of these fiscal policy changes (a feedback effect) is less than $10 billion. As shown in figure 33–2 the solid line is at a constant level of *direct* budget cost of $10 billion and the broken line is the net effect (feedback effect). The feedback can be described through circular reasoning.

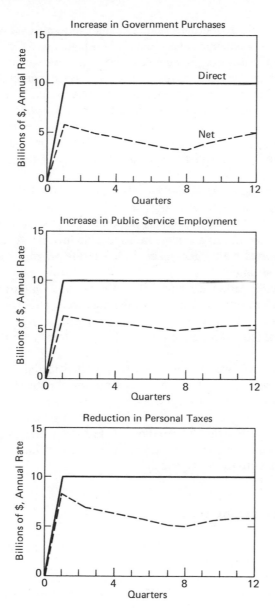

Source: Congress of the United States, Congressional Budget Office, *Understanding Fiscal Policy*, background paper (Washington, D.C.: U.S. Government Printing Office, April 1978), figure 3, page 19.

Figure 33–2. Direct and Net Budget Costs of $10 Billion Step Changes in Government Purchases, Public Service Employment, and Personal Taxes: CBO Multipliers Model.

The fiscal policies followed lead to higher federal revenues by causing higher levels of real and current dollar GNP. A higher real GNP also tends to reduce outlays for transfer payments, such as unemployment compensation. Furthermore, higher prices increase those federal expenditures which are sensitive to inflation, such as social security payments. Therefore, the net outcome of these feedback forces is equal to direct budget cost ($10 billion) minus the induced increases in revenues, minus the induced reduction in transfer payments, plus the induced increase in inflation-adjusted programs. The feedback effects ranges from 35 to 55 percent of the direct cost ($10 billion).

Relevant examples on state and local government responses would include general revenue sharing. In terms of time profile of the general revenue sharing program, state and local governments respond slowly, somewhat slower than the household response to a change in disposable income. A long lag in state and local responses makes general revenue sharing programs a less effective stabilization instrument.

Another stabilization instrument is a public service employment program, which can be a powerful instrument if the time profile (time lag) in setting up local programs and hiring qualified persons is short and rate of displacement (substitutions of federal for state and local money to pay for the program) is very low.

The last example we consider is the recent effort to simulate the economy through public works—that is, by new construction of public facilities, such as schools, hospitals, dams, sewage treatment plants, and mass transportation structures. According to almost all models, spending here is more powerful than general tax cuts or transfer payments. However, the long lag of public works seem to suggest that such programs must be a portion of long-term plans to improve productivity of the society.

Policy and Forecasting Uses

Macroeconomic models, if correctly specified in terms of parameter estimates, provide an ideal procedure for evaluating the total impacts of alternative economic policy measures. Total impacts consist of immediate or direct effects of policy actions and of indirect effects in the form of the whole chain of interactions throughout the system initiated by policy action. As already illustrated, the direct effect in the form of direct budget cost and indirect effect is called the feedback effect.

In a static (one-period) model, it is a straightforward exercise to identify these policy impacts. Complications arise when dynamic models with multiple policy objectives are used. In the dynamic case, the estimated parameters are not exactly known and are subject to random disturbances. Policy simulation experiments have been undertaken to overcome these problems in the dynamic case. These experiments are not only relevant in macroeconomic modeling, but also in models of regions, industries, firms, and even some engineering systems. In conducting such experiments, a model must have an explicit policy parameter, such as tax rates, transfer payments rates, matching ratio in federal grant programs, and tax rebates. Then, by changing these fiscal instruments, we simulate (that is, we compute the values of exogenous variables based on the changes in the values of exogenous variables) to evaluate policy impacts.

In a multiple objective case, trade-off problems develop—for example, improving some economic indicators (inflation) and worsening others (unemployment). This kind of classic trade-off (the Phillips curve, which is simply plotting inflation against unemployment rate) is indeed difficult to identify from the present data base. The data do not reflect fully price expectations and present exogenous inflationary shocks, such as rising world oil prices and domestic oil policies.

Forecasting is fundamental to all planning activity. Any help that modeling activity can provide in the development of forecasts can be very helpful, even though systematic forecasting is inevitably subject to errors. Errors are centered usually in the data base and the estimation method. Error in the data base includes inaccurate estimation of capital stocks (tangible assets), which include structures, equipment, inventories, and estimated land values. Vacant lots are excluded from the land value base because their values are derived from the expectation of future use. Furthermore, the value of nonresidential farm land is computed on the basis of the estimated value of farm land (U.S. Department of Agriculture estimate), minus an estimated 25 percent of the value of farm dwellings (structure only) for a farm dwelling site allowance.

Estimates of the value of nonfarm, nonresidential business land is computed by multiplying the value of nonfarm residential structures by estimated ratios of the value of land to the value of structures. These estimated ratios are based on various judgmental methods, including interpolation. The accuracy of these estimated values of land are directly relevant to state and local governments in their efforts to read macroeconomic indicators.

Errors in the estimation method impose further restrictions on the accuracy of parameter estimates. These shortcomings include misidentification, nonlinearity, misspecification, and many other statistical as well as econometric difficulties. Finally, because the economy is continuously subject to random shocks (errors), there is a need to develop long-run trends so that deviation generated by such shocks can be properly evaluated.

With all these shortcomings, some doubt must exist as to whether economic forecasting is helpful to policymakers. If usefulness is judged on the basis of potential improvement that can be made systematically, based on past performances as it should be, then modeling must be given a passing grade. A systematic improvement on macroforecasting technique seems preferable to a naive method of forecasting that is not susceptible to improvement.

The various errors in the forecasting method indicate that a cautious assessment of macroeconomic activities should be made, particularly in analyzing the indirect effects on state and local fiscal consequences. For example, suppose there is an error in estimating capital stock, especially land values estimates. The indirect effects of inflation on land values are shifts in the portfolio composition of the household sector at the local level. The persistent inflationary process will induce more people to invest in land, which will drive up the land values.

At the macroeconomic level, however, land values are just a certain ratio of the value of structures. This will certainly result in strikingly different state and local fiscal expectations than the actual observations (at the local level), where land values (which is one of the components of capital stocks) are rising rapidly. This is just one example to demonstrate the need for a full understanding of the macrodata base.

Classes of Models

In addition to macroeconomic models, there are whole classes of models that have a practical usefulness to state and local governments.

Regional Projections

The Water Resources Council of the federal government, together with the Regional Economic Analysis Division of the Department of Commerce and the Department of Agriculture, have completed a very helpful detailed projection of income, employment, and population to 1990. All the data are given in constant 1967 dollars. The data basically reports on the basis of residence of the population. However, one major exception is the earnings data, which are reported on the where-worked basis.

The models used develop data for 173 economic areas, 20 water resources regions, and 205 water subareas, the 50 states, 253 SMSAs, plus other portions of some economic areas and water subareas. Income for the United States is projected to rise by 119 percent (real dollars) and population by 22 percent by 1990.

Operations Research

Operations research models are frequently developed to determine which of a group of possible locations is best for a new fire station or a waste disposal center. The definition of best must exclude political and social expediency needs. As developed in these location and transportation models, best is limited to cost minimization, plus some consideration of traffic densities and the like. Establishing the best solution is a *linear programming model problem* usually solved by using standard computer codes.

Linear programming can also be used to model optimal distribution of, for example, energy from a group of energy-producing sources. This type of model can yield the least-cost combination of plant usage to meet various use demands during a period of fluctuating fuel prices and environmental requirements.

Another procedure for efficient use of capital, fuel, and workers in carrying out an assignment might concern itself with the routing of school buses, gas lines, or garbage trucks. In this situation, the *heuristic technique* is apt to be used. Because a model cannot be completed at reasonable cost because of mathematical difficulties, plausible arguments and examples are developed that are not mathematically complete.

Heuristic techniques often turn out to be the most helpful procedure to use in developing a model useful to city and local government managers in setting up an efficient routing or distribution network. The heuristic techniques require as careful gathering and application of data as a mathematically complete model; however, the additional efficiency of a mathematically complete model would cost more than any additional efficiency provided over a heuristic model.

To develop optimal efficiency in the use of materials, equipment, and energy, these models are not helpful if they result in a reduction of labor cooperativeness. The various ways a devoted worker can increase performance of tasks must be encouraged along with the modeling of tasks. Modeling of the routes and timing of school buses is no substitute for driver attention to efficiency in loading and unloading of students.

Model Evaluations and Limitations

A macroeconomic model should pass certain technical criteria. A reasonable model is at least able to generate simulated values, which conform (within 2 to 5 percent error) to the actual data. Because there are various simulation techniques, at minimum requirement a model should be able to produce simulated values (generated by a deterministic single period) that conform with actual observation within and outside the sample period.

More demanding tests for those models that have already passed this minimum requirement determine whether a model can respond to various policy initiatives as perceived by economic theory or independent historical observation. Because model builders have some more or less vague ideas about the magnitude of various policy impacts, it is difficult to catalog what seems to be a minimum requirement. It varies according to actual needs of the model users and different technical preferences of the researchers. Similarly, model users tend to expect unrealistic, quick results with a certain degree of confidence. It must be recognized that errors will remain in any macroeconomic model and that operations research and linear programming is incomplete. Models produce different time profiles and forecast impact, depending on the economic assumptions and the number of conditions.

Earlier macroeconomic models of the economy were constructed by single individuals or a small group. However, with the increasing complexity of the economy and with the advancement of computer technology, modeling requires a full staff of mathematically oriented economists and computer specialists.

State and local governments can gain access easily to all kinds of macroeconomic models by subscription or by purchasing a forecasting package, or by acquiring a minicomputer at a minimum cost. However, although the initial cost of a macroeconomic model is attractive, the maintenance costs (including updating the macrodata base, improving forecasting techniques, and other software and hardware costs) will be substantial. Usually, model users will become technically dependent on the modeling industry. This can reduce the independence of decision makers. Preliminary and independent studies should be made before deciding to purchase a modeling package.

Summary

Various macroeconomic models that have been developed and simulated against historical observation have proved to be useful instruments in the evaluating of policy impacts. State and local governments have these models at their disposal for use either by direct subscription to major macroeconomic modeling groups or by acquiring a simple forecasting technique that requires a desk calculator or minicomputer.

The effort of the federal government to influence the economy and public and private sector economists to forecast the level of economic activity have stimulated efforts at modeling the economy. The results have not been good at turning points, but new knowledge of economic relationships has been developed. More understanding of social elements such as nerve, will, optimism, confidence, and morale is needed.

Operations research and the use of linear programming have proved to be useful in making operational decisions and are in general use.

34 Macroeconomic Activities and State and Local Government Fiscal Responses

As discussed in the last chapter, the development of macroeconomic models has led to the examination of state and local government fiscal responses to economic change. These analyses concentrate on the fiscal responses of state and local governments to federal grants and the indirect effects of macroeconomic shifts on state and local government finances.

At the macroeconomic level, state and local governments have been the source of expanding aggregate demand. Total government purchases of goods and services have risen at an annual average of 9.2 percent over the last five years. The state and local governments purchases component have growth rates of slightly more than 10 percent. In fiscal year 1978, state and local governments spent $250 billion, about half the federal government spending, but over 20 percent is financed with federal grants of various types. It accounts for 13 percent of real gross national product (GNP).

Federal grants to state and local governments were obviously one of the most important elements for such growth. Modeling the effects of federal grants to state and local governments not only opens up various dimensions of state and local budgeting responses, but also helps the state and local governments assess the direct and indirect effects of macroeconomic shifts upon their budgetary position. Three selected topics that have been the subject of considerable modeling effort are considered here: (1) the types of state and local government fiscal responses, (2) the link between current and capital accounts and budgetary surplus, and (3) the short-run versus long-run trade-off faced by state and local governments.

State and Local Fiscal Responses

State and local governments would like to spend more, but are prevented from doing so by the difficulty of raising taxes to cover these expenditures. This very simple statement plays an important role in understanding state and local fiscal responses. The notion of budget constraints, similar to a financial constraint faced by a consumer, was first introduced into modeling by James H. Henderson, who conceptualized that community expenditures are limited by local taxes, intergovernmental revenues, and new debt.

Edward Gramlich refined this concept and concluded that the budget constraint has an important bearing on the way state and local governments

231

respond to external forces, such as movements in GNP, interest rates, and federal grants-in-aid. He arrived at this macroeconomic conclusion via both a mathematical process of maximization and a reconstruction of state and local budgetary process for hypothetical state and local governments. Both approaches concluded that expenditures depend on taxes and taxes on expenditures.

The underlying theory behind the relationship is that state and local governments are treated as decisionmaking bodies. Their behavior can be approximated by a utility maximization exercise for the citizens of state and local governments subject to budget constraints. The utility maximization considered here is simply a maximization of the state and local government preferences, including, for example, higher current expenditures, higher private disposable income, greater flows of services from the tangible assets owned by states and local governments, and greater flows of service from the financial assets.

All modeling of state and local fiscal responses hinges on the notion of this type of utility maximization and budget constraints. The empirical results are encouraging (in terms of responses of revenues and expenditures pattern to exogenous shocks), despite the fact that different data bases are used, such as cross-sectional county data for a single year (Henderson), states over time (Gramlich), aggregate state and local sector, quarterly data (Gramlich and Galper, Eckstein and Halvorsen), and central city annual data (Inman and Galper et al.).

Displacement Effects

Displacement effects refer to a *change* in sources of funds from nonfederal to federal as a consequence of federal spending programs (either lump sum transfers, such as general revenue sharing, or categorical grants). The main concerns here are, first, the existence of economic effects and whether a particular federal program has 100 percent displacement effects. The economic effects are, for example, in the form of an increase in total financial assets.

Second, displacement effects are not equivalent to neutral effects (no effects) of federal grants. Third, displacement effect is an important concept to use in evaluating the effects of a change in the federal budget on state and local government finances. Modeling state and local fiscal responses is, among others, intended to estimate the detailed displacement impacts.

Effects of Various Types of Federal Grants

Federal and state grants can be disaggregated into three distinct types of grants with different matching ratios. The matching ratio is, of course, a fiscal instrument to influence local fiscal responses. We are here concerned only with federal grants, but the concept applies to both state and federal grants.

Type A grants are the open-ended matching grants, where federal government alters the relative price structure facing state and local governments. These are grant programs under which the federal government shares the cost of certain categories of local expenditures with no limit on the amount of matching funds that will be provided. Such programs reduce the cost of these expenditures to the state and local governments by the fraction of the expenditure that the federal government is willing to pay. Therefore, the federal government determines the matching rate and the state and local governments determine the dollar amount of funds it wants at that matching rate.

Type B grants are the lump-sum grants, such as general revenue sharing programs. The grants have no matching requirements and no or few restrictions as to the use of funds. Thus, they represent general government support rather than support for particular expenditure programs.

Type C grants are the closed-ended categorical grants. These grants specify both the share of the expenditures that the federal government will provide as well as the maximum amounts of funds that will be made available as matching grants. These grants are similar to type A grants in that they are for particular purposes and matching is involved. However, unlike A grants, C grants are limited in the amounts made available at the specified matching rate. In terms of this limitation, C grants resemble B grants. Hence, in a sense, C grants are a hybrid of the other two types.

The data base used in the following findings of the impacts of A, B, and C type federal grants to state and local governments in quarterly time-series observations given below is based on data from the national income and product accounts from 1954 to 1972 (see, for example, *Survey of Current Business*, July issues) of total state and local governments finances. The data include only general government revenues and expenditures and exclude retirement fund transactions. Total state and local government expenditures have been broken down (comparable to revenue side) into discretionary expenditures and mandated expenditures. The latter are expenditures mandated by the federal grant (for example, type C federal grants). Discretionary expenditures are essentially initiated by state and local governments. Further breakdown of these expenditures categories are made to reflect the three types of federal grants of revenue, as well as current and capital outlays and interest payments.

State and local governments respond with a time lag. Thus, the *direct* effect of changes in the flow of federal grants (for example, a rise of $1 lump-sum type B grants) will increase the current surplus by $0.96 in the first quarter, with only a slight increase in expenditures and a small reduction in taxes. In the case of type C grants, the *direct* impacts of a rise in C grants will immediately increase total expenditures by the amount of mandatory expenditures.

The *long-run* effects of lump-sum grants (type B grants) is that after one year, the increase of $1 lump-sum grants will increase the current surplus by $0.75, with $0.25 going into expenditure increases and tax reductions. After two years, the proportional impacts of $1 rise in lump-sum grants will be fifty-fifty for current surplus and combined expenditures increases and tax reductions.

The *long-run* effects of C grants is that after one year the impacts of $1 increase in C grants will be $0.32 decline in discretionary expenditures. This decline is also reflected in the rise of the current surplus.

The *feedback* effects of lump-sum grants arises as the current surplus increases in the first quarter, the budgetary allocations in the subsequent quarters will be influenced by the current surplus. In the long run, the ultimate effects of $1 lump-sum grants will raise state and local governments expenditures by $0.43 and will reduces taxes by $0.57.

The *feedback* effects of C grants is that having increased current surplus (with an $0.32 decline in discretionary expenditures), the surplus will eventually raise discretionary expenditures by a small amount. If we set matching rates equal to one, a $1 rise in C grants will stimulate $0.88 total expenditure in the first quarter, about $0.70 in the fourth quarter when the displacement effects have had time to work, and about $0.75 in the eighth quarter, by which time the increase in the surplus has begun to feedback on expenditures. The ultimate effect, with a matching ratio equal to unity, is $0.80 increase in total expenditures (which is almost twice as much as the effects of lump-sum grants).

A second data base consists of pooled time-series and cross-section annual financial series for ten large central cities (Baltimore, Boston, Denver, New Orleans, New York, Philadelphia, Providence, St. Louis, San Francisco, and Washington, D.C.). The data used cover the 1962–1970 period.

The long-run effects of a dollar of revenue sharing on expenditures is weaker than in time-series data, with only $0.25 going to expenditures and $0.75 in tax reduction. The long-run effect of a dollar in C grants to these cities is to stimulate between $0.54 and $0.58 of additional spending for education and social services.

Current and Capital Accounts and Budgetary Surplus

The obvious link between current and capital accounts of state and local government finances is via debt services payments (including debt repayments and interest payments). The following analysis is not based on empirical examination of such a link but is based on casual observation.

On national income and product accounts basis, state and local government budget surpluses have been increasing steadily since the fourth quarter of

1972. This surplus can be viewed from both the short-run and long-run perspectives. In the short run, state and local government surplus (at least, in general government accounts) plays a role as a fiscal adjustment mechanism through which the lagged response of the state and local governments to macroeconomic activities, including federal government's fiscal policy instruments (such as matching grants rates or transfer payments) operate.

State and local governments respond to exogenous forces with a time lag. The surplus, therefore, provides a temporary shock absorber that gives state and local governments sufficient time to adjust their fiscal planning. This implies that in the long run, the surplus has no role in fiscal adjustments. Once the state and local governments have made a full fiscal adjustment to any macroeconomic activities, then the surplus should be reduced and eventually eliminated in the long run. The fiscal adjustment includes accumulation of financial assets and tangible capital. This accumulation of assets will then be allocated either by reduction of tax collection or by increase of certain expenditures.

The long-run question of the surplus is a question of choice between reduction of tax rates and/or tax bases or an increase of expenditures; it is not a problem of the surplus size.

Debt Services Payments

The next link of fiscal adjustment mechanism is debt services payments. The interest payments of state and local governments grew at the rate of 10 percent during the 1974–1977 period, which corresponds to the growth rate of total state and local government expenditures. On the average, in this period, state and local governments paid out about $10 billion in interest payments and received interest on investments of almost $16 billion. The substantial difference between interest payments and interest receipts is due to two factors. The low interest rate on municipal securities induces more borrowing. The low direct cost of borrowing is one of the features of tax-exempt state and local government bonds.

In 1977, about 20 percent of total long-term borrowing of state and local governments was financed through advance refunding. The bulk of this refunding consisted of revenue bonds. This arbitrage technique widens the scope of the choice between tax reduction and expenditure increase via current surpluses available to state and local governments.

Short-run versus Long-run Trade-off

As has been shown, different types of federal grants have a variety of effects in the long run on both the revenue and expenditure pattern of state and local governments. Similarly, at the macroeconomic level, the effects of a step-increase in federal nondefense purchases on aggregate economic activities (GNP, employment, price level) vary. One feature of this type of analysis is that we are interested in the effects (direct, indirect, and total effects) of *one-shot* policy action (for example, general revenue sharing introduced at the first quarter, such as a step-increase of federal nondefense purchases at the first quarter).

Empirically, work remains to be done on the effects of various revenue-raising policy actions introduced at different or subsequent periods. Currently, theoretical studies in the macroeconomic field analyze the dynamic aspects of financing government expenditures, but the empirical implementation is still in progress.

Also, theoretical work on the influence of various revenue measure on expenditure patterns is incomplete. However, we do know that because various financing methods have different effects on revenues and expenditure patterns, there should be an optimal pattern of state and local government finances arising from such mixed financing introduced at different times.

Reading Macroeconomic Activity Signals

Macroeconomic indicators are often compared to a barometer, because they register some significant aspects of the performance of the economy. A single economic indicator, like a barometer, measures only one characteristic of the economic climate and it is sensitive only to changes in this one aspect. But unlike a barometer, economic indicators now embrace almost all the quantitative measures of economic change that are continuously available, such as daily, weekly, monthly, quarterly, and annual indicators on such factors as production, prices, incomes, and employment. The forecaster is faced with a multiplicity of barometers.

Some of these indicators are calculated on the basis of sample surveys, such as the indexes of stock market prices, consumer price index, and the index of land prices. Users must, therefore, assess in some systematic way what the information says about the local environment, at present and in the future. The National Bureau of Economic Research has classified economic activities into a few broad categories of closely related processes that are significant for the business cycle. The principal categories are included in the *Business Condition Digest* (published by the U.S. Department of Commerce); they include employment, unemployment, income, consumption, and the federal government's deficit. However, such categories do not include all aspects of the economy; for example, statistics on agriculture, state and local government, and wealth are omitted.

Also, as noted previously, an error in estimating capital stock exists because the index of land ignores quality changes. Students of land values have further noted that it is desirable to make some adjustments for changes in the quality of agricultural, mineral, and forest land. These adjustments are not yet feasible.

When using macroeconomic activity signals, one should be aware of what is included or excluded in the macroeconomic indices. Also, of course, what is relevant at the macrolevel may not be significant at the local level.

Summary

Modeling state and local government finances hinges on the nature of the budget constraints. State and local governments are treated as a decision-making body that acts on behalf of the local community to get the most from (1) higher current expenditures to ensure a good quality of local public services delivery; (2) higher private disposable income for the community; (3) greater flows of services from capital stocks; and (4) greater yields from accumulated financial assets.

In the process of achieving these objectives, state and local governments face budget constraints. Through these budget constraints, we are able to analyze the state and local fiscal responses to macroeconomic activities, including federal grant policies. Another crucial aspect of the financing of state and local governments is the presence of the current surplus and the choice between tax reduction and expenditure increases in the long run.

Further empirical work is necessary on the relationship between current and capital accounts via debt services payments and on the evaluation between short-run and long-run trade-offs faced by state and local governments. Both theoretical and empirical work must also be done on the dynamic aspects of the financing methods used by state and local government.

A systematic and careful reading of macroeconomic indicators by state and local government administrators is recommended. Careful analysis can be very helpful since most macroindicators suppress local information and ignore certain quality changes that are very relevant to state and local government decisions, such as changes in land values.

35 Measuring Productivity of Government

The concept of zero-base budgeting is one aspect of an often expressed attitude that government resources may be used to accomplish goals that are not given a high priority by the community. The number of children graduating from the third grade is only productive if this is what the community wants. If the community wants its children to be able to read the daily newspaper and summarize a story at age 9, then the number completing the third grade is not an appropriate measure of productivity. Production is always as defined by the producer, the user, or by any of a number of groups interested in the results of a certain quantity of inputs.

A much more limited concept of productivity has been advanced by those attempting to measure productivity of government. One definition is the ratio between the units produced or services provided by an organizational unit (output) and the resources consumed in production (input) during a specified period of time. It is assumed in this situation that agreement exists on the unit of output, and that, in addition, there is no need to consider undesirable side effects arising from efficiency in reaching a high unit of productivity level. In the third grade reading example, undesirable side effects might be nervous disorders among the children, no understanding of history, no opportunity to play games, and little development of skills in the use of numbers. Some people may look at the side effects, relate them to improved productivity, and conclude that increased productivity was not worth the externality price.

Concept

Measured productivity in both the public and private sectors is limited to relating output to direct labor input. Productivity increases arising as the direct result of the introduction of improved lighting, the provision of visual aids to stimulate interest, or machines that replace dozens of workers while keeping output constant are always allocated to the persons employed in the project. All production arises from the direct action of workers. Therefore, the definition that includes capital inputs does not correspond with the concept of production of the Bureau of Labor Statistics (BLS). Production in government, as in business, is expressed in terms of output per staff year.

The three aspects of the level of productivity measured by BLS are categorized as *people*, *process*, and *product*. A better way to express the multifaceted aspects of a production package is *total performance measure-*

239

ment. Both verbalizations express the idea that productivity includes efficiency of labor use, resources, and user satisfaction maximization. When all of these are maximized, the operation is highly productive.

Economics considers product and service user satisfaction under welfare economics. A highly productive office in the welfare economic sense is a highly *effective* office. A highly productive office in the technical sense is a highly *efficient* office or department.

The productivity concepts of efficiency and effectiveness are difficult to apply in the public sector because so much of its output involves nonrivalry and nonexclusive products. For example, all of us can use a park, and because I use it does not mean you cannot use it—nonrivalry. The nonexclusive concept is exemplified by government's provision of national defense: when one is defended, we are all defended.

The productivity of the park depends on the number of people who use it. The productivity of defense expenditures depends on the aggressiveness of other nations. Both types of expenditures are very wasteful if a need does not exist as measured by use. But perhaps there is a considerable unmeasurable satisfaction in knowing that a park is close and that an enemy attack would be repulsed.

Outputs and Consequences

Some progress in visualizing public sector productivity can be gained by using simplified systems analyses. The highway and roads responsibility, for example, can be divided into five sectors.

1. The environmental sector measures the needs of the district to provide roads to move certain quantities of passengers and freight traffic at a given population and industrial intensity. These needs will be affected by the concentration of the traffic flow during certain periods of the day. The distribution, as well as the quantity, of traffic will be affected by the age distribution of the population and the type of industry located in the area.

2. The input sector requires a most efficient combination of highway lanes and traffic control. Also, the strength and durability of the construction of the highway must be related to weight and speed of vehicles using it and the destructive effects of the weather.

3. In the activities sector, a decision must be made as to (1) types of repairs to be applied to the roadbed; (2) the quality of traffic signals; (3) the intensity of road patrols to pick up stalled or abandoned vehicles; and (4) the degree to which traffic lanes are switched to meet shifting directional traffic levels. The efficiency of these operations can be measured in terms of average time required to complete a trip and the degree of roughness of the surface of the road.

4. In the output sector measurement is based on traffic count of private passenger vehicles, small and large trucks, and the like. Ratios developed out of this sector and from the activities sector can be used to provide some insight into productivity.

5. In the consequences sector, the efforts to move traffic more efficiently may be countered by increased concentration of vehicle use, so that traffic movement is not improved but the quantity of traffic handled is increased. The productivity realized is not the type of productivity increase desired by the original users and providers of the road.

Net productivity, even in this simple example, is much more complex than envisaged in the five-sector system. For example, the increase in traffic will also increase the fumes and noise arising from the road. These undesirable spinoffs will, in turn, reduce the value of property bordering the road and affect the health of both those who use it and nearby residents.

Employee Participation

The two basic elements in productivity expansion in the public sector are (1) the efficient use of new techniques and machines, and (2) the impact the introduction will have on employee attitudes. Full productivity of the innovation cannot be attained unless the employee is anxious to demonstrate the full potential inherent in the new approach. To gain this cooperation, the employee must be included as a necessary portion of the decision process. If management is inefficient in the use and necessary reallocation of resources, it is good for the employee to know this. The resulting employee pressure on management can increase productivity through an increase in management alertness.

The productivity ethic is deeply engrained in the decision processes of the private sector. Cost accounting and related well-established cost and productivity analyses are widely used and accepted. The private sector has available the price of inputs and the selling price the market will accept to judge productivity. Although the degree of control over the selling price by a particular firm or an industry varies, the ability to increase price to cover costs is limited. In most instances in the private sector, one will, by becoming more efficient, increase its share of the total market for the good. Also, it is always possible for a particular industry to improve the quality of its product and lower the cost of production so that it can claim a larger portion of the GNP.

On the other hand, in the public sector the management and many employees are always tempted to grow by demonstrating that more resources are needed to meet established goals. Under this sort of perception of success and advancement, the productivity ethic is smothered. The continuing importance of this approach in the public sector is demonstrated by the fact that major productivity gains in New York City, despite a strong productivity program, were not experienced until massive cuts were made during the fiscal crisis.

Taxpayer Participation

Taxpayers should consider themselves as using certain employees to provide needed goods and services that are best obtained through the public sector. They can learn, through organization of fact-finding committees, if productivity is as high as feasible.

The taxpayer has top policymakers of government available in any effort to increase productivity. The behavior of these top level taxpayer employees, as modified by taxpayer efforts, can have a strong impact on middle-level managers and employees. Therefore, the management cannot advocate increased productivity and lower costs while placing inefficient employees on the payroll and increasing their own salaries. Taxpayers must not permit this behavior nor be fooled and lulled into complacency by business-expert committees.

Cooperation among the taxpayers, government employees, and business management will probably help reinforce the productivity ethic. Short-term raids and public relations thrusts, on the other hand, are likely to bring forth negative productivity impacts. The elected officials—whether legislators, city council members, or county board members—can be effective in initiating and carrying out management and productivity improvement programs.

Summary

Productivity efficiency, measured on the basis of the number of units of service (however defined) produced per $1,000 of labor cost, plus certain costs for capital equipment, supplies, and energy, takes into account only production and distribution. Determination of the costs of supplying a unit of service is an important aspect of measuring the productivity of government, but it is not the end of the story. The service or goods being provided must also represent a productive use of resources for bringing forth citizen satisfaction. The intensity of the needs felt, and the degree to which they are satisfied, are a necessary aspect of the measurement of government productivity.

Outputs and consequences rely on relatively simple systems analysis and appear to possess considerable potential in developing really useful measurements of government productivity. At least this procedure avoids the weakness inherent in looking only at units produced per expenditure unit. The use of prices and a competitive market, plus a rather dominant single goal of a good bottom line, make measuring productivity in the private sector far easier, despite its inherent complications, compared to the difficulties encountered in the public sector.

36 Efficiency, Equity, and Equality

The price of public goods paid by interested parties must be the same, just as is true in the private sector. Unless the quantity of taxes is closely associated with the quantity of desired public good available, the justice of the two transactions—bargaining for a particular tax system and enjoying a particular package of public goods—cannot be settled. Relative political power of those groups desiring different packages of public goods will be matched with different groupings favoring one or another tax package until acceptable compromises have been completed. The process, as well as the result of the determination of what public services are provided and how much they cost, is very similar to the private sector process.

Price and Product

The running political and public relations fight between those groups advocating the poverty burden be carried entirely by the national government and those favoring considerable state and local government responsibility is an excellent example of the allocation of costs and benefits in the public sector. New York government fiscal analysts point out that 23 percent of New York City's own-source revenues support social programs. The poor are said to come to New York from Alabama because assistance levels are higher. New Yorkers advocate either a national uniform social spending program or additional federal assistance for New York.

When the bargaining becomes more intense, the very substantial wealth of New York City and the relatively low property taxes as a percentage of this wealth are brought into the discussion. Not far behind is the consideration of the desirability of the manner in which New York City uses its tax collections. Differences of opinion arise as to the desirability of relatively liberal welfare programs. Finally, the efficiency of the entire New York City public sector as demonstrated by union contracts is questioned.

As a result, those benefiting from the services of a particular public sector find it increasingly difficult to enjoy the political backing of those directly involved in supporting the operation. One avenue open to this group so they can continue to enjoy the expenditure benefits is to gain support of a broader political sector. The effort includes appeals to justice and dreaded consequences if support is refused. This wider group is at first dominated by the information distribution activities of the users of government services losing direct political support. Later the larger group initiates an examination to determine what sacrifices they must make. When this process is completed a payment and public service equilibrium is reestablished.

The type of revenue sources used can affect the attitude toward tax collection levels and services to be provided by the public sector. Some forms of taxation and tax administration procedures reduce citizen antagonism toward giving up for government purposes some of their wealth and income. When these tax policies are followed, expenditures possessing marginal support can be initiated or strengthened.

Unless a tax or a fee is attached to the provision of a particular service (for example, the state and local gasoline taxes) it is very difficult to identify exactly what service is provided by what tax collection. The association between tax and service can be improved through budgetary activity aimed at cutting out or decreasing marginal services. Zero-based budgeting is a particularly thorough approach to the use of cost-benefit analyses (see chapter 6).

When the tax is largely used to finance a basic service, such as education with the property tax, the different approaches to providing the service and the varying attitudes toward the property tax become an important portion of the decision process. One approach sees society as a whole benefiting from a well-educated population and property gaining its value from the increased productivity of educated people. Although wide acceptance of these propositions makes for a rather tranquil education-spending-financing system, several concepts have a potential for considerable negotiation between users and providers of the service.

Tax and Service

The property tax is paid by individuals and enterprises. The amount paid does not quickly and directly vary with cash flow or direct benefits. Considerable injustice can be perceived in the standard property tax by those with low incomes, a rather substantial real estate holding, and no children being educated. Justice and acceptance of a working relationship between property taxes and education involves continual bargaining between those who benefit from the system and those perceiving damage to their general well-being.

If education were taken out of the public sector, the cost per adult would vary depending on number of children, desire for education attainment, and the relative luxury with which the activity was accomplished. The state could set education minimum standards that all parents were required to support if they had the means. Parents unable to finance the costs of educating their children would be subsidized. The schools providing instruction would be licensed and inspected by the state, and a conveniently located and desirable type of school could be chosen by parents for their children.

The satisfactions and dissatisfactions of private education systems have been weighed and the decision has come down on the side of public education. Obviously, a decision as basic as this cannot be shifted on the whim of the moment. Therefore, the degree of efficiency, equity, and equality that the system provides can be only varied within the limits set by the basic decision the schools should be public.

The provision of education by the government is a basic, costly undertaking requiring substantial and stable revenues. Also, because education is the basic source of productivity, it should rest on the wealth of a community, while not discouraging innovative and progressive undertakings. Also, because incomes are somewhat related to education, income and standard of living should be reflected in the education financing procedures.

A general tax based on land and income is an equitable approach to the financing of public education. This approach does little, however, to guarantee efficiency. Also, the equity of the burden as measured by cost per dollar of wealth or spending level depends on the number of children relative to wealth and income using the public education facilities. The failure of the property tax to perform ideally in the area of efficiency and equity has triggered basic reexamination of financing and providing education. Bargaining to relate financial support to efficiency and to equalize the economic burden of education are constantly in progress. The best guarantee of a continuing closer approach to the ideal relationship is an informed public opinion and tighter control over public officials through the budgetary process (see chapter 44).

Justice and Liberty Requirements

Liberty is thought widely by political leaders to be a primary social good that the public sector, in carrying out its activities and completing the financing needed, must maximize and not destroy. Yet the public sector, in reaching its economic security and equality goals, tends to restrain pursuit of individual aspirations. The public sector needs to beware of evolving control systems that go beyond the goal of sharply reducing the harm some can do. If evil is held in check, then much less needs to be done for the good people to enjoy the fruits of efficiency and equity along with an unreduced level of liberty.

Liberty obviously cannot be complete. The provision of liberty has long been recognized to be limited to the level that can be enjoyed without preventing others from reaching a similar level. Liberty, when considered in this sense, is limited to social arrangements and does not refer to such concepts as "free will" or the restrictions of nature.

The public sector often finds itself confronting appeals for greater or less activity in an area such as education or medicine. The big spenders see justice being thwarted unless *every* individual with the possibility of developing through education or enjoying a longer life through medical expenditure is fully supported. To accomplish these goals would require considerable funds and the allocation of additional resources to these selected areas. Because economics and its traditional emphasis on the allocation of limited resources among unlimited wants is not dead, the provision of a full opportunity in education and medical care would mean less resources for other areas.

There can be little disagreement that a program that increases justice and liberty while also increasing efficiency, equity, and equality should be given the highest priority. Nevertheless, failure to support new programs meeting these requirements, or failure to abandon old programs not up to these standards, is common. The failure partly arises out of problems in defining each concept. More importantly, however, progress is limited by the extreme difficulty of doing what is required within the limitations of the five recognized basic characteristics of good social policy.

The granting of maximum benefits to the disadvantaged within a state or a city cannot be accomplished without affecting many established political and economic groupings. More than likely, the establishment of any program that truly maximized equality would require a sharp reduction of what most people consider to be liberty and would, in addition, lead to reduced efficiency and therefore, ability to support other programs. Social engineering responses to the making of a better society do not have a 100 percent record in improving the degree to which basic social and economic goals are reached.

Tax Burden and Justice

Using taxes to cover costs is unique to the public sector. Generally, a tax is defined to be a compulsory payment that is not largely spent by the collecting agent to meet the personal needs of the payer. The effect this tax payment has on the distribution of real incomes in the private sector is what incidence is all about. The impact under consideration arises entirely from price shifts caused by the tax payment. Examining these price shifts enables one to say where the burden or incidence of the tax rests.

A tax that largely reduces the incomes and wealth of the rich by reducing the real price or value of income and wealth would act to increase equality. If, at the same time, this equalization pressure was applied, better use of resources is also stimulated, the tax would be increasing efficiency. Though these desirable results could be associated with the incidence of a tax, it would also be true that equity, justice, and liberty as judged by some, would be reduced. The person, group, or institution bearing the incidence of the tax could develop strong arguments, based on classical liberal tenets, that what they had produced or inherited was *rightfully* theirs. This was true because in the long run a stable responsible and efficient society is of benefit to everyone, and this type of society is dependent on private property, the right of inheritance, and each person to benefit fully from his or her productivity.

Determining where the burden of a tax rests, and therefore its justice, are important because the payment is forced and the productivity financed does not directly benefit the taxpayer. Price, on the other hand, is a voluntary payment made to purchase certain goods and services that will satisfy specific wants, and therefore, the benefit is equal to or greater than the cost.

The location of the burden of a tax is important politically. Taxes are used to reallocate income, consumption and wealth, as well as to provide government with funds needed to finance services. If the burden of a tax can be demonstrated to fall on a few wealthy persons with large incomes, while the benefits of government expenditures are distributed rather evenly, then the tax has increased equality and has attracted voter support.

The analysis of tax incidence frequently goes beyond the person writing the check to the government or paying the extra amount that is added to the price of a purchase. If the quantity of a product purchased decreases rapidly when a tax is added and the price goes up (that is, elastic demand), the producers will have a surplus. To cut back on the surplus, the producers will cut prices. To cover costs at these reduced sales prices, they will bargain for lower prices for supplies and lower wages. If the suppliers and workers depend on sales of the taxed product, they will be forced to accept lower prices and wages. The result will be a lower price for the product so that the product plus tax is about the same as price alone before the tax was enacted. The process described is called tax shifting. It can result in the burden of the tax resting on economic elements quite different from the person paying the tax as an addition to price.

The justice of taxes as well as the equality impact of taxes depends on many elements affecting the process of shifting. The general public finds the whole concept of tax shifting and incidence so complex and uncertain that they largely accept the obvious; taxes are a burden to those who make the payment. The payment of taxes, of course, tend to generally reduce liberty while posing important unanswered questions of equity and efficiency.

Summary

The finance and allocation of public sector spending is determined by a continuous process of bargaining. If the public keeps itself well informed, and if efficient legal channels for action are kept open, the result is not far different from what results in a competitive market economy.

The social goals included in the words *efficiency*, *equity*, and *equality* need to be modified. The appropriate modification is justice and liberty. Justice and liberty are the necessary and primary social goods, and they cannot be sacrificed to speed along progress toward efficiency, equity, and equality. The success of social engineers or a rationalist-constructivist have not been sufficiently impressive to justify abandonment of liberty or the reduction of individual freedom and justice.

Taxes are nearly always talked of in terms of burdens and also as important economic tools. The production processes are affected by taxes in a very complex way. This complexity, plus the tendency of the political process to demand that the burden and effect of taxes be considered to rest where collected, has made tax justice largely a catchword. Everyone favors tax justice, but its measurement and definition in operational terms has proved to be very illusive.

37 General Purchasing Management

Carrying out general purchasing management goals starts with the budgetary preparation process and ends with the postaudit, which is made after transactions have been completed. The proper administration of all purchasing activities is best assured if organized around two essential elements: fiscal control and management control.

Fiscal Control

Basic to fiscal control is a simple but effective allotment system for all expenditures from appropriations. The procedure set down in the operational instructions and manual should always be the steps actually followed before the commitment of funds.

The recommendation of the use of the allotment procedure to enjoy good fiscal control does not mean one allotment procedure should be used by all. The basic problem in allotment is to enjoy both control and efficiency in terms of goal accomplishment. Actually this is a quality of management problem, and is inherent in the use of the allocation procedure only in the sense that some system of allocation is a basic building block to fiscal control.

A very detailed allocation system sets down the monthly or quarterly amount to be spent on specific items, such as telephone and automobile use. In some cases, it has proved helpful to even break down these uses—for example, telephone services into local, regional, national, and international calls. The detailed allocation encounters the problem of procedures for granting exceptions, for example, when a basic ongoing activity is held up because the long distance telephone allocation has been used up.

An allocation procedure that is so general that it amounts to not much more than dividing the department appropriation into months or quarters, based on the sums used within each previous time frame, requires in-depth management skills within each division that has expenditure commitment power. Even the general allocation procedure continues to provide the central budgeting and accounting office with expenditure level trends they need. This information, when intelligently used, can avoid breakdowns in vital service levels. The need for unexpected heavy expenditures in one area should be met with active and early allocation amendments. The same is necessary when fund need declines in a certain area whether due to unexpected grants or to reduced need and costs.

Laws that sharply restrict shifting of allocations to meet changed conditions are seldom defensible. Modern accounting practices generally support shift of funds when conditions warrant such action. It is the difficulty in carrying out this decision to the satisfaction of all parties that keeps legislation on the books which restricts modification of allocations once established. It is obvious, for example, that large additional police expenditures to control rioting in the streets does not decrease need for funds to purchase modern office equipment. Nevertheless, one result of rioting may turn out to be reduced funds for modernizing office procedures. Legislation that makes reallocation nearly impossible protects basic continuing need from real or trumped-up emergencies and forces more intensive search for additional funds.

Management Control Alternatives

The centralization of purchasing seems to be an attractive approach to uniformity, quality assurance, and diversification of bidders and therefore obviously the best approach to the basic organization of the important purchasing function. Although this is largely true the approach has its pitfalls.

The Large and the Small Picture

One difficulty of centralization is the mere problem of communication and the related time and delay of getting bureaucratic detail straightened out. An important example of this difficulty lies in the general requirement that the lowest bid must be accepted. A centralized purchasing group is unable to recognize all the costs that are directly and indirectly related to a particular purchase choice.

For example, one cost not included in price and difficult to evaluate for a particular piece of equipment by a centralized purchaser is the speed with which replacement parts can be provided. Another is the availability of inventory replenishment. The saving through use of quantity discounts may be more than eaten up in excess storage costs and inconvenience of getting supplies from a warehouse rather than the back room.

On the other hand, decentralized purchasing may result in expensive dead inventories scattered around different operating units. Also, decentralized purchasing wastes time in reinventing the wheel, as it were, by the different departmental purchasing officers.

Often, many of the inherent advantages of both centralized and decentralized purchasing can be enjoyed by developing uniform government-wide ordering and bidding procedures and leaving the remainder of the process in the hands of the departments. The purchasing activity at whatever level it takes place must have access to supplier information and be able to deal with the representatives of the various firms. The departments, therefore, cannot expect to enjoy the increased control over purchases that arises through decentralized procedures without a willingness to develop effective purchasing data and personal contacts.

Periodic Statements

Whether purchasing is highly centralized or basically decentralized, top management (that is, the legislative group and chief executive) needs the information that arises from purchasing activity. This information, when given in terms of actual cash outgo, completed purchasing transactions with date payment is due, and purchases under negotiation with both total cost and contemplated payment schedules reported, provides a large portion of the management information required to evaluate operational activities.

Much of this information can be reported and included in computer printouts without relying on management judgment after development of the model. The area of purchase negotiation and new directions and new approaches to old directions cannot be met satisfactorily without evaluation by those immersed in the operation. The desire to make reports automatic and unencumbered with judgmental comments reduces evaluation potentials at the highest decision level. Obviously this is counter to the basic aim of periodic statements and must be avoided.

Another aspect of the need for evaluation input in periodic statements arises from the common phenomenon that a given purchasing decision both increases and decreases costs. The favorable impact on total costs of a decision varies with the shifts in the relative strength of the cost increase and the cost decrease impacts. The costs, for example, typically decline if fewer and larger orders are placed. High interest rates would cut into these savings; however, accurate storage cost data might do the same. On the other hand, rising prices and inflationary expectations could increase the cost benefits arising from large purchases above those existing under stable prices. Large purchases by the purchasing agent that is decided upon on the basis of higher price expectations has made the purchasing agent an unhedged futures buyer who bets that prices in the future will be above current quotes.

Routine Duties

Purchasing must have a developed routine procedure for circulating notices and advertising for bids. Bids received require evaluation beyond price and delivery, although these are two fundamental aspects of any bid. Other elements that need to be considered routinely in the decision process include quality characteristics, supply emergency potential, and flexibility of payment arrangements.

Coverage

Purchasing is very different from contracting for the construction of a tennis court. The tennis court specifications are made available to all bidders and the contract can be awarded with confidence to the lowest reliable bidder. Construction must be completed as established in specifications and according to design. When something is purchased the product is designed by the seller, and services, delivery time, and capabilities vary between different sellers. Bid price is only one very important characteristic to be considered in making the decision to buy.

In today's world of rapidly changing and complicated technology the purchaser must be able to separate frills from useful improvements. There is always a new model to buy, but is it worth the outlay required?

The "new federalism" of the national government emphasizes giving state and local governments more authority and responsibility in spending grant funds. This development has brought to light that state and local government regulations and legal guidelines are very varied and also apt to be inappropriate.

Control

Efficient purchasing requires a centralized purchasing group that enjoys complete purchasing authority and ease of communication with the various departments of the organization. To avoid haphazard collection of information for the purchasing decision process, a clear statement of principles and steps to be taken is a necessity. All delegated activities must be closely monitored and checked for correct procedures. More than likely, even such purchases as those of procurement of specialists of various types should be centralized in the general purchasing department.

The regulations establishing the centralized purchasing group should provide for waivers of competitive bidding. The rules governing this purchasing approach must be set down in detail.

Purchasing is a vital aspect of governmental operations. It must be performed in a professional fashion and located near the top of the government hierarchy. Because professional training does not really exist in the area of purchasing, the needed professional competence is nearly always developed through learning on the job. Each purchasing department is duty bound to do its part in the training of new people in this vital area of government management.

Information

The data utilized by a purchasing group must be provided in a regular and organized fashion by the various departments. The different users of purchases are the best source of information about how the material or service met the needs of the agency. All this experience is much more useful when collected in a regular and organized fashion. To do this properly, users must be trained to keep a set of records that can be used to tell the story at regular intervals.

To make certain the best possible estimates of quantities needed are available the purchasing group should make its estimate and send it to the operating unit. The manager of the division should check these data with division information. When a difference exists a conference to arrive at a consensus should establish the best purchase level or result in an agreement that more information is needed.

Bidders

The firms qualified to bid as suppliers must be established on an open basis. The prequalification requirements to bid need to be made available to all potential sellers. Also all qualified bidders should know what will be considered in action to remove a bidder from the qualified list.

Bid invitations can be targeted toward only potential suppliers if the commodity organization is divided into the lowest practicable item level. Each time a purchase is put out to bid, information about new possible suppliers should be solicited. This action increases chances for lower costs and also makes everyone aware that purchases are on an open competitive market.

Specifications

The specification process is less important when purchase of regularly marketed commodities is contemplated than when unique nonstandard products or services are to be acquired. The supplier should generally not be asked to set specifications. Sometimes a supplier is able to demonstrate that the particular specification established by the department is not required to meet the need and that a cheaper product can do as good a job. The purchasing agent must always be alert to waste arising from over- or underpurchase of quality.

The use of a brand name as the specification is usually a shorthand approach that can only be used with care. A performance requirement specification is always desirable. When a new product is being purchased, however, the performance record of the offered products is bound to be scanty. Difficulties encountered in acquiring a completely satisfactory service or product should not stand in the way of normal operations of a division. A cool head and willingness to take a calculated risk is sometimes of utmost importance in carrying out purchasing requirements—if an operating unit is to meet its goals.

One responsibility of the purchasing department is to use information developed by other governments. Large states, cities, and the federal government frequently have developed specification and other useful information. Keep the lines of communication open to other fellow purchasing agents.

Invitation for Bids

The key document in the purchasing process is the invitation for bids (IFB). It provides the legal basis for offering and accepting a bid. Frequently, bidders are required to put up bid bonds or a certified check in a state or local government. More than likely normal purchasing activities make this an unnecessary expense to the supplier. All the requirement does is increase the costs of government.

When the bids come in those not meeting the requirements set down in the IFB should be discarded. All the factors mentioned previously that affect cost in addition to price must be given evenhanded and appropriate weights. All the items that will be considered in the bid review process should be made clear to the bidders in the IFB document. In addition, guidelines are needed so that the purchasing agent can determine if a deviation from IFB is a minor technicality or a substantial nonconformance.

Competition

Competition is the key to low-cost and high-quality state and local government purchases. Suspected collusion should be reported to the department of justice with all details and an indicated willingness to follow up the original suspicion.

Identical bidding should be discouraged by finding within the conditions set down in the IFB some way to give all the business to one of the bidders. Tossing a coin or dividing up the business encourages identical bidding, which reduces efficiency of the bidding process.

Inspection

Inspection reports of condition of goods on arrival and date of arrival is the final step of the purchasing function. It is appropriate to develop testing procedures to make certain quality meets the requirements of the IFB. What is learned should be disseminated within the organization and to other purchasers located in organizations unable to carry out their own testing procedures.

Summary

Allotment procedure, when properly done, should not sacrifice efficiency to enjoy control. It is necessary to have the allotment process sufficiently detailed to place pressure on wasters, while at the same time not cause delays because one minor but necessary functional area has used up its allocation.

The efficiency of the purchasing activity of a government is a basic element of the management mix. A government unit carrying out its purchasing by crony rather than through procedures carefully developed and followed is wasteful and is certain to suffer from a general reduction of morale.

Part IX
Financing Economic
Security and
Special Programs

38 Financing and Managing Pension Commitments

State and local government pension programs are typically financed partially out of deductions from employee wages and contributions from the general revenues of the employing government unit. A local government making contributions to its retirement system at a level judged to be adequate to meet full funding requirements based on an actuarial evaluation is not out of the pension financing woods.

Funded System

Under conditions of inflation and a more rapid general productivity increase in the private than the public sector, earlier negotiated pension levels become unacceptable. The result is that levels of pension and disabiity payments are negotiated upward. The increase is usually justified on the basis of inflated prices and the right to receive an undiminished purchasing power. The funds to finance this expansion of dollar payments would not have been accumulated under the most liberal actuality sound funding system.

A manager of a contributory system, under conditions of considerable inflation and increasing living standards, is fighting a losing battle when he attempts to meet the real benefit levels originally established, without reducing the actuarial soundness of the system. The reduction of the adequacy of the fund in meeting newly negotiated pension levels can be rectified by increasing the share of payments coming from general revenues or by increasing deductions from the salaries of employees.

The difficulties inherent in funding a retirement and disability payments system have required an increased visibility as the systems have matured. In the early stages, funds are adequate and claims are easily met. The fiscal adequacy begins to be doubted as claims expand in line with a mature system, inflation, and existing salary levels. Nevertheless, the complexity of the concept of being actuarially sound, plus some difference of opinion as to earnings to be expected on invested funds, often hide the development of conditions pointing to default.

Pay-As-You-Go System

These types of problems can be avoided by a system relying on current collections to meet disability and retirement outlays. Under a payment from current collections system, the revenue-providing base is already adjusted to the payment level appropriate to maintain the support agreed on, if the size and age of the work force has not changed. Current revenue financing requires a well-recognized basic responsibility that cannot be abandoned when the economy is down or when employee-citizen relations are strained.

Current financing rather than relying on fund accumulation would tend to reduce the communities' savings available for investment in securities. Also, the third source of retirement and disability payments—earnings and appreciation in the value of investments—would not be available. To a considerable extent, of course, this third source of revenues has turned out to be ephemeral. The dividends and interest receipts have frequently failed to compensate for value loss through inflation and the market value of the pension fund investments have not enjoyed a regular upward price movement.

Payment Adjustment

Procedures for keeping retirement and disability benefits at a constant or increasing purchasing power vary considerably between state and local governments. All programs have found it necessary to increase money payments above the level initially guaranteed by the system.

Some governments rely entirely on ad hoc adjustments voted by the legislative body. These adjustments have become more liberal and more frequent as the high inflation rate and the related increasing state and local government salaries have continued.

The ad hoc adjustments governments typically don't establish definite guidelines for action. The increases in the CPI have been looked at frequently as one adjustment guideline. The other basis is the percentage the pension is of current salary levels being received.

The number of states and local governments that increase pension and benefit payments along with newly negotiated salaries of current workers has been growing. This approach to payment adjustment recognizes the growth of government worker unions and the continuing relationship of government as an employer to its former employees who are eligible for benefits.

When adjustments are tied to CPI changes, no provision is made for a decrease of payments if the CPI declines. Limits to annual benefit increases are frequently set so that a very substantial increase in the CPI for one year is only partially compensated for. If the CPI in following years becomes relatively stable, the pension payments of these governments would gradually regain their original purchasing power level.

A few states and some cities provide for an automatic increase with an upward movement of CPI. Under this procedure, a limit is sometimes set on the size of the pension payment that would benefit from this automatic adjustment. When this is done, the CPI is a realistic basis of adjustment on only that portion of the payment required to purchase basic needs.

The funds for all of the postretirement and disability benefits adjustments cannot be taken out of the fund reserves without weakening the actuarial soundness of the system. This fact of life is too often realized only partially as a portion of payment adjustment legislative action because the withdrawal of funds is considered to be only a delay until better financial conditions prevail. Other times, too optimistic estimates are made of earnings and capital gains on investments.

A large portion of the problem of financing benefit adjustments is avoided under a pay-as-you-go financing system established as a given percentage of total payroll. The feeling that this financing approach represents reduced commitment and other shortcomings mentioned above is less persuasive today than was true a few years ago. For example, Atlanta, Indianapolis, and Seattle, all three well-financed cities, have current financing systems. Also, frequent adjustments of payouts reduce the usefulness of fund accumulations. The funds of many government pensions systems have not been well managed. Frequently the earnings are less than employees could earn depositing their savings in a savings account. Finally, pay-as-you-go financing would prevent the unconscionable raids on pension funds to support deficit governments.

Contribution Levels

In 1960 the receipts of state and local employee retirement systems (SLERS) was $3.4 billion. The contributions were divided between about one-third employee and two-thirds government. Today employee contributions are down to about one-fourth of the total. This decline has been made up with larger employer contributions. During the past twenty years, total contributions have increased by about 500 percent.

The rapid growth of SLERS plus the high inflation levels, weak security markets, and pension overcommitment in labor contracts have led to several careful examinations of the system. A comparison of the funding of SLERS with the funding of pension systems in the private sector shows that SLERS are in a relatively sound financial condition. Nevertheless, additional federal supervision along the lines now in effect relative to private sector pension funds can be expected.

Investment of SLERS Funds

The SLERS have been investing over half of their funds in corporate bonds and about 5 percent in federal government securities. For a number of years, the

SLERS expanded the portion of their total investments consisting of corporate common stocks. This trend was reversed by the very weak equity investment market in the late 1970s.

The approximately $100 billion of SLERS funds available for investment is large enough to affect financial markets when investment policy is shifted. Also, these business investments are large enough to legitimately claim some participation in business decisionmaking.

Summary

State and local government retirement and disability compensation programs were originally built on the idea of government's responsibility being limited to substantial contributions to the pension fund out of which all benefits would be paid. Inflation and liberal pension provisions in labor contracts have combined to cause accumulated funds to be inadequate to make payment commitments. The adequacy of current levels of fund contribution and vesting and financing arrangements are being questioned. A result of these developments has been a reconsideration of pension funding and payment arrangements.

If state and local governments of the nation continue to experience fiscal relationships of the type that became common in the 1970s, one can expect reconsideration of the shortcomings of financing payments from revenues collected currently. Cutting back on the reliance on fund accumulation to pay pensions will reduce savings available to finance corporate indebtedness and increase voter awareness of the cost of pension programs. These developments can be expected to cause retirement ages to be increased and the payments to employees of ten or so years to be much less than to those of thirty or forty years. Finally, pay-as-you-go financing has the potential of increasing uniformity of SLERS around the country and sharply reducing the problem of portability.

39 Welfare Spending, Financing, and Managing

Government expenditures to provide the necessities of life to the poor have become an ever-growing portion of GNP. The expenditures to support the poor have been declining relatively at the local government level and increasing at the state and federal level. A number of categories of expenditures are usually included totally or nearly so when aggregates of public welfare activity are developed.

The term *welfare* is generally applied to payments received by mothers of dependent children. Another group of recipients of income maintenance payments come under the title Supplemental Security Income. The federal program provides funds to assist the aged, blind, and disabled. The allocation of health and hospital care expenditures is appropriately divided between welfare expenditures and general social expenditures similar to education. Food stamps and public housing plus rent and mortgage interest supplements are more closely related to welfare distributions than to general social expenditures.

The complexity of the welfare expenditure and welfare-related government activities arises from both the number of separate programs and the variety of sources of financing. The cash and service provision programs are not integrated, so each has its own administration. The economic definitions of such concepts as income, wealth, and accounting period also vary between programs. Social definitions of concepts of the family unit, independent household, and social situation benefit rate also vary between programs. As a result, benefit receipts frequently vary without a justifiable cause. Some of these difficulties arise because of existing shared fiscal responsibility of different government levels.

The federal government, outside the general area of public assistance, is an active cooperator with private nonprofit organizations. These activities include food stamps, surplus food for the needy and for institutions, child nutrition, institutional care, child welfare, economic opportunity and manpower programs, veterans' welfare services, vocational rehabilitation, and housing. About two-thirds of the funds for these programs come from the federal government. The money value of volunteer services and quarters is not included in the calculation.

The effectiveness with which the welfare provision function is carried out is determined by the degree to which basic fiscal-functional criteria are followed. A program must possess four generally recognized qualities to a high degree if it is going to adequately meet basic fiscal-functional criteria: (1) fiscal equity, (2) economic efficiency, (3) administrative effectiveness, and (4) political accountability. Each of these general goals is fraught with problems of definition and difficulties in measuring progress. They are useful primarily in passing judgement on contemplated changes.

Shortcomings

Welfare is typically limited to programs where a means test of one sort or another is administered to determine eligibility. All these means maximums use a net income definition, but every program uses different net income definitions. The allowable deductions and exemptions and net income calculation are not the same in any two programs. Therefore, the information required to establish eligibility in one program will not satisfy the needs of another. In addition to the net income limits, there are also net asset tests. Such limits and tests reduce the degree to which applicants can benefit, as was intended by Congress.

The multiple program base under which welfare is provided results in about 67 percent of the poor receiving benefits from two or more programs and some 12 percent of the poor get benefits from six or more programs. For the poor to bring their income through welfare up to the poverty level, they must go through an obviously inefficient as well as demeaning process.

Welfare is sometimes referred to as the Middle East of the public sector. To the extent a satisfactory solution proves to be most illusive the analogy is apt. It is also apt when reference is made to the governance provided. Some twenty-one Congressional committees and nine executive agencies have been allocated a portion of the oversight and administrative function. In addition, each state and territory has its own agencies concerned with welfare allocation. Despite a myriad of rules and regulations, a large amount of discretion is enjoyed by over 3,000 welfare agencies. All these agencies dispense about $50 billion to the poor as defined by each program and administered by each agency. See figure 39–1 for a summary of relative importance of different income maintenance programs.

In several states, a family man working full time and being paid a minimum hourly wage will not earn as much as welfare entitlements would provide. In Wisconsin, if a man works halftime with a family of four and receives welfare benefits—aid for dependent children, food stamps, medicaid—his income will be about $2,000 greater than if he worked full time at minimum wages. The disincentive impact of the welfare system is a serious weakness that cannot be eliminated as long as a means test is used in allocating welfare funds.

As a recipient begins to earn money, and 30 to 40 percent of the total living in poverty escape every year, 67 percent of each dollar earned goes to reduce

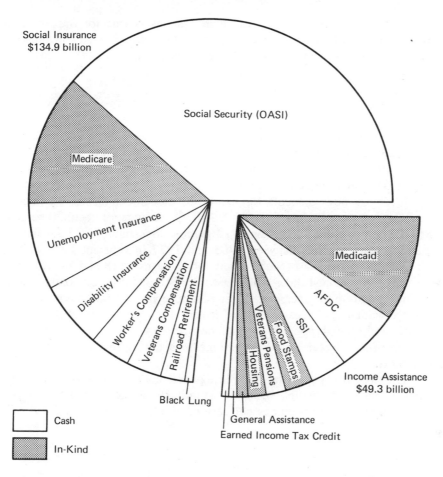

Source: *Special HEW Report on Welfare Reform*, Ways and Means Hearing (May 4, 1977): 15.

Figure 39–1. Income Maintenance Programs, Fiscal Year 1977.

AFDC receipts. Only a 10 percent reduction is applied to food stamps. Out of the $100 of additional earnings only a $5 income improvement is enjoyed.

The substantial variation in the level of welfare benefits between states continues largely unabated despite urban revenue crises. The Aid for Families and Dependent Children (AFDC) payment by the federal government to the poor of a state depends on the average per capita income of the residents of a state. This situation plus variation in state decisions to pay AFDC at a particular level result in welfare payment to a family of four to vary from $720 to $6,668. The program's benefits are not integrated nationally. Where

integrated, payments are sometimes in cash as is true for Supplemental
Security Income (SSI) and some programs payoff in subsidized rent and food.
Such variations are another administrative headache.

Participants

Amazingly, the definition of poor has remained the same as long as studies
have been made. It is 20 percent of the population, which also works out to be
those with an income that is one-half the median wage. This group consists
largely of women and children and the aged.

Medicaid now accounts for nearly 40 percent of the federal income
maintenance program based on need. AFDC accounts for about 30 percent,
SSI 18 percent, and food stamps 12 percent. See figure 39–2 for income
maintenance programs between 1965 and 1977 in constant 1976 dollars.

About 1.5 percent of women between the ages of 18 and 54 will go on
welfare each year, just under 1 million women. About 5.5 percent of the women
in this age group are members of families receiving welfare payments. The
average woman that goes on welfare goes off for various periods of time and
actually only spends about four out of the next ten years on welfare. About 14
percent of all women spend some time in a family that receives welfare
payments.

The two principal causes that place people under welfare are weak labor
demand and family disruption, usually a marital breakup. Each of these causes
are temporary. The nation has not developed a large welfare class.

Reform

Most welfare reform programs either tie welfare to the social security program
or largely eliminate the means test in gaining eligibility for federal funds. These
approaches are first of all procedures for developing national uniformity. The
result would make the financing of all other welfare programs entirely a state or
local government responsibility.

The tie to social security most frequently advocated is to divide the system
into two parts. A flat social security payment that is large enough when added
to a per person tax credit or refund to provide minimum subsistence. This is an
income floor available to everyone who has reached a certain age or is
otherwise entitled to assistance.

It is estimated that an expanded social security and accident support
program plus an individual tax credit program and an active employment
stability program can reduce the welfare load in the United States to around 8
million beneficiaries from the present level of around 20 million.

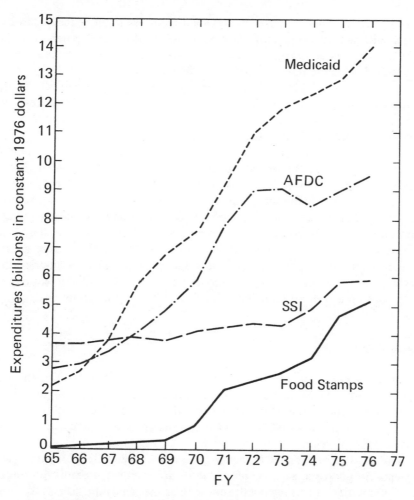

Source: *Special HEW Report on Welfare Reform*, Ways and Means Hearing (May 4, 1977): 17.

Figure 39–2. Growth of Income Assistance Programs.

A quite different approach to reform of the welfare program would emphasize eradication of urban decay while fostering urban conservation and development. An economically sound urban area core is seen to be the source of an improved individual earning potential. In this environment, the need for welfare assistance declines, and a major portion of the need for welfare programs in the public sector is removed.

In Massachusetts, for example, several agencies guarantee and provide business development financing. The Massachusetts Industrial Mortgage Insurance Agency grants loans to companies in need of financing to continue their expansion. The state uses its assistance powers in the areas of sewers, school buildings, recreation area grants, transportation development, and the siting of state government offices. These actions improve the economic environment existing in urban area core districts.

The governor of Massachusetts through a development cabinet is constantly examining how their decisions can assist central business areas. In some instances, this is done by denying improvements to suburban areas in favor of business location in the urban core area.

None of the efforts to develop a state or city growth and redevelopment strategy are aimed exclusively at reducing the general welfare problem. What is new and what makes these activities a welfare reform activity is the realization by the economic planners that decaying urban areas produce welfare spending needs. The next step is to examine ongoing public and private sector investment decisionmaking processes to determine how they can improve the economic health of urban core areas. The third step is to gather together appropriate political and financial tools. Finally, of course, the programs must include provisions that assure the activity will strengthen the urban core area without reducing efficiency of the entire community.

Accountability

Washington, D.C., includes much of the District of Columbia. The government of the city and the district are subject to oversee control by Congress. This relationship resulted in the General Accounting Office (GAO) examining the provision of welfare assistance and recommending four steps to improve management of welfare in the district.

The steps recommended to reduce overpayments and illegal payments are conventional good management procedures—for example, prompt reporting of errors, immediate searching out the cause of errors, analyzing causes of error, and prompt reporting of findings to management.

The comptroller developed three systems to manage the AFDC program. One system is designed to identify recipients who are overpaid by $100 a month or more. Another system picks up all overpayments, regardless of amount. The third system identifies ineligible cases. Each system ranks cases for review according to their error potential.

Erroneous welfare payments have declined since 1973, but the national total is still substantial. GAO estimates that nationwide nearly $500 million of federal funds are being misspent annually in the welfare area.

Medicare and Medicaid

Medicare is a nationwide health insurance program for the aged and some of the disabled. The program has two parts. Part A is available automatically to all citizens when they reach age 65. It is also available to the disabled at any age after they have been covered by the disability insurance portion of the Social Security program. The coverage in the hospital and skilled home care is about 200 days.

Part B is a voluntary program financed through monthly charges of about $10 paid by enrollees and with general federal government revenues. All persons age 65 and over including those enrolled in Part A may join Part B. Under this program payments are made for X-ray and laboratory costs and out-patient hospital care of an additional 100 days. The programs pay 80 percent of reasonable charges for covered services.

The annual cost of the medicare program is about $28 billion. Despite this substantial budget, Medicare is estimated to cover somewhat less than half the cost of medical care for the elderly. A portion of this uncovered total arises from the deductible amount of $60 (1979).

Medicaid is a federal-state matching grant program. The program is only available to the disabled, blind, aged, or members of families with dependent children. The level of matching provided by the federal government is affected by the average level of per capita income of the state. The matching percentage minimum is 50 percent for highest per capita income states and 83 percent for the lowest.

To be eligible, states must offer a program similar to Medicare. The programs available in different states vary widely but must be available to all poor people. Around 20 million of the poor are included under the program. It is estimated that the average annual cost per family is $1,500. The level of aid per family available in states varies from less than $500 per year in Mississippi to over $2,000 in New York. The program is costing over $5 billion a year.

Both Medicare and Medicaid were given their current legislated form in 1965. The programs have not fulfilled the expectations of those who developed the legislation. The costs are much higher than expected, partially because of fraud, but more the result of inability to set enforceable price ceilings and to limit care prescribed by medical personnel. Access to the services of the program is uneven between the races and between geographical areas. The high-income states, despite the reduced federal matching percentage, are relatively larger users of Medicaid.

Health Care Trends

The provision of health care continues to be divided between the private and public sectors. The private sector, however, does not function in the same manner as it does in the provision of food or clothing.

The health care provided to around 90 percent of the population is paid out of a prepayment health plan of some sort. The user of health services typically does not pay for them as he uses them. This separation in time of payment from service offered, as well as the lack of a close relationship between payment and service benefits enjoyed, is a major source of difficulties encountered in keeping health care costs under control.

The rapid development of private health insurance, plus the expensive government Medicare and Medicaid programs, has stifled support for a national health service by providing two very different types of experience.

Medicare and Medicaid as government-provided medical services have proved to be so expensive and so overlaid with rules and restrictions that there is little desire to move further in this direction. Medicaid is a state program benefiting from substantial federal assistance. Medicare is a portion of the federal social security system and is financed as a portion of the old age security and disability insurance (OASDI) payroll tax that is paid half by the employer and half by the employee as a percentage of wages.

The private insurance health programs have, on the other hand, provided a very satisfactory level of service. Surveys show that 90 percent of the people are very satisfied with medical service provided. Few people are severely affected by costs of a fee for service system.

The health insurance companies, in cooperation with large employers, government bodies, hospitals, and Individual Physicians Association (IPA) are developing a new type of health provision system. Choice of doctor is largely preserved and quality of service is assured through negotiated agreements between IPA, employers, and insurance companies. A part of the developing procedure will be a systematic review of hospital costs and practices by Blue Cross and the other health insurance companies. Re-insurance by the government of catastrophic illness can be expected as a portion of this typically American approach—decentralized and disorderly.

New areas of development will be contribution programs covering dental care and costs of prescription drugs. All these programs will develop deductible levels of $100 per family per year. The next insurance area will include costs of the common medical appliances—dentures, hearing aids, and corrective glasses. Most contracts can not be expected to include emotional problems. Confidence in psychotherapy is too low and it is too costly.

The health maintenance organization (HMO) concept now being actively supported by the federal government is perhaps an idea whose time has passed. The HMO requirement that a physician be a part of an organization taking patients as they come along is not satisfactory to most doctors and most patients. The centralized location reduces administration costs somewhat for the health care providers, but because of the scattered employment locations of husbands, wives, and schools of the children, a centralized location is inconvenient and costly to patients.

Health care cost data show costs in the United States have risen very rapidly, but in Germany and Sweden, for example, the increase has been even more rapid. Medicaid and Medicare requirements account for a substantial portion of the fact health costs have increased so fast. Actually, in Europe, hospital stays are on the average longer than in the United States and the daily costs are higher (based on current exchange rates).

The care of the aged is a growing portion of the costs of our society. The elimination in 1978 of compulsory retirement at age 65 through federal legislation was wise. It will reduce the financial drain on pension funds and increase the size of the productive work force without decreasing parental time to care for the upbringing of children.

Currently about 1.5 million people live in long-term health, hospital, and nursing facilities. There are some 24,000 institutions offering long-term care. The monthly cost per patient is about $500. The main support of nearly 40 percent of these institutions is Medicaid. About 75 percent of these people are in nursing homes.

Summary

The welfare expenditure level has been rising but not as fast as the confusion between programs and complexity of administrative procedures. The core of the difficulty arises from the effort in this area of government to ensure that each state, and even to a degree every local government, has some program flexibility in both the financing and expenditure side.

Welfare spending is usually limited to government expenditure programs that require a means test. That is, benefits are withheld if income or wealth is above prescribed limits. The means test reduces costs while injecting social and moral problems of serious proportions. Much of the cost reduction support for use of means test will be eliminated when the social security system in the United States is divided into two parts, as in much of Western Europe. The first part provides an income floor under everyone who reaches a certain age or for other reasons is entitled to assistance. The second part is like an annuity and is based entirely on contributions.

Welfare spending is determined by the prosperity of the economy and the strength of the institution of the family. Government can only be helpful, and even here to a limited degree, in the provision of a sound economy. It is this limitation of government's effectiveness that makes action to improve the economic soundness of the urban core such a viable approach to the welfare problem.

40 Metropolitan Fiscal Experience

The development of metropolitan area governments has been advocated as the best approach to providing urban services of a relatively uniform quality to a number of population and industrial centers making up a geographical and economic unit. What often starts out as a two-tiered system, with the metropolitan government financing limited to only a few areawide services with the original governmental units retaining real authority over a variety of activities, often evolves into a nearly complete consolidation of local units within the metropolitan structure.

The organization of services under a level of government covering a broader area nearly always has the upgrading of the level of service available in certain areas as one of its goals. Another often expressed goal is greater economy arising from consolidation through a more efficient use of equipment and of personnel. If a number of units with the same basic operational purpose are combined as a result of these two forces, the level of government expenditures increases by less than the quality of services of low service areas is increased. The result is higher government costs, along with a better level of services in low service areas and greater efficiencies in all areas.

The history of metropolitan development has been toward greater centralization of spending and collecting of funds. This history is somewhat less supportive of the generalized conclusion that metropolitan development results in an improvement of the relative level of services in low service area and a greater general efficiency in the use of funds and personnel.

Toronto

A careful study of the Toronto, Canada, metropolitan development concludes that redistribution toward the low service areas did take place as the theory forecasts. The study did not turn up any savings resulting from greater efficiency under consolidation. Therefore, those areas gaining in service levels which were already being taxed above the overall tax level gained both lower taxes and improved services. These gains were fully capitalized into higher property values at a discount rate of 10 percent in 1967.

These higher property values in the areas gaining significantly from consolidation into a metropolitan area, with a uniform metropolitanwide property tax rate, result in a return of some of these gains to the residents of the no-gain areas included in the consolidation. The balance that develops under

275

the new uniform tax and expenditure relationship results in a one-time only capital gain with a one-time compensating capital loss in the areas where tax liabilities are increased more than service benefits are improved.

The municipalities that received negative subsidies after consolidation generally either retained the previous expenditure level or reduced expenditures by less than the negative subsidy. The municipalities receiving positive subsidies increased expenditures by more than the subsidies. Therefore, the general level of expenditures of all combined municipalities increased as the metropolitan area of Toronto was combined with the center city of Toronto.

New York

The catastrophe of New York unfolded during 1976 and remained unresolved through 1978. June 30, 1978, was the date originally set by Congress for New York to get its house in order.

The Concept of the City

The New York difficulties are in sharp contrast to Toronto's success story. Also, cities of the United States vary sharply in the efficiency with which services are provided and financed. The newer cities of the South and Southwest, plus aggressive citizen participation cities like Seattle and Minneapolis do better than the older cities of the Northeast. Every large city has its Harlem or Watts or Hough. The destructiveness of the slum or the ghetto depends on the extent of the impact it has on the political and social life of a city.

If enough people see the core of the city and the closely associated residential areas to be a godforsaken heath, then that is likely to be what it becomes. Throughout the 1960s a vast multitude of the gifted and prosperous left New York for the islands and hills where the ideals of the American lifestyle as developed by the Sierra Club and others could be practiced. The true city dweller and New Yorker accepts crime, corruption, noise, and dirt as the leaf mold of civilization—that is, a fair price to pay for a free market of ideas and an environment that encourages a multitude of choices.

Debt Default

The bankruptcy of New York was barely avoided on Friday, October 17, 1975. It was widely forecasted that default on the $453 million of short-term notes would push the municipal bond market and the stock market into disarray. No such thing occurred, even though default in fact happened. The word used was "moratorium," but it meant no payment.

The minimum impact of the New York crisis on the municipal bond market demonstrated to the satisfaction of many that federal financial help to New York City was unnecessary. The support needed to bring New York back into the money markets was available in improved management of New York City's property tax and a tightening of the management procedures. In addition, the State of New York had to accept the burden of its responsibility as the government responsible for the fiscal soundness of local governments of the state. Citizens throughout the nation came to realize during the 1974–1978 period that the price our society will pay is high, if the federal government takes over the fiscal and financial decisionmaking process at the state and local levels.

New York fiscal records of 1975–1976 showed a cash flow deficit so large that even if all debt service payments—both principal and interest—were suspended, a shortfall in excess of $1 billion would occur. At the same time it was reported that New York land values, particularly those with access to improved public transportation, had increased dramatically. It was also reported that land valuations are generally underassessed relative to other properties.

Property Tax

The property tax system of New York was and continues to be based on the idea that Manhattan is a cornucopia of wealth and income that can be tapped as funds are needed. In many cases, the assessment on residential property in New York has not been changed for forty years. An older house with a sales value in excess of $50,000 will have an annual tax bill under $1,000 at a property tax rate of about 9 percent. What the New York crisis has done is to make all the boroughs of New York City more similar to Manhattan. The special ability of the central portion of all cities, including New York, to finance activities of outlying areas is declining. The central city cornucopia has become just another borough, able to pay its share, but not much more.

City Property Tax

A study of twenty-one selected large cities that was aimed at determining the record of the property tax as a revenue raiser in cities encountering some financial troubles concluded that the property tax performed very well.

One test of whether the property tax burden is high and whether the owners of property are prosperous is the current property tax collections as a percentage of current property tax levies. If the property tax burden is too great, tax delinquencies arise and the tax collections fall considerably below the tax levies.

In the twenty-one cities, collections were over 90 percent of levies in all cities but one. That one city was Chicago, where levies are made the year before collections. More than likely this unusual administrative procedure was largely responsible for the below 90 percent tax collection-to-levy ratio.

When the property tax collection–levy ratio is examined over a recent five-year period, the change turns out to be very small. One must conclude they were largely due to happenstance rather than to any fiscal improvement or deterioration. Actually, in twenty cities examined, the tax collection–levy ratio improved in eight, the ratio declined in eleven cities, and remained constant in one.

Changes in the assessed base to which the property tax is applied reflects the economic well-being of the area being taxed. In a study of twenty-nine large cities, thirteen of them enjoyed an increase in their assessed base of over 4 percent. The assessed property tax base in four cities increased by over 10 percent. The tax base decreased in only three cities, and the declines were small—0.1, 0.7 and 1.3 percent.

Assessed property valuations typically lag behind market values, which gives the property tax helpful stability during an economic decline. However, it is an exceptional city where property tax revenues without a rate increase rise as rapidly as government costs during an inflation period. Recently land values and construction costs have been increasing more rapidly than the consumer price index. If these increased market values of real estate are made a portion of the assessed base by applying a uniform inflation rate between assessment dates (usually six years apart), property tax collections can keep up with normal expenditure increases without higher tax rates.

Generally city property taxes have not been increasing in real terms. Only in a few cities, Newark and East St. Louis for example, have property tax collections increased more rapidly than the value of the dollar has been falling. This relationship has been partially due to increased use of other tax sources, such as sales and income taxes, and partially due to increased revenue aid to the cities from the federal and state governments.

The property tax continues to provide substantial revenues from the application of reasonable rates. The tendency to place too large a portion of the assessed valuation on the structure and too small a portion on the land has retarded modernization of older sections of cities. Another tax relationship that acts in the same undesirable way is the federal government's allowance of depreciation on structures sold on the basis of the purchase price, rather than on the remaining undepreciated value base.

Direct Aid to Cities

The state and federal governments have been busy passing legislation that resulted in expanded city government costs. At the same time, the cities have become the recipients of additional fiscal support.

In 1957, federal and state direct aid to the 47 largest cities was about $2.33 per capita. Since then, the per capita level to these 47 cities has increased to about $175. This seventy-five-fold increase took place largely after fiscal year 1970. The development has caused about 50 percent of the expenditures of these largest cities to be financed with funds directly provided by federal or state governments. It is estimated that for every dollar these large cities raise from their own sources they will receive 50 cents from the federal government. Approximately 15 percent more aid was received from the federal government than from the government of their home state.

This huge and largely recent expansion of the flow of direct federal aid to the cities arose mainly from four pieces of federal legislation. First came the war on poverty programs of President Johnson in the 1960s. Next came the passage of general revenue sharing legislation in 1972. Revenue sharing was seen as a method to effectively utilize the substantial surpluses the federal government was expected to realize during prosperous periods. The war on poverty was a program to be carried out during periods of peace to rid the nation of pockets of poverty among racial minorities and backward geographical areas.

The third source of direct federal aid to the cities was provided by the enactment of the community development program in 1974. Economic stimulus packages have also been used to fight local pockets of unemployment.

Many of these federal programs providing funds to cities require relatively low provision of matching funds, but the money must be spent as established in federal legislation. The pattern of distribution of these grants results in the states with higher per capita incomes and smaller rural populations receiving larger per capita amounts. These, however, are also the states that contribute higher per capita amounts to the federal government through income tax payments. This revenue receipt and aid provision relationship provides a rough sort of fiscal justice.

State-dominated fiscal systems tend to be used by the less urban states. These states also tend to have lower per capita incomes and to receive higher grants. This relationship, however, only modifies, and does not reverse the fact that relatively larger grants go to the richer and more urban states. The federal direct aid programs aimed particularly at cities account for much of the higher federal grant receipts of the more urban states.

A substantial portion of federal direct aid and grant programs were first developed to meet city needs. Much of the rural allocation arose to meet political rather than economic requirements.

Shifting to the State Level

The cities have tended to look to the federal government for financial assistance. Their reluctance to press for state assistance arises from a combination of political weakness in many state legislatures and a vague feeling the federal level was economically appropriate.

The overrepresentation of rural and suburban residents in state legislatures has been largely remedied. The economic horn of plenty at the federal level is empty. These two developments of the past ten years should cause the cities to press for useful state-city fiscal cooperation.

The amount of state-city intergovernmental assistance can therefore be expected to continue to expand. Another shift that has taken hold moves much of the financial responsibility for local schools and public welfare away from the city and local government level.

State assumption of responsibility for schools would transfer a bit more funds to suburbs than to the core city. In the case of welfare the transfer would be substantially toward the core city.

The finance of education and public welfare by the state would move the revenue source from largely property taxes to largely sales and income taxes. The true property tax rates of urban areas would decrease to about the level prevailing in farming areas. The additional sales and income taxes necessary to cover these new state expenditure commitments would rest relatively more heavily on urban residents. The state could rectify this revenue raising disparity by introducing a low rate statewide land tax and through strengthening its inheritance tax. There has been some action toward a state land tax, for example, in Vermont, Maine, and California, but new legislation has reduced the application of the inheritance tax.

Several estimates have been made about what the movement of education and public welfare to the state would do to relative core city fiscal effort. For the nation's twenty-two largest metropolitan areas the disparity between core city and suburbs would be approximately halved; for New York the disparity would be decreased by two-thirds.

Assessment Procedures in Chicago and Portland

Both Portland and Chicago are well-financed cities using a property tax to supply regular and substantial revenues. The property tax administration procedure used in the two cities is, however, very different.

Chicago, in making its assessments, very nearly completely abandons market value, whereas in Portland properties are assessed with the single goal in mind of reaching market value. Chicago has an assessment cycle of four years aimed only at the structure's reconstruction cost and depreciation. The Portland cycle is five years. The reassessment process is aimed at placing a value on specific improvements since the last assessment and the overall changes in the neighborhood that have affected community property values.

Chicago's reassessment process makes no effort to evaluate effects of shifts in the neighborhood or changes in the income-producing capability of the property. Portland has introduced an annual adjustment of 4 percent to keep the base and rates approximately at the level expected after the reassessment cycle.

Chicago accepts in appeal hearings evidence of changes in neighborhood conditions and income earnings. These appeals, of course, are only initiated when assessed values are believed to be too high. Portland considers appeals on the same basis as the original adjusted assessed value.

Chicago's procedure results in substantial underassessment of properties in improving neighborhoods and overassessment of properties in declining neighborhoods. The Portland procedure should treat both neighborhoods the same. If speculation is decreasing values of property in a declining neighborhood more rapidly than long-run effects justify, and if the opposite relationship exists for improving neighborhoods, then the Portland procedure would widen the disparity in taxpayer liabilities of the two neighborhoods. Portland's declining neighborhoods would be stimulated by relatively low taxes and the improving neighborhoods would be held back by relatively high taxes.

To catch all improvements that required a building permit, the Portland assessor has a list of all building permits issued for each parcel of property. However, if the improvement did not result in a general increase in the value of the property it would not affect valuation. In Chicago, on the other hand, improvements are very likely to be added to the assessed value and to be depreciated on a regular schedule as is the original structure in arriving at assessed value. Some cities list improvements that will not be reassessed if made.

Chicago's approach to assessment places a greater emphasis on investment in structures than does Portland. In Portland, land is given a value based on optimal use. If the structure on the land must be torn down to arrive at optimal use, the existing improvement could have a negative value. The parcel would have a higher value if the improvement were not on the land.

The appeals procedure is available in both Chicago and Portland as it is in all states. The use of the potential of appealing an unjust tax burden varies somewhat from year to year and between jurisdictions. Typically, large investors make the most use of the appeals system. The impact of changes as a result of appeals is seldom sufficient to change a situation where a certain group of properties are making relatively large tax payments.

Current Urban Demands of the Federal Government

The cities continue to look to the federal government for continuation and expansion of aid programs. The turn toward state cooperation is now becoming apparent as revenue realization actualities at the federal and state level are being realized.

Some requested urban assistance can only be provided by the federal government. Examples of this are (1) targeting federal procurement to areas in unusual need, (2) additional investment tax credits percentage to private investors placing new investments or improvement of old investments in a declining area, (3) control the rate of inflation, and (4) keep the existing flexibility in Comprehensive Employment and Training Act (CETA) policy.

A large number of city needs that have been identified by the United States Conference of Mayors are appropriate programs for joint management and financing by states and cities, for example: (1) community care and treatment centers for the elderly, (2) specific arts programs, (3) countercyclical capital investment programs, (4) active programs to preserve and rebuild American cities, (5) studies to identify how taxes can be reformed and services more efficiently provided, and (6) taxes and subsidies that encourage industry and citizens to reduce pollution of all kinds.

Credit problems of local governments normally arise because of persistent budget deficits and declining local economic conditions. Most students of local government finance have concluded that a danger sign to be ignored only at great risk is the accumulation of short-term operating loans.

The three developments likely to cause operating deficits are sharp decreases in assessed property values and in population, plus a sudden increase in property tax delinquency. When these shifts take place credit difficulties are nearly certain to develop if local governments with state assistance fail to act decisively in meeting the new economic and fiscal conditions.

In addition, poor financial management and underfunding of retirement programs can cause credit problems for a local government, even though the area is not plagued with other shortcomings. The officials should have available, and use in making decisions, information reflecting the government's entire financial responsibility.

Summary

The former independent financial position of cities have been undermined by federal expenditure programs and grants. If the federal grants are reduced, the city is left with federal-initiated programs that often possess a low priority. A gradual replacement of federal fiscal support with state support, plus modernization of city revenue systems seems to be the appropriate direction for urban fiscal reform.

The revenue potential of the property tax as applied in the cities is strong as demonstrated by the low delinquency level. The injection of federal programs that are drafted to meet general aims are necessarily misfits and accomplish much less than similar resources raised locally for a high-priority community project.

The municipal governments have started to develop closer ties with the states. This shift in emphasis has occurred because programs better tailored to the needs of particular cities can be developed through the home state than through the federal government. This opportunity can now be realized because state revenue sources have been strengthened.

Variation in assessment procedures can affect the efficiency of land use and the perceived justice of the property tax. The Portland approach perhaps generates a higher justice perception level than does the Chicago system.

41

Revenue Sharing and Grants

Special purpose grants to local governments from the states are dominated by funds granted under various formulas to support education from community colleges down to day nursery schools (see chapter 43). In addition to greater flexibility of its grants, the federal government since the State and Local Fiscal Assistance Act of 1972 (revenue sharing) has begun to bypass the states and to make grants directly to local governments. By the time the 1976 legislation extending and amending the state and local fiscal assistance act of 1972 was adopted, more than half of federal grants (excluding welfare) went directly to local governments—cities, counties, towns. Nevertheless, state-dominated finance systems participate more in most forms of federal grants than do more locally dominated fiscal systems.

Federal Revenue Sharing

The idea of the federal government assisting states to carry out designated projects was born along with the nation. Thomas Jefferson in his second inaugural address spoke out for federal assistance to help the states finance a variety of improvement projects. President Madison vetoed as unconstitutional legislation to distribute to the states the dividends available from the Second National Bank. President Jackson in 1836 through the Surplus Distribution Act carried out a program quite similar to the Walter Heller Plan of 1964.

The 1972 federal revenue sharing legislation contains spending priorities and limitations that seem on the surface to be quite restrictive. In practice the restrictions are largely cosmetic because all normal areas of government activity can be indirectly supported with revenue sharing funds. About two-thirds of the recipients use the funds granted to avoid new taxes or to lessen the existing rates.

The 1972 federal legislation provided funding for a five-year period. The 1976 legislation followed this practice of avoiding annual appropriations and extended the program for three years and nine months with a $25.6 billion appropriation for the extended period. Two-thirds of the funds go to local governments and one-third to the states.

Analyses of experience under the 1972 legislation were made available to Congress as it considered the extension of revenue sharing. Two basic areas for administrative improvement were identified. One by the General Accounting

Office (GAO) stressed the difficulties involved in determining the use of shared revenue. The other by the Ford and Carnegie Foundation pointed out the tendency of the format used to stimulate retention and expansion of limited function government units. The procedures remain, however, basically the same as the original legislation.

Single-purpose local governments remain eligible for grants and are therefore propped up by the legislation—particularly townships in the Midwest. Also, all efforts to use revenue sharing to stimulate modernization of state and local government administration were rejected. The GAO lost ground in its desire to know how revenue-shared funds were actually being used.

The funds are allocated on the basis of a statutory formula. This formula takes into account population, per capita income, and tax effort.

From the beginning, revenue sharing was seen by Walter Heller and George Peckman, both federal fiscal specialists, to be related to the development of an improved government revenue-raising system. The federal government was envisaged as a more efficient taxing unit than state and local governments. The progressive personal income tax, the principal federal tax, was seen to be a more just approach to taxation. Therefore, what could be more appropriate than for the state and local governments to rely on revenues collected under the federal tax system. Also, it had been expected in the 1960s that there would be a federal surplus that could be best managed by increasing grants to state and local governments, the big spenders.

Although the expectations of Heller and Peckman were not realized, revenue sharing on a relatively small scale continues to function, and by 1980 will have returned over $50 billion to state and local governments. Many supporters of the program see it as a procedure to finance an expanded level of a state and local government service. This point of view conflicts with that which emphasizes revenue sharing as a method of reducing the level of state and local taxes through provision of more federal funds. The actual experience has been a considerable emphasis on new expenditures and particularly on capital projects. County governments have been most apt to finance new and advanced services with funds from revenue sharing. Tax reduction or prevention of a tax increase was the most common reported impact of revenue sharing by central cities and their suburbs.

Revenue sharing under present procedures and at approximately the current level has not significantly affected the structure of state and local governments. A program that continued along the present lines, that became permanent, and that acquired additional funds, could be expected to stimulate formation and expansion of small local governments. The incentives that would develop under these conditions could slow down consolidation and regional approaches to the offering of public services.

The temporary nature of the federal government's commitment to provide substantially the same program has affected expenditure emphasis and reduced the willingness to carry out planning needed for efficient expenditure. The director of the Federal Office of Revenue Sharing believes the limited authorization period has stimulated use of funds on capital programs. Capital spending is not bad in itself, but could represent in some instances a lost opportunity.

The "no strings" description of revenue sharing should mean that local governments can plan to use these funds on a par with other funds available. The fact the federal government is footing the bill means this can never quite be true, but it seems to many the program could come closer to meeting its billing. One useful step would be the elimination of spending by priority categories. Another would cut out the restriction on the use of revenue sharing funds to match federal grants received under other programs. Finally, the restriction on the percentage maximum and minimum of the allocation formula might be eliminated to increase the equalization impact of the program.

Other Federal Grants

At one time there were over 1,000 federal categorical grant programs. The development of revenue sharing and block grants tends to reduce the federal government's use of categorical grants. They are, however, still very much a part of the fiscal relationship between the federal government and state and local government project spending selection priorities.

Block Grants

There are only a few of these new types of block grant programs. The eight in existence as this is written are:

1. Comprehensive Employment and Training Act (CETA)
2. Educational Support and Innovation (ESEA)
3. Law Enforcement Assistance Administration (LEAA)
4. Community Development
5. Comprehensive Public Health Services
6. Social Services Title XX
7. Temporary Economic Stimulus Package
8. Urban Development Action Grant (UDAG)

One of the more important impacts of the introduction of federal block grants and the assumption of a larger portion of welfare costs by the federal government has been the very substantial increase in aid to large cities (see chapter 39).

Each block grant program enjoys broadly defined objectives, eligibility requirements, and a formula based on social and economic characteristics. CETA is the most administratively liberal program and the selection of the management agency is entirely in the hands of the grantee. LEAA specifies a state planning agency but not a single state agency as does Title XX.

CETA is also the most liberal fiscally. Matching funds are not required but an annual plan must be prepared and accepted. For LEAA and Title XX matching funds from nonfederal sources of 10 to 50 percent are required.

The availability of block and other grants from the federal and state governments to local governments does not ensure the funds will actually be distributed on the basis of eligibility. Political factors, sophistication of local government administrators, and community desires and expectations from use of the grants affect application effort and success. As a result, need for the assistance provided by the grant does not correspond with the actual allocation of the funds. Federal policy is carried out through grants in a blurred and incomplete fashion. Conservative approaches to local government functions find federal grants unacceptable. Where this attitude is strong, the local political leadership has rejected some federal grants and accepted and applied for others. The American federal system of local control has not turned over and played dead with the expansion of state and federal grants.

The Housing Assistance Plan (HAP) is a portion of the community development block grant. There has been a continuing tussle between those wishing to establish detailed conditions to be met to get the program's benefits, and those believing the minimum intrusion test is defeated and the block grant concept destroyed if elaborate regulations are introduced. It is truly difficult for federal and state governments to provide grants without also establishing spending controls.

UDAG, which was introduced in 1978, demonstrates again that complicated procedures seem to be necessary when general grant legislation is adopted to achieve certain specific federal goals. To be eligible for UDAG, a city or urban county must be a distressed community. Seven factors determine distress, for example, at least 34 percent of year-round housing was constructed before 1940.

The announced purpose of UDAG is to make certain that HUD grants under the program go only where needed and where the record of the community demonstrates good performance in carrying out community development programs. In this effort to break away from the high total cost of general programs the federal government has introduced a nearly unworkably complicated eligibility and management procedure.

The whole concept of block grants is to strike a happy middle ground between the need to push for national objectives and giving the applicant discretion. Under HAP the U.S. Senate was unwilling to abandon completely its designation of national goals. The act, therefore, requires that a majority of the funds be spent to benefit low- and moderate-income persons or blighted areas. UDAG has demonstrated again the practical impossibility of using grants to reach specific goals.

Categorical Grants

The goals of categorical grants programs extend from the preservation of historical properties to sewage treatment construction. The recent growth in dollar amounts has occurred largely in several general government activity areas: countercyclical programs, sewage treatment construction, Medicaid, income security programs, and community development block grants.

The largest grant and assistance program to state and local governments by the federal government is for public welfare. About half of total federal grants support welfare spending. An additional substantial portion is used to support various social programs. For example, temporary employment assistance has become an important program, absorbing about 4 percent of the total federal grant program funds.

State and local governments have felt that categorical programs forced them to spend funds in areas with relatively low priorities. The federal government has found that categorical grants stimulate state and local governments to carry out national priority programs that are closely related to traditional state and local government activity areas. Another point of view relative to federal and to some extent state grants relates the dollar quantity of grants to the dollar amount of taxes paid. This latter relationship has resulted in the calculation of the tax costs per dollar of aid received by a state.

The tax cost per dollar of aid goes from the high in Indiana, where each dollar of federal aid has a tax dollar cost of $1.43, to Vermont, where the tax burden per dollar of aid is only $.53. Another calculation shows that own-source revenues equal to about one-third of the federal aid must be raised to enjoy the benefits of the federal largess. Despite these two obvious aspects of unfairness in the state and local government grant program, and the unwillingness of some local governments to accept national goals, categorical grant spending continues to be among the fastest growing outlays of the federal government. Recent total grant rates of growth (revenue sharing, block grants, and categorical grants) have been 50 percent greater than the growth rate of total federal spending.

Summary

The concept of federal revenue sharing rests on two basic assumptions. First, both the state or the federal level either find it easier to raise tax revenues and/or tax revenues collected by them possess built-in desirable characteristics—that is, they are more closely related to ability to pay, or place a lower level of hardship on industry. Second, national spending programs outside of the traditional areas—that is, defense, international relations, and the judiciary—are frequently more efficient and more acceptable politically when managed by lower level governments.

Federal revenue sharing, block grants, and categorical grants are to an extent also used in a modified form by states. These grant types basically vary in the degree of spending freedom they permit successful applicants. The revenue sharing grant can be spent most freely, and therefore has the best chance of being used in a manner that maximizes benefits as seen by the politically dominant group within the jurisdiction of the government receiving the grant. It is also true revenue sharing is least likely to advance the goals of the grant-providing government if they should happen to differ from local priorities. In block and categorical grants, spending freedom is reduced and goal achieving potential is increased.

The return of the statewide land tax and the use of land as a local tax base could increase the relative attractiveness of revenue-raising at the state and local government level. The large federal deficits and the growing tax wedge between bargained income and aftertax income point to greater problems being associated with federal grant spending commitments financed with income and payroll taxes.

Part X
Accounting and
Resource Allocation

42 Municipal Accounting

The cities and other local governments are reconsidering their accounting procedures and establishing evaluation approaches to learn whether recent changes are helpful. Seven areas of municipal accounting will be examined: financial reporting, fund accounting, budgetary accounting, cost accounting, performance measurement, auditing, and grant-in-aid accounting.

These divisions of the accounting function overlap to some extent. In addition, the importance of each division to sound management and financing of local government vary greatly. The order in which the divisions are placed represents only to a degree their relative importance.

Financial Reporting

The accounting reports of a city are compared by investors with those available from business firms. Actual and potential investors in municipal securities are interested in annual reports that bring together in one place all the revenues and expenditures of the organization. They are interested in a standard format so that the financial condition of cities can be compared. The taxpayers of the city and potential taxpayers have approximately the same interest.

One study group of this area of municipal accounting came up with a group of recommendations that can be summarized as follows.

1. Adopt the standard format available in *Government Accounting, Audition and Financial Reporting* which is made available by the Municipal Finance Officers Association. (Currently, fewer than one-third of local governments with the power to tax and borrow have adopted the system.)
2. Establish procedures for reporting in footnotes pension and employee-benefit data in such a form that the future burden of these contracts can be evaluated.
3. Initiate accounting disclosure requirements of the same comprehensiveness as required of businesses by the Securities and Exchange Commission.
4. Use a set of generally accepted accounting principles appropriate for reporting to the public.
5. Present the city's fiscal condition, including lease obligations and assets and liabilities on a full-accrual basis, in a concise set of financial statements.

The financial reporting of a government unit is always bothered by the fact fund accounting (see the next section) does not generally permit the transfer of revenues from a fund with a surplus to a fund experiencing a deficit. Also the revenue estimate is always considered too conservative by those desiring additional expenditures.

The chief function of financial accounting is to tie together changes in the various fund balances. The availability of liquid resources to the municipal government is determined by the aggregate fund balance. This balance is frequently seen as the financial margin of safety available to the city in carrying out its obligations.

Under the current financial accounting approach of most local governments, the proper use of an encumbrance system is of prime importance. An encumbrance system provides for deduction from available funds of every expenditure when contracted. The correct use of encumbrances prevents payment of bills of one period from appropriations of a subsequent budget period. A city on an encumbrance system cannot develop a large floating debt.

Unencumbered balances at the end of the fiscal year are frequently committed to avoid loss of these monies to the department. These practices can be wasteful. To keep track of the problem all outstanding encumbrances at the end of the year should be included in a special balance sheet account called "reserve for encumbrances."

The computer systems installed in some large cities go beyond payroll and tax collection to link all spending and income departments directly to the finance department. When correctly programmed and with personnel cooperation, a computer financial control system should be able to give the finance department current information on the exact financial position of the city. However, large cities with their very complex financial structures have largely defied effective use of computer management systems. At one time the federal Department of Housing and Urban Development attempted to develop such a system. After eight years and $26 million it gave up. Although progress has been slow, some cities have after a number of years adjusted their fiscal system to the capabilities of available computers.

Fund Accounting

All accounting systems can be broken down into three general jobs: recording, reporting, and auditing. In the use of fund accounting the need for careful attention to the recording aspect is of particular importance. The secretary or manager of an operation carrying out activities included in a number of different funds is often unaware of the importance of making certain the activity is credited to the proper fund and that the correct budgeting code number is used on a requisition form.

Fund accounting is aimed particularly at meeting management's need for control. The activities of a city are carried out through a number of departments that have been allocated certain functions and certain funds. It is the prime duty of the city government to make certain that revisions of the budget and other legislation related to each department are carried out. Certain funds are made available, and these funds must be used to carry out certain programs established by law.

To a degree, then, a city government consists of a number of specialized and largely self-managed operations. Each activity is allocated to a suitable fund for accounting. One recommended breakdown of funds is made up of eight different groups: general fund, special revenue funds, capital project funds, enterprise funds, trust and agency funds, intergovernmental service funds, and special assessment funds.

How each of a local government's funds are best managed varies widely. The general fund, which is also usually the largest, is best managed along the lines of a system of encumbrances. The funds concerned with capital financing are usually not directly affected by annual appropriation ordinances. However, if revenues become inadequate to meet debt service arrangements accepted when the capital commitment was made, the annual appropriation ordinance may have to reduce revenues dedicated to the general fund.

Most cities operate commercial type activities. The accounting of these operations is carried out as it would be in a wholly owned subsidiary corporation. The budgets under which the revenues are collected and spent generally function as does a budget of a private commercial operation. This means the amounts to be spent are not legal limits. Many of these enterprises, like golf courses and utility plants, are financed with user charges that are similar to prices used to finance private sector activities. Everything possible should be done to make everyone aware that certain revenue goals must be met through the user charges collected. This means prices must be increased when general inflation exists.

The management of retirement and disability pension funds requires operational procedures that strictly separate these monies from general operational funds. Also, the adequacy of the funds to meet commitments must be continuously reexamined and the findings made public. A city with a surplus in its general fund but with an actuarially unsound pension fund is not basically in any better financial condition than a city with a deficit in its general fund but an actuarially sound pension fund.

Special Assessments

City improvements are frequently financed with special assessments. However, when the improvement is made, financing is with borrowed funds.

Gradually, year by year, as established when the undertaking was decided on, the collections from the special assessments retire the indebtedness. The management of these arrangements requires making certain the funds are collected as agreed, and that they are wisely invested for the short period between receipt and application to retirement of the serial bonds issued to finance the improvement (see chapter 30).

Internal Payments

One interesting aspect of fund accounting is the collection of costs from different governments using the services of other government units. The use of the services of the legal office to collect taxes becomes a cost to the tax department. A large portion of the costs of having a city legal department might be met in this manner. The procedure limits waste of internally provided services.

The same procedure can be used to finance office buildings and duplicating services, for example. The management of the transfer of these funds also provides use data that can be helpful in analyzing the efficiency of operations of the different departments.

Expanding Usefulness

Fund accounting is useful in controlling operations through receipts and expenditures. To maximize benefits, the data must be available quickly and must be accurately reported at the basic source level. The effectiveness can be destroyed if so many funds are separately reported that a picture of basic trends is badly blurred. The advantage in knowing how particular units are doing has recently been recognized by business leaders, finance analysts, and the Securities Exchange Commission. As a result, corporations are more frequently breaking down their outlay and revenues by particular use and source.

Budgetary Accounting

The appropriations included in the budget document make up a large portion of a government's legal power to spend. The fiscal year starts out with a certain quantity of funds provided in the budget to do certain things. As the year progresses, salaries are paid and purchases of materials and equipment are made. The allocation for salaries must be checked each quarter to make certain overspending through overtime and special situations is not exceeding the budget allocation. As each purchase commitment is made, the amount set aside for this purpose is encumbered and the available funds reduced by that amount.

The line item budgetary approach sets aside a certain amount for each authorized position and certain amounts for materials, social security payments, and the like. When the expenditure level reaches these totals, further expenditure is not possible until procedures established for variation from the budget are carried out. An aim of encumbered budgeting is to give a warning prior to an actual shortage of funds.

Cost Accounting

The science of cost accounting is highly developed in the private sector because it is fundamental in determining the basic goal—profits. In the public sector, cost accounting is of much less importance, but is necessary in carrying out a number of management functions.

Cost accounting permits comparison of costs of certain activities in different government units. If accurately done, these comparisons can be used to judge the efficiency of a particular department. The comparison is often weakened by basically unmeasurable differences in the quality of service provided.

Because the person in charge of an operation frequently must meet costs over which he or she has little control, the concept of responsibility costing has been introduced. Comparisons under the responsibility costing concept are limited to costs over which managers have control. The use of the concept of responsibility costing demonstrates the shortcoming of cost accounting in the public sector. In the private sector, management can't be excused because costs are not controllable. Management had better work out a procedure through cost and selling price policy so that the firm makes a profit. The easy out, when prices rise, of an increase in the operating budget is much more available in the public sector. In the private sector, cost cuts to compensate for a price increase of one product is likely to be pressed more actively.

Another common question related to cost accounting is how much more will it cost to do something different. The incremental cost of adding to the quality and availability of a service helps management make several decisions. Sometimes incremental cost is limited to only the variable costs obviously associated with the shift. Other costs related to capital equipment use level and burden placed on related services by increasing peak use loads must be considered. The impact of decreasing the portion of capacity use of staff and capital of competing services, must also be included in correct estimates of the additional cost.

The common practice of internal charging for use of services of other departments requires cost information in the setting of prices charged. In some cases, full cost pricing is used. Under this procedure, a portion of the general overhead and depreciation costs is added to incremental or out-of-pocket costs in setting price. Often the service offered is also available in the private sector. When this is the case, these prices will usually be approximated by in-house prices.

Performance Measurement

The establishment of costs per unit of production under cost accounting is an important aspect of performance measurement. The quality of the service provided must also be measured; this can be learned through sample surveys. Finally, the areas of activity left undone need to be analyzed to make certain performance levels are not partially the result of "skimming"—that is, completing the easy assignments and leaving the tough ones undone.

When management uses the quantity of work completed as a measurement of efficiency, it must also decide whether the services wanted by the public are being provided. The public sector usually does not have the assistance of the price system in determining user priority. Every public sector manager must be aware of this basic public sector weakness in the efficient allocation of resources.

Auditing

The auditing function is often completed by an agency of the state or by the auditor's department of a city government. Outside accounting firms are being utilized more often as the frequency of local government financial difficulties increase. Most states require its subdivisions to complete a uniform summary of their financial operations. This document is filed with the designated department of state government.

Auditing, as envisaged under ideal conditions, provides three services. The first, and the traditional one, is to determine if financial operations have been properly conducted. The second is to evaluate the efficiency with which the activities were managed. The third goal of a good auditing program is to determine how well the aims of the governing body have been met and how this could be done at a lower cost. Auditors are limited to making recommendations; the manager must see that improvement is realized.

Auditing is usually carried out by accountants. Their training emphasizes the items that can be measured and counted. This, of course, is also the emphasis of the auditing evaluation of a city and each of its departments. This procedure is entirely appropriate in checking the inventory on hand and whether public funds were spent illegally. The approach has weaknesses when applied to goals such as a safe city in which to work and play or a school system graduating useful citizens.

Grant-in-Aid Accounting

Federal revenue sharing and grants-in-aid are providing an increasing portion of the funds of local governemnts, particularly in large cities. The federal government's grants programs, but not revenue sharing, requires a certain amount of matching funds. These programs can be used also to finance services related to the carrying out of the program that are provided by regular government departments.

The emphasis of the federal government on an efficient system of internal controls and measurement of goal achievement has influenced city accounting procedures. For example, the federal requirement of external audit has increased the use of private auditing firms. These firms develop unusual competence in developing the data needed by the city accounting department when the final federal evaluation of the grant performance is carried out.

The costs of an operating government that can be counted as matching funds to meet requirements of federal grant programs has become an important influence on local government accounting practices. The first requirement in maximizing the availability of matching funds is to make certain that all payments are made by check and that the purpose of the payment is shown. Another is to keep proper records to prove that a person is engaged in sufficient grant related activities to justify use of his salary as matching funds. Records need to be kept so that the cost of library and technical equipment use counted as matching support can be substantiated. Records of the same nature are required when contributions of personnel and facilities are being paid for out of grant funds.

Summary

Local government accounting needs have proved to be so complex that a complete electronic data processing (EDP) system that establishes a central data base still escapes the efforts of the specialists. The requirement that income from one source may have to be allocated to five different funds and reallocated when certain limits are reached proves to be more than EDP can handle along with more routine activities.

Relating city use of fund accounting to the allocations established in the budget and the requirement of special legislation, commercial operation needs, and federal procedures (where federal funds are used) adds up to a very complex revenue provision and use system. In addition to these largely fund management responsibilities, local government accounting should attempt to determine the efficiency of the government departments in meeting the needs of its residents. The public sector does not generally have available the convenient price system to use in matching benefits with costs and bottom line profits to use in judging efficiency. Also, the public sector can only spend and collect revenues as provided by law, which requires much greater emphasis on control and legality than does commercial accounting.

43 Intergovernment Revenue Sources and Spending

The federal Constitution allocates specific powers to the central government and all residual powers belong to the states, which could be expected to maintain and expand state powers. The social welfare, economic, and political developments brought about by the wars and depressions of the past sixty-five years, aided by a constitutional amendment granting the federal government power to use a graduated income tax, have combined with the relaxation of the restrictions on the money supply to reverse the expectations of the framers of the Constitution. The trend of relative government power during the twentieth century has been continuously away from state and local authorities to the national government bureaucracy.

Shift of Direction

Evidence shows that results below expectations in a number of problem areas have reduced citizen support of national government's continued relative growth. Perhaps the most far-reaching and least perceived of this reduced support is demonstrated in the frequency of large annual federal budget deficits. Popular support for federal programs has proved to be insufficient to provide the taxes needed to cover the costs.

A thumbnail evaluation of the relative strengths and weaknesses of the federal government and of the states and their government creations goes like this. The federal government, because of the national and international character of the economy, possesses superior abilities in collecting taxes. The states and local governments, because the achievement of expenditure goals are nearly always tied closely to local conditions, prove to be the government level best suited to the requirements of efficient public expenditure.

Exceptions, of course, exist, and they are important in understanding the developing role of state and local governments in the United States. One can accept the fact that the federal government is technically the better tax gatherer. But does this necessitate that states and local governments abandon tax collecting and the political acceptability of tax collection at this level of government and opt to rely ever more on revenues granted by the federal government?

Dominant Use of Property and Sales Taxes

One very important tax, the property tax, is available to the federal government without a constitutional amendment only if liabilities are set on a per capita basis. (The federal Constitution requires in Article I, Section 9, that direct taxes must be apportioned among the several states according to the census.) Also, this tax, particularly the portion resting on land, has proven to be an excellent, if often unloved, source of revenue for local governments. Obviously, the federal government is most unlikely to invade this revenue source. It also so happens that the property tax before the great depression of the 1930s was a much more important source of state revenues than it is today. As we shall indicate, it may be that the states will return to at least that portion of the property tax resting on land to reduce the inequalities in education finance and to hold back somewhat the burden of taxes resting on wages.

As the states largely released the property taxes for use by local government units, and particularly by school districts in the 1930s, they moved into the retail sales tax collection business. The sales tax, after the bulge in adoption after World War Two, became the largest source of state revenues. Because this tax is paid on local transactions and because states have been active in its development, it is often assumed this is a tax best used at the state and local government level. Nevertheless, this tax might function better if shifted to the national level. The reasons for support of such a shift rest on both administrative and economic grounds (see chapter 24).

The administration of sales taxes on goods purchased outside the jurisdiction using the tax has proven most troublesome. All states wish to encourage out-of-state sales to reduce local unemployment and to encourage economic growth. This encouragement of local business has prevented the taxation of out-of-state sales the same as in-state sales. The state of residence of the purchaser, in addition, wishes to assess a sales tax of its own on goods purchased outside the state. States have been doing this by applying a "use" tax. This "pick-up" tax and other devices are used to solve administrative problems related to lack of uniformity of state and local government sales tax laws. The exemption of out-of-state sales are more than just bothersome; they result in substantial efficiency reductions and related cost increases.

VAT Transactions Tax

A basic economic weakness of the state and local retail sales tax rests on the inability of a transactions tax of this type to offer the international economic advantage available if a national tax on commercial sales is used. The value-added tax (VAT) used generally in Europe is such a tax. VAT under the regulations of the General Agreement on Tariffs and Trade (GATT) can be refunded on exports and assessed as a border tax on imports. This, of course, is impossible under state and local retail sales taxes and largely so under a national retail sales tax. In fact, Sweden, which for a number of years made substantial use of a national retail sales tax, abandoned the tax for a VAT. The shift was made largely because of the economic advantages of VAT.

The federal Constitution allocated to the federal government the power to levy indirect taxes—that is, taxes based on sales. This basic tax power was broadened by the Sixteenth Amendment, which granted the power to levy a graduated income tax.

It is unfortunate but understandable that the states moved into the general retail sales tax area in the 1930s. Real estate prices were down, mortgages were being foreclosed, and the states, by removing themselves largely from use of the property tax, could give some economic relief to owners of real estate. In addition, the federal government had not developed a general indirect tax. Eventually, the retail sales tax contributed to the inflation of consumer prices that is causing severe economic dislocation. The state departure from real estate taxation stimulated land and real estate speculation generally, which has in turn drained savings from productive investment in modern equipment and energy production.

In the 1930s, when the retail sales tax caught on, the Brookings Institution recommended to Alabama and Iowa that they introduce a value added tax (VAT) and not a retail sales tax (see chapter 28). The 1932 recommendations were not followed, but the business taxation economists continued to recommend that states levy a land tax and if more revenues were needed, move to VAT.

In 1940, Paul Studensky, the leading business taxation economist, in a basic study aimed at developing a theory of business taxation, advocated major use of VAT. Nevertheless, the federal government did not move to share, and certainly not usurp, the use of indirect taxes by the states.

A substantial use of VAT by the federal government could be combined with an allocation to states based on source of collection or portion of national personal income allocated to the state. The federal government could even go one step farther and tie allocation of VAT revenues to portion of personal income being collected by the state and its subdivisions as sales and transaction taxes. A procedure might be adopted that would reduce the basic allocation by some percentage, say 25 percent, for each 1 percent of personal income being collected as sales and transaction taxes.

The desirability of having the federal government share with state and local governments a substantial portion of VAT collections rests on two principal positions. First, it would neutralize arguments like those used by the National Governors Conference that a federal VAT would compete with state and local sales taxes. Second, the federal government could collect a substantial VAT without an equal increase in the size of the public sector. The United States is the only major commercial nation that does not make extensive use of a national VAT or similar taxes that are assessed on imports as border taxes and refunded on exports. This lack of tax harmonization was not of great importance when government tax collections were less than half the current level. One way to recognize the changed international impact of divergent tax programs and, in addition, increase the administrative desirability of indirect tax collections, is to legislate in this direction. Certainly the approach cannot be legitimately opposed on the basis that it constitutes an unwarranted intrusion into the fiscal areas staked out by state and local governments. Actually, except in the taxation of wealth (that is, property tax), overlapping rather than separation of tax sources is the typical practice.

Dominant Federal Use of Income Tax

The personal income tax as a modern tax has its roots in the Wisconsin tax of 1911. The taxation of income in various ways from assuming an income level from personal profession or expertise, to the number of windows in a house, dates back to medieval times. The federal government's use of the income tax basically dates from the Sixteenth Amendment (1913) to the federal Constitution. (The amendment is simple and to the point: "The Congress shall have power to lay and collect taxes on incomes, from whatever source derived, without apportionment among the several states, and without regard to any census or enumeration." Alabama was the first state to ratify the amendment and Delaware was the last.) However, an income tax was used in both the North and the South during the Civil War. The federal government collected a personal income tax from 1862 through 1872 (see chapter 26).

Although the personal income tax was used by both the federal and state governments, the tax became primarily a federal tax after World War One and the federal dominance expanded substantially during World War II and the introduction of tax withholding. The state activity continued but at a relatively low level. State legislation in this area expanded as revenue needs grew out of the birth bulge after World War II, but states remain relatively inactive. (There is a great variation in the relative use of the personal income tax by the states. In Oregon, the tax provides about 50 percent of total state revenues while in Louisiana and Maine the percent is 9 percent and 10 percent, respectively.)

It has been suggested that state and local income taxes be treated as credits against federal income taxes while other taxes remain either nondeductible for individuals or only deductible from gross income in arriving at the taxable income base. Congress has not seen fit to enact this legislation, but if it did, state and local government use of income taxes would skyrocket. The treatment of only state and local government income tax payments in this fashion would make the treatment of taxes domestically the same as international treatment. Therefore, some justification exists for the change.

The rationale for federal dominance in the income tax field rests largely on administrative requirements of the use of graduated rates and the need for substantial federal revenues. To arrive at all sources of income and therefore to permit the application of really progressive rates, taxpayer income from throughout the nation and the world must be included in and collected from the base.

As the degree of progressivity of federal income tax collections has declined, and the importance of foreign income tax payments increased, the federal government's very heavy reliance on the personal income tax has become less justified. This does not mean, however, that additional opportunities for state and local government use are developing. What it does demonstrate is that the collection of income taxes at sufficiently high real progressive levels to bring about income redistribution is much more difficult than was envisaged by the tax reformers of 1913.

The considerable variation in the use of the income tax by states stimulates business and personal decisions dictated at least partially by income tax variation. The high federal personal income tax and the desire to place income under the lower capital gains rates are even more important in deciding consuming and investing decisions. These deadweight costs of collecting the income tax are resulting in advocacy of state income taxes that are a flat rate of federal tax liabilities that will be deductible from federal taxes due up to a certain set percentage, say 10 percent. There is also considerable agitation for use of a flat rate federal income tax that would treat all incomes alike and that would allow only a few basic deductions in arriving at taxable income from gross personal income.

Movement in these directions demonstrates a reduction in the ability-to-pay support for the use of personal income as a tax base. Under these shifts, the federal income tax becomes very similar to the existing state income taxes. Tax harmonization between states, communities, and nations has become a tax policy goal so important under current high tax collections that it cannot be abandoned in efforts to apply an income tax that adheres to some sort of ability-to-pay tax procedure developed by a particular government.

Pyramiding Government Debt

An important support of the relative growth of federal portion of the public sector has been the interaction between what has come to be called Keynesian economics and the political attractiveness of spending without the political pain of taxation. State and local governments are restricted in their borrowing by perceived ability to repay the debt as well as meeting interest costs; this is not so of the federal government's spending of borrowed funds. Deficit spending is, therefore, more readily available to the federal government.

Although actual borrowing is more readily carried out at the federal level, the state and local governments have been expanding their borrowing as well. To a degree, state and local borrowing finds its economic support in federal debt. This relationshiop is shown by the financial aid the federal government has extended to state and local governments. These federal-sourced revenues of state and local governments have expanded rapidly; one result of this growth has been a substantial increase in the ability of state and local governments to support borrowing.

State and local borrowing ability rests to a considerable degree on federal grants that were, at least indirectly, financed out of federal borrowing. A pyramiding of debt has tended to be one result of federal support of services and projects carried out by state and local governments.

This fiscal relationship, which basically sees federal grants and revenue sharing as borrowed funds that act to spawn additional state and local debt, is not widely perceived. The politically accepted relationship sees federal fiscal assistance as coming from federal tax collections that reduce the borrowing of state and local governments by reducing their fiscal burden. The hoped-for relationship between deficit financing and federal grants to state and local governments will become the actual situation when the federal budget is in balance, and state and local government borrowing is not being limited by available funds to meet interest and debt retirement requirements.

Summary

Revenue-raising social goals are being modified and postponed as administrative and economic impacts of government deficits and tax rate and base diversity grow with expanded revenue needs. Diversity in the use of income and transaction (production) taxes cause tax determined business and individual decisions. The taxation of land values largely avoids this problem and is therefore well suited for diversity of application.

The large tax collections required point to reevaluation of the manner in which general indirect taxes are collected. The federal government, by adopting a substantial VAT, can both harmonize the American tax system with that of other major industrial nations and sharply reduce domestic tax administrative costs.

44 Managing the County

Federalism—A Layer Cake or a Marble Cake

All states except Connecticut and Rhode Island have counties. There are about 3,000 counties (called parish in Louisiana and borough in Alaska). The population and territory covered varies widely. About 127 counties include half the total population of the nation.

Because of the great variety in county activities and population density a fourfold classification has been suggested and has gained some acceptance. A county would be judged rural if population density was less than 100 per square mile; semirural if the population density was between 101 and 250 persons per square mile; semiurban if the population was between 251–1,000 persons; urban when above 1,001 persons per square mile density. The average density of the counties of states vary from 953 persons per square mile in New Jersey to 4 persons per square mile in Nevada.

The variation in types of services provided and the revenue sources used by counties is largely the result of differences in population density. The three general basic areas of county responsibility are (1) administrative district of the state, (2) government and proprietary function as a unit of local government similar to a municipality, and (3) coordinator of government programs such as planning and pollution control. The first area is the traditional county role. It exists in all counties but is the limit of county activity in the rural counties only. The other two areas are highly developed in the urban and semiurban counties.

The county government executive and legislative functions are usually combined in a single body. This is called the commissioner form and is used in about two-thirds of the counties. Pennsylvania originated the approach in 1724. Beginning in 1893 in Cook County, Illinois, counties have used the executive form, which provides for an elected chief executive office as well as an elected board. The county manager form of government was first introduced in Iredell County, North Carolina, in 1927. Some 50 counties in nearly 20 states currently use this form of government.

The basic legislative powers of the county board, by whatever name it is called, are fiscal and regulatory. The two principal officers responsible for carrying out these two basic county board functions—that is, assessor and sheriff—are frequently elected by the people and are therefore politically independent of the board. Both these officers and other elected department heads are limited to their independence, however, because the fiscal and budgetary powers remain in the board.

Revenues

County government property tax receipts amount to somewhat less than one-third of total revenues. During recent years nonproperty tax revenues have been increasing about three times as rapidly as property taxes. Intergovernmental revenues are about 40 percent above property taxes. Recently, the growth of intergovernmental revenues has fallen below the property tax expansion rate. During this period the portion of intergovernmental revenues coming from the federal government expanded substantially.

The per capita revenues of county government are about half as great as those of cities. The counties receive a smaller portion of the revenues from own sources than do the cities. Cities are much greater users of nonproperty taxes than counties, but counties are heavier users of current charges. Recently both counties and city governments have enjoyed total general revenues in excess of general expenditures.

The continuation of federal assistance programs, such as revenue sharing and block grants, generally assure the counties of an ample revenue base. The reduction in real terms of county intergovernment revenues from the states demonstrates that, to a degree, customary levels of intergovernment revenues have not been exceeded because the states cut back as federal assistance expanded.

The counties have been receiving a larger number of grants from state and federal governments than the cities for a number of reasons. One is the fact counties cover the entire state. Therefore grants to counties assure that all portions of the state will have an opportunity to benefit. Another explanation is that counties are the level of local government just below the state.

The categorical grants were reported in some local and national studies to skew spending more than block grants. Apparently the additional flexibility of block grants actually do, at least in the case of counties and cities, result in a greater likelihood of expenditures on things the local people want.

Pivotal Role

The most pervasive local government development is the increase in local government cooperation in the provision of services and related use of grants and own-source revenues. These arrangements have frequently been aimed at reaching a desired economic and service goal, while having a minimum impact on the local government structure. The three procedures that have been finding favor result in an expanding role for the county.

The interlocal service contract is a simple business contract with the county to provide police or some other services. Another is the joint service agreement between several governments operating under an agreement supervised by the county. In the third procedure, functional transfer, several local governments might turn over the operation of their separate playgrounds and parks to the county and the county accepts the responsibility of financing the operation.

Urban County Functions

Counties falling in the semiurban or urban category should be allocated appropriate duties through specific state legislation. The ACIR has suggested legislation that would authorize the county to perform the following responsibilities in addition to its traditional responsibilities:

1. trash and refuse disposal
2. sanitary and storm sewer collection, treatment, and disposal
3. library services
4. water supply and distribution
5. airports

These services would be made available to all unincorporated areas. Where appropriate the county would cooperate with the cities as another local government entity.

Because a considerable portion of the new county responsibilities are enjoyed exclusively by residents living outside incorporated municipalities, the revenue source to finance these undertakings should exclude the municipal-sited tax base. Financing allocation raises problems as small cities and rural-urban areas like to retain existing municipal and urban benefits generally without paying their share of the cost. Here a sound accounting and cost-benefit system can be of great assistance in arriving at an agreement that fits the individual situation.

Special Districts

About three-quarters of the counties have special districts, which do not seem to vary with the type of county administration. The extent of county control over district decisions is determined in most cases by the portion of financing coming from the county.

A large portion of the special districts have taxation power, often limited by the availability of the initiative. About 70 percent of drainage, education, fire protection, and irrigation districts have taxing powers. The same taxing power is enjoyed by about 40 percent of districts concerned with parks, school buildings, sewage, water supply, libraries and hospitals.

The power of special districts to borrow varies greatly between types and the way grants are made available. Very few soil conservation districts can borrow whereas two-thirds of the solid waste districts have this power.

The concept of specialized districts that are not limited by local government boundaries to carry out needed services is very attractive. The procedure also complicates the administration of the property tax and develops powerful political and economic groups unwilling to recognize the need to equalize expenditure burdens. A rich district financing its own irrigation project or schools is able to provide a high level of service with a lower property tax rate than required in a poorer district. In the case of schools (see chapter 44), the courts have reduced this undesirable aspect of special districts. The use of special districts generally should be restricted so that a government operation does not take on many of the exclusion characteristics of a private sector operation.

Taxing and provision of services by government should be generalized. If generalization is not appropriate or desired, then the activity belongs in the private sector. Stopping the proliferation of special districts that criss-cross counties and to make firmly established districts responsive to general needs must be high on the county reform priority list.

Summary

Counties have become much more important allocators of public funds during the past ten years. This growth is supported by a strong property tax that rests on a booming real estate market. However, even more of the revenue growth has come from increasing intergovernmental revenue.

The counties are being modernized in their administrative procedures and in the allocation of decisionmaking power. The growth of home rule counties is in response to the need felt by many local government administrators that county governments are pivotal in working out interlocal government arrangements meeting the particular needs of the area. The county seems destined to become as important in meeting urban government needs as it has traditionally been in the performance of rural government needs.

States and counties need to work closely together in meeting the requirements of urban and rural areas for government services—the expanded level of federal aid has expanded these needs. It has proved to be very difficult to tailor federal aid to local conditions. The problems created when national programs attempt to meet local needs give strength to advocacy of county-state cooperation in revenue-raising and spending.

45 The Unique Problems of Public School Finance

Education, except during periods of war, has been the largest single-purpose expenditure of government. A well-educated population has since the days of Aristotle been considered the basic requisite for democracy and a productive society. In the United States, the financing of this basic function has rested largely with local school districts. During the depression of the 1930s, state governments increased their financial commitment to education. The trend has been continuing since then. Thirty years later another surge of funding from states and the national government was made available to support primary and secondary education.

Since the nineteenth century, postsecondary education in agriculture and engineering has been substantially assisted by federal expenditures, with a large increase in the 1960s. Higher education has become largely a joint product of the national and state governments. The two-year junior and community colleges are, however, recipients of substantial financing from school districts, the states and the federal government.

Cost-Benefit

The historical background of school support and the deeper involvement of governments above the school district level would lead one to expect school spending to enjoy full public support. This has never been the general case, although periods of great enthusiasm for education have occurred.

In the 1920s, college education and state universities enjoyed great support. In the late 1950s and early 1960s school districts enjoyed nearly unreserved support for their programs. From the 1970s on, however, education quality has been questioned. Research findings have shown the upper middle class to be the great beneficiaries of public finance of colleges, in particular, but also of primary and secondary education. This was counter to the folklore that saw public education as lifting the lower classes up to equality with the middle class. Education, financed with taxes that fell heavier on the poorer people, could be justified because these were also the people who benefited most by the expenditure financed with the taxes collected.

These reappraisals of education as a government-provided and -subsidized service pointed to a rethinking of the trend away from property taxation as the major source of funds for primary and secondary education. The state, in this new context, was an appropriate major contributor only if its revenue base rested to a substantial extent on those enjoying economic surpluses. The federal government became a more appropriate financer of education on a purely revenue-to-service relationship. But there was, of course, more to the question of how education should be financed than the relative progressivity of the revenue and relative regressivity of the expenditure.

The middle and higher income receivers and wealth owners found state and local tax-supported education advantageous because of federal income tax provisions. Expenditures made for tuition, books, and special training were not deductible from taxable income. Tax payments to state and local governments, on the other hand, were deductible. The poor and relatively poor with their flat allowable deductions do not benefit from this procedure.

Even though education as a service is used more by those well-off economically than by the poor, the benefit to the poor is nevertheless greater. The well-off could be taught at home or by voluntary neighborhood groupings or by organized tuition-supported schools. These alternatives are not available to the poor. The provisions of schooling under the existing tax-financed procedure does not exclude the poor completely, as might be largely true under private provision. In addition, a private system would nearly entirely prevent the poor children from associating with the well-to-do. These traditional advantages of public education have proven to be much more limited than advertised.

The neighborhood school in the larger urban areas, and also even in smaller towns, has resulted in segregated schools by race and economic position. Learning from the fortunate by the poor even when they attend the same classes is apparently much less than has been assumed. This situation does not appear to be materially improved by making more funds available to the schools of poorer school districts. Research has found nothing that consistently assures achievement improvement. Whether a student comes from a poor or a wealthy family, learning depends on incentives. The assumption that the incentives of the poor would be greater, if ever existing, are not visible in current studies.

School District

The school district has become much more than a convenient procedure to finance and manage basic education made available to everyone. The setting of school district boundaries became a method to ensure that very valuable real estate was located in areas where the costs of providing education was minimal because few residential properties were located there. The property taxes required per $1,000 of assessed value to provide minimal education to the children of different school districts varies greatly within a state and even within a county or an urban area.

The revenues provided by the state retail sales taxes of many states are partially dedicated to reducing school district fiscal inequalities. State activity in reducing education finance fiscal inequities had to pay the political price of also providing additional funds to the relatively low tax rate districts. The states, as would be expected, are no more able politically to target assistance to only those requiring it than the federal government. Nevertheless, the existing inequitable conditions required a state effort, which has meant bureaucratic regulations and a school finance system nearly no one understands.

The *Serrano versus Priest* Supreme Court decision in 1971 spurred California to act more vigorously to equalize school-related property tax rates. The decision requires basically that equal tax effort provide equal revenues, in the philosophy that education is so important to the nation that its quality should not be dependent on the wealth of a child's parents or of the school district in which the family resides.

Since the *Serrano* decision, several similar court decisions have been made across the country and the original *Serrano* case has been reaffirmed in California. The concept of power equalization was developed to avoid state control and financing of education and to preserve the power of the local school district board members and their constituents.

Under power equalization schemes, each school district sets its budget and determines the tax rate required to meet it. If the tax rate required is higher than the average rate necessary to raise the average cost per student, the state would provide funds until the tax rate is reduced to this average level. If the tax rate to provide funds needed is less than the average rate required, then the state raises the tax rate to the state average. These additional funds become the source of state revenues to supplement revenues raised in a school district where a rate higher than the average is needed to support an average level of education.

The scheme breeds modifications of all kinds and tends to become extremely complicated. In this characteristic, at least, it is similar to the Strayer-Haig model of the mid-1920s, which started out as a procedure to guarantee a basic level of school finance. This was to be done through state aid to areas that did not raise the base amount when applying a given property tax rate.

It is generally agreed that the theory of state aid to education has become more egalitarian, but there is also a history of emasculation of state aid to education programs. It was thought in the mid-1970s that state court decisions could result in legislation that followed the new education finance theory. In the *San Antonio Independent School District versus Rodriguez* case of 1973, the U.S. Supreme Court took itself out of litigation in this area.

The idea of 100 percent state finance of education with assistance provided by the national government and with local extras provided by student-parent donations remains politically unacceptable. A few states, such as Hawaii, have been able to move farther than others. Locally controlled and locally financed education, at least a substantial portion, remain a vital portion of the American way of life. The roots of this attitude are complex and tangled.

Education provides a service very close to basic family, racial, and institutional goals. Each state and urban area is made up of a number of neighborhoods with goals and attitudes of their own. They find it desirable that at least indirectly the schools assist the families and neighborhoods in maintaining what is considered to be the good life. Even the poorer neighborhoods see this to be an important aspect of education they wish to preserve.

Combined with this neighborhood education involvement desire is a practical school tax minimization goal. The school districts with substantial property valuations and relatively few children can enjoy a low school tax rate under local control and local finance. In a typical state, these richer areas that make up a school district of their own can avoid carrying education costs equal to the average school tax rate.

These forces have combined effectively to keep school financing an important local use of property taxes. Some progress in tax rate equalization and in the reduction in the number of school districts has taken place, but resistance is strong. Another aspect of the local finance of education has arisen out of the general belief that taxes generally are too high. Voters have been refusing to approve school budgets as a method of protest. Schools are held in bondage as a means of making a political point. The schools are finding their role as the melting pot and also as the preservers of racial and community differences very difficult and often the basic goal of providing an educated citizenry is forgotten in the melee.

Private Sector Education

In these days of grassroots tax rebellion, a new and generally more sympathetic look is being taken at the possibility of moving education to the private sector. The private sector schools could receive some assistance in the financing of new facilities and the like. Basically, however, costs would be covered by tuition, donations, and charges for books, athletic equipment, and laboratory use.

In addition to financing new facilities, the state's role would be primarily in granting scholarships to children from lower income families and inspecting schools to ensure education meets state standards. Because this education cost is apt to rest largely on rather young income receivers, the state could establish a minimum interest loan program to be repaid only after the child is 18.

The funds used by the state could be collected as a special education gross receipts tax levied on all business firms that are a portion of a group having gross receipts in excess of $500,000. Some other type of business tax might be used, but the tax would have to be levied on business only.

Each school would be managed by selected elders from the neighborhood. Hiring and firing would be the obligation of the elders as would the financing of the activities of the school from the various sources available. No uniformity of procedure would be required other than those necessary in meeting state standards. Under this procedure, each school district would consist of a single primary school. Several primary school districts would combine to provide middle schools, high schools, and junior colleges.

The advantage of placing education in the private sector is that real local control can be exercised. The school would become a stronger influence in the development of neighborhoods and citizen input would be stimulated.

The disadvantage lies largely in the relatively narrow finance base available. The procedures outlined or similar approaches would provide the needed finance safety valves without giving up the basic characteristics of a private sector operation.

Summary

Schools were nearly entirely financed by property taxes levied on property within the school district in the 1920s. Today, financing also includes funds from the state and the federal governments. During this major shift in school financing, the enrollments expanded at a rapid pace and the concept of the neighborhood school became an example of segregation.

The traditional belief that public education was the American way to integrate the rich and the poor, the immigrant and the native-born, the black and the white lost much of its acceptance. The loss of a belief in education has reduced acceptance of education funding needs by the taxpayers. Because the states, in their distribution of aid, have not been able to withhold aid from the richer districts, many states have people in poor school districts making funds available to rich districts from the collections of a regressive sales tax. This is a prescription for trouble, and it has worked.

The education system of the country may be ready for its first major change in the past hundred years. Education may move very substantially toward the private sector.

46 Historical Interdependence of the Public and Private Sectors

At the conclusion of this observation of the management and financing of state and local government, a brief effort to place economic activity and the obligations of the private and the public sectors in historical perspective is appropriate. Every society works out procedures to meet its economic desires within a social and political framework that has been adopted as numerous problems needed attention. Many of these problems were not basically economic in nature, and therefore the management approaches developed only partially met the needs of those interested in solving the existing economic inefficiencies.

Taxation and government or social spending through the ages have been both a positive and a negative factor in the improvement of the well-being of the members of a political unit. Much of society's spending has financed defensive and offensive military operations. The obviousness of this sector of the public economy in the preservation of ethical aspirations and its basic heroic nature has tended to hide the fact success was dependent on the day-to-day, relatively peaceful pursuit of the private sector, and the less heroic government services that cooperate with the private sector in carrying out the work required in everyday economic activities.

The public economy becomes more deeply embedded in a society during periods when a nation is united in the pursuit of a well-understood goal. In the past, this united effort has usually existed when the goal has been dominated by prestigious religious or military aims. Currently, welfare and production goals are gaining acceptance as social aspirations. Nevertheless, the myriad of tasks required to provide medical care through social spending rely as completely on private sector activities as did the placing of a stone in place for an ancient temple or the assembling of bombers for World War II.

The public economy now, as in archaic times, must gather the resources needed for social goals. And this must be done without destroying the individual initiative the private sector needs to be efficient and productive. The farmer must continue to raise more than he eats and bring his grain to town, and the miller must make the flour needed by the people of the city.

Men have been dealing for ages with three basic economic issues. What shall we produce? How shall we divide it? How can we produce more? The Great Pyramid of Egypt gives some clues to the solutions that were worked out in the civilization of the pharaohs some 5,000 years ago. This immense structure, covering 13 acres, was built of great blocks of stone that had to be hauled by unaided human labor from quarries on the other side of the Nile to the construction site. Vast numbers of architects, craftsmen, and laborers worked for the better part of a generation to build it. The cost, in terms of food, shelter, and raw materials provided to the workers, must have been fantastic. Today we see it as no more than a tomb in which the reigning ruler, at his death, could be laid away with proper observance of religious prescriptions to assure his entrance into an afterlife.

Government-Directed Economies

To the ancient Egyptians, however, the pyramid was much more. It symbolized their power and their organizational ability. Its construction was a highly acceptable use for their productive talents, and it was an economic achievement of great significance.

Royal privilege and religious doctrine had much to do with the decision of what goods would be produced in the Egyptian economy. One might also conclude that the pharaoh was able to determine the direction of a major share of the productive activity. In fact, the determination of what goods and services should be produced and how they should be divided was made by the pharaoh, the nobles, and the temple priests. A large portion of production and also of education was aimed at preserving the Egyptian civilization.

The efforts of thousands were directed toward the construction and maintenance of a widespread irrigation system. The system benefited the ruling class, but it also benefited the common man, for a productive Nile Valley kept them from starving. This was a god-ruled state. Change was very slow. It was also, however, a well-ordered state, and it met the basic economic needs of the people and provided employment for everyone on projects considered worthwhile—a basic social need that eludes modern industrial societies relying on market signals alone.

Trading Economies

In the later civilizations of Greece and Rome, free markets for goods and services broadened, and the uncertainties of the market increased. When goods are offered for sale by their producers or by retailers, anyone who has sufficient money can buy them. When buyers show by their purchases that a certain product is in great demand, the price of that product increases and producers are encouraged to bring more to the market. Similarly, when a product goes unsold, its price decreases and producers are discouraged from producing more. With this kind of market, salesmanship becomes very helpful, and consumers must learn to recognize quality and to budget their money.

Although markets became important in the Greek and Roman civilizations, they did not become the means by which all basic economic issues were decided. Slaves continued to provide the labor foundation of the economy. They did not earn incomes, however; they were maintained by their owners. Their consumption preferences entered the market only as their owners permitted. Legally enforced distinctions of social class also often restricted a person's choice of employment.

The relatively powerful free market of early Rome was gradually reduced in scope. The state came to hold immense economic power through regulation of economic activities and through active participation in production, transportation, and even in selling to consumers. The growth of state economic activities seemed necessary to hold the empire together. Though some decisions could still be made by the consumer in the markets of imperial Rome, and, though many individual producers might decide for themselves how much to save and invest, the major weight of decisionmaking lay with the state. In Rome, as in Egypt, education was not aimed at technical improvement. Its main function became to show why the current social, political, and religious systems had to be continued.

Producing Economies

In early medieval times, after the Roman Empire and its state-directed economy had crumbled, trade and the transport of goods were sharply reduced. Roads fell into disrepair, and robber bands roamed the countryside.

Local economies, restricted to the household or manor of one noble or landlord, became the common economic unit. The lord organized the activities of serfs, who could not legally leave the land to which they were bound. The serfs worked their fields and gave a portion of the produce to the lord. In addition, they worked the lord's own land without wages. The lord employed craftsmen to produce the manufactured goods needed on the manor. Decisions on all economic matters rested by custom and law with the lord of the manor. This system, like earlier ones, met basic human economic and social needs. But the price was high. Lord and serf alike were unable to live except according to a prescribed set of guidelines.

Part of the lord's income might be given to the church or to a greater lord to whom he owed allegiance, but he did not produce for the market. His products did not have to compete. He consumed, invested, and produced according to the feudal customs, and he received the lion's share. Again, education was aimed largely at justifying the current state of affairs.

With the decay of the Roman Empire, towns and cities shrank in size and importance. Gradually, however, conditions suitable for trade redeveloped. Cities grew and the market place again assumed importance. More and more economic decisions were made by buyers and sellers in the market. By early modern times the economies of the market were beginning to dictate what was produced and consumed. The market broke through royal regulations and feudal restrictions. The economic system that was developing was called capitalism, because private producers used capital, either their own or borrowed from other private owners, to produce goods for the market. The motive for using privately owned capital in production for the market was, of course, the hope of making a profit; that is, receiving more than one paid out in producing goods sold on the market.

Freedom-of-Market Economies

The free market grew more important as businessmen gradually escaped old restrictions on their enterprise. The American and French revolutions were at least partially struggles to free the rising system of capitalistic decision making from old royal approaches to economic decisions.

By the end of the eighteenth century, capitalism predominated in Western Europe and North America. The economists of the period proclaimed the free, competitive market as an automatic mechanism that would resolve all the basic economic issues. Adam Smith's *Wealth of Nations* appeared in 1776, and his theory of the "invisible hand" began to gain favor. Everything would be in order and everything would be done right, but without regulations and controls.

According to the theory, buyers would determine by their purchases what would be produced. Sellers would decide freely how to use their earned incomes to maximize satisfactions. Producers would supply goods according to the demands of the market and invest capital in the production of goods that would earn the best profits. In making decisions on this basis, producers were also doing what would give consumers the greatest satisfaction.

As producers competed with one another, the search for profits would lead them to use the most efficient methods of production. Wages of labor would be fixed by the supply and demand of labor in the market. Rents charged by landowners and interest charged by persons who loaned money would also be set by supply and demand. Only the receivers of rent would enjoy incomes not needed to continue the efficient and just operation of the system.

Competition among buyers and sellers of all goods and services in free markets would determine what should be produced, how it would be produced, how income would be distributed, how much could be saved, and for what purposes savings would be invested. The one who prospered most was the one who changed to a better method of distribution or production first, the world would beat a path to the door of the man with the better mousetrap. There was no need for economic decisions on the part of the government, and in fact, government would upset the whole system if it interfered.

This is the theory of laissez-faire, which held that the state should play a minimal economic role. All decisions should be worked out by the automatic mechanisms of competitive markets and the "invisible hand" they provided. The concept as developed in the nineteenth century continues to be widely advocated, and the changes introduced during the past eighty years are, as perceived by many observers, merely modifications.

The Welfare State

The United States, more than the European Economic Community member states, claim to be following the theory and practice of nineteenth-century capitalism. The simple economic theories of the nineteenth century, however, have become the complex economic interrelationships of the 1980s. This institutional complexity has required the adoption of laws to regulate and guide economic activities and the introduction of government action to stimulate and assist certain economic areas.

Laws and government regulations are necessary because perfect competition among producers and users is very difficult to maintain. Also, competition by itself does not always lead to what many consider a socially desirable use of resources or to an adequate degree of economic stability or growth. Therefore, the United States and other industrial nations have adopted laws specifying minimum wages and maximum hours of work, setting pure food and drug standards, regulating stock exchanges and investments, and setting guidelines for many business practices.

To stimulate the economy, the federal government, along with state and local governments, is active in distributing purchasing power to a variety of groups, from investors in solar energy to students. Highways and airports are constructed to facilitate movement of goods. Foreign market information is sent to American exporters. Perhaps even more important is the function the federal government has assumed by acting as a sort of balance wheel to the private sector of the economy.

The 1946 Congress adopted the Employment Act. This legislation pledged policies that would help create economic conditions conducive to a high level of employment and sufficient purchasing power. The enjoyment of economic prosperity by citizens became a major government goal. The country had learned in the 1930s that employment could not be provided by the free enterprise system alone. In the 1970s, we have learned that it is an elusive goal even when a huge government budget is being actively used to reach employment and prosperity goals.

Summary

The role of government spending and the role of collecting revenues change with the requirements for the "good life" as seen by leaders and their followers.

The theory of laissez-faire and the necessity for active government involvement in the economy can live side-by-side. For this to occur, however, adequate revenues must be available for both business and government without destroying the foundation of their economic power.

In the private sector the operational base is profits; for the public sector, it is stable revenues adequate to meet society's material needs not provided sufficiently through the decisions of the market.

Appendix

Introduction

In the body of the descriptive and analytical materials of this book, data details have been kept at a minimal level. This was done to prevent overburdening descriptions of alternatives and developing trends with statistics that at the very best give only an accurate idea of the situation when the data were gathered. Most state and local government fiscal data are apt to be a year or more after conditions reported in the data existed. Another year or so is likely to pass before the data can be included in the analyses of a book for general reference.

The tables and figures of this statistical appendix have been selected for inclusion because of the fundamental nature of the activity being quantified. In some cases "fundamental" consists of historical data of basic fiscal quantities. In other instances tables were considered "fundamental" and selected when they dealt with an emerging aspect of state and local government management and finance.

The primary source of state and local data is the Bureau of the Census of the U.S. Department of Commerce. The Advisory Commission on Intergovernmental Relations (ACIR), another federal government agency, analyzes and presents in its publications Bureau of the Census data plus statistics from other sources, including some data originating with the ACIR. In addition, of course, state and local governments prepare and release general economic and fiscal data arising from their activities and relating to their areas of responsibility.

Several private groups are concerned with gathering and analyzing state and local government finance and management activities. The *Bond Buyer* presents and gathers data primarily concerned with debt outstanding and being offered by state and local governments. The Tax Foundation, Inc., and The Brookings Institute make basic government finance and management studies that frequently result in tables that are published in books and pamphlets. Other private groups active in publishing and analyzing state and local government economic data include the U.S. Chamber of Commerce, The American Institute for Public Policy Research, the Committee for Economic Development (CED), and the Conference Board. The findings of all these organizations are included in the body of this book and examples of their work are included in this statistical appendix.

A–1. State Relationships between Tax Capacity and Effort and Amount Collected per Capita, General Sales Taxes, 1975.

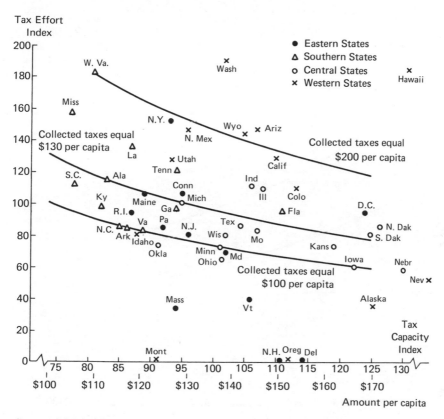

Source: Advisory Commission on Intergovernmental Relations calculations.

A–2. State Relationships between Tax Capacity and Effort and Amount Collected per Capita, Individual Income Taxes, 1975.

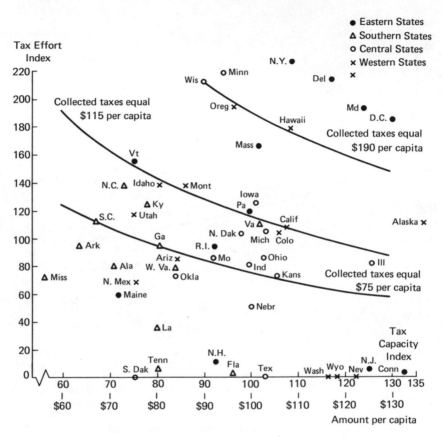

Source: Advisory Commission on Intergovernmental Relations calculations.

A–3. State Relationships between Tax Capacity and Effort and Amount Collected per Capita, Residential Property (Nonfarm) Taxes, 1975.

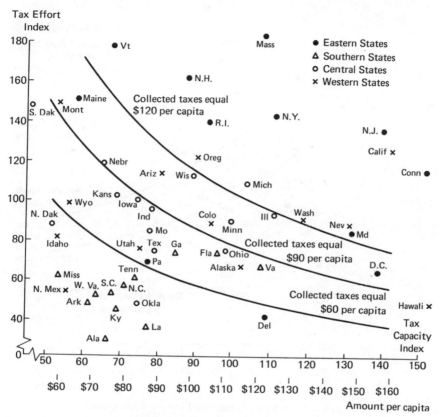

Source: Advisory Commission on Intergovernmental Relations calculations.

A–4. State Relationships between Tax Capacity and Effort and Amount Collected per Capita, Commercial and Industrial Property Taxes, 1975.

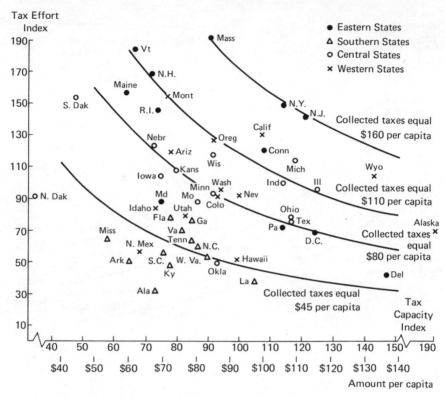

Source: Advisory Commission on Intergovernmental Relations calculations.

A–5. Capacity and Effort Measures for All Taxes of State and Local Governments, by State, 1976.

State	Tax Capacity Per Capita	Tax Capacity Index (1975)	Potential Tax Yield	Taxes Collected Amount	Taxes Collected Per Capita	Tax Effort Index	Amount Collected Less Potential Tax Yield
Alabama	$572.57	78	$2,069,825	$1,668,300	$461.49	81	$−401,525
Alaska	1,048.10	143	382,556	417,800ᵃ	1,144.66	109	35,244
Arizona	683.47	93	1,511,842	1,660,400	750.63	110	148,558
Arkansas	575.53	78	1,214,364	956,900	453.51	79	−257,464
California	810.77	110	17,186,624	20,749,500	978.84	121	3,562,876
Colorado	767.28	104	1,949,666	1,880,400	740.02	96	−69,266
Connecticut	831.15	113	2,576,555	2,424,500	782.10	94	−152,055
Delaware	894.62	122	517,986	447,100	772.19	86	−70,886
D.C.	883.17	120	630,493	648,700	906.01	103	18,207
Florida	718.06	98	5,943,377	4,764,600	575.64	80	−1,178,777
Georgia	648.22	88	3,196,371	2,726,800	552.99	85	−469,571
Hawaii	799.02	109	693,549	829,100	955.18	120	135,551
Idaho	636.36	87	517,357	490,600	603.44	95	−26,757
Illinois	839.89	114	9,404,215	8,639,800	771.62	92	−764,415
Indiana	718.41	98	3,816,908	3,118,300	586.92	82	−698,608
Iowa	759.87	103	2,173,999	2,010,800	702.83	92	−163,199
Kansas	773.18	105	1,762,855	1,504,400	659.82	85	−258,455
Kentucky	657.54	90	2,227,075	1,880,800	555.30	84	−346,275
Louisiana	760.05	103	2,892,759	2,342,400	615.45	81	−530,359
Maine	544.59	74	576,174	718,400	679.02	125	142,226
Maryland	747.81	102	3,082,488	3,374,300	818.61	109	291,812
Massachusetts	691.39	94	4,019,713	5,243,800	901.93	130	1,224,087
Michigan	741.59	101	6,756,663	6,819,300	748.47	101	62,637
Minnesota	722.65	98	2,833,528	3,261,900	831.91	115	428,372
Mississippi	512.14	70	1,198,917	1,144,500	488.89	95	−54,417
Missouri	689.41	94	3,286,420	2,724,400	571.51	83	−562,020
Montana	720.01	98	537,124	533,800	715.55	99	−3,324
Nebraska	754.47	103	1,164,896	1,021,300	661.46	88	−143,596

A-5 Continued

State	Tax Capacity		Potential Tax Yield	Taxes Collected		Tax Effort Index	Amount Collected Less Potential Tax Yield
	Per Capita	Index (1975)		Amount	Per Capita		
Nevada	1,108.52	151	654,028	500,400	848.14	77	-153,628
New Hampshire	716.26	97	581,600	469,700	578.45	81	-111,900
New Jersey	817.79	111	5,996,833	5,816,200	793.15	97	-180,633
New Mexico	685.95	93	784,727	698,600	610.66	89	-86,127
New York	747.48	102	13,511,416	20,883,600	1,140.44	153	7,103,184
North Carolina	614.97	84	3,346,042	2,883,600	529.98	86	-462,442
North Dakota	725.51	99	462,153	428,800	673.16	93	-33,353
Ohio	750.51	102	8,056,749	6,262,100	583.33	78	-1,794,649
Oklahoma	751.53	102	2,040,392	1,465,300	539.71	72	-575,092
Oregon	719.75	98	1,643,901	1,638,200	717.25	100	-5,701
Pennsylvania	693.01	94	8,219,112	8,112,500	684.02	99	-106,612
Rhode Island	631.47	86	587,903	658,700	707.52	112	70,797
South Carolina	564.88	77	1,590,693	1,393,200	494.74	88	-197,493
South Dakota	665.25	91	453,033	409,100	600.73	90	-43,933
Tennessee	606.04	82	2,259,022	2,078,200	498.01	82	-180,822
Texas	828.09	113	10,134,227	7,258,600	593.12	72	-2,875,627
Utah	628.17	86	755,684	727,700	604.90	96	-27,984
Vermont	619.99	84	292,634	353,200	748.31	121	60,566
Virginia	684.42	93	3,409,072	3,065,500	615.44	90	-343,572
Washington	731.67	100	2,604,008	2,629,600	738.86	101	25,592
West Virginia	658.98	90	1,185,498	1,063,600	591.22	90	-121,898
Wisconsin	683.45	93	3,136,337	3,643,700	794.01	116	507,363
Wyoming	1,076.56	147	404,788	330,200	878.19	82	-74,588
U.S. Total	$734.64	100	$156,504,200	$156,504,200	$734.62	100	0

Source: Advisory Commission on Intergovernment Relations calculations.

Note: Potential tax yield, amount collected, and amount collected less potential tax yield are in thousands of dollars. Per capita is in dollars.

[a]Excludes $306,429,000 state special property taxes levied on oil and gas reserves on property used for the exploration for, production of, or pipeline transportation of gas or unrefined oil.

A-6. State Tax Collections, by Source, Selected Years, 1902–1976, Estimated
(Dollar amounts in millions)

Year	Total Excluding Employment Taxes	Individual Income Taxes	Corporation Income Taxes	Death and Gift Taxes	General Sales Taxes
1902	156	—	—	7	—
1913	301	—	—	26	—
1922	947	$43	$58	66	—
1927	1,608	70	92	106	—
1932	1,890	74	79	148	$7
1934	1,979	80	49	93	173
1936	2,618	153	113	117	364
1938	3,132	218	165	142	447
1940	3,313	206	155	113	499
1942	3,903	249	269	110	632
1944	4,071	316	446	110	720
1946	4,937	389	442	141	899
1948	6,743	499	585	179	1,478
1950	7,930	724	586	168	1,670
1952	9,857	913	838	211	2,229
1954	11,089	1,004	772	247	2,540
1956	13,375	1,374	890	310	3,036
1957	14,531	1,563	984	338	3,373
1958	14,919	1,544	1,018	351	3,507
1959	15,848	1,764	1,001	347	3,697
1960	18,036	2,209	1,180	420	4,302
1961	19.057	2,355	1,266	501	4,510
1962	20,561	2,728	1,308	516	5,111
1963	22,117	2,956	1,505	595	5,539
1964	24,243	3,415	1,695	658	6,084
1965	26,126	3,657	1,929	731	6,711
1966	29,380	4,288	2,038	808	7,873
1967	31,926	4,909	2,227	795	8,923
1968	36,400	6,231	2,518	872	10,441
1969	41,931	7,527	3,180	996	12,443
1970	47,962	9,183	3,738	996	14,177
1971	51,541	10,153	3,424	1,104	15,473
1972	59,870	12,996	4,416	1,294	17,619
1973	68,069	15,587	5,425	1,431	19,793
1974	74,207	17,078	6,015	1,425	22,612
1975	80,155	18,819	6,642	1,418	24,780
1976 est.	89,100	21,500	7,300	1,500	27,500

Source: Department of Commerce, Bureau of the Census.

A–6 Continued

Selective Sales and Gross Receipts							
Motor Fuel Taxes	Alcoholic Beverage Taxes	Tobacco Taxes	Amusement Taxes	Public Utility Taxes	Property Taxes	Motor Vehicle and Operators' Licenses	All Other
—	—	—	—	—	$82	—	67
—	—	—	—	—	140	$5	128
$13	—	—	—	—	348	152	267
259	—	—	—	—	370	301	410
527	—	$19	—	—	328	335	373
687	126	44	—	—	228	360	426
777	176	55	—	—	244	359	549
839	193	97	—	—	260	387	564
940	257	130	$29	$100	264	431	492
684	267	159	53	125	243	394	554
886	402	198	116	132	249	439	644
1,259	425	337	129	155	276	593	828
1,544	420	414	118	185	307	755	1,039
1,870	442	449	153	228	370	924	1,230
2,218	463	464	189	263	391	1,098	1,440
2,687	546	515	219	3	467	1,295	1,736
2,828	569	556	240	343	479	1,368	1,891
2,919	566	616	244	345	533	1,415	1,860
3,058	599	675	257	352	566	1,492	2,040
3,335	650	923	283	365	607	1,573	2,189
3,431	688	1,001	296	401	631	1,641	2,337
3,665	740	1,075	306	420	640	1,667	2,385
3,851	793	1,124	342	437	688	1,780	2,501
4,059	864	1,196	379	498	722	1,917	2,756
4,300	917	1,284	409	498	766	2,021	2,924
4,627	985	1,541	439	552	834	2,236	3,160
4,837	1,041	1,615	456	600	862	2,311	3,350
5,178	1,138	1,886	447	664	912	2,485	3,597
5,644	1,246	2,056	526	763	981	2,685	3,884
6,283	1,420	2,308	573	918	1,092	2,956	4,318
6,628	1,527	2,536	622	1,012	1,126	3,174	4,672
7,216	1,684	2,831	646	1,215	1,257	3,340	5,356
8,058	1,817	2,112	663	1,347	1,312	3,637	5,887
8,207	1,909	3,250	717	1,445	1,301	3,755	6,493
8,255	1,963	3,286	775	1,740	1,451	3,941	7,084
8,634	2,115	3,540	835	2,090	1,475	4,345	8,266

A–7. Average Effective Property Tax Rates, Existing Single-Family Homes with FHA-Insured Mortgages, by States, 1975.[a]

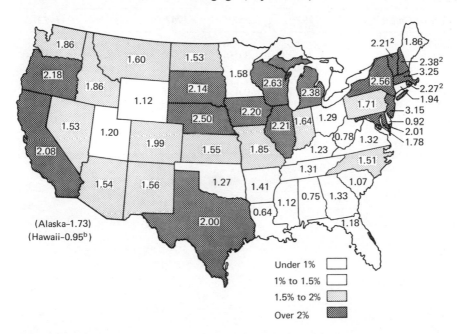

(Alaska–1.73)
(Hawaii–0.95[b])

Under 1%
1% to 1.5%
1.5% to 2%
Over 2%

Source: Computed by Advisory Commission on Intergovernmental Relations staff from data contained in U.S. Department of Housing and Urban Development, Federal Housing Administration, Management Information Systems Division, *Data for States and Selected Areas on Characteristics of FHA Operations Under Section 203(b).* 1975.

[a]Effective tax rate is the percentage that tax liability is of the market value.

[b]1974 rates.

A–8. Number of State and Local Government Units by Type, Selected Years, 1952–1972.

Type of Unit	1952[a]	1957[a]	1962	1967	1972
State	50	50	50	50	50
County	3,052	3,050	3,043	3,049	3,044
Municipality	16,807	17,215	18,000	18,048	18,517
Township	17,202	17,198	17,142	17,105	16,991
School district	67,355	50,454	34,678	21,782	23,885
Special District	12,340	14,424	18,323	21,264	23,885
Total	116,806	102,391	91,236	81,298	78,268

[a]Adjusted to include Alaska and Hawaii.
Source: Advisory Commission on Intergovernmental Relations, Understanding the Market for State and Local Debt, M-104, May 1976.

A–9. Historical Summary, Finances of State and Local Governments: 1972–73 to 1975–76.

Item	Amount (millions of dollars)				Per Capita		
	1975–76	1974–75	1973–74	1972–73	1975–76	1974–75	1973–74
Revenue							
Total	304,678	261,592	237,856	217,616	1,416.82	1,227.43	1,125.20
Total General Revenue	256,176	228,171	207,670	190,214	1,193.41	1,070.62	982.40
Intergovernmental Revenue	55,589	47,034	41,820	39,256	258.97	220.69	197.83
Revenue from Own Sources	249,089	214,558	196,360	178,360	1,160.39	1,006.74	927.37
General Revenue from Own Sources	200,586	181,137	165,850	150,958	934.44	849.93	784.57
Taxes	156,813	141,465	130,673	121,102	730.52	663.78	618.16
Individual Income	24,575	21,454	19,491	17,994	114.48	100.67	92.20
Corporation Net Income	7,273	6,642	6,105	3,388	31.17	28.45	
Sales and Gross Receipts	54,547	49,815	46,098	42,047	254.11	233.74	218.07
General	32,044	29,102	26,314	22,992	149.28	136.55	124.48
Selective	22,502	20,713	19,784	19,054	104.83	97.19	93.59
Property	57,001	51,491	47,705	45,283	265.54	241.60	225.67
Other	13,417	12,063	11,364	10,354	62.50	56.60	53.76
Charges and Miscellaneous General Revenue	43,774	39,668	35,177	29,856	203.92	186.13	166.41
Utility Revenue	12,573	10,867	9,392	8,622	58.57	50.99	44.43
Liquor Stores Revenue	2,553	2,468	2,355	2,276	11.90	11.58	11.14
Insurance Trust Revenue	33,376	20,086	18,439	16,504	155.48	94.25	87.23
Employee Retirement	14,533	12,354	10,900	10,064	67.70	57.97	51.56
Unemployment Compensation	16,575	5,734	5,729	4,964	77.22	26.90	27.10
Other	2,269	1,998	1,809	1,476	10.57	9.37	8.56
Expenditure, by Character and Object							
Total	305,268	266,483	226,032	205,336	1,422.11	1,250.38	1,069.27
Current Operation	204,387	180,976	154,810	138,974	952.15	849.17	773.96
Capital Outlay	46,531	44,824	38,084	35,272	216.77	210.32	180.16
Construction	38,299	36,356	30,542	28,251	178.42	170.59	144.48
Equipment	5,373	5,101	4,192	3,741	25.04	23.93	19.83
Land and Existing Structures	2,857	3,367	3,350	3,279	13.31	15.80	15.85
Assistace and Subsidies	12,494	11,146	11,290	12,180	58.21	52.30	53.41
Interest on Debt	11,681	10,087	8,840	7,828	54.42	47.33	41.82

A-9 Continued

Item	Amount (millions of dollars)				Per Capita		
	1975–76	1974–75	1973–74	1972–73	1975–76	1974–75	1973–74
Insurance Benefits and Repayments	28,994	18,475	12,667	11,074	135.07	86.69	59.92
Exhibit: Expenditure and Personal Services	116,466	106,168	94,054	86,042	542.56	498.16	444.93
Expenditure, by Function							
Total	305,268	266,483	226,032	205,032	1,422.11	1,250.38	1,059.27
General Expenditure	256,731	230,721	198,959	181,227	1,195.99	1,082.58	941.19
Education	97,216	87,858	75,833	69,714	452.89	412.24	358.74
Local Schools	67,674	61,485	53,059	48,789	315.26	288.50	251.00
Institutions of Higher Education	24,304	21,702	18,884	17,370	113.22	101.83	89.33
Other Education	5,239	4,670	3,890	3,555	24.41	21.91	18.40
Highways	23,907	22,528	19,946	18,615	111.37	105.71	94.36
Public Welfare	32,604	28,155	25,582	23,582	151.89	132.11	118.67

Source: U.S. Department of Commerce, Bureau of the Census.

A–10. Trends in Local Government Finances, Fiscal Years 1966 and 1976

	1966	1976	Percentage Change 1966–1976
	Direct General Expenditure[a] *(billions)*		
All Units, Total	53.7	159.7	+198
Counties	10.8	35.4	+228
Municipalities	17.0	52.9	+210
Townships	2.0	5.5	+169
School districts	21.2	58.2	+175
Special districts	2.7	7.8	+194
	Number of Units		
All Units, Total	81,248	80,120	− 1
Counties	3,049	3,042	—[c]
Municipalities	18,048	18,856	+ 4
Townships	17,105	16,822	− 2
School districts	21,782	15,260	−30
Special districts	21,264	26,140	+23
	Source of General Revenue[a] *(billions)*		
All Units:	$53.2	$162.9	+206
General revenue, total	35.4	93.2	+163
Taxes	27.4	67.6	+147
Property tax	23.4	54.9	+130
Other taxes	3.5	12.7	+260
Charges and miscellaneous	8.0	25.6	+219
Intergovernmental revenues, total	17.8	69.7	+292
Federal	1.4	13.6	+885
State	16.4	56.2	+242

Sources: Tax Foundation computations based on data from Bureau of Census, U.S. Department of Commerce.

[a]"General" operations exclude transactions of utilities, liquor stores, and insurance-trust funds.
[b]Number as of 1967 and 1977.
[c]Less than 1%.

A–11. The Growth of the State-Local Sector, 1948–1977.
(State-Local Expenditures and Taxes as a Percentage of State Personal Income)

| Fiscal Year | State-Local Direct General Expenditures | | State-Local Tax Revenue | Exhibit: State-Local Employees per 10,000 Population |
	Total	From Own Funds (excluding federal aid)		
1948	9.32%	8.34	7.03%	240[a]
1958	12.93	11.53	8.85	298
1968	16.38	13.64	10.81	393
1976	20.32	15.90	12.47	475
1977 est.	20.75	16.05[b]	12.87	485

Source: Advisory Commission on Intergovernmental Relations staff computations based on U.S. Bureau of the Census, Governments Division, various reports, and staff estimates.

[a]Based on population including armed forces overseas.

[b]This 1976–77 slight increase varies from an earlier ACIR finding of a slight decrease in the relation of state and local spending to gross national product. This tabulation used census data, fiscal year, and personal income. The earlier analysis used national income accounts, calendar year, and gross national product.

A–12. Costs and Participation Rates of State Property Tax Circuit-Breaker Programs, Fiscal Years 1974 and 1977.

Year	Total Cost of programs (in thousands)	Number of Claimants	Average Cost per Claimant	Cost per Capita
1974 (21 states)	$446,970	3,020,755	$147.97	$4.41
1977 (29 states + D.C.)	949,561	5,112,738	185.72	6.90
Percentage increase	112.4	69.3	25.5	56.5

Source: Advisory Commission of Intergovernmental Relations.

A–13. The State and Local Revenues Systems, Fiscal Years 1954 and 1976.

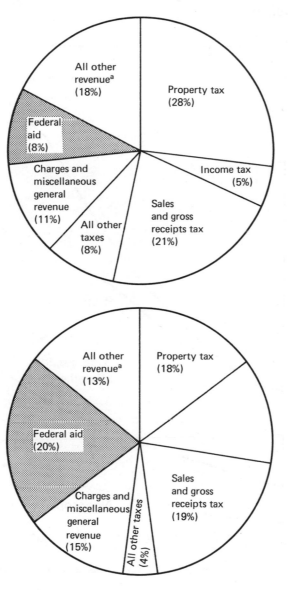

Source: Advisory Commission on Intergovernmental Relations, *Significant Features of Fiscal Federalism, 1976 Edition*, Vol. 1, *Trends* [M–106], Washington, D.C.: U.S. Government Printing Office, 1976, p. 34.

[a]Includes utility, liquor store, and insurance trust revenue.

A–14. Trends in County General Revenue from Selected Major Sources, 1966–67 to 1975–76.
(Billions of dollars)

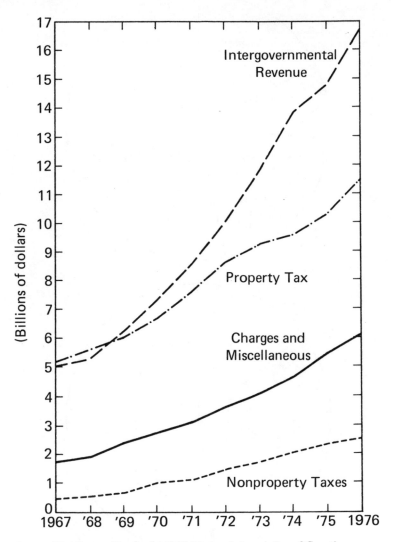

Source: *The County Yearbook, 1977*, National Association of Counties.

A–15. Trends in County Direct General Expenditure for Selected Major Functions, 1966–67 to 1975–76.
(Billions of dollars)

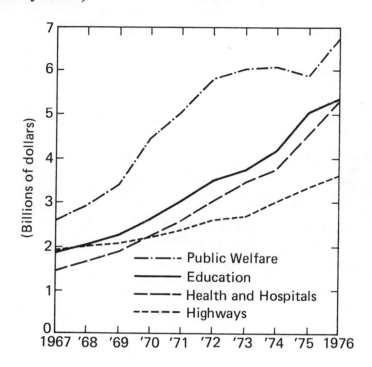

A–16. County Government Liquid Assets, 1974–1975.

Item	Amount (millions of dollars	Percentage	Percentage Increase or Decrease (−) from 1974–75
Cash and security holdings at end of fiscal year	14,631	100.0	0.3
Insurance trust:			
Employee retirement	4,059	27.7	5.5
Other than insurance trust	10,572	72.3	−1.5
By purpose:			
Bond funds	2,299	15.7	−10.5
Offsets to debt	912	6.2	13.6
Other and unallocable	7,361	50.5	(z)
By type:			
Cash and deposits	8,899	60.8	−2.3
Securities	1,674	11.4	3.0
Federal	1,319	9.0	7.8
State and local government	14	(z)	−17.6
Other (nongovernmental)	341	2.3	−11.4

Source: *The County Year Book, 1977,* (Washington, D.C.: National Association of Counties and International City Management Association), reprinted with permission.
Notes: − Represents zero or rounds to zero.
     z Less than half the unit of measurement shown.

A–17. Trends in State Government Tax Collections, Fiscal 1974 to 1977.

Type of Tax	Collections (millions of dollars)				Percentage Distribution			
	1977 (preliminary)	1976	1975	1974	1977	1976	1975	1974
Total	$101,026	$89,256	$80,155	$74,207	100.0	100.0	100.0	100.0
Sales and gross receipts taxes	52,351	47,391	43,346	40,556	51.8	53.1	54.1	54.7
General	52,351	27,333	24,780	22,612	30.6	30.6	30.9	30.5
Selective	21,481	20,058	18,566	17,944	21.3	22.5	23.2	24.2
Motor fuels	9,087	8,66	8,255	8,207	9.0	9.7	10.3	11.1
Tobacco products	3,500	3,462	3,286	3,250	3.5	3.9	4.1	4.4
Other	8,894	7,936	7,025	6,487	8.8	8.9	8.8	8.7
License taxes	7,141	6,899	6,289	6,055	7.1	7.7	7.8	8.2
Individual income	25,453	21,448	18,819	17,078	25.2	24.0	23.5	23.0
Corporation net income	9,187	7,273	6,642	6,015	9.1	8.1	8.3	8.1
Other	6,895	6,245	5,059	4,502	6.8	7.0	6.4	6.0

Source: Bureau of the Census, State Government Finances in 1976.

Note: Because of rounding, detail may not add to totals.

A–18. The Interstate Range for Average per Capita Amounts of State Tax Revenue.

Per Capita State Tax Revenue	Number of States	
	1977 Fiscal Year	1976 Fiscal Year
$600 or more	4	3
$550 to $599	5	1
$500 to $549	6	4
$450 to $499	9	7
$400 to $449	15	11
$350 to $399	7	12
$300 to $349	2	10
Less than $300	2	2

Source: Department of Commerce, Bureau of the Census

A–19. Trends in State Revenue from Selected Types of Taxes, 1972–1977.

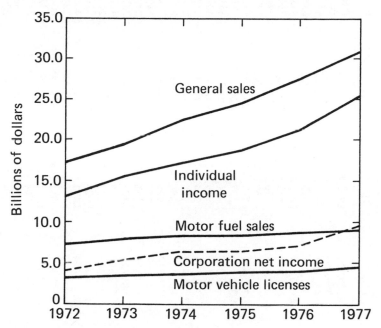

Source: Department of Commerce, Bureau of the Census.

A-20. Total Federal Aid to States—Fiscal Years 1973–1977.
(in thousands)

States and Other Areas	1973	1974	1975	1976	T.Q.	1977
Alabama	$795,952	$829,475	$820,235	$992,934	$303,462	$1,120,519
Alaska	209,316	234,207	260,457	318,553	89,305	382,004
Arizona	381,226	426,956	462,604	530,309	136,720	648,435
Arkansas	468,895	470,181	511,273	613,667	152,225	638,790
California	4,626,872	4,665,989	4,930,433	5,802,854	1,448,326	6,813,730
Colorado	504,572	503,328	601,832	672,597	206,957	714,543
Connecticut	550,746	669,431	672,844	723,950	192,889	894,981
Delaware	119,891	119,155	120,216	160,607	51,893	187,302
District of Columbia	604,574	610,012	722,529	749,043	265,795	942,136
Florida	1,114,688	1,160,863	1,318,518	1,527,688	426,110	1,988,414
Georgia	902,948	1,123,869	1,179,061	1,421,097	342,370	1,861,105
Hawaii	210,535	245,308	246,778	309,151	82,267	400,144
Idaho	174,592	187,252	211,639	264,600	71,637	287,675
Illinois	2,159,129	2,265,065	2,226,480	2,795,467	777,293	3,202,188
Indiana	676,024	710,720	805,790	996,144	284,439	1,095,093
Iowa	438,304	450,754	555,820	659,337	183,964	714,420
Kansas	391,383	385,468	445,087	517,947	123,481	548,524
Kentucky	773,195	826,290	837,128	1,016,474	274,463	1,018,066
Louisiana	940,332	946,504	881,429	1,135,477	332,463	1,237,128
Maine	245,848	277,862	292,288	376,041	88,850	411,510
Maryland	785,722	750,187	965,565	1,119,935	319,042	1,244,922
Massachusetts	1,251,609	1,311,763	1,456,161	1,820,676	473,189	2,079,940
Michigan	1,743,481	1,816,207	2,113,454	2,615,605	680,219	2,915,254
Minnesota	780,388	871,023	900,213	1,088,723	325,347	1,224,464
Mississippi	680,402	685,910	637,967	783,174	205,146	800,688
Missouri	847,006	852,859	908,771	1,038,936	316,406	1,142,323
Montana	225,198	212,860	230,604	288,475	79,763	347,632
Nebraska	238,228	271,810	338,244	396,312	125,173	367,820
Nevada	123,712	126,951	139,056	194,142	48,985	206,027
New Hampshire	144,536	149,617	171,345	212,591	57,986	233,703
New Jersey	1,233,970	1,316,469	1,501,252	1,861,537	522,298	2,199,862

New Mexico	346,553	337,182	399,300	427,588	102,655	449,345
New York	4,797,242	5,221,037	5,682,478	6,417,280	1,827,843	7,446,787
North Carolina	937,331	975,396	1,049,787	1,275,040	341,991	1,511,942
North Dakota	163,515	152,208	170,856	204,909	65,439	224,401
Ohio	1,592,115	1,760,225	1,788,060	2,134,818	616,141	2,510,305
Oklahoma	589,233	597,776	654,808	688,866	257,361	782,019
Oregon	577,789	557,718	659,597	795,997	241,514	836,132
Pennsylvania	2,357,661	2,390,490	2,697,909	3,121,571	870,144	3,628,059
Rhode Island	238,667	248,846	248,917	311,639	92,442	357,546
South Carolina	556,630	559,268	574,740	697,106	174,493	802,540
South Dakota	198,675	210,032	213,232	228,249	62,775	240,454
Tennessee	816,365	851,141	910,734	1,083,348	294,002	1,188,617
Texas	2,055,628	2,128,082	2,200,105	2,604,263	647,169	2,885,381
Utah	260,802	275,247	294,104	359,361	100,132	387,837
Vermont	138,112	150,773	154,252	176,963	61,836	222,501
Virginia	828,077	890,559	1,004,305	1,185,831	304,747	1,311,454
Washington	829,474	792,930	798,108	979,689	258,177	1,118,893
West Virginia	536,022	581,623	551,472	689,874	176,918	631,233
Wisconsin	778,284	817,868	919,714	1,165,409	326,427	1,493,308
Wyoming	115,059	119,426	132,289	166,657	61,532	185,644
Puerto Rico	579,160	543,431	630,007	812,951	182,662	939,008
Virgin Islands	104,363	109,210	127,879	163,389	63,323	179,576
Other	104,363	109,210	127,879	163,389	63,323	179,576
Adjustments or undistributed to States	140,181	197,675	200,340	198,328	313,167	999,483
Total	43,963,648	46,040,381	49,723,153	59,111,874	16,443,830	68,436,840

Source: U.S. Treasury, Federal Aid to States.

A–21. Federal Grants-in-Aid to State-Local Governments and Estimated Tax Burden of Federal Grants by State,[a] Fiscal Year 1977

| State | Millions | | Tax Burden per Dollar of Aid |
	Grants	Tax Burden for Grants[b]	
Indiana	$1,094.5	$1,563.4	$1.43
Connecticut	895.0	1,215.3	1.36
Kansas	547.6	735.7	1.34
Ohio	2,509.4	3,277.9	1.31
Texas	2,877.4	3,770.6	1.31
Illinois	3,200.7	4,039.9	1.26
New Jersey	2,199.7	2,759.0	1.25
Nebraska	367.1	453.3	1.23
Florida	1,985.4	2,430.5	1.22
Iowa	714.3	847.4	1.19
Missouri	1,140.1	1,353.2	1.19
Maryland	1,244.8	1,438.6	1.16
Virginia	1,308.9	1,497.7	1.14
Washington	1,108.2	1,261.2	1.14
Colorado	695.6	781.7	1.12
Delaware	187.3	210.2	1.12
Nevada	199.6	223.3	1.12
California	6,779.9	7,350.7	1.08
New Hampshire	233.0	249.6	1.07
Michigan	2,911.6	2,929.8	1.01
Pennsylvania	3,626.5	3,639.2	1.00
Wyoming	139.0	138.0	.99
Arizona	638.7	604.4	.95
Minnesota	1,222.0	1,162.7	.95
Oklahoma	779.8	722.6	.93
Tennessee	1,144.9	1,057.6	.92
Oregon	783.0	702.9	.90
Massachusetts	2,079.8	1,852.5	.89
Wisconsin	1,491.2	1,313.8	.88
North Carolina	1,509.2	1,320.4	.87
Rhode Island	357.5	302.2	.85
Kentucky	1,011.2	834.3	.83
New York	7,446.0	6,096.0	.82
North Dakota	222.5	177.4	.80
South Carolina	801.1	637.2	.80
Idaho	274.0	216.8	.79
Louisiana	1,235.1	978.8	.79
Utah	380.0	295.6	.78
Alabama	1,102.6	840.8	.76
Hawaii	400.0	295.6	.74
West Virginia	630.0	459.8	.73
Arkansas	636.0	446.7	.70
New Mexico	406.4	282.5	.70
Georgia	1,858.1	1,221.8	.66
South Dakota	237.9	157.7	.66
Maine	409.8	262.8	.64
Alaska	376.4	229.9	.61
Montana	331.9	203.6	.61

Mississippi	795.2	453.3	.57
Vermont	222.0	118.2	.53
Washington, D.C.	942.1	275.9	.29
U.S. Total	$65,690.0	$65,690.0	$1.00

Source: Tax Foundation's computations based on data from U.S. Treausry Department and Office of Management and Budget.

[a]Excludes shared revenues, e.g., payments in lieu of taxes on federal lands in certain states; but includes general revenue sharing grants.

[b]The total tax burden for aid payments is assumed to equal aid payments.

A–22. Federal Aid in Relation to State and Local General Revenue from Own Sources, 1966 through 1976.

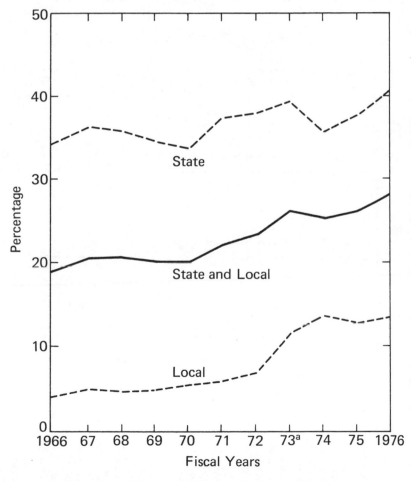

[a]Beginning in 1973, includes federal general revenue sharing.

Source: Advisory Commission on Intergovernmental Relations.

[a]Beginning in 1973, includes federal general revenue sharing.

A–23. Percentage of State-Local General Revenue from Federal Aid, by State, Selected Years, 1942 through 1975.

State	1975	1971	1967	1962	1957	1953	1942
United States, Total	20.6	18.0	16.9	13.5	10.1[a]	10.5[a]	8.2[a]
Alabama	27.0	27.6	24.6	24.0	19.9	17.8	11.5
Alaska	32.1	32.5	51.8	33.8	(24.4)	n.a.	n.a.
Arizona	18.5	17.7	21.6	16.6	12.8	14.4	15.2
Arkansas	29.0	25.8	27.8	24.1	18.8	22.2	11.4
California	18.6	19.3	19.0	14.0	10.7	11.4	8.2
Colorado	21.3	19.9	18.7	16.2	14.7	15.1	14.4
Connecticut	18.8	14.5	13.5	10.7	5.4	6.6	6.2
Delaware	18.8	13.4	13.4	9.8	9.1	9.8	10.6
Dist. of Columbia	51.2	41.3	31.8	26.8	18.0	12.6	15.4
Florida	18.1	14.1	14.9	11.0	10.0	9.8	8.2
Georgia	24.7	21.7	21.0	19.6	14.3	17.6	10.1
Hawaii	23.5	20.4	23.2	19.4	(14.6)	n.a.	n.a.
Idaho	24.7	21.2	18.8	21.4	15.9	15.5	14.8
Illinois	18.2	16.4	13.5	11.2	6.9	8.5	6.9
Indiana	15.2	13.2	12.3	10.8	6.8	7.5	9.1
Iowa	19.6	14.2	15.0	12.4	9.8	9.6	7.7
Kansas	19.4	17.1	14.9	13.0	11.7	12.7	10.7
Kentucky	25.6	27.6	27.0	20.3	14.5	17.2	11.0
Louisiana	22.6	20.4	21.2	19.7	14.8	17.1	9.3
Maine	27.0	21.7	19.2	15.7	12.1	10.9	9.6
Maryland	19.1	15.4	12.8	12.2	8.4	7.9	6.7
Massachusetts	19.0	16.8	14.0	11.0	7.2	7.9	7.0
Michigan	20.5	15.4	14.6	11.2	7.9	8.3	7.1
Minnesota	19.7	16.2	16.4	12.2	9.8	9.6	9.1
Mississippi	28.7	26.5	25.4	20.7	17.0	18.5	12.9
Missouri	20.9	19.4	18.5	17.9	16.5	18.1	12.0
Montana	26.4	28.1	24.7	20.9	17.7	17.6	12.5
Nebraska	19.3	15.4	18.4	15.0	12.1	11.2	11.8
Nevada	17.8	16.4	24.0	18.2	17.4	19.6	25.8

New Hampshire	23.1	17.8	16.9	17.9	9.3	9.6	9.3
New Jersey	17.7	15.0	11.2	8.7	4.6	5.0	4.2
New Mexico	27.1	27.7	30.1	22.3	22.5	18.0	13.3
New York	17.9	13.9	11.1	7.1	5.5	5.4	3.8
North Carolina	26.4	20.6	18.2	15.1	16.3	11.6	8.1
North Dakota	21.4	24.0	19.8	16.5	12.3	13.0	8.9
Ohio	18.8	14.4	14.4	12.7	8.0	7.9	8.2
Oklahoma	25.5	24.4	24.9	21.5	17.5	19.0	14.4
Oregon	26.6	24.6	19.3	18.8	13.9	12.7	11.8
Pennsylvania	20.6	17.2	14.6	11.0	6.4	7.4	8.3
Rhode Island	24.0	19.6	19.7	13.6	12.2	10.6	6.5
South Carolina	24.1	21.2	19.2	17.6	13.3	14.4	15.1
South Dakota	27.8	21.3	21.7	23.7	16.6	16.2	11.4
Tennessee	24.6	24.8	23.8	20.3	14.3	17.3	10.5
Texas	20.7	19.2	18.0	13.8	12.8	12.6	9.7
Utah	26.9	26.4	25.9	19.9	14.6	17.6	17.3
Vermont	27.6	25.5	25.0	28.8	13.1	12.9	10.8
Virginia	21.6	19.1	18.5	16.1	9.3	10.7	8.7
Washington	21.4	17.4	16.9	14.2	11.2	12.3	14.5
West Virginia	29.9	31.8	27.0	19.2	12.7	16.1	11.4
Wisconsin	29.9	31.8	27.0	19.2	12.7	16.1	11.4
Wisconsin	18.1	11.9	12.3	11.2	7.1	7.7	6.9

Source: Advisory Commission on Intergovernmental Relations staff computations based on various reports of U.S. Bureau of the Census, Governments Division.

Note: n.a. = Not available.

[a]Excluding Alaska and Hawaii.

A-24. Classification of States by Participation in Various Types of Federal Grant Programs.

Type of Grants	High Participation[a]	Low Participation[b]
Project	Arizona, California, Minnesota, New Jersey, Wyoming, Alaska, Maryland, Ohio, Arkansas, Oklahoma	Illinois, Indiana, Iowa, Montana, Nebraska, Nevada, North Carolina, Utah, Wisconsin, Vermont
Formula	California, Kentucky, Minnesota, Missouri, New Jersey, Tennessee, Texas, Wyoming, West Virginia, Alaska	Connecticut, Delaware, Indiana, Iowa, Montana, Nevada, New York, Utah, Wisconsin, Illinois
State Recipient	Alaska, California, Louisiana, Mississippi, Montana, New Mexico, New York, Utah, West Virginia, Wyoming	Connecticut, Indiana, Iowa, Kansas, Maryland, Nebraska, New Hampshire, North Carolina, Vermont, Wisconsin
Local Recipient	Alabama, Arkansas, California, Georgia, Minnesota, New Jersey, Ohio, Pennsylvania, Tennessee, Arizona	Connecticut, Delaware, Illinois, Indiana, Montana, Nebraska, Nevada, Utah, Wisconsin, West Virginia
High Matching	Alabama, Alaska, Arkansas, Delaware, Florida, Kentucky, Minnesota, New Jersey, New Mexico, Pennsylvania	Connecticut, Georgia, Iowa, Missouri, Nevada, North Dakota, Oklahoma, Oregon, West Virginia, Wisconsin
Low Matching	Alaska, California, Kentucky, Minnesota, Missouri, New Jersey, Texas, West Virginia, Wyoming,	Connecticut, Delaware, Illinois, Indiana, Iowa, Maine, Montana, New York, Wisconsin
No Matching	Alaska, California, Kentucky, Minnesota, Missouri, New Jersey, Texas, West Virginia, Wyoming, Tennessee	Connecticut, Delaware, Illinois, Indiana, Iowa, Maine, Montana, Nevada, New York, Wisconsin

Source: Metropolitan Studies Program, Maxwell School of Citizenship and Public Affairs, Syracuse University. Calculated from various data sources.

[a]Ten states with the largest positive residuals.

[b]Ten states with the largest negative residuals.

A–25. Recent State Restrictions on State Tax Spending Powers.

| State | Type of Restriction and Year of Enactment | | Remarks |
	Constitutional	Statutory	
Colorado		1977	Allows a 7% increase in general fund spending with an additional 4% to reserve fund. Amounts over 11% refunded to taxpayers.
		1978	Indexation of the state personal income tax to prevent inflation from pushing taxpayers into higher tax brackets.
Michigan		1977	Budget stabiliation fund provided. Percentage in excess of 2% of adjusted personal income multiplied by previous year general purpose revenue to determine amount to be deposited in budget stabilization fund. Withdrawals are provided if there is a decrease in adjusted personal income.
New Jersey		1976	Spending increase limited to increase in the state personal income (federal series). Increase of between 9% and 10% for this year.
Tennessee	1978		Spending increase limited to growth in the economy. Increase approximately 11% this year. Provisions for full or shared costs for mandated programs to local governments.
California	1978		Proposition 13 (Jarvis-Gann), by consitutional revision, provides that any changes in state taxes enacted for the purpose of increasing revenues must be imposed by an act passed by not less than two-thirds of all members elected to each of the two houses of the legislature, except that no new ad valorum taxes on real property or sales or transaction taxes on the sales of real property may be imposed.

Source: Advisory Commission on Intergovernmental Relations.

A-26. Individual States, Intergovernmental Expenditure by Function, 1976
(thousands of dollars)

State	Total Intergovern- mental Expenditure	Function						
		Education	Public Welfare	General Local Government Support	Highways	Hospitals	Corrections	All Other
All States	57,858,241	34,083,711	9,476,411	5,673,843	3,240,806	95,738	120,129	5,167,603
Alabama	700,064	549,004	—	17,907	70,166	4,802	1,719	56,466
Alaska	207,088	143,534	—	27,032	—	642	568	35,312
Arizona	694,268	476,504	—	130,506	58,078	35	—	29,145
Arkansas	418,197	286,265	1,515	23,177	56,328	3,147	—	47,765
California	8,135,469	3,910,060	2,309,598	987,133	367,788	2,977	27,781	530,132[a]
Colorado	675,431	416,053	151,692	15,587	41,667	2,345	—	48,087
Connecticut	525,225	346,716	20,913	66,401	17,166	—	—	74,029
Delaware	188,428	163,504	961	—	2,000	—	—	21,963
Florida	1,834,215	1,445,887	—	199,909	111,719	1,230	—	75,470
Georgia	845,591	694,325	2,133	16,117	40,149	2,303	3,113	87,451
Hawaii	- 22,772	—	4,438	18,247	—	87	—	—
Idaho	187,358	130,292	—	24,337	24,676	—	—	8,053
Illinois	2,652,553	1,785,192	232,662	127,982	224,808	166	2,404	279,339[b]
Indiana	1,253,233	587,384	120,646	312,011	160,764	1,967	—	70,461
Iowa	797,891	545,304	20,291	72,791	114,659	1,195	301	43,350
Kansas	404,805	321,568	836	23,701	38,170	183	—	20,347
Kentucky	510,160	442,198	788	692	13,535	—	—	52,947
Louisiana	998,899	698,008	6,191	179,712	71,564	1,370	—	42,054
Maine	320,491	266,954	7,583	16,624	3,668	—	—	25,662
Maryland	1,460,454	761,707	245,650	82,915	172,147	46	—	197,989
Massachusetts	1,429,110	774,355	119,062	28,307	68,655	2,187	—	436,544[c]
Michigan	2,306,268	1,297,444	207,091	307,544	314,798	1,950	784	176,657
Minnesota	1,602,859	975,706	196,679	262,836	87,341	2,102	4,311	73,884
Mississippi	582,224	424,665	—	69,995	59,602	1,786	208	25,968
Missouri	693,542	552,564	14,945	4,741	44,380	539	—	76,373

Montana	147,181	116,490	717	1,040	6,575	196	—	22,163
Nebraska	257,768	113,605	13,723	59,176	29,320	267	12	41,665
Nevada	143,910	111,377	2,788	15,073	5,857	55	715	8,045
New Hampshire	87,832	37,088	92	28,338	5,141	—	—	17,173
New Jersey	1,634,972	757,322	483,958	193,495	16,505	25,499	—	158,193
New Mexico	363,060	271,922	—	67,982	9,992	86	—	13,078
New York	9,977,102	3,650,944	4,176,234	926,299	111,687	1,200	44,562	1,066,176[d]
North Carolina	1,652,666	1,185,737	201,479	69,011	29,366	6,109	—	160,964
North Dakota	148,253	101,960	4,320	13,696	18,512	71	—	9,694
Ohio	2,095,547	1,330,982	141,071	361,078	178,199	2,965	1,534	79,718
Oklahoma	491,460	364,602	1,086	6,997	77,797	548	2	40,428
Oregon	421,079	290,143	2,399	29,644	74,716	737	—	23,440
Pennsylvania	2,762,409	1,922,223	205,028	28,593	117,685	438	7,978	480,464[e]
Rhode Island	148,660	104,515	25,073	10,868	387	—	—	7,817
South Carolina	530,983	385,600	71	54,373	33,747	2,003	—	55,189
South Dakota	68,306	47,793	356	4,375	4,405	902	—	10,475
Tennessee	657,567	458,363	2,453	56,546	104,343	5,067	5,077	25,718
Texas	2,161,147	2,085,706	—	11,373	14,600	1,404	168	47,896
Utah	288,129	235,267	194	1,000	11,615	1,812	535	37,706
Vermont	81,941	55,179	4,460	200	5,786	—	—	16,316
Virginia	1,010,572	660,770	212,637	21,525	51,646	5,280	18,335	40,379
Washington	947,921	722,389	21,463	43,885	69,688	1,040	—	89,456
West Virginia	356,823	338,988	—	—	—	240	—	17,595
Wisconsin	1,868,145	675,803	313,086	628,039	88,501	8,683	22	154,011
Wyoming	108,213	63,750	49	25,033	10,908	77	—	8,396

Source: Department of Commerce, Bureau of the Census.

Note: — Represents zero or rounds to zero.

[a] Includes $262,276,000 health and water pollution grants to local governments.

[b] Includes $122,406,000 transportation aid and $75,296,000 pollution control and health grants to local governments.

[c] Includes $192,165,000 payment to the Massachusetts Bay Transportation Authority, and $76,261,000 C.E.T.A. grants and $73,223,000 lottery commission grants to local governments.

[d] Includes $237,919,000 health grants and $170,995,000 water pollution and sewerage grants to local governments, and $250,000,000 advance of funds to New York City.

[e] Includes $111,024,000 health grants and $108,207,000 mass transportation grants to local governments.

A-27. Comparison of Federal Funds by States with State Rankings of Selected Demographic Characteristics.

State	Total State Funds (Millions)	FY 1977 Federal Funds %	Rank	FY 1977 per Capita Federal Funds (Dollars)	Rank	Per Capita Income in 1976[a] %	Rank	Resident Pop. of States in 1976[b] %	Rank	Federal Income Tax, Net FY 76 & TQ[c] %	Rank	Number of Unemployed as of August, 1977[d] %	Rank
Alabama	6,127	1.5	21	1,695	33	79.3	48	1.7	21	0.9	27	1.5	21
Alaska	1,545	.4	44	4,389	2	158.0	1	0.2	51	0.2	41	0.3	47
Arizona	4,506	1.1	28	2,026	15	90.3	32	1.1	32	0.5	32	1.2	26
Arkansas	3,289	.8	34	1,554	42	78.8	49	1.0	33	0.4	34	0.8	31
California	47,195	11.9	1	2,233	10	111.2	8	10.0	1	9.5	2	12.3	1
Colorado	5,228	1.3	26	2,063	12	101.0	16	1.2	28	1.4	20	1.0[l]	28
Connecticut	5,921	1.5	23	1,913	32	225.6	4	1.5	24	2.0	15	1.7	19
Delaware	800	.2	49	1,538	43	113.2	6	0.3	48	0.5[j]	33	0.3	42
District of Columbia	11,510	2.9	10	16,075	1	134.3	2	0.3	44	[j]	—	0.5	39
Florida	14,457	3.9	6	1,852	25	94.8	29	3.9	8	2.5	12	4.1	9
Georgia	8,767	2.2	16	1,780	28	86.5	36	2.3	13	1.5	19	2.4	11
Hawaii	2,066	.5	39	2,388	6	108.2	12	0.4	40	0.3	38	0.5	38
Idaho	1,689	.4	42	2,057	14	88.9	33	0.4	41	0.3	40	0.3	43
Illinois	17,337	4.4	5	1,556	41	115.4	3	5.2	5	8.4	3	4.4	8
Indiana	6,649	1.7	19	1,252	51	97.1	25	2.5	12	2.3	13	1.9	17
Iowa	3,671	.9	33	1,279	50	100.0	20	1.3	25	1.0	26	0.7	34
Kansas	4,215	1.1	30	1,859	24	100.8	18	1.1	31	0.9	28	0.7	33
Kentucky	5,902	1.5	24	1,738	31	81.4	45	1.6	23	1.4	22	1.2	27
Louisiana	5,478	1.4	25	1,445	45	83.6	43	1.3	20	1.1	25	1.9	16
Maine	1,910	.5	40	1,804	27	83.6	43	0.5	38	0.2	42	0.6	36
Maryland	9,875	2.5	13	2,410	5	109.2	10	1.9	18	2.8[k]	10	1.8	18
Massachusetts	11,462	2.9	11	1,970	18	102.2	15	2.7	10	2.6	11	2.8	10
Michigan	12,308	3.1	8	1,344	48	108.6	11	4.2	7	5.7	7	4.9	6
Minnesota	6,147	1.6	20	1,566	40	95.5	28	1.8	19	2.1	14	1.4	24
Mississippi	4,048	1.0	31	1,725	32	71.0	51	1.1	29	0.4	37	0.9	29
Missouri	9,809	2.5	14	2,059	13	93.2	30	2.2	15	2.8	9	1.9	14
Montana	1,691	.4	41	2,261	9	86.9	35	0.3	43	0.2	47	0.3[l]	45

State	C1	C2	C3	C4	C5	C6	C7	C8	C9	C10	C11	C12	C13
Nebraska	2,458	.6	37	1,594	39	96.9	27	0.7	35	0.7	30	0.3	46
Nevada	1,184	.3	48	2,000	16	113.9	5	0.3	47	0.2	44	0.4	41
New Hampshire	1,426	.4	47	1,743	30	92.7	31	0.4	42	0.2	45	0.3	44
New Jersey	11,166	2.8	12	1,526	44	112.9	7	3.4	9	3.7	8	4.7	7
New Mexico	3,068	.8	35	2,675	3	80.9	46	0.5	37	0.2	43	0.7	35
New York	33,992	8.6	2	1,876	23	110.2	9	8.4	2	13.2	2	10.7	2
North Carolina	7,872	2.0	18	1,444	46	84.0	40	2.5	11	1.6	18	2.1	12
North Dakota	1,476	.4	45	2,318	8	83.8	41	0.3	40	0.2		0.2	49
Ohio	14,641	3.7	7	1,361	47	99.9	21	5.0	6	5.9	5	4.9	5
Oklahoma	5,156	1.3	27	1,901	22	87.8	34	1.3	27	1.2	24	0.9	29
Oregon	3,836	1.0	32	1,676	34		22	1.1		0.9	29	1.4	23
Pennsylvania	19,205	4.9	4	1,624	37		19	5.5	4	5.9	4	5.6	3
Rhode Island	1,629	.4	43	1,758	29	100.9	17	0.4	39	0.4	35	0.5	37
South Carolina	4,498	1.1	29	1,596	38	79.6	47	1.3	26	0.6	31	1.2	25
South Dakota	1,429	.4	46	2,092	11	74.5	50	0.3	45	0.1	48	0.2	50
Tennessee	8,218	2.1	17	1,962	19	84.3	39	2.0	17	1.2	23	1.5	21
Texas	20,196	5.1	3	1,651	35	96.9	26	5.8	3	5.7	6	5.1	4
Utah	2,383	.6	38	1,976	17	85.3	37	0.6	36	0.3	39		40
Vermont	872	.2	50	1,851	26	85.1	38	0.2	49	0.1	50	0.2	48
Virginia	11,783	3.0	9	2,373	7	97.4	24	2.3	14	1.7	17	2.1	13
Washington	8,879	2.2	15	2,503	4	105.1	13	1.7	22	1.4	21	1.9	15
West Virginia	2,942	.7	36	1,632	36	83.7	42	0.8	34	0.4	36	0.7	32
Wisconsin	6,027	1.5	22	1,309	49	97.7	23	2.1	16	1.9	16	1.6	20
Wyoming	729	.2	51	1,949	20	104.4	14	0.2	50	0.1	49	0.1	51

A–27 continued

State	Low Income Individuals in 1975[e]		Average Expenditure per Pupil in Attendance 1976[f]		Living Veterans in 1975[g]		Federal Civilian Employment in 1975[h]		Land Area in 1970[i]		Federal Owned Land in 1975[j]		Number of Hospital Beds in 1974[k]	
	%	Rank	%	Rank	%	Rank	%	Rank	%	Rank	%	Rank	%	Rank
Alabama	2.4	15	79	42	1.4	23	2.1	15	1.4	29	0.1	30	1.8	21
Alaska	0.1	51	151	2	0.1	51	0.5	51	16.2	1	46.3	1	0.1	51
Arizona	1.3	26	102	21	1.0	31	1.2	25	3.2	6	4.1	7	0.7	36
Arkansas	1.6	22	63	50	0.9	32	0.7	37	1.5	27	0.4	17	0.8	33
California	9.1	1	95	25	11.1	1	11.0	2	4.4	3	6.0	3	8.2	2
Colorado	1.0	30	102	20	1.2	28	1.7	20	2.9	8	3.2	11	1.0	31
Connecticut	0.9	33	120	6	1.6	21	0.8	35	.1	48	m	50	1.3	23
Delaware	0.2	49	116	8	0.3	46	0.2	50	.1	49	m	48	0.3	45
District of Columbia	0.4	40	141	3	0.4	41	12.6[h]	1	m	51	m	49	0.8	34
Florida	3.7	8	80	38	2.1	14	2.7	10	1.6	21	0.3	21	2.2	16
Georgia	3.7	8	80	38	2.1	14	2.7	10	1.6	21	0.3	21	2.2	16
Hawaii	0.3	44	111	9	0.3	44	0.9	31	.2	47	0.1	39	0.3	43
Idaho	0.4	42	80	37	0.3	43	0.3	45	2.3	13	4.4	5	0.2	48
Illinois	4.8	5	105	18	5.3	5	4.0	6	1.6	24	0.1	37	5.4	4
Indiana	1.8	20	84	35	2.5	11	1.5	22	1.0	38	0.1	38	2.4	12
Iowa	0.9	31	105	17	1.3	26	0.7	36	1.6	25	m	43	1.4	22
Kansas	0.7	35	106	16	1.1	30	0.8	35	2.3	14	0.1	33	1.3	26
Kentucky	2.5	14	71	48	1.4	24	1.3	23	1.1	37	0.2	26	1.3	24
Louisiana	3.0	11	78	44	1.5	22	1.1	28	1.3	31	0.1	32	1.8	20
Maine	0.5	37	86	31	0.5	37	0.4	41	.9	39	m	45	0.5	37
Maryland	1.3	27	109	11	2.1	16	2.4	13	.3	42	m	44	2.0	19
Massachusetts	1.7	21	(not available)		3.0	10	2.1	14	.2	45	m	47	3.5	9
Michigan	3.4	9	98	24	4.1	7	2.0	17	1.6	23	0.4	14	3.7	7
Minnesota	1.4	25	109	12	1.9	19	1.1	27	2.3	12	0.4	15	2.2	17
Mississippi	2.5	13	72	47	0.8	33	0.9	33	1.3	32	0.2	25	1.1	28
Missouri	2.4	17	85	33	2.4	12	2.4	12	1.9	19	0.3	22	2.4	11
Montana	0.4	41	111	10	0.3	42	0.4	42	4.1	4	3.6	9	0.3	46

State													
Nebraska	0.6	36	94	26	0.7	35	0.6	38	2.1	15	0.1	35	0.7	35
Nevada	0.2	48	91	28	0.3	44	0.3	48	3.1	7	8.0	2	0.2	49
New Hampshire	0.3	46	85	34	0.4	40	0.3	46	.3	44	0.1	34	0.4	40
New Jersey	2.4	16	136	4	3.7	9	2.6	11	.2	46	m	45	3.3	10
New Mexico	0.9	32	91	28	0.5	39	1.0	29	3.4	5	3.4	10	0.4	39
New York	7.0	3	154	1	8.6	2	6.4	3	1.4	30	m	42	11.1	1
North Carolina	3.3	10	79	239	2.1	15	1.5	21	1.5	28	0.3	23	2.3	14
North Dakota	0.3	45	87	30	0.2	48	0.3	47	2.0	17	0.3	20	0.4	42
Ohio	4.2	7	91	27	5.1	6	3.4	7	1.1	35	m	40	4.9	6
Oklahoma	1.5	23	81	36	1.3	25	1.8	19	1.9	18	0.2	28	1.2	27
Oregon	0.9	34	108	13	1.2	27	0.9	32	2.7	10	4.3	6	0.8	32
Pennsylvania	4.7	6	120	5	6.0	3	4.9	5	1.3	33	0.1	36	6.7	3
Rhode Island	0.3	43	107	15	0.5	36	0.4	43	m	50	k	51	0.5	37
South Carolina	2.0	19	74	46	1.1	15	1.1	26	9	40	0.2	29	1.3	25
South Dakota	0.4	39	79	40	0.3	46	0.4	44	2.1	16	0.4	16	0.4	41
Tennessee	2.8	12	70	49	1.8	20	1.9	18	1.2	34	0.2	24	2.1	18
Texas	7.8	2	79	40	5.5	4	5.6	4	7.4	2	0.4	18	5.2	5
Utah	0.4	38	78	43	0.5	38	1.3	24	2.3	11	4.6	4	0.3	44
Vermont	0.3	47	101	22	0.2	49	0.2	51	3	43	m	41	0.3	47
Virginia	2.1	13	86	31	2.2	13	2.8	8	1.1	36	0.3	19	2.4	13
Washington	1.1	29	104	19	2.0	17	2.1	16	1.9	20	1.7	12	1.1	29
West Virginia	1.2	28	77	45	0.8	34	0.5	39	.7	41	0.1	31	1.1	30
Wisconsin	1.5	24	117	7	2.0	18	1.0	29	1.6	26	0.2	27	2.2	15
Wyoming	0.1	50	107	14	0.2	50	0.2	49	2.7	9	3.9	8	0.2	50

Source: U.S. Community Services Administration, Geographical Distribution of Federal Funds (FY–1977).

a Survey of Current Business, August 1977, Volume 57, No. 8, page 17, Bureau of Economic Analysis, U.S. Department of Commerce (National per Capita Income $6,441 = 100%). b Current Population Report, series P-25, No. 642, December 1976, Bureau of the Census, U.S. Department of Commerce. c Statistical Appendix to Annual Report of the Secretary of the Treasury for Fiscal Year Ended June 30, 1976 and Transition Quarter. (Taxes minus refund 5.) d State and Metropolitan Area Unemployment, August 1977, Bureau of Labor Statistics, U.S. Department of Labor. e Survey of Income and Education, Spring 1976, Bureau of the Census, U.S. Department of Commerce. f Statistical Abstract of the United States, 1976 (U.S. Average expenditure per pupil $1,388 = 100%). g Statistical Abstract of the United States, 1976. h Includes Maryland and Virginia counties in Washington, D.C., Md., and Va. SMSA. i Included in Maryland. j Excludes counties in Washington, D.C., Md. and Va. SMSA. k Includes District of Columbia. l Estimated. m Less than one-half of one percent.

A–28. Current Property Tax Collections as a Percentage of Current Levy, 21 Selected Large Cities, 1970.

Denver	99.4
Dallas	98.5
San Diego	98.2
San Francisco	98.4
Phoenix	98.3
Detroit	97.8
Kansas City	97.6
Baltimore	97.6
Cincinnati	97.5
Minneapolis	97.4
Jacksonville	97.2
Seattle	96.9
Buffalo	96.8
Nashville	96.0
Philadelphia	95.6
Atlanta	94.1
Pittsburgh	94.0
Houston	91.7
Boston	90.8
San Antonio	90.5
Chicago	84.5

Source: Published financial reports.
Note: information about the other nine large cities is not available on a comparable basis.

A–29. General Fund, Accumulated Fund Balance or Surplus, 30 Large Cities.

	As Reported by City ($ millions)	Pro Forma Cash Basis ($ millions)	Cash Balance or Deficit as a Percentage of Annual Resources
New York City	0	(657.6)	(9.2)
Chicago	2.2	(188.3)	(47.5)
Los Angeles	N.A.	N.A.	
Philadelphia	(30.1)	(29.2)	(6.1)
Detroit	(20.5)	(17.2)	(3.7)
Houston	12.6	13.6	(3.7)
Baltimore	6.5	9.2	2.4
Dallas	4.8	3.8	4.3
Cleveland	(13.6)	(13.6)	(16.6)
Indianapolis	2.0	2.0	4.5
Milwaukee	28.5	17.5	12.3
San Francisco	48.1	79.9	15.8
San Diego	4.8	4.8	7.3
Boston	27.8	42.0	13.4
Memphis	4.0	5.6	6.7
St. Louis	(3.5)	(3.5)	(2.9)
New Orleans	.5	(.8)	(1.2)
Phoenix	2.7	3.0	4.4
Columbus	1.7	1.7	3.3
Seattle	10.0	14.7	22.9
Jacksonville	14.5	15.4	26.3
Pittsburgh	3.4	7.3	7.9
Denver	7.2	7.2	8.2
Kansas City	.6	.7	1.2
Atlanta	5.7	10.1	17.3
Buffalo	2.5	1.6	2.1
Cincinnati	.5	.5	2.1
Nashville	2.9	2.8	6.3
Minneapolis	4.4	5.4	12.9

Source: Most recently available published financial reports of individual cities.

Note: Figures in parentheses represent deficits.

A–30. State and Local Debt Outstanding by Type of Governmental Unit, Selected Years, 1955–1975.
(expressed as percentage of state and local debt outstanding)

Year	State	County	Municipality	Township	School District	Special District	Total
1955	25	7	36	2	17	13	100
1962	27	7	33	2	17	14	100
1967	28	7	32	2	16	15	100
1968	29	7	31	2	16	15	100
1969	30	7	30	2	16	15	100
1970	29	8	30	2	16	15	100
1971	30	8	30	2	15	15	100
1972	31	8	30	2	14	15	100
1973	32	8	30	2	13	15	100
1974	32	8	29	2	13	16	100
1975	33	9	29	2	12	15	100

Source: Advisory Commission on Intergovernmental Relations, *Understanding the Market for State and Local Debt*, M-104, May 1976 (updated).

A–31. State and Local Long-Term Debt Classified by Purpose, Selected Years, 1959–1974. (Percentage)

Year	Schools	Utilities	Transportation	Public Housing	Industrial Aid	Pollution Control	Other	Total
1959	30%	15%	12%	4%	—%	—%	39%	100%
1962	35	15	14	4	1	—	31	100
1967	31	14	8	3	9	—	35	100
1968	29	12	10	3	10	—	36	100
1969	28	12	14	3	0[a]	—	44	100
1970	28	13	8	1	0[a]	—	50	100
1971	24	15	11	4	1	—	45	100
1972	23	13	9	4	2	—	49	100
1973	21	15	6	5	1	9	43	100
1974	22	14	4	2	2	10	46	100

Source: Advisory Commission on Intergovernmental Relations, *Understanding the Market for State and Local Debt*, M-104, May 1976 (updated).
[a]Less than .5 percent.

A–32. Statutory Interest Rate Ceilings on State and Local Bonds.

	State GO (%)	State Revenue (%)	State Agency (%)	State Notes (%)	Local GO (%)	Local Revenue (%)	Local Agency (%)	Local Notes (%)	Urban Renewal Notes (%)	Low-Rent Housing Notes (%)
Alabama[a]	V	U	V	U	V	V	V	V	0	0
Alaska[b]	7	8	V	V	V	V	V	V	7	7
Arizona[c]	0		0	0	0	0	0	0	0	0
Arkansas[d]	U	U	V	V	6	V	V	V	8	8
California[e]	7	V	V	7	8	V	8	0	8	7
Colorado[f]	0	0	0	0	0	0	V	0	0	0
Connecticut	0	0	0	0	0	0	U	0	0	0
Delaware	0	0	0	0	V	V	V	V	6	V
Florida[g]	7½	7½	7½	7½	7½	7½	7½	7½	7½	7½
Georgia	0	0	0	0	0	9	9	0	8	8
Hawaii[h]	8	0	N	8	7	7	N	7	6	8
Idaho	7	U	0	6	0	U	0	6	0	0
Illinois[i]	0	U	V	N	V	V	V	V	7	7
Indiana[j]	N	N	0	N	0	0	0	0	0	0
Iowa	7	7	U	U	7	7	7	7	7	7
Kansas[k]	N	0	0	U	8	9	N	U	N	0
Kentucky	0	0	0	0	0	9	0	N	0	0
Louisiana[l]	0	0	V	0	8	9	8	0	8	8
Maine	0	0	V	0	0	0	V	0	6	8
Maryland	0	V	0	0	V	V	V	V	V	8
Massachusetts	0	0	0	0	0	0	0	0	0	0
Michigan[m]	0	10	10	0	10	10	10	10	10	10
Minnesota[n]	0	U	0	N	7	7	7	7	7	7
Mississippi[o]	7	7	7	U	7	8	7	U	8	8
Missouri[p]	8	8	8	U	8	8	8	U	8	8
Montana	0	0	0	0	7	9	7	0	0	0
Nebraska[q]	0	0	0	9	0	0	0	9	0	0
Nevada	9	9	N	9	9	9	0	0	9	9
New Hampshire	0	9	0	9	0	9	0	0	8	8
New Jersey[r]	0	0	0	N	0	0	U	0	0	0

State								
New Mexico	8	8	8	8	8	8	U	8
New York[s]	0	N	8	0	N	8	0	0
North Carolina	0	0	0	0	0	0	0	0
North Dakota[t]	0	0	0	0	0	0	8	8
Ohio[u]	0	8	V	8	0	8	8	8
Oklahoma[v]	6	U	U	7½	N	0	N	7½
Oregon	10	0	U	10	U	0	0	0
Pennsylvania[w]	0	0	6	0	U	6	0	6
Rhode Island	0	7	0	0	U	0	7	0
South Carolina	7	7	7	7	7	7	7	7
South Dakota	0	U	8	8	U	8	U	8
Tennessee[x]	10	10	10	10	10	V	10	8
Texas[y]	10	10	10	10	10	10	U	8
Utah	0	0	9	0	0	0	0	0
Vermont	0	U	0	0	0	U	0	0
Virginia[z]	0	0	0	0	0	0	0	0
Washington	0	7	0	0	0	0	U	0
West Virginia	0	U	7	8	7	7	0	0
Wisconsin[aa]	0	0	0	0	0	0	V	0
Wyoming	0	0	0	0	0	0	10	0

Source: The Bond BUyer's "Municipal Finance Statistics," Vol. 14, June 1976. Reprinted with permission.

Note: 0 = none; U = none issued; N = none authorized; V = various.

[a] Alabama: Sect. 60 of Title 9 of Alabama code sets 8% statutory ceiling, but respective statutes authorizing particular bonds set various limits; i.e., 2% on sinking fund bonds and rates up to 15% on loans of $100,000 or more by nonprofit corporations, the State Board of Education, and trustees of state educational institutions. While bonds of local agencies are subject to 8% statutory usury limitation, bonds of local industrial development boards and medical clinic boards are exempt and may bear unlimited rates.

[b] Alaska: Ceiling on state bond anticipation notes is 7%: there is no limit on state revenue anticipation notes. No municipal bond or note may bear interest exceeding the legal usury rate which is fixed at four percentage points above the discount rate of the 12th Federal Reserve District. A contract or loan commitment in which the principal amount exceeds $100,000 is exempt from this limitation.

[c] Arizona: Maximum interest rate must be specified on ballot. If political subdivision has authority to issue bonds without an election, there is 9% ceiling. There is $300,000 ceiling on amount of bonded indebtedness state may incur. On urban renewal notes, the interest is set by each local authority. All authorities have set a limit of 8% or the loan and grant contract rate, whichever is higher.

A-32 Continued

[d]Arkansas: School district bonds have 7% ceiling. About 20 types of bonds for street and parking facilities, public building corporations formed to construct municipal facilities, municipally sponsored bonds for waterworks, sewer, parks, recreation agencies, convention centers, and construction and refunding bonds for eight state-sponsored colleges and universities, and county and municipal bonds for hospitals, nursing and rest homes may be issued for 10%. County and municipal industrial development revenue bonds, airport revenue bonds for cities, metropolitan (multijurisdictional) port revenue bonds may be issued at 10%. Municipal Improvement Districts may issue bonds for, among other purposes, drainage with a ceiling of 10%.

[e]California: Any rate permitted on specific issue approved by two-thirds vote of each house of legislature and by governor. Municipalities' GOs have 8% limit in some instances.

[f]Colorado: Maximum interest rate must be part of proposal submitted to voters along with amount of authorization.

[g]Florida: Some local, county, municipal authority bond authorizations have an interest rate above 7½% or no interest ceiling. Upon request of issuing unit State Board of Administration may authorize a rate of interest in excess of maximum rate set by law.

[h]Hawaii: 8% limitation for state bonds effective until April 1, 1976, at which time it will revert to 6%. Counties with population in excess of 100,000 have 7% limit; counties under 100,000 have 8% limit. On urban renewal notes, state attorney general says interest ceiling does not apply to borrowing from federal government for direct loans. Limit on housing notes reverts to 6% on May 16, 1976.

[i]Illinois: Municipal, school and district bonds, except for isolated instances, have 7% limit. When bonds are voted, ballot is permitted to set maximum rate within the 7% rate. Home rule units may establish own maximum, but may not exceed 8% usury rate—not to be confused with 9½% home mortgage ceiling.

[j]Indiana: Certain town bonds, Barret Law assessment bonds, and grade separation taxing district bonds have 6% ceiling; airport authorities except Indianapolis have 7% ceiling; school bus notes and security agreements have 5% ceiling.

[k]Kansas: Interest on universities and colleges limited to best competitive bid rate in lieu of statutory rate.

[l]Louisiana: Certain state agencies have no interest rate limit while others have a ceiling of 9%.

[m]Michigan: 10% maximum on municipal bonds. On state bonds the ceiling is set at the time voters approve the individual authorizations. Currently there is no ceiling on state GO bonds or operating notes with the exception of authorized and unissued water resources and recreation bonds voted with a 6% ceiling. State housing Financew Agency and state college and university bonds have no rate ceiling.

[n]Minnesota: 7% under a statute superseding all lower limits in any law or charter, but not affecting laws or charters authorizing the issuer to fix higher rates. Laws authorizing the issuer to fix rates apply to state bonds (except highway bonds constitutionally limited to 5%); to virtually all bonds now authorized to be issued by state agencies (Housing Finance Agency, Higher Education Facilities Authority and Higher Education Coordinating Commission, but not the Armory Building Commission); and to municipal industrial revenue bonds.

[o]Mississippi: Interest rates on state and local bonds revert to 6% on March 31, 1976, except for local hospital revenue bonds which will remain at 7%. State park improvement and water pollution abatement GO bonds have 6% ceiling. Local industrial revenue bonds have 8% limit. Under 1973 statute, public building bonds have 7% ceiling.

[p]Missouri: Bonds cannot be sold less than 95% of par. Negotiated sales cannot exceed 6%, except industrial aid bonds which have 8% ceiling.

[q]Nebraska: No state general obligation public debt. As of Aug. 25, 1975, the usury limitation changed from 9% to 11%. This limitation does not apply to obligations of all issuers. A few types of local bonds are governed by specific rate limitations.

[r]New Jersey: 6% ceiling suspended through June 30, 1978 for counties, municipalities, school districts, state agencies and other public authorities and agencies. State GOs have 6% limit except those sold under Recreation and Conservation Development Act of 1974 which have 8% limit.

[s]New York: 5% ceilings suspended for state and local bonds and notes until July 1, 1976. Public authority obligation ceiling is 8% until July 1, 1976 except housing authority obligations on which there is no ceiling until July 1, 1976.

[t]North Dakota: Obligations sold privately are restricted to net interest cost rate of 8%; sales at up to 2% discount reduce coupon rates accordingly.

[u]Ohio: Some state agencies, such as the Ohio Turnpike Commission and State Underground Parking Commission have 8% limit. Urban renewal project notes, if GO, have 8% limit. Low rent housing notes have 8% limit.

[v]Oklahoma: Some state agencies such as public trusts have no interest ceiling. Ceiling on turnpike bonds is 6%. Local industrial development bonds have 6% ceiling and state industrial development bonds have 6½% ceiling.

[w]Pennsylvania: 6% ceiling on obligations of state and local authorities suspended until June 30, 1976. Philadelphia is excluded from provisions of Local Government Unit Debt Act of 1972 and thus has no ceiling on interest costs, except for 6% limitation on port, transit, and street bonds. Urban renewal note ceiling reverts to 6% on June 30, 1976.

[x]Tennessee: Local utility districts are limited to 8%. All others have 10% ceiling.

[y]Texas: Bonds sold by Water Development Board, Veterans Land Development, Park Development and Wildlife bonds have a weighted average annual interest rate ceiling of 6%.

[z]Virginia: Ceiling reverts to 6% after June 30, 1976.

[aa]Wisconsin: Local notes can run for 10 years. Local promissory notes for vocational, technical and adult education school dsitricts have 7% limit.

A–33. Functional Distribution of Governmental Employment, October, 1976.

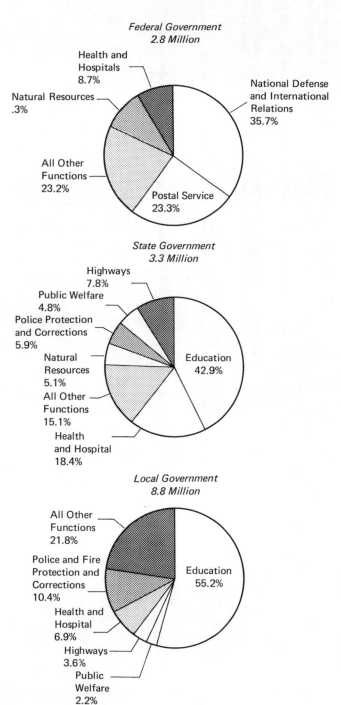

Federal Government
2.8 Million

Health and
Hospitals
8.7%

Natural Resources
.3%

National Defense
and International
Relations
35.7%

All Other
Functions
23.2%

Postal Service
23.3%

State Government
3.3 Million

Highways
7.8%

Public Welfare
4.8%

Police Protection
and Corrections
5.9%

Natural
Resources
5.1%

All Other
Functions
15.1%

Health
and Hospital
18.4%

Education
42.9%

Local Government
8.8 Million

All Other
Functions
21.8%

Police and Fire
Protection and
Corrections
10.4%

Health and
Hospital
6.9%

Highways
3.6%

Public
Welfare
2.2%

Education
55.2%

A-34. National Totals of Employee-Retirement System Finances, 1975–1976 and 1974–1975. (millions of dollars)

Item	1975–1976					1974–1975				
	All Systems	State-Administered Systems	Locally Administered Systems			All Systems	State-Administered Systems	Locally Administered Systems		
			Total	Municipal	Other			Total	Municipal	Other
Receipts	21,637	16,415	5,222	2,786	2,436	18,898	14,208	4,690	3,464	1,226
Employee Contributions	4,808	3,854	954	620	334	4,488	3,552	936	603	333
Government Contributions	10,502	7,641	2,861	1,094	1,767	9,116	6,597	2,519	2,004	515
From States	4,748	4,672	76	29	47	4,093	3,974	119	30	89
From Local Governments	5,754	2,969	2,785	1,065	1,720	5,023	2,623	2,400	1,974	426
Earnings on Investments	6,327	4,920	1,407	1,072	335	5,294	4,059	1,236	858	378
Benefits and Withdrawal Payments	8,422	6,045	2,377	1,878	499	7,490	5,207	2,283	1,828	455
Benefits	7,507	5,327	2,180	1,737	443	6,540	4,480	2,060	1,674	386
Withdrawals	915	718	197	141	56	950	727	223	154	69
Cash and Security Holdings at End of Fiscal Year,										
Total	111,501	85,979	25,522	19,037	6,484	98,064	74,703	23,361	17,475	5,886
Cash and Profits	1,418	728	690	404	286	2,020	800	1,220	977	243
Governmental Securities	12,357	8,457	3,900	3,188	712	7,296	5,105	2,191	1,776	415
Federal	9,207	7,234	1,973	1,307	666	6,569	4,898	1,671	1,300	371
United States Treasury	3,632	2,426	1,207	783	424	2,215	1,315	900	646	254
Federal Agency	5,575	4,808	766	524	242	4,354	3,583	771	654	117
State and Local	3,150[a]	1,223	1,927	1,881	46	728	207	521	477	44
Nongovernmental Securities	97,726	76,794	20,932	15,445	5,486	88,747	68,798	19,949	14,721	5,228
Corporate Bonds	57,389	45,123	12,266	8,985	3,281	53,600	41,693	11,907	8,956	2,951
Corporate Stocks	24,605	19,002	5,603	4,270	1,333	21,762	16,431	5,332	4,039	1,293
Mortgages	7,903	7,225	678	403	275	7,328	6,503	825	420	405
Other Securities	6,406	4,496	1,909	1,611	298	5,397	3,946	1,451	1,163	288
Other Investments	1,423	948	475	176	299	660	226	434	143	291

Source: Department of Commerce, Bureau of the Census.

Note: Because of rounding, detail may not add to totals.

[a]Reflects short-term investments by New York State and New York City retirement systems.

A-35. Finances of State-Administered Public-Employee Retirement Systems, 1976.
(thousands of dollars)

State	Receipts		Government Contributions				Cash and Security Holdings				
	Total Receipts[a]	Employee Contributions	State Government	Local Government	Earnings on Investments	Benefits and Withdrawals	Total Holdings	Cash and Deposits	Federal Securities	State and Local Government Securities	Other Securities
All States	16,598,656	3,914,656	4,427,947	3,336,322	4,919,731	6,045,197	85,810,581	727,744	7,234,025	1,223,203	76,625,609
Alabama	264,294	62,859	122,407	13,239	65,789	79,636	1,026,936	305	173,863	—	852,768
Alaska	83,997	23,938	24,362	17,698	17,999	16,919	279,630	6,331	84,929	—	188,370
Arizona	168,127	50,588	20,084	43,191	54,264	27,564	1,076,775	132	221,673	—	854,970
Arkansas	113,763	32,476	41,633	10,941	28,713	36,957	468,003	11,243	20,370	492	435,898
California	2,529,115	688,424	530,902	549,320	760,469	835,616	13,264,981	63,483	1,370,776	28,486	11,802,236
Colorado	193,722	48,477	25,520	49,461	70,264	54,002	1,142,722	1,348	82,702	—	1,058,672
Connecticut	221,756	55,738	107,389	7,042	51,587	114,817	1,003,653	8,064	61,911	—	933,678
Delaware	41,862	6,053	29,046	—	6,763	14,652	100,358	3,951	5,439	—	90,968
Florida	486,406	17,361	87,238	225,398	156,409	140,264	2,063,773	16,237	367,576	239	1,679,721
Georgia	256,270	65,946	91,992	26,811	71,521	94,185	1,432,164	20,797	67,912	—	1,343,455
Hawaii	157,596	45,868	39,498	12,716	59,514	57,501	750,083	80,952	26,818	852	641,461
Idaho	49,251	16,408	9,948	15,366	7,529	20,423	171,475	12,131	10,884	—	148,460
Illinois	732,463	244,038	230,498	74,946	182,981	303,043	3,193,417	8,005	124,503	8	3,060,901
Indiana	196,090	44,056	83,054	15,551	53,429	102,364	761,769	63,525	243,028	—	455,216
Iowa	131,451	37,919	10,110	34,386	49,036	42,078	727,154	1,529	66,853	—	658,772
Kansas	123,769	33,778	31,429	36,650	21,912	39,645	449,324	791	15,931	7,153	425,449
Kentucky	189,267	58,000	67,845	13,189	50,233	71,866	878,993	12,998	61,121	1,499	803,375
Louisiana	297,605	91,335	90,615	3,832	111,823	143,974	1,701,888	34,058	150,066	11,905	1,505,859
Maine	61,591	23,888	20,457	7,994	9,252	52,088	201,551	11,919	34,234	—	155,397
Maryland	272,825	87,660	102,873	8,679	73,613	111,746	1,577,772	—	99,075	—	1,478
Massachusetts	299,135	87,166	159,900	470	51,599	184,363	953,755	21,375	39,260	180	892,940
Michigan	644,981	121,389	297,981	30,969	194,642	207,905	3,335,552	156,797	505,551	2,306	2,670,898

Minnesota	280,987	87,911	82,726	51,376	58,974	78,068	1,517,927	1,259	46,782	8,918	1,460,968
Mississippi	124,099	40,443	20,787	29,142	33,727	46,247	492,346	1,568	122,402	—	368,376
Missouri	202,841	55,888	25,225	52,262	69,466	64,561	1,103,038	2,592	115,609	—	984,837
Montana	53,950	19,506	5,345	11,614	17,485	27,202	269,791	1,770	10,148	1,179	256,694
Nebraska	23,685	7,751	5,712	1,852	8,370	9,021	123,836	4,405	9,811	—	109,620
Nevada	88,135	20,208	11,699	29,560	26,668	15,398	330,916	785	985	—	329,146
New Hampshire	34,939	12,981	4,505	4,705	12,748	14,552	219,753	18,698	55,776	—	145,279
New Jersey	662,529	166,633	149,094	119,409	227,393	232,541	3,958,397	9,439	144,220	2,257	3,802,481
New Mexico	93,432	29,665	12,845	22,715	28,207	30,328	436,262	11,075	125,556	—	299,631
New York	2,009,892	33,963	419,584	902,192	654,153	694,080	12,270,089	528	319,307	1,095,577	10,854,677
North Carolina	416,067	108,317	124,031	42,725	140,994	109,254	2,436,559	1,403	68,362	20,410	2,346,384
North Dakota	16,499	6,596	2,141	4,220	3,442	8,689	80,856	614	30,433	—	49,809
Ohio	1,303,377	362,763	121,654	421,494	397,466	506,375	7,294,405	2,152	327,015	3,912	6,961,326
Oklahoma	103,274	22,022	52,780	3,095	25,377	57,808	387,150	6,548	22,249	—	358,353
Oregon	174,501	57,296	28,625	47,492	41,088	43,880	871,490	2,055	21,105	649	847,681
Pennsylvania	995,847	225,518	326,273	146,838	297,218	509,558	4,990,784	85	150,516	194	4,839,989
Rhode Island	63,900	18,507	16,427	11,431	17,535	33,200	281,854	3,980	55,932	680	221,262
South Carolina	186,708	56,522	55,640	25,020	49,526	54,523	1,131,787	34,621	210,058	14,839	872,269
South Dakota	36,753	12,254	8,470	6,953	9,076	6,365	111,158	1,598	41,322	—	68,238
Tennessee	196,545	49,724	84,309	9,408	53,104	79,074	840,372	42,793	50,547	—	747,032
Texas	707,836	213,990	304,024	—	189,822	227,647	3,386,500	7,705	782,293	—	2,596,502
Utah	83,321	29,447	9,566	23,214	21,094	20,158	353,150	257	17,040	—	335,853
Vermont	24,609	6,813	7,521	81	10,194	9,036	146,019	2,971	56,026	—	87,022
Virginia	203,559	91,168	13,338	36,553	62,500	87,800	1,334,000	—	232,000	17,443	1,102,000
Washington	398,222	109,700	127,821	51,796	108,905	151,645	1,780,418	26,011	169,648	—	1,567,316
West Virginia	129,520	32,268	65,923	6,260	25,069	78,729	394,572	5,045	146,891	285	242,351
Wisconsin	438,322	83,115	113,658	70,099	171,450	90,065	2,574,361	3	16,359	3,740	2,554,259
Wyoming	29,971	10,222	3,443	6,967	9,339	7,785	131,063	1,813	51,157	—	78,093

Source: Department of Commerce, Bureau of the Census.

Notes: Amounts for purchase and liquidation of investments are excluded.
— Represents zero or rounds to zero.

A–36. Comparative Racial Composition and Growth of the 72 Largest SMSAs, 1960–1970.

Region and SMSA	% Nonwhite in Central City		Change White Population 1960–70		CC Share of SMSA's Nonwhite Growth 1960–70
	1960	1970	CC	OCC	
Northeast	17%	25%	−19%	22%	81%
Hartford, Conn.	15	28	−18	24	89
Wilmington, Del.	26	43	−37	33	77
Washington, D.C.	54	71	−39	58	60
Baltimore, Md.	35	46	−21	36	91
Boston, Mass.	9	16	−17	13	84
Springfield, Mass.	8	13	−12	16	94
Jersey City, N.J.	13	21	−15	3	91
Newark, N.J.	34	54	−37	11	56
Pat.-Clif.-Pas., N.J.	9	17	−9	18	72
Albany-Schen.-Troy, N.Y.	5	8	−11	22	78
Buffalo, N.Y.	13	20	−21	14	91
New York City, N.Y.	14	21	−9	24	88
Rochester, N.Y.	7	17	−17	41	88
Syracuse, N.Y.	5	11	−15	26	92
Allentown-Beth.-Easton, Pa.	1	3	−3	20	84
Harrisburgh, Pa.	19	31	−28	18	114
Philadelphia, Pa.	26	34	−13	22	72
Pittsburgh, Pa.	17	20	−18	4	50
Providence, R.I.	3	5	−18	15	72
Midwest	17	23	−8	25	89
Chicago, Ill.	23	33	−19	34	85
Gary-Hammond-E. Chi., Ind.	25	33	−17	34	100
Indianapolis, Ind.	15	18	7	31	96
Wichita, Kansas	8	10	6	−12	95
Detroit, Michigan	29	44	−29	28	90
Flint, Michigan	18	28	−15	37	83
Grand Rapids, Michigan	8	11	7	20	94
Minneapolis-St. Paul, Minn.	3	4	−9	55	87
Kan. City, Mo.	18	22	0	21	85
St. Louis, Mo.	29	41	−32	27	48
Omaha, Neb.	8	10	13	22	88
Akron, Ohio	13	18	−10	29	100
Cincinnati, Ohio	22	28	−17	21	74
Cleveland, Ohio	29	38	−27	23	50
Columbus, Ohio	16	19	11	32	92
Dayton, Ohio	22	31	−18	30	71
Toledo, Ohio	13	14	19	−1	108
Youngstown-Warren, Ohio	17	22	−16	19	140
Milwaukee, Wisconsin	8	15	−10	27	98
South	24	26	8	40	94
Birmingham, Ala.	40	42	−15	22	66
Mobile, Ala.	32	35	−11	22	103
Jacksonville, Fla	23	29	17	0	100
Miami, Fla.	22	23	14	43	21
Tampa-St. Pete., Fla.	15	18	5	66	78
Atlanta, Ga.	38	51	−20	73	87
Louisville, Ky.	18	24	−14	40	88

A–36 Continued

Region and SMSA	% Nonwhite in Central City		Change White Population 1960–70		CC Share of SMSA's Nonwhite Growth 1960–70
	1960	1970	CC	OCC	
New Orleans, La.	37	45	−18	68	73
Greensboro-W.S.-H.P., N.C.	28	29	14	18	109
Oklahoma City, Okla.	12	14	9	45	94
Tulsa, Okla.	9	11	22	−8	146
Knoxville, Tenn.	19	13	67	−13	128
Memphis, Tenn.	37	40	21	−6	174
Nashville-David., Tenn.	19	20	11	52	98
Dallas, Texas	19	25	14	66	98
Fort Worth, Texas	16	20	4	71	97
Houston, Texas	23	216	26	63	96
San Antonio, Texas	7	8	10	63	75
Norfolk-Ports., Va.	28	31	−6	78	76
Richmond, Va.	42	42	13	25	80
West	5	8	21	47	77
Phoenix, Ariz.	5	5	31	74	90
Anaheim-S.A.-G.G., Cal.	1	2	51	133	75
Fresno, Cal.	8	10	19	5	181
Los Angeles-L.B., Cal.	12	17	5	14	59
Sacramento, Cal.	6	11	24	25	88
San Bernardino-R., O., Cal.	6	7	34	40	51
San Diego, Cal.	6	8	17	41	82
San Francisco-Oak., Cal.	14	21	−17	28	60
San Jose, Cal.	1	3	111	38	65
Denver, Colo.	6	9	0	63	91
Honolulu, Hawaii	0	1	37	52	43
Portland, Ore.	4	6	0	39	90
Salt Lake City, Utah	5	7	−8	47	26
Seattle-Everett, Wash.	5	7	−6	63	83
Total (unweighted average)	17	21	−1	35	86

Source: U.S. Bureau of the Census, *General Demographic Trends for Metropolitan Areas, 1960 to 1970* (PHC-2 Series), Table 1.

Note: Nonwhite population declined in both central city and outside central city areas of the Birmingham SMSA.

A–37. Millions of Persons in Poverty in Each Type of Household in All Metropolitan Areas, 1966.

Type of Household	Adults	Children	Total	Percentage of Total
Headed by females under 65	1.974	2.347	4.321	28.4
Headed by unemployed males under 65	1.137	1.133	2.270	14.9
Headed by disabled males under 65	0.479	0.477	0.956	6.4
Headed by employed males under 65	2.393	2.384	4.777	31.4
Headed by persons 65 or over	2.876	—	2.876	18.9
All Persons	8.859	6.341	15.200	100.0

Source: Committee for Economic Development Supplementary Report No. 26. Reprinted with permission.

A–38. The Worst Tax.

Which Do You Think Is the Worst Tax—That Is, the Least Fair?

	Percentage of Total U.S. Public				
	May 1977	May 1975	April 1974	May 1973	March 1972
Federal Income Tax	28	28	30	30	19
State Income Tax	11	11	10	10	13
State Sales Tax	17	23	20	20	13
Local Property Tax	33	29	28	31	45
Don't Know	11	10	14	11	11

When 1977 national totals are broken down by region, they reveal the following striking contrasts:

	Percentage of Total U.S. Public	Percentage of Respondents by Region			
		North-east	North Central	South	West
Federal Income Tax	28	20	32	33	25
State Income Tax	11	17	9	10	7
State Sales Tax	17	23	15	17	15
Local Property Tax	33	28	37	25	45
Don't Know	11	13	8	14	7

Source: Advisory Committee on Intergovernmental Relations, Changing Public Attitudes on Government and Taxes.

Questions

Chapter 1

1. Why does the federal government use grants and aid to state and local governments to accomplish its aims?
2. Look up the concept of the negative income tax and explain how it would meet citizen basic economic needs.
3. How has urban growth affected the original concept of federalism as included in the federal Constitution?
4. What was the original role assigned to states in the federal Constitution?
5. What is meant by the "new federalism"?
6. What are the basic concepts of an unitary government?
7. Why does a federal program to meet a particular need often become so expensive?
8. How has federal income tax legislation affected state and local tax legislation?

Chapter 2

1. List the services you believe should be provided on the basis of need.
2. Define the concept of merit wants.
3. What is the exclusion principle?
4. What are the advantages of government-required consumption level over government-provided consumption level?
5. Explain the ways in which the use of price to ration goods and services is bad? is good?
6. What is the concept of externalities?
7. If a choice had to be made between free primary education and free college education, which would you choose? Why?
8. What is the basic philosophical difference between a food stamp program and a welfare minimum income program?
9. If the counties were to take over welfare spending, what changes in approach on both the expenditure and revenue raising side would you expect?
10. What is cooperative federalism supposed to provide in the way of allocation of federal funds?
11. What are the basic differences between a social security approach and a welfare approach to adequate incomes?
12. Explain the Western European two-step social security program.
13. Explain the "world of the underclass" and the "grants" economy.

14. Summarize the growth of transfer payments plus welfare and medical assistance government outlays during the past ten years.

Chapter 3

1. Describe the different effects arising from the use of "macro" and "micro" approaches to fiscal policy.
2. Summarize the basic characteristics of land as a form of wealth.
3. Why is land control apt to result in more monopoly power than control over growing timber?
4. What are the advantages of private ownership of land over government ownership?
5. What are the basic features of the United Kingdom's Development Land Tax (DLT)?
6. What problems do you see developing from this system?
7. On the whole why do you favor (disfavor) betterment tax legislation?
8. Land value taxation (LVT) and its annual tax based on market value of land tends to reduce the price of land. Do you think this is a strength of LVT? Why?
9. Explain the land betterment procedures adopted by some U.S. states.
10. Do you think society and not individual action determines the value of land more than the value of a machine? Why?
11. Describe Sweden's preemptive purchase of real estate legislation. Do you favor it? Why?
12. Describe Korea's land readjustment law.
13. Describe the Dutch surface basis urban real estate tax.
14. Why does market value continue to be a better approximation of value than the value produced with multivariate analysis?

Chapter 4

1. How has the automobile changed urban life?
2. What fiscal problems would you expect to increase if a city attempted to increase its effectiveness in holding and attracting industry?
3. How do high property taxes discourage new construction? What kind of a property tax base would encourage new construction? How does the treatment of structure depreciation by the federal income tax discourage structure replacement?
4. What are the advantages and disadvantages of tying a particular tax or a surcharge to a particular expenditure?

5. What are the advantages and weaknesses of local government collecting needed funds in much the same way as industry?
6. Justify the use of the property tax on the basis of benefits for the taxpayer.
7. Special districts have been criticized because they frequently overlap. Discuss this problem.
8. Why is the flexibility of the property tax useful? Why can these same characteristics be the source of waste?
9. Would you favor placing police and highways under the federal government? Why?
10. Intergovernment programs have grown rapidly since the 1930s. What alternatives would you suggest to reduce cost and complications?
11. Develop a chart showing the sources and quantities revenues from various sources used to finance education in your state.
12. Develop a growth rate expectation for each of the seventeen city government groups used by the Bureau of the Census.

Chapter 5

1. Distinguish between a projection and a forecast.
2. Project the trend of expenditures of own-source taxes and other revenues using national or local data.
3. Why should the use of a general price index be avoided in forecasting revenues or expenditures?
4. List types of city developments or new legislation that would affect the projected quantities in the fire inspection block.
5. Why can it be said a careful preparation of a forecast is worth the effort even though the accuracy is low?
6. Explain various ways in which the source of employment affects the stability of the economic base of a local government or a state.
7. What are the sources of information that can be used to forecast the assessed value of real estate?
8. Why is the yield of the property tax more difficult to forecast than income or sales taxes?
9. What have been the sources of unusual growth in state and local government expenditures during the past ten years?
10. If state and local government expenditures decline, why will this be largely reflected in property tax reductions?
11. List four elements of the existing situation that make state and local government fiscal forecasting unusually risky.
12. How does a PPB system act to increase forecasting accuracy?

Chapter 6

1. What are the six steps in moving from a citizen consensus to an actuality?
2. What are allotments?
3. What are the five categories into which expenditures are divided in carrying out an activity?
4. What is meant by sunset laws?
5. What is accomplished under ZBB?
6. What are the advantages and weaknesses of incremental budgeting?
7. What shortcomings and strengths does the ZBB approach provide?
8. Why shouldn't all financing efforts be allocated to the finance department?
9. How is decision making improved by tying expenditures more closely to revenues?
10. Why is citizen participation now being realized as important for public sector efficiency?

Chapter 7

1. Define a budget.
2. What is the difference between the budget as a management plan and as a financial plan?
3. Why is setting priorities the basic purpose of the budget?
4. How are priorities established in the private sector?
5. What would you do to rank government expenditures by productivity?
6. What factors would you take into consideration in determining whether something should be done in the public sector?
7. What is meant by marginal cost? How is it useful in making expenditure decisions?
8. What are the two roles of the budget process?
9. What are the unique characteristics of PPB?
10. What are the processes carried out in preparing the program memorandum (PM) within the PPB System?
11. Why is the use of a number of years important to the PPB system?
12. What are the six categories of analysis used by the PPB system?
13. Briefly explain two ways in which PPB would fundamentally change traditional budgetary procedures?
14. How will PPB work to improve relations between voters and bureaucrats?
15. How is the final budget document organized and presented under PPB?

Chapter 8

1. What are the advantages and disadvantages of the three different basic approaches to cutting the budget?

2. How can new financing approaches avoid reduction of service level?
3. Demonstrate how basic services can be preserved under a reduced budget.
4. Explain the problem of maximizing use of grants and the most efficient use of resources.
5. How do reliable five-year projections assist in adjusting to reduced budgets?
6. Explain the likely sources of innovation and why it is important.
7. What is meant by full social cost?
8. Why might optimization of user choice bring about a poor use of public resources?
9. Why does concern with full social cost push us into the age of externalities?
10. What areas of resource use are likely to decline with a reduction in the relative size of the public sector? Which ones increase?

Chapter 9

1. Give examples of public sector services that cannot be financed with pricelike charges. What common characteristics do they share?
2. What are the justifications for limiting voting on property taxes to those owning property?
3. Give the principal justifications used for property tax limitations.
4. What has been the trend during the past ten years in the portion of total taxes consisting of property taxes?
5. What is the relationship between property tax limitations and state and local government expenditures?
6. Compare the existence of property tax limitation and the relative level of own-source financing of local governments.
7. Explain why the levy limitation is considered superior to the rate limitation.
8. How can rate limitation be prevented from accommodating inflation?
9. How does full disclosure limit local government spending?
10. Under what conditions are service levels of local government too high? Too expensive?
11. The same person will say the property tax is a wealth tax and the tax is paid out of income. Why is this done? Is it correct? How?
12. Which groups of our society are likely to suffer most from expenditure limits? Why?
13. Under what conditions do levy restrictions result in reduced property tax rates?
14. Explain the advantages and weaknesses of the "caps" approach based on a certain percentage of GNP.

Chapter 10

1. Identify some of the reasons for state and local government indebtedness. What private uses of these savings do you believe would be more productive? Why?
2. What is meant by the intergeneration burden of debt?
3. Under what conditions is current payment of capital improvements appropriate?
4. Select a community capital project and find out how the decision to act was made.
5. Select three of the seven general aspects of a bond offering and carry out a detailed study.
6. Would you favor direct federal subsidy of state and local government interest costs rather than exemption of interest on state and local government debt from federal income taxes? Why?
7. What is the method of financing a capital improvement that is most just to all present and future residents? Why?
8. Why are municipal projects justified in being more capital intensive than those of the private sector?
9. What is the concept of the social discount?
10. What is the opportunity cost concept? Do you think it should be important in setting public investment policy? Why?
11. Why is the value of the natural environment increasing?
12. What are revenue bonds? Do you favor their use? Why?
13. How would you calculate the earnings of a sewage project to see if they were equal to the social discount rate?
14. Why is it generally believed the social rate of discount should be set below the market rate of interest?

Chapter 11

1. What types of information are essential for the development of a capital budget?
2. What are the characteristics of items included in a capital budget?
3. Explain why capital investment decisions are often also basic land use decisions.
4. Analyze the usefulness of planning capital projects that meet the needs of areas outside the typical government units.
5. What are spillovers?
6. Define the concept net present value (NPV).
7. How does "free" money affect the efficiency of allocation of capital funds?
8. What conditions affect the willingness of voters to vote for new capital projects?

9. What are some useful measurements to use in determining whether a government unit is overspending?
10. Under what conditions are revenue bonds appropriate?
11. What are some elements of a debt management policy that can lead to minimum interest costs?
12. Why is indebtedness to cover capital costs more appropriate than debt to meet operating expenses?
13. During the past ten years what have been the shifts in the quantities of new indebtedness?
14. Develop an explanation of why a growing city should go into debt now to improve its water system.

Chapter 12

1. How is deficit financing related to economic stability?
2. What has changed relative to timing of borrowing to get low interest rates and also decreased unemployment?
3. What is involved in arbitrage borrowing?
4. Why do local governments frequently issue industrial bonds?
5. Why is a call provision in the borrowing instrument useful?
6. What is a serial bond?
7. What is a yield curve?
8. Trace the growth of state and local debt during the past ten years and compare the change in quantity with several economic quantities.
9. Why has stagflation reduced the ability of local governments to borrow and spend to stabilize the local economy?
10. Why might a bond rejection hurt the credit rating of a government more than additional indebtedness?
11. Why do high interest rates on the early maturing portion of a serial bond issue seem to save interest costs?
12. How can the market be used to set varying interest rates on the different maturity portions of a serial bond issue?
13. What does a flat yield curve indicate?
14. What should be done to make certain financial reporting is adequate?

Chapter 13

1. What was the history of local government defaults in the 1930s?
2. Why should property tax limitations discourage debt defaults?
3. What have been the major causes of municipal and local government debt defaults?
4. What have been the principal causes of rising municipal costs? How could a state review board be of assistance?

5. What are the major causes of higher per capita costs in the central city?
6. How would you forecast per capita CC and OCC expenditures in the future? Why?
7. What is the "infrastructure"?
8. What portion of expenditures in CC and OCC go for education?
9. How does home rule work?
10. Why is having considerable local government financial freedom important?

Chapter 14

1. What are the characteristics of transaction costs?
2. What are the opportunity and real costs related to a cash balance?
3. Why might a slowdown in paying bills be appropriate when interest rates are rising rapidly?
4. What is a money market security?
5. How can a loss be experienced on federal government securities?
6. What risks are invovled in investing in a one-year $100,000 CD?
7. What is a warrant? How does its use reduce the need for demand deposit balances?
8. Why are some securities best left with the treasurer and others with a broker?
9. Describe commonly used cash control procedures of local governments.

Chapter 15

1. What was the original purpose for introducing zoning in the United States?
2. Briefly state the legal base for city use of the power to determine how land will be used.
3. Why hasn't zoning attracted more attention from the U.S. Supreme Court?
4. How would you support a case that zoning affects the rights of people?
5. Explain how "contract" zoning works.
6. How can urban planning and zoning be mutually helpful? Mutually harmful?
7. How does zoning tend to reduce the efficiency of property appraisal?
8. If you were an elected official, why might you favor zoning of the special permit type? Not favor it?
9. What is a "variance"?
10. What is meant by the following statement? Zoning is a useful procedure to handle spillover effects.

11. How has Houston, which is unzoned, developed differently from highly zoned cities?
12. Why can an economist say that zoning reduces the economic efficiency of an urban area?

Chapter 16

1. Briefly summarize the good and bad aspects of the automobile in the enjoyment of urban living.
2. How has government policy stimulated suburban development?
3. How would you justify high gasoline taxes to be spent for general purposes?
4. Draw a chart illustrating the growth of gasoline tax collections at all levels of government during the past ten years.
5. Is Stockfish's attack on those favoring spending gasoline taxes on roads fair? Why?
6. Gasoline is a nonreplaceable resource provided without production costs—only recovery costs. Who should enjoy this bounty of nature? Why?
7. A large portion of U.S. income goes into highways and housing. Do you consider these investments productive? Why?
8. Why has private home ownership reduced the acceptance of the property tax?
9. Briefly explain how federal and state income taxes have encouraged condominiums.
10. Weak construction unions and no insurance of mortgages could have been the housing industry's economic setting. How do you think this would have affected urban lifestyle?
11. Were you a suburban child? How did this environment affect you?
12. Why might a property tax on land only have reduced urban sprawl?

Chapter 17

1. Explain the source of the basic concept that affected the planning of many American cities.
2. What were the causes of the breakdown of the checkerboard pattern of development?
3. What are the triumphs of urban renewal?
4. How have local governments contributed to the financing of urban renewal?

5. What are the necessary steps in getting an urban renewal project underway?
6. How can the application of the income tax and the property tax affect urban renewal?
7. How can city governments operate to make urban renewal more helpful?
8. Explain the new town satellite development of Western Europe and Japan.
9. Do we have a new town development in the United States? Explain.
10. What is the justification and usefulness of keeping government ownership of land in new town developments?

Chapter 18

1. What are the five generally recognized steps in building consensus?
2. What are the basic characteristics of the types of persons damaged by a planning decision?
3. How can a betterment tax aid in planning?
4. Compare the potential wastefulness of market land use decisions with the potential inherent in planning.
5. What are some ways that costs within the service area can be reduced?
6. Explain the cornucopia effect and how it can be encouraged through use of a property tax emphasizing land values.
7. What is the net effect on land use of federal intergovernment activities in the housing area?
8. Describe the ideal role of land use planning.
9. How can the adoption of a property tax on land only reduce the pressures on planning?
10. What were the basic shortcomings of urban renewal?
11. What are some procedures that have proved useful in reducing property tax delinquency in older urban areas?
12. What is "redlining"?
13. What is the best way to keep urban property taxes current?
14. What is the basic change in allowable depreciation on structures in calculating taxable income that is needed to prevent deterioration of built-up urban areas?

Chapter 19

1. Summarize the development of the property tax in the United States.
2. What is intangible property? Why is a different treatment justified?
3. Real estate taxable to the owner does not provide for the deduction of indebtedness. Do you favor this procedure? Why?

4. Placing a tax on each item without regard to value is *ad rem* taxation. What are the advantages and weaknesses of this approach to that of the *ad valorem* procedure?
5. What is meant by the following statement? The supply of land is very inelastic.
6. What is meant by use value?
7. Explain why a tax on land tends not to increase costs while a tax on buildings tends to increase costs.
8. Compare investing in land to investing in gold. How do these investments differ and how are they the same?
9. It is said high-priced land drains away investment funds that could be used to increase productivity and supply jobs. Analyze this position.
10. Why does an increase in the property tax rate on land affect land prices in the same way as increases in interest rates?
11. Why does the incidence of a land tax rest entirely on the owner of the land at the same time the tax rate was increased?
12. What would be the overall effect on funds available to the private sector if land taxes replaced some sales and income tax collections? Why?

Chapter 20

1. If your property is assessed at less than its market value can you successfully plead to have the assessment lowered? Why?
2. What are the four tests applied by the courts to determine if real market value was set by a sale?
3. Why isn't it necessary that similar properties be neighboring properties?
4. Explain how land value is assessed by the residual approach.
5. What are the two procedures for setting land value by the abstraction method?
6. What are the characteristics of ripening land?
7. Why does speculation in land values make the assessor's job more difficult?
8. What are the advantages and disadvantages of using annual rent rather than capital value in setting the base to which the property tax rate is applied?
9. Why does an owner of real estate wish to have more of the total value allocated to structure than is justified?
10. List the pluses and minuses relative to ease of assessment of setting a value on both structure and land or only land.
11. Check the assessed values placed on several properties with which you are familiar and on which you have set a value.

12. Personal property is being removed from the property tax base in many states. Do you favor this? Why?
13. Why don't raw farmland sales data often represent true value?
14. Why shouldn't the cost of land or the interest on funds invested be included as an expense in calculating net income from gross receipts?

Chapter 21

1. What is meant by use value assessment?
2. Explain the arguments used to support use value assessment rather than market value assessment.
3. How is use value calculated?
4. Explain how higher property taxes could make it easier for persons of modest means to purchase land.
5. List five additions to city efficiency that could arise from taxing city and fringe area land on full market value.
6. Why is a high land tax sometimes considered unjust?
7. If land were only taxed indirectly on the capital gain when sold, how would this affect cost of housing? Why?
8. Explain why taxes levied on the land are less likely to increase prices than taxes levied on machines.
9. Why is the price of land sometimes called a rationing device, whereas a tax on machines is an addition to the cost of production that must be included in price?
10. Explain why farm subsidies may not increase the profits new farmers can make out of their operations.
11. What has the trend of land prices been during the past ten years?
12. Relate land price increases to the increase in the price of gold, consumer price index, and the price of a black and white television set.

Chapter 22

1. Describe the content of the rent figure contained in the Statistics of Income published by the U.S. Treasury.
2. Define economic rent as used in economics texts.
3. Compare the justice of the U.S. and the Spanish approach to control and ownership of natural resources.
4. What is a severance tax? Compare the economic pressures it generates with those generated by the property tax.
5. In what respect is a tree, a crop, or a wood-fiber-producing factory a natural resource?

6. Do you think different types of wealth should be taxed differently? Why?
7. Define the yield tax applied to timber.
8. How does school district financing of education reduce, below the average, the contribution per dollar of real estate wealth of timber and mineral properties?
9. How is present value of a capital asset estimated by using the quantity of production in the future?
10. How were all the people of Minnesota able to share in the economic rent of their iron mines?
11. How can timber-producing areas be best taxed to maximize wood fiber production while distributing much of the economic rent to society?
12. What would lead a state to use value of production as the base for a property tax? How does this approach change the impact of a property tax?
13. How does a low cost of holding natural resources affect efficiency of resource use?
14. Define depletion. How does it differ from depreciation?

Chapter 23

1. List costs of open space for parks and playgrounds that are often neglected.
2. Open space for parking can be self-supporting in direct revenues and costs. This is less true of open space as flower gardens. Analyze the true picture of the costs-benefits relationship of these two open space possibilities.
3. How does emphasis on a land tax increase the possibility of developed open spaces without increasing the area covered by a city?
4. Control over land use reduces the rights of ownership. Would government ownership be better? Why?
5. What are the bad effects and good effects of cheap energy?
6. In what way are all decisions of individuals and businesses land use decisions?
7. List some of the more important elements to be considered in setting policy for establishing fair share of land space for particular uses.
8. How can a market allocation of land be made more democratic and more efficient?
9. How does the EPA move toward clean air and unpolluted water?
10. What considerations enter the decision process of whether pristine quality air should be polluted or air already dirty be made somewhat dirtier?
11. Compare the use of fines with tax stimulants to speed up industry's reduction of pollution.
12. List five broad areas of concern that will develop if pollution control activities are expanded.

Chapter 24

1. Why did the classical economists consider the sales tax a bad tax?
2. Why would a national sales tax with receipts allocated to the states be favored by the business community?
3. What are the three fundamental areas of sales tax policy?
4. Describe the principal function of the use tax.
5. Why don't the states limit sales tax liability to the location of the vendor and eliminate all the problems associated with exemption of out-of-state sales?
6. What are the basic conditions required for an efficient city sales tax?
7. What are the three requirements for an ideal sales tax?
8. What are the principal retail sales exempted and treated differently under state sales tax legislation?
9. What is the basis for the belief that sales taxes paid by businesses are passed on to consumers?
10. How can sales taxes be collected from only the nonpoverty groups of society?
11. Where do you believe the relatively strong political support for sales taxes comes from? Why?
12. What do you believe the relative popularity of the sales tax will be ten years from now? Why?
13. Trace the trend in sales tax collections in your city, state, and nation during the past ten years.
14. Would you oppose or favor payment of the sales tax at the wholesale rather than the retail level? Why?
15. Why do small retailers tend to favor the retail sales tax?
16. Why do voters opt for sales taxes to reduce reliance on the property tax when most people own little or no real estate?
17. Why should services be included in the sales tax base? Why are they seldom or only partially taxed?
18. What taxes should the central city impose if it needs additional revenues? Why?

Chapter 25

1. What are the two basic reasons for the relative decline in the collections from the state corporate income taxes?
2. What is the basic problem in the allocation of corporate profits to taxing jurisdictions?
3. Even though all states have a corporate income tax, why is the total base available to states less than the national base?

4. Explain how the concept of marginal utility justifies progressive income tax rates.
5. Would the two-component formula of the Willis Bill work to the advantage of your state? Why?
6. What is the Multistate Tax Commission attempting to do? Do you favor the approach? Why?
7. The incidence of CIT is often assumed to be divided equally between profits, wages, and prices. Attack or support this approach.
8. Summarize the various points to be considered in evaluating the effect of CIT on the level of profits.
9. What is the marginal firm concept in evaluating the location of the burden of CIT?
10. Why do many believe it is undesirable to have a tax that increases the return required on an investment?
11. Why has CIT lost a considerable portion of the favor it formerly enjoyed?
12. How has CIT affected business management? Why?

Chapter 26

1. Why is income difficult to define?
2. Justify the use of progressive income tax rates.
3. Give four reasons why you believe the income tax has grown to be the largest tax source in the United States.
4. Explain how the concept of marginal utility justifies progressive income tax rates.
5. Summarize the growth of federal and state income tax receipts during the past ten years.
6. What is the Myrdal argument against the use of marginal utility to justify a progressive income tax?
7. What is meant by horizontal justice?
8. What are the three principal causes of the relatively rapid increase in state sales tax collections?
9. How does the treatment given to federal income taxes affect the progressivity of state income taxes?
10. Why would the availability of income tax returns improve the accuracy of property value assessments?
11. Explain how out-of-state and interstate earnings are treated.
12. What administrative reasons largely force city income taxes to be less progressive than national income taxes?
13. Point out the justifications for a commuter income tax.
14. Set down the basic provisions you believe an ideal local income tax should possess.

Chapter 27

1. How far can business taxes legally go in applying different rates and taxes to different types of businesses?
2. Is it possible to make a gross receipts tax have about the same impact as a net receipts tax? Explain.
3. How does the "commerce clause" limit the levy of business taxes? What is the general level permitted?
4. In what way are local governments most likely to violate the commerce clause in the application of business taxes?
5. When is a business tax unjust?
6. Would you recommend a city make substantial use of business taxes on retail and service industries but none on manufacturing and transportation industries. Why?
7. What are the advantages and shortcomings of a flat rate license charge?
8. What are the advantages of a variety of tax rates applied to the gross receipts of different businesses?
9. Explain the problem in differentiating between business and nonbusiness taxes.
10. What are the two principal approaches to induce businesses to reduce the pollutants they are putting in the air and water?
11. What is meant by "throwback"?
12. What is the unitary rule? Why is it important?
13. Do you favor action along the lines set out by the Multistate Tax Commission? Why?

Chapter 28

1. What must be assumed if the tax stool has only one leg—income?
2. Give examples of how higher rates make weaknesses of a tax more serious.
3. Why would you favor an expenditure tax with progressive rates over an income tax with progressive rates?
4. What is the conservative side of the expenditures tax?
5. List four examples of where the level of spending would not indicate the ability-to-pay taxes.
6. What are the shortcomings of procedures to estimate the level of expenditures to be used as the base of an expenditures tax?
7. Explain how an expenditure tax encourages savings and an income tax discourages savings.
8. What are the big advantages seen for SVT (LVT)?
9. How can a landowner prevent an increase of taxes as a percentage of real estate owned when SVT (LVT) is introduced?

10. What are the strong points of a value-added tax?
11. To what degree is VAT a tax on production?
12. How does VAT differ from a tax on gross receipts?

Chapter 29

1. What are the basic unique characteristics of the allocation of goods and services within the public sector?
2. What are the advantages of relating tax payments closely to ability to pay and the benefits of government spending to ability to use?
3. What is a transfer payment?
4. How can taxes be levied on business to reduce the tax included in the prices of goods purchased by the poor?
5. What is the "price yardstick" government policy?
6. What characteristics are often a part of government price-cost problems?
7. How does the federal income treatment of user charges differ from that of local taxes?
8. What must be the principal justification for public sector production?
9. If user charges of all kinds, from tuition to fire protection fees, finance services of local government, what is the justification of keeping the activity in the public sector?

Chapter 30

1. What are the characteristics of a compelled purchase?
2. What assumptions are made when necessary government services are only available on payment of a fee?
3. Why would setting fees to cover all property allocated costs help to decrease urban scatteration?
4. What are four other major costs of the automobile in addition to the costs of roads?
5. Work out a license and automobile use permit system that would enable collection of full automobile use costs.
6. What are the basic arguments used to support the existing automobile use finance system?
7. What is the difference between price justice and tax justice?
8. Describe the principle features a sewage finance system should possess.
9. Why do many cities fail to collect a high enough sewage charge that covers both capital and operating costs?
10. What are some advantages and disadvantages of using private contractors to collect garbage and bring it to the disposal facility?

11. What are some possible explanations for the same charges for electric and telephone charges to outlying and downtown customers?
12. How would you set up a procedure for full cost pricing of fire protection?
13. What are the major strengths and weaknesses of earmarked revenues?
14. Define an earmarked tax and explain what is necessary for a tax to become an earmarked tax.
15. Why has the use of special assessments declined?

Chapter 31

1. How would your community benefit and be hurt by the loss of a major industry?
2. What are industrial aid bonds?
3. What would be gained and lost if the federal government removed the tax exemption on interest paid on industrial aid bonds?
4. What basic needs of an established industry might cause it to migrate?
5. How would investment be stimulated or reduced if the property tax raised as much revenues as currently but rested only on land?
6. List four aspects of comparative tax burden studies that have reduced their usefulness.
7. What is the area of taxation where the right kind of action is certain to be useful to everyone? Why?

Chapter 32

1. If local governments are able to finance and manage education, why can't they finance other services as they are introduced?
2. Compare income and property taxes on the basis of stability, local control, and revenue potential.
3. How have the concepts of spillovers and externalities justified social spending at the federal level?
4. Explain the so-called chaos of federal programs depending on state and local government support.
5. Why do social expenditures vary more than other government service expenditures?
6. What is meant by fiscal pressure?
7. How does the federal income tax favor use of state and local taxes in high-income areas?
8. Why has the federal government become deeply involved in financing social programs?

Chapter 33

1. What are the four major types of macroeconomic models?
2. Give the major elements that affect the size of a macroeconomic model.
3. What were the five advancements of the second-generation large-scale econometric model?
4. What do input-output accounts attempt to do?
5. Why should macroeconomic models be used with great caution?
6. What is involved in the feedback effect of a change in the level of spending and taxing?
7. Explain why public works programs are not good programs to stabilize the economy?
8. How are changes in land prices treated in the macroeconomic models in use today?
9. Describe the types of decisions that can be assisted by using operations research.
10. How could you avoid reduction of labor cooperativeness when requiring abandonment of old and familiar procedures so that more technical efficiency could be enjoyed?

Chapter 34

1. How do you analyze the effects of macroeconomic activities on state and local government finances?
2. What is the nature and the role of budget constraints in modeling state and local government finances?
3. Discuss various types of federal grants to state and local governments. Which of these federal grants has the most stimulating effect on state and local expenditures in the long run?
4. What is the economic meaning of displacement effects of a change in the federal budget?
5. What is the feedback effects of general revenue sharing?
6. Give an example of unintended effects of macroeconomic activities on state and local government finances.
7. Do you think state and local government surplus is a healthy aspect of state and local finances? What is the economic role of surplus in the long run?
8. Why do state and local governments increasingly tend to use the advance refunding technique in borrowing?
9. What is the relevant use of macroeconomic indicators for state and local government when macroindicators exclude important local information?

Chapter 35

1. How would you compare the productivity of an accountant and a truck driver?
2. Can productivity be used to set the level of pay? Explain.
3. How can productivity be used to determine how to eliminate a department?
4. What is meant by product and user satisfaction as a measure of productivity?
5. How is productivity of workers measured by the BLS?
6. What might be the reasons for a decrease in the productivity of workers?
7. What is the difference between a highly effective office and a highly efficient office?
8. Explain how more effective, low-cost government is best brought about.

Chapter 36

1. Describe the bargaining process that takes place as benefit levels and contribution levels are established in the public sector.
2. How does the determination of the price and payment process in the public sector correspond to price determination in the private sector?
3. In what way is the existing education finance system just?
4. What can be done within the context of the existing school finance system to increase pressures for greater efficiency?
5. What areas of spending could be reduced to provide greater support for medicine and education? How could this change be accomplished?
6. What is the purpose of social engineering?
7. What is meant by incidence and shifting of taxes?
8. Explain the basic justice of the free market system.
9. On what basis can the redistribution of income and wealth through the collection of taxes be considered a just act?
10. What is the shifting process required for a new tax to be paid without increasing price?

Chapter 37

1. What is meant by fiscal control?
2. What are some of the problems encountered in a relatively exact allocation system?
3. Why does legislation often remain in effect that seriously restricts modification of allocations once made?

4. What are some pitfalls in centralized purchasing and taking advantage of quantity discounts?
5. What is the purpose of the invitation for bids (IFB)?
6. How can purchasing information be prepared to be most useful to management?
7. What are some of the inefficiencies that can arise under decentralized purchasing?
8. What are the basic routine duties of purchasing agents?
9. When is a purchasing agent acting as an unhedged futures buyer?
10. What is the purpose of the bid review process?
11. What are some of the records the centralized purchasing group should keep?
12. What is the difference between contracting and purchasing?
13. Why should identical bidding be discouraged?
14. Why must the purchasing group examine the recommendations of operating units?
15. What can a purchasing agent or group do to make certain materials and services purchased will lead to least-cost provision of government services?

Chapter 38

1. Why does inflation make an adequately funded pension program ten years ago inadequately funded today?
2. What are the possible weaknesses of a pay-as-you-go system?
3. How have governments acted to keep the real value of pension payments at the level relative to salaries being paid and purchasing power existing at the time of the original contract?
4. What has been the growth rate of SLERS?
5. How large a percentage of contributions are generally made by employees?
6. What would be some of the broad economic effects if all SLERS went on the pay-as-you-go basis?
7. What is meant by pension portability?

Chapter 39

1. List the principal types of welfare programs and the percentage of the total that is accounted for by each.
2. Summarize the growth of public welfare programs during the past ten years.

3. What is the usual basis for separating public welfare programs from regular social programs?
4. Explain why it is appropriate to refer to public welfare as the Middle East of the public sector.
5. What is meant by the disincentive impact of the public welfare system?
6. What are the two principal causes that place women on welfare?
7. What is the most frequent approach to welfare reform through a tie-in with social security?
8. Explain how welfare and urban renewal can become cooperative programs.
9. How can management of public welfare be improved?
10. Explain how the social security of a number of Western European countries is divided into two parts.

Chapter 40

1. Why do high tax areas frequently benefit more from metropolitan area development than low tax areas?
2. How would you explain the fact that more efficient provision of community services does not reduce housing costs?
3. What seems to be the determining factors that set the livability of an urban area?
4. What do you think is the explanation for the manner in which the New York problem was approached?
5. What are some of the weaknesses of the New York property tax system?
6. Explain the concept and the roots of the belief that the core area is able to subsidize residential areas.
7. What proof is there that city property taxes are not too high?
8. How can higher property tax rates be avoided even where city salaries are increasing along with the CPI?
9. Why have city property tax collections generally failed to keep up with the inflation rate?
10. Give and briefly explain three reasons why a federal program to aid a particular community for a particular purpose expands into a general and far more expensive program.

Chapter 41

1. Why isn't the impression of restriction in the use of revenue sharing correct?
2. How does revenue sharing prop up small single purpose governments?
3. How are most revenue sharing funds spent?

4. What is a categorical grant?
5. What is a block grant? What is its main purpose?
6. Why is it difficult for governments to provide grants without also establishing spending controls?
7. What are the difficulties encountered when an effort is made to target a grant to a particular small group?
8. What have been the weaknesses of categorical grants as seen by local governments?
9. What are the two basic assumptions on which the revenue sharing policy rests?
10. What is the tax wedge?

Chapter 42

1. What is the chief function of financial accounting?
2. What is one conception of an appropriate standard accounting format to be used by all cities?
3. How should the wasteful practice of committing all unencumbered balances at the end of the year be substantially reduced?
4. Explain what is meant by fund accounting?
5. What is the main reason for the use of fund accounting?
6. What is the prime duty of city government?
7. Explain the accounting approach most cities use in the management of enterprise type operations.
8. What is the approved approach in the management of pension funds?
9. How does the accounting system of state and local governments generally assure the meeting of debt and capital financing obligations?
10. What has become a common procedure of accounting for internally provided services?
11. What is a strength of fund accounting that is being adopted in the business world?
12. How does the line item budget work along with a fund accounting system?
13. What is the concept of responsibility costing?
14. What is the practice of "skimming" to gain a high performance measurement of a department?
15. How do government units know they are doing something sufficiently useful that citizens would buy the service in the open market?

Chapter 43

1. How did the provisions of the federal Constitution point toward a national government of restricted powers?
2. How is the federal government restricted in its use of the property tax?

3. What are the economic advantages of a national VAT over a state sales tax?
4. Why is deficit spending more available to the federal government?
5. How does a pyramiding of debt result from federal revenue sharing and other grants to state and local government?
6. Why might fiscal action to reduce the relative well-being of the wealthy be accomplished more effectively through spending than taxing?
7. What advantages do you see in the harmonization of the income taxes used by state and national governments?
8. Why is diversity of land tax legislation the cause of fewer problems than diversity of income taxes?
9. How do the characteristics of VAT permit diversity of rates between nations while encouraging additional harmonization?
10. Do you believe it would be desirable for the federal government to rely largely on transaction taxes as originally contemplated in the federal Constitution? Why?
11. How can additional federal government borrowing provide the base for additional state and local government debt?

Chapter 44

1. What are the advantages of the county as the government below the state level?
2. What are the advantages and disadvantages of special districts?
3. Explain the three types of county government.
4. What are the advantages and disadvantages of election of the sheriff and county assessor?
5. Compare the revenue level on a per capita basis of county government with that of the federal, state, and city governments.
6. What are the three procedures for additional local government cooperation that are being used rather widely?
7. Select three new areas of county development and analyze each in relation to growth potential and direction of growth.

Chapter 45

1. How has the type of public revenues used to support education been affected by the type of student body?
2. Why has the sales tax been considered an inappropriate source of finance of state universities?
3. What has been the extra benefits the children from poor families have enjoyed by attending the same classes as children from rich families?

4. If the neighborhood school is a segregated school does that make it bad? Why?
5. How has the school district become a method of avoiding a fair share of eduation costs?
6. What was the finding of the *Serrano* decision?
7. Explain the concept of power equalization.
8. Explain the Strayer-Haig model of giving school aid.
9. Collect information on the trend of the per student cost in a local school district and compare it with the national and state trends.
10. Find out the percentage of revenues coming from various sources that make up the budget of your local school district.
11. How would you change the education system?

Chapter 46

1. How would you decide that this is for government; this is for business?
2. How does modern education differ from education of ancient times? On this basis why is it appropriate or inappropriate that education be in the public sector?
3. The federal Constitution provides for a federal government with relatively powerful states. Do you believe states are using this power to the full extent desirable? Why?
4. How do you think some of the basic trends in state and local government are going to affect our society?
5. If you had the power of a pharaoh, what changes would you make in the state and local governments function and the categories of responsibilities they assume?

References
and Notes

Chapter 1
References

Advisory Commission on Intergovernmental Relations, "The Presidency and Intergovernmental Relations," in *Intergovernmental Perspective* 2 (Summer, 1976).

———, "Restraint and Reappraisal: Federalism in 1976," in *Intergovernmental Perspective* 3 (Winter, 1977).

———, "Urban Policy: Initial Readings," in *Intergovernmental Perspectives* 4 (Spring, 1978).

Canadian Tax Foundation, *Provincial and Municipal Finances, 1977*, Toronto: Canadian Tax Foundation, 1977.

Jianakoplos, Nancy Ammon, "The Growing Link Between the Federal Government and State and Local Government Financing," in *Federal Reserve Bank of St. Louis Bulletin* (May 1977):13–20.

Maddox, Russel W., and Fuquay, R.F., *State and Local Government*, 3rd ed. New York: D. Van Nostrand, 1975.

Reynolds, Morgan, and Smolensky, Eugene, *Public Expenditures, Taxes and the Distribution of Income*. New York: Academic Press, 1977.

Chapter 2
References

Beveridge, W.H., *Full Employment in a Free Society*. New York: W.W. Norton, 1945.

Kohler, Heinz, *Scarcity Challenged*. New York: Holt, Rinehart and Winston, 1968.

Ornati, Oscar A., "Poverty in the Cities," in *Issues in Urban Economics* (ed. Harvey S. Perloff and Lowdon Wingo, Jr.). Baltimore, Md.: Johns Hopkins Press, 1968.

Pigon, A.C., *Socialism vs. Capitalism*. London: Macmillan, 1937.

Ozawa, Martha N., *Jubilee for Our Times*. New York: Columbia University Press, 1977.

Sharhansky, Ira, *The Politics of Taxing and Spending*. Indianapolis: Bobbs-Merrill, 1969.

Chapter 3
References

Denman, D.R., "Public Appropriation of Unearned Land Values." Vancouver, B.C.: British Columbia University, 1969.

Floyd, Joe S., Jr., *Effects of Taxation on Industrial Location*. Chapel Hill: University of North Carolina Press, 1952.

Holmes, Dallas, "Assessment of Farmland Under the California Land Conservation Act and the 'Breathing Space' Amendment," *California Law Review* 55 (April 1967):273–282.

Honjo, Nashakiko, "City Planning Administration," in *Trends in Japanese Development Planning*, 1970.

Land (Green Paper), Cmnd 5730. London: HMSO, 1975.

Lindholm, Richard W., *Value Added Tax and Other Tax Reforms*. Chicago: Nelson-Hall, 1976.

Meyer, J.R., et al., *The Urban Transportation Problem*. Cambridge, Mass.: Harvard University Press, 1966.

Swedish Preemptive Purchase Law, Law 868, 1967.

Tanabe, Noboru, "The Taxation of Net Wealth," *IMF Staff Papers* 14 (1967):151–152.

Vickrey, William S., "Defining Land Value for Taxation Purposes," in *The Assessment of Land Value* (ed. D.M. Holland). Madison: University of Wisconsin Press, 1970), 25–36.

Chapter 4
References

Arrow, Kenneth, *Social Choice and Individual Values*. New York: John Wiley, 1951.

Bish, Robert L., and Ostrom, Vincent, *Understanding Urban Government*. Washington, D.C.: American Enterprise Institute of Public Policy Research, 1973.

Box, Dieter, "Federalism and Intergovernmental Problems of Urban Finance," in *Issues in Urban Finance*. Saarbruchen: International Institute of Public Finance, 1972:56–81.

Buchanan, James M., "The Economics of Earmarked Taxes," *Journal of Political Economics* (1963):457–469.

Lindholm, Richard W., "The Dynamic State Revenue Systems," *The Tax Executive*, 29 (October 1976):14–18.

Morag, Amotz, *On Taxes and Inflation*. New York: Random House, 1965.

Rollins, John C., *Special District Governments in the United States*. Berkeley: University of California Press, 1957.

Wallich, Henry C., *The Cost of Freedom*. New York: Harper & Row, 1960.
Wall Street Journal, "Grass-Roots Revolt" (Sept. 7, 1977):1, 28.

Chapter 5
References

Council of Economic Advisers, *Economic Report of the President*. Washington, D.C.: U.S. Government Printing Office, 1978.
Hirsch, Werner Z., *The Economics of State and Local Government*. New York: Appleton, 1971.
McLoone, Eugene P., et al., *Long-Range Revenue Estimation*. Washington, D.C.: George Washington University, 1967.
Levy, Michael E., *Major Economic Issues of the 1970s*. New York: Conference Board, 1973.
Tax Foundation, *The Financial Outlook for State-Local Government to 1980*. New York: Tax Foundation, 1973.
Watters, Elsie M., *Fiscal Outlook for State and Local Government to 1975*. New York: Tax Foundation, 1966.

Chapter 6
References

Advisory Council on Intergovernmental Relations, *Sunset Legislation and Zero-Based Budgeting* 76-5. Washington, D.C.: ACIR, 1976.
Cheek, Logan M., *Zero-Base Budgeting Comes of Age*. New York: AMACOM, 1977.
Cleveland, F.A., and Buck, A.E., *The Budget and Responsible Government*. New York: Appleton, 1921.
Lindholm, Richard W., "The Budgetary Process in Management Policies in Local Government Finance." Washington, D.C.: ICMA, 1975.
Moak, Lennox L., and Killian, Kathryn W., *A Manual of Techniques for the Preparation, Consideration, Adoption and Administration of Operating Budgets*. Chicago: Municipal Finance Officers Association, 1973.
Mowitz, Robert J., "Some Problems in Dealing with Government Productivity," *Tax Review* 37 (August-September 1976):29–32.
Mushkin, Selma J., and Cotton, John F., *Sharing Federal Funds for State and Local Needs*. New York: Praeger, 1969.
Niskanen, William A., "Improving U.S. Budget Choices," *Tax Review* 32 (November 1971):41–44.
Peat, Marwick, Mitchell & Co., "An Automated Line-item Budgeting System

for Local Government," *Management Controls* (November 1976):270–273.

Schick, Allen, *Budget Innovation in the States*. Washington, D.C.: Brookings Institution, 1971.

Singleton, David W., et al., "Zero-based Budgeting in Wilmington, Delaware," *Governmental Finance* 5 (August 1976):20–29.

Smithies, Arthur, "Conceptual Framework of the Program Budget," in *Program Budgeting*, ed. David Novick. Washington, D.C.: U.S. Government Printing Office, 1965:2–32.

U.S. Congress, *Compendium of Materials on Zero-Base Budgeting in the States*. Washington, D.C.: Senate Subcommittee on Intergovernmental Relations, 1977.

Chapter 7
References

Brazer, Harvey E., "The Variable Cost Burdens of State and Local Governments," in *Financing State and Local Government*. Boston: Federal Reserve Bank of Boston, 1970:93–106.

Cleveland, F.A., and Buck, A.E., *The Budget and Responsible Government*. New York: McGraw-Hill, 1970:217–254.

Schick, Allen, "Multipurpose Budget Systems," in *Program Budgeting and Benefit-Cost Analysis* (ed. H.H. Hinricks and G.M. Taylor). Pacific Palisades, Calif.: Goodyear, 1969:358–372.

Sitton, Paul, "Comments," in *Measuring Benefits of Government Investments* (ed. Robert Dorfman). Washington, D.C.: Brookings, 1965:277–288.

Chapter 8
References

Baker, Gordon E., "The Impulse for Direct Democracy," *National Civic Review* 66 (January 1977):19–23, 35.

Beck, Morris, "The Expanding Public Sector: Some Contrary Evidence," *National Tax Journal* 29 (March 1976):15–21.

Business Week, "Returning the Riches to State Taxpayers" (March 20, 1978):42.

Farmer, Richard N., "The Death of Cities and What to Do About It," *MSU Business Topics* 19 (August 1971):11–18.

Heller, Walter, "Meat-Axe Radicalism in California," *Wall Street Journal* (June 5, 1978):20.

Leff, Laurel, "Deep Budget Cuts in California County Reflect Fiscal Agonies of Proposition 13," *Wall Street Journal* (June 28, 1978):25.

Levin, David J., "State and Local Government Fiscal Position in 1977," *Survey of Current Business* (December 1977):16–18, 23.

Time, "Sound and Fury Over Taxes" (June 19, 1978):12–21.

Wall Street Journal, "California Clears $5 Billion Allocation to Lessen Fiscal Pinch of Proposition 13" (June 26, 1978):9.

Chapter 9
References

Advisory Commission on Intergovernmental Relations, *State Limitations on Local Taxes and Expenditures* A–64. Washington, D.C.: U.S. Government Printing Office, 1977.

_____, *Information Bulletin, No. 77-1* (Cost to local government of proposed state legislation). Washington, D.C.: February 1977.

Cattanach, Dale, et al., "Tax and Expenditure Controls: The Price of School Finance Reform" in *School Finance Reform: A Legislator's Handbook*. Washington, D.C.: National Conference of State Legislators, 1976.

Gabler, L. Richard, and Shannon, John, "State Controls on Local Government Revenues: Punch and Counter Punch," *Governmental Finance* 6 (November 1977):9–14.

Hillhouse, A.M., and Welch, R.B., *Tax Limits Appraised* 55. Chicago: Public Administration Service, 1937.

Howards, Irving, "Property-Tax-Rate Limits: A View of Local Government" in *Property Taxation—USA* (ed. R.W. Lindholm). Madison: University of Wisconsin Press, 1967:165–185.

Ladd, Helen F., "An Economic Evaluation of State Limitations on Local Taxing and Spending Powers," *National Tax Journal* 31 (March 1978):1–18.

Shannon, John, et al., "Recent State Experience With Local Tax and Expenditure Controls," *National Tax Journal* 29 (September 1976): 276–285.

Chapter 10
References

Advisory Commission on Intergovernmental Relations, *Significant Features of Fiscal Federalism, 1976–77 Edition* M-110, vol. 2—*Revenue and Debt*. Washington, D.C.: U.S. Government Printing Office, 1977.

_____, *Understanding the Market for State and Local Debt* M-104. Washington, D.C.: U.S. Government Printing Office, 1976.

Arrow, Kenneth J., and Kurz, Mordecai, *Public Investment, the Rate of Return and Optimum Fiscal Policy*. Baltimore: Johns Hopkins University Press, 1970.

Bureau of the Census, Current Industrial Reports, "Pollution Abatement Costs and Expenditures 1976." Washington, D.C.: U.S. Government Printing Office, 1977:6.

Eckstein, Otto, "Investment Criteria for Economic Development and the Theory of Intertemporal Welfare Economics," *Quarterly Journal of Economics* (February 1957):56–58.

Herfindahl, Orris, C., and Kneese, Allen V., *Economic Theory of Natural Resources*. Columbus, Ohio: Charles E. Merrill, 1974.

Lerner, Abba P., "The Burden of Debt," *Review of Economics and Statistics* 43 (May 1961):139–141.

Marglin, Stephen A., "The Social Rate of Discount and the Optimal Rate of Investment," *Quarterly Journal of Economics* 77 (February 1963):95–111.

Mikesell, Raymond F., *The Rate of Discount for Evaluating Public Projects*. Washington, D.C.: American Institute for Public Policy Research, 1977.

Chapter 11
References

Aronson, Richard, "A Comment on Optimality in Local Debt Limitations," *National Tax Journal* 24 (March 1971):107–108.

Hirsch, Werner I., ed., *Regional Accounts for Policy Decisions*. Baltimore: The Johns Hopkins Press, 1966.

Lichfield, Nathaniel, and Margolis, Julius, "Benefit-Cost Analysis as a Tool in Urban Government Decision Making," in *Public Expenditure Decisions in the Urban Community* (ed. H.G. Scholler). Baltimore: The Johns Hopkins Press, 1963:118–146.

Maxwell, James A., and Aronson, Richard, "The State and Local Capital Budget in Theory and Practice," *National Tax Journal* 20 (June 1967):165–170.

Musgrave, Richard A., "Should We Have A Capital Budget?" *Review of Economics and Statistics* 45 (May 1963):134–137.

Mushkin, Selma J., and Gabrielle C. Lupo, "Is There A Conservative Bias in State-Local Sector Expenditure Projections?" *National Tax Journal* 20 (September 1967):282–291.

Schwartz, Eli, "The Cost of Capital and Investment Criteria in the Public Sector," *Journal of Finance* 25 (March 1970):135–142.

Chapter 12
References

Advisory Commission on Intergovernment Relations, *Understanding the Market for State & Local Debt*, (Washington, D.C.: ACIR, 1976).

Center for Capital Market Research, *Improving Bidding to Reduce Interest Costs in the Competitive Sale of Municipal Bonds*. Eugene: University of Oregon, College of Business Administration, 1977.

Hopewell, Michael H., and Benson, Earl D., *Alternative Methods of Estimating the Cost of Inefficient Bids on Serial Municipal Bond Issues*. Eugene: University of Oregon, College of Business Administration, 1975.

Jantschet, Gerald, *The Effects of Changes in Credit Ratings on Municipal Borrowing Costs*. New York: Investment Bankers Association, 1970.

Kidwell, D.S., "An Analysis of the Call Provision in Municipal Bonds," unpublished doctoral dissertation, University of Oregon, 1975.

Robinson, Roland I., "Debt Management" in *Management Policies in Local Government Finance*. Washington, D.C.: International City Management Association, 1975:229–247.

West, E.G., "Public Debt Burden and Cost Theory," *Economic Inquiry* 13 (June 1975):179–190.

Chapter 13
References

Advisory Commission on Intergovernmental Relations, *City Financial Emergencies*. Washington, D.C.: ACIR, 1973.

Bird, Frederick L., "Cities and Their Debt Burden," *National Municipal Review* 25 (January 1936):12–19.

Brazer, Harvey E., "Variable Cost Burdens of State and Local Governments," in *Financing State and Local Governments*. Boston: Federal Reserve Bank of Boston, 1976:93–106.

Hempel, George H., *The Postwar Quality of State and Local Debt*, NBER General Series 94. New York: Columbia University Press, 1971:19–39.

Lewis, Peter. "The Case for the Urban Development Bank," in *Financing State and Local Government*. Boston: Federal Reserve Bank of Boston, 1970:159–180.

Sacks, Seymour, *City Schools/Suburban Schools: A History of Fiscal Conflict*. Syracuse: Syracuse University Press, 1972.

Chapter 14
References

Advisory Commission on Intergovernmental Relations, *Investment of Idle Cash Balances by State and Local Governments: Report A-3 and Supplement*. Washington, D.C.: ACIR, 1961, 1965.

Aronson, J.R., "The Idle Cash Balances of State and Local Governments: An Economic Problem of National Concern," *Journal of Finance* 23 (June 1968):499–508.

Baxter, N.O., "Marketability, Default Risk, and Yields on Money Market Instruments," *Journal of Financial and Quantitative Analysis* 3 (March 1968):75–85.

Ecker-Racz, Laszlo L., *The Politics and Economics of State-Local Finance*. Englewood Cliffs, N.J.: Prentice-Hall, 1970.

Jones, John A., and Kenneth, Howard S., *Investment of Idle Funds by Local Governments: A Primer*. Chicago: Municipal Finance Officers Association, 1973.

Martin, James W., and Gibson, James L., *Administration of Petty Cash*. Lexington: Bureau of Business Research, University of Kentucky, 1960.

Moak, Lennox L., and Hillhouse, Albert M., *Concepts and Practices in Local Government Finance*. Chicago: Municipal Finance Officers Association, 1975.

Roberts, Samuel M., and Gill, Donald G., *Treasury Cash Management and the Investment of Idle Funds*. Berkeley: League of California Cities, 1956.

Chapter 15
References

Babcock, R.F., *The Zoning Game*. Madison, Wisconsin: University of Wisconsin Press, 1969.

Crecine, J.P., Davis, D.A., and Jackson, J.E., "Urban Property Markets: Some Empirical Results and Their Implications for Municipal Zoning," *Journal of Law and Economics* (1967).

Linowes, R. Robert and Allensworth, Don T., *The Politics of Land Use*. New York: Praeger Publishers, 1973.

Myers, Phyllis, *Zoning Hawaii*. Washington, D.C.: The Conservation Foundation, 1976.

Siegan, Bernard H., *Land Use Without Zoning*. Lexington, Mass.: Lexington Books, D.C. Heath, 1972:116–122.

_____, *Other People's Property*. Lexington, Mass.: Lexington Books, D.C. Heath, 1976:56.

Chapter 16
References

Meyer, J.R., Kain, J.F., and Wohl, M., *The Urban Transportation Problem*. Cambridge, Mass.: Harvard University Press, 1965:109.
Stockfish, J.A., "The Outlook for Fees and Services Charges," *Proceedings of 60th Annual National Tax Association Conference* (1967):86–102.
Thompson, Wilbur R., *A Preface to Urban Economics*. Baltimore: The Johns Hopkins Press, 1968:116.
Udall, Stewart L., *1976: Agenda for Tomorrow*. New York: Harcourt, Brace and World, 1968:67.

Chapter 17
References

Aastrom, Kell, *City Planning in Sweden*. Stockholm: The Swedish Institute, 1967.
Clark, Colin, *Population Growth and Land Use*. New York: St. Martin's, 1967.
Flink, James J., *The Car Culture*. Cambridge, Mass.: MIT Press, 1975.
Galantay, Ervin Y., *New Towns: Antiquity to the Present*. New York: George Braziller, 1975.
Levine, Robert A., *Public Planning*. New York: Basic Books, 1972.
Moynihan, Daniel P., "What is Community Action?" *The Public Interest* (Fall 1966):3–8.
Prentice, Perry, "Better Assessment for Better Cities," *Nation's Cities*, May 1970.
Rabinovitz, Francine F., *City Politics and Planning*. New York: Atherton Press, 1969.
Rae, John B., *The Road and the Car in American Life*. Cambridge, Mass.: MIT Press, 1971.
Tyrwhitt, Jacqueline, "The Size and Spacing of Urban Communities," *Journal American Institute of Planners* 15 (Summer 1949):10–17.
Wilson, James Q., ed., *Urban Renewal*. Cambridge, Mass.: MIT Press, 1966.
Wingfield, Clyde J., "City Planning," in *Managing the Modern City* (ed. J.M. Banovetz). Washington, D.C.: International City Manager's Association, 1971.

Chapter 18
References

Aaron, Henry, *Shelter and Subsidies: Who Benefits from Federal Housing Policies*. Washington, D.C.: Brookings Institution, 1972.

Godschalk, David R., and Ahler, Norman, *Carrying Capacities Applications in Growth Management:A Reconnaissance*. Chapel Hill: HUD, 1977.

Le Corbusier, *The City of Tomorrow and Its Planning*. New York: Paysen and Clark, 1929.

Haar, Charles M., *Land Use Planning: A Casebook on the Use, Misuse and Re-use of Urban Land*. Second edition. Boston: Little, Brown, 1971.

Lichfield, Nathan, Peter Kettle, and Michael Whitbread, *Evaluation in the Planning Process*. London: Pergamon Press, 1975.

Lincoln Institute of Land Policy "Conference on Tax Delinquency and Land Policy" (unpublished), October 17, 1977, Cambridge, Massachusetts.

Meyer, John R., ed., *Local Public Finance and the Fiscal Squeeze: A Case Study*. Cambridge, Mass.: Ballinger, 1977.

Sterne, Michael, "Squatter-Thieves May Force South Bronx Businesses Out," *New York Times*, November 1, 1977:1, 30.

Sternlieb, George, and Burchell, Robert W., *Residential Abandonment: The Tenement Landlord Revisited*. New Brunswick, N.J.: Rutgers University, 1973.

Sussman, Carl, *Planning the Fourth Migration*. Cambridge, Mass.: MIT Press, 1976.

U.S. Department of Housing and Urban Development, *Abandoned Housing Research: A Compendium*. Washington, D.C.: U.S. Government Printing Office, 1973.

U.S. Department of Transportation, *Effective Citizen Involvement in Transportation Planning*, vols. 1 and 2. Washington, D.C.: U.S. Government Printing Office, 1976.

Chapter 19
References

Advisory Commission on Intergovernmental Relations, *Significant Features of Fiscal Federalism, 1976–77, vol. 2*. Washington, D.C.: ACIR, 1977.

Bogart, E.L., *Financial History of Ohio*. Urbana: University of Illinois, 1912.

Break, George F., ed., *Metropolitan Financing and Growth Management Policies*. Madison, Wisconsin: University of Wisconsin Press, 1978.

Jensen, Jens P., *Property Taxation in the United States*. Chicago: University of Chicago Press, 1931.

Lindholm, Richard W., ed., *Property Taxation—USA*. Madison: University of Wisconsin Press, 1967.

———, "Twenty-one Land Value Taxation Questions and Answers," *American Journal of Economics and Sociology* (April 1972):153–160.

Netzer, Dick, *Economics of the Property Tax*. Washington, D.C.: The Brookings Institute, 1966.

Orr, Daniel, and Ramm, Wolfhard, "Rawls' Justice and Classical Liberalism," *Economic Inquiry* 12 (1974):377–397.

Polanyi, Karl, *Primitive, Archaic and Modern Economies* (ed. George Dalton). New York: Doubleday, 1968; Garden City, Anchor Books, 1968.

Sacks, Seymour, et al., "Competition Between Local School and Non-School Functions for the Property Tax Base," in *Property Taxation and the Finance of Education* (ed. R. Lindholm). Madison: University of Wisconsin Press, 1974:147–161.

Seligman, E.R.A., "The General Property Tax" in *Essays in Taxation*, 10th ed. New York: Macmillan, 1921:19–62.

Chapter 20
References

American Institute of Real Estate Appraisers, *The Appraisal of Real Estate*, 6th ed. Chicago: National Association of Real Estate Boards, 1974.

Burkhard, Earl E., "The Taxation of Business Personal Property," in *Property Taxation—USA* (ed. Richard W. Lindholm). Madison: University of Wisconsin Press, 1965:103–115.

Dasso, Jerome, *Computerized Assessment Administration*. Chicago: International Association of Assessment Officers, 1973.

International Association of Assessing Officers, *International Property Assessment Administration*. Chicago, 1971.

Kinnard, William N., and Messner, Stephen D., *Industrial Real Estate*, 2nd ed. Washington: Society of Industrial Realtors, 1971.

Mikesell, John L., "Property Tax Assessment Practice and Income Elasticities," *Public Finance Quarterly* 6 (January 1978):53–65.

Murray, William G., *Farm Appraisal and Valuation*, 5th ed. Ames: Iowa State University Press, 1969.

Unger, M.A., *Real Estate*, 3rd ed. Cincinnati: South-Western, 1964.

Woolery, Arlo, *The Art of Valuation*. Lexington, Mass.: Lexington Books, D.C. Heath, 1978.

Chapter 21
References

Corusy, Paul V., "Improving Assessment Performance: Key Findings of Recent Research," in *Proceedings of NTA/TIA, 69th Annual Conference*. Columbus, Ohio: NTA/TIA, 1976:125–129.

Goleman, Harry A., ed., *Financing Real Estate Development*. Englewood Cliffs, N.J.: Aloray, 1973.

Harriss, C. Lowell, ed., *Government Spending and Land Values*. Madison: Univerity of Wisconsin Press, 1971.

Houthakker, Hendrick S., "The Great Farm Tax Mystery," *Challenge* (February, 1967):12–13 and 38–39.

Lindholm, Richard W., "Hawaii and Oregon: Graded Property and Land Value Taxation," in *Property Taxation and the Finance of Education* (ed. R.W. Lindholm). Madison: University of Wisconsin Press, 1974: 104–111.

_____, *Taxation and Assessment of Rural and Fringe Area Lands in Nevada*. Reno: University of Nevada, 1974.

Netzer, Dick, "The Incidence of Property Taxation Revisited," *National Tax Journal* 26 (December 1973):515–535.

Schultze, Charles, *The Distribution of Farm Subsidies*. Washington, D.C.: The Brookings Institution, 1971.

Chapter 22
References

Fred Rogers Fairchild & Associates, *Forest Taxation in the United States*. Washington, D.C.: U.S. Department of Agriculture, 1935.

Gaffney, Mason, "Editor's Conclusion," in *Extractive Resources and Taxation* (ed. M. Gaffney). Madison: University of Wisconsin Press, 1967: 333–419.

Joint Economic Committee, *Measuring the Nation's Wealth*, Washington, D.C.: U.S. Government Printing Office, 1964.

Kansas Legislative Council, *Ad Valorem Taxation of Oil and Gas Property 78 Kansas Counties* 222 (January 1959).

Lindholm, Richard W., *Taxation of Timber Resources* (Eugene:BBER, College of Business Administration, University of Oregon, 1973).

McGrew, James W., "The Present Pattern of State-Local Oil and Gas Taxation" in *Proceedings of National Tax Association*. Harrisburg, Pa.: NTA, 383–393.

National Institute of Education, *Tax Wealth in Fifty States* (Washington, D.C.: Department of Health, Education and Welfare, 1978).

Trestrail, R.W., "Forest and the Property Tax—Unsound Accepted Theory," *National Tax Journal* 22 (1969):347–356.

Williams, Ellis T., "Trends in Forest Taxation," *National Tax Journal* 14 (June 1961):124–130.

Chapter 23
References

Break, George F., ed., *Metropolitan Financing and Growth Management Policies*. Madison: University of Wisconsin Press, 1978.

de Neufville, Judith Innes, *Social Indicators and Public Policy: Interactive Processes of Design and Application*. Amsterdam: Elsevier, 1975.

Haefele, Edwin, *Representative Government and Environmental Management*. Washington, D.C.: Resources for the Future, 1970.

Hibbard, B. Horace, *A History of Public Land Policies*. Madison: Univerity of Wisconsin Press, 1969.

Lindholm, Richard W., "Property Taxation and Land Use Control Policies in Oregon," in *Metropolitan Financing and Growth Management Policies* (ed. George F. Break). Madison: University of Wisconsin Press, 1978: 31–49.

Mack, Pamela C., "Piecemeal Approach Dilutes Federal Environmental Laws," *The Mortgage Banker* 1974:6–17.

Ottoson, Howard W., *Land Use Policy and Problems in the U.S.* Homestead Centennial Symposium. Linccln: University of Nebraska Press, 1963.

Pfeiffer, Ulrich, "Market Forces and Urban Change in Germany," in *The Management of Urban Change in Britain and Germany* (ed. Richard Rose). Beverly Hills: Sage, 1974.

Roberts, Neal Alison, *The Government Land Developers*. Lexington, Mass.: Lexington Books, D.C. Heath, 1977.

Strong, Ann Louise, *Private Property and the Public Interest: The Brandywine Experience*. Baltimore: Johns Hopkins Press, 1975.

Susskind, Lawrence, *The Land Use Controversy in Massachusetts: Case Studies and Policy Options*. Cambridge: MIT Press, 1976.

Chapter 24
References

Barrett, Thomas J., "Multistate Sales and Use Taxation," *Journal of Corporate Taxation* 3 (Spring 1976):5–27.

Due, John, *Sales Taxation*. Urbana: University of Illinois Press, 1957.

Ebel, Robert D., *The Michigan Business Activities Tax*. East Lansing: Michigan State University Business Studies, 1972.

Galbraith, John Kenneth, *The Affluent Society*. Boston: Houghton Mifflin, 1958.

Hamovitch, W., "Sales Taxation: Analysis of the Effects of Rate Increases in Two Contrasting Cases," in *National Tax Journal* 24 (December 1966):411–420.

Lindholm, Richard W., "Integrating a Federal Value Added Tax with State and Local Sales Levies," *National Tax Journal* 24 (September 1971): 403–411.

Mikesell, John L., "Problems of Local Sales Tax Coordination," *Akron Business and Economic Review* 2 (Spring 1971):16–22.

_____, "Central City Sales and Sales Tax Rate Differentials," *National Tax Journal* 23 (June 1970):206–213.

Morgan, Daniel C., Jr., "Reappraisal of Sales Taxation: Some Recent Arguments," *National Tax Journal* 16 (March 1963):89–101.

Nelson, Carl L., Blakey, Gladys C., and Blakey, Roy G., *Sales Taxes*. Minneapolis: League of Minnesota Municipalities, 1935.

Siska, F.V., Jr., "An Appraisal From One Business Viewpoint" in *Business Taxes in State and Local Governments*. Lexington, Mass.: Lexington Books, D.C. Heath, 1972:27–35.

Chapter 25
References

Advisory Commission on Intergovernmental Relations, *Significant Features of Fiscal Federalism*. Washington, D.C.: U.S. Government Printing Office, 1978.

Break, George F., and Peck, Joseph A., *Federal Tax Reform*. Washington, D.C.: The Brookings Institution, 1975.

Committee for Economic Development (CED), *A Better Balance in Federal Taxes on Business*. New York: CED, 1966.

Krzyaniak, Marian, and Musgrave, Richard A., *The Shifting of the Corporation Tax—An Empirical Study of Its Short-Run Effect on the Rate of Return*. Baltimore, Md.: The Johns Hopkins Press, 1963.

Lent, George, *The Impact of the Undistributed Profits Tax*. New York: Columbia University Press, 1948.

Lindholm, Richard W., *The Corporate Franchise as a Basis of Taxation*. Austin, Texas: University of Texas Press, 1944.

_____, "Value Added Tax vs. Corporate Income Tax," *Business Economics* 5 (January 1970):62–65.

Multistate Tax Commission, *Annual Report*. Boulder, Colorado: MTC.

U.S. Senate, Committee on Finance, *State Taxation of Interstate Commerce, Hearings*, September 18–19, 1973.

Chapter 26
References

Advisory Commission on Intergovernmental Relations, *Local Revenue Diversification: Income, Sales Taxes and User Charges*. Washington, D.C.: ACIR, 1974.

———, *Significant Features of Fiscal Federalism*, vols. 1, 2. Washington, D.C.: ACIR, annual publication.

———, *Tax Overlapping in the United States: 1974*. Washington, D.C.: ACIR, 1974.

Blakey, Roy G., and Blakey, Gladys C., *The Federal Income Tax*. New York: Longmans, Green, 1940.

Domar, Evsey D., and Musgrave, R.A., "Proportional Income Taxation and Risk Taking," *Quarterly Journal of Economics* (May 1944):388–422.

Federal Reserve Bank of Boston, *Financing State and Local Governments*. Boston: Federal Reserve Bank of Boston, 1970.

Goode, Richard, *The Individual Income Tax*, rev. ed. Washington, D.C.: The Brookings Institution, 1976.

Myrdal, Gunnar, *The Political Element in the Development of Economic Theory*. London: Routledge and Kegan Paul, 1953.

Vickery, William, *Agenda for Progressive Taxation*. New York: Ronald Press, 1947.

Chapter 27
References

Advisory Commission on Intergovernmental Relations, *Local Taxation and Industrial Location*. Washington, D.C.: U.S. Government Printing Office, 1967.

Alsop, Ronald, "Property-Tax Breaks for Firms Proliferate, But Need Is Disputed," *Wall Street Journal* (June 30, 1978):1, 20.

Ballaine, Wesley C., *Why Business Firms Located in Oregon, 1948 through 1957*. Eugene: University of Oregon, Bureau of Business Research, 1958.

Due, John, "Studies of State-local Tax Influences of Location of Industry," in *National Tax Journal* 19 (June 1961):163–173.

Grieson, Ronald E., "The Effect of Business Taxation on the Location of Industry," *Journal of Urban Economics* 4 (April 1977):170–185.

Harriss, C. Lowell, *Handbook of State and Local Government Finance*. New York: Tax Foundation, 1966.

Tax Foundation, *Pollution Control: Perspectives on the Government Role.* New York: Tax Foundation, 1971.

Tax Institute of America, *State and Local Taxes on Business.* New York: Tax Institute, 1965.

_____, *Business Taxes in State and Local Governments.* Lexington, Mass.: Lexington Books, D.C. Heath, 1972.

Thompson, James H., and Issack, Thomas S., *Factors Influencing Plant Locations in West Virginia.* Morgantown: University of West Virginia, Bureau of Business Research, 1956.

Yaseen, Leonard, *Plant Location*, rev. ed. New York: American Research Council, 1956.

Chapter 28
References

Becker, Arthur, *Land and Building Taxes; Their Effect on Economic Development.* Madison: University of Wisconsin Press, 1969.

Fisher, Irving, *Constructive Income Taxation.* New York: Herper, 1942.

George, Henry, *Progress and Poverty.* New York: Schalkenbach Foundation, 1955.

Kaldor, Nicholas, *An Expenditure Tax.* London: Unwin, 1955.

Lindholm, Richard W., *Value Added Tax: and Other Tax Reforms.* Chicago: Nelson-Hall, 1976.

Sullivan, Clara K., *The Tax on Value Added.* New York: Columbia University Press, 1965.

Chapter 29
References

Brinnes, Roger E., and Clotfelter, Charles T., "An Economic Appraisal of State Lotteries," *National Tax Journal* 28 (December 1975):395–404.

Goetz, Charles J., "The Revenue Potential of User-Related Charges in State and Local Governments," in *Broad Based Taxes: New Options and Sources* (ed. R. Musgrave). Baltimore: Johns Hopkins Press, 1973.

Mann, Patrick, "The Application of User Charges for Urban Public Services," *Review of Urban Economy* 1 (Winter 1963):25–42.

Tax Foundation, *Nontax Revenues.* New York: Tax Foundation, 1968.

Williamson, Oliver E., "Peak Load Pricing and Optimal Capacity," *American Economic Review* 56 (September 1966):810–827.

Chapter 30
References

Bab, Herbert J.G., *Land Services Taxes Can Help to Overcome the Crisis of Cities*. (mimeographed) Los Angeles: 1969.

Gaffney, Mason, "Containment Policies for Urban Sprawl," in *Approaches to the Study of Urbanization*, ed. R. Stauber. Lawrence, Kan.: University of Kansas, Government Research Service 27, 1974.

Jacobs, Jane, *The Death and Life of Great American Cities*. New York: Random House, 1961.

Johnson, James A., "The Distribution of the Burden of Sewer User Charges Under Various Charge Formulas," *National Tax Journal* 22 (Deember 1969):472–485.

Kafaglis, Milton Z., "Local Service Charges," in *State and Local Tax Problems* (ed. Harry L. Johnson). Knoxville, Tenn.: University of Tennessee Press, 1969:164–186.

Mann, Patrick, "The Appliation of User Charges for Urban Public Services," *Review of Urban Economics* 1 (Winter 1963):25–42.

Manvel, Allen D., "Land Use in 106 Large Cities: in National Commission on Urban Problems," *Three Land Research Studies* (Research Report 12). Washington, D.C.: U.S. Government Printing Office, 1968.

Mohring, Herbert, "Land Values and the Measurement of Highway Benefits," *Journal of Political Economy* 69 (June 1961):236–249.

Muth, Richard F., *Cities and Housing: The Spatial Pattern of Urban Residential Land Use*. Chicago: University of Chicago Press, 1969.

Saunders, Robert J., "Urban Area Water Consumption Analysis and Projections," *The Quarterly Review of Economics and Business* 9 (Summer 1969):5–20.

Tax Foundation, *Special Assessment and Service Charges in Municipal Finance* (Government Finance Brief 20). New York: Tax Foundation, 1970.

Vickery, William W., "General and Specific Financing of Urban Services," in *Public Expenditure Decisions in the Urban Community* (ed. Howard G. Schaller). Baltimore: Johns Hopkins Press, 1963.

Warford, J.J., "Water Requirements: The Investment Decision in the Water Supply Industry," *Manchester School of Economic & Social Studies* 34 (January 1966).

Notes

1. Joint Report, Fundamental Considerations in Rate and Rate Structure for Water and Sewage Works," *Ohio State Law Journal* (Spring 1951).

2. Gary L. Buschow and Dwight Brown, unpublished study, University of Oregon, December 1969.

Chapter 31
References

Alyea, Paul E., "Property Tax Inducements to Attract Industry," *Property Taxation—USA*, ed. Richard Lindholm. Madison, Wisconsin: University of Wisconsin Press, 1967:139–158.

Bridges, Benjamin, Jr., "State and Local Inducements for Industry," *National Tax Journal* 18(1):March 1965.

Lipsky, Mortimer, *A Tax on Wealth*. New York: A.S. Barnes, 1977.

Puryear, David, and Bahl, Roy W., *Economic Problems of a Nature Economy*. Syracuse, N.Y.: Syracuse University Maxwell School of Public Affairs, 1976.

Ross, William D., "Tax Exemption in Louisiana as a Device for Encouraging Industrial Development," *The South-Western Social Science Quarterly* 34 (June 1953):14–22.

Schaller, Howard G., ed., *Public Expenditure Decisions in the Urban Community*. Washington, D.C.: Resources for the Future, 1963.

Soule, Don M., *Comparative Total Tax Loads of Selected Manufacturing Corporations with Alternative Locations in Kentucky, Indiana, Ohio and Tennessee*. Lexington: Bureau of Business Research of University of Kentucky, 1960.

Chapter 32
References

Advisory Commission on Intergovernmental Relations, *Fiscal Balance in the American Fiscal System*. Washington, D.C.: U.S. Government Printing Office, 1967.

Alexander, Sidney S., "Opposition to Deficit Spending for the Prevention of Unemployment," in *Income, Employment and Public Policy*. New York: W.W. Morton, 1948:177–198.

Break, George F., *Intergovernmental Fiscal Relations in the United States*. Washington, D.C.: Brookings Institute, 1967, chapter 3.

Eldridge, Douglas H., "Equity, Administration and Compliance and Intergovernmental Fiscal Aspects," in *The Role of Direct and Indirect Taxes in the Federal Revenue System*. Princeton, N.J.: Princeton University Press, 1964.

Keynes, J.M., *The General Theory of Employment, Interest and Money*. New York: Harcourt-Brace, 1936:11–32.

Lindholm, Richard W., *Value Added Tax and Other Tax Reforms*. Chicago: Nelson-Hall, 1976:119–124.

National Institute of Education (HEW), *Tax Wealth in Fifty States*. Washington, D.C.: U.S. Government Printing Office, 1978.

Osman, Jack W., "The Dual Impact of Federal Aid on State and Local Government Expenditures," *National Tax Journal* 19 (December 1966.

Pluta, Joseph E., "Growth Patterns in the U.S. Government Expenditures," *National Tax Journal* 27 (March 1974):71–92.

Reisehauer, Robert D., "The Federal Govenrments Role in Relieving Cities of the Fiscal Burden of Low-Income Persons," *National Tax Journal* 29 (September 1976):293–311.

Vickrey, William, "Conference Review Hour," in *Property Taxation and the Finance of Education*, ed. Richard W. Lindholm. Madison: University of Wisconsin Press, 1974:63–74.

Note

1. Walter W. Heller, "A Sympathetic Reappraisal of Revenue Sharing," in *Revenue Sharing and the City*, ed. Harvey S. Perloff and R.P. Nathan (Baltimore: Johns Hopkins Press, 1968), p. 23.

Chapter 33
References

Ando, Albert, et al., "Government Revenues and Expenditures," in *The Brookings Quarterly Econometric Model of the United States* (ed. James S. Duesenberry et al.). Chicago: Rand McNally, 1965.

Brown, T. Merritt, *Specifications and Uses of Econometric Models*. New York: Macmillan, St. Martin's Press, 1970.

Congressional Budget Office, *The CBO Multipliers Project: A Methodology for Analyzing the Effects of Alternative Economic Policies*, A CBO Technical Analysis Paper. Washington, D.C.: U.S. Government Printing Office, August 1977.

Congressional Budget Office, *Understanding Fiscal Policy, Background Paper*. Washington, D.C.: U.S. Government Printing Office, 1977.

Dennison, Edward, *Accounting for United States Economic Growth—1929–1969*. Washington, D.C.: The Brookings Institution, 1974.

Duesenberry, James S., and Klein, Lawrence R., "Introduction: The Research Strategy and Its Application," in *The Brookings Quarterly Econometric Model of the United Sttes* (ed. J.S. Duesenberry et al.). Chicago: Rand McNally, 1965.

Greenberger, Martin, et al., *Models in the Policy Process, Public Decision Making in the Computer Era*. New York: Russell Sage Foundation, 1977.

Hillier, F., and Lieberman, G., *Introduction to Operations Research*, 2nd ed. San Francisco: Holden-Day, 1974.

Hirsch, Albert A., et al., *The BEA Quarterly Economic Model*. Washington, D.C.: U.S. Department of Commerce, 1973:1–5.

Klein, L.R., *An Essay on the Theory of Economic Predictions*. Markham

Klein, L.R., *An Essay on the Theory of Economic Predictions*. Chicago: Markham Publishing Company, 1971.

Kraemer, Kenneth L., and King, John L., *Computers and Local Government*, 2nd ed. New York: Praeger, 1977.

Moore, Geoffrey H., "The Analysis of Economic Indicators," *Scientific American* (January 1975).

Surrey, M.J.C., and Ormerod, P.A., "Formal and Informal Aspects of Forecasting With an Econometric Model," *National Institute Economic Review* 81 (August 1977):67–71.

Chapter 34
References

Blinder, Alan S., and Solow, R.M., "Analytical Foundations of Fiscal Policy," in *The Economics of Public Finance*, essays by Alan S. Blinder and Robert M. Solow, George F. Break, Peter O. Steiner and Dick Netzer. Washington, D.C.: The Brookings Institution, 1974:3–115.

City Need and the Responsiveness of Federal Grants Programs, Subcommittee on the City of the Committee on Banking, Finance and Urban Affairs House of Representatives, 95th Congress, Second Session, August 1978.

Denison, Edward F., *Accounting for United States Economic Growth: 1929–1969*. Washington, D.C.: The Brookings Institution, 1974 (in particular, appendix J, pp. 266–267, on the method of estimating land values).

Eckstein, Otto, and Halvorsen, Robert F., "A Behavioral Model of the Public Finances of the State and Local Sector," *Discussion Paper* 170, Harvard Institute of Economic Research, Harvard University, February 1971.

Galper, Harvey, Gramlich, Edward, Scott, Claudi, and Wignjowijoto, Hartojo, "A Model of Central City Fiscal Behavior," in *Proceedings of the International Institute of Public Finance*. Saarbruken, 1973: pp. 187–207.

Gramlich, Edward M., "State and Local Government and Their Budget Constraints," *International Economic Review*, June 1969:163–182.

Gramlich, Edward M., and Galper, Harvey, "State and Local Fiscal Behavior and Federal Grant Policy," *Brookings Papers on Economic Activity* (First Quarter 1973):150–165.

Henderson, James M., "Local Government Expenditures: A Social Welfare Analysis," *Review of Economics and Statistics*, May 1968:156–163.

Levin, David J., "State and Local Government Fiscal Position in 1977," *Survey of Current Business*, December 1977:16–18, 23.

Wignjowijoto, Hartojo, and Galper, Harvey, "Data Appendix on the Finances of Ten Large Central Cities," *Urban Institute Working Paper* 506-4 (November 1973).

Chapter 35
References

Bowers, Gary E., and Bowers, M.R., *The Elusive Unit of Service*. Human Service Monograph Series 1. Washington, D.C.: U.S. Department of Health, Education, and Welfare, 1976.

Burkhead, Jesse, and Miner, Jerry, *Public Expenditures*. Chicago: Aldine, 1971.

Gannon, Martin J., and Paine, Frank F., "Factors Affecting Productivity in the Public Service: A Managerial Viewpoint," *Public Productivity Review* (September 1975):44–50.

Greiner, John M., et al., *An Assessment of the Impacts of Five Local Government Productivity Programs*. Washington, D.C.: Urban Institute and the Labor Management Relations Service, 1976.

Hayes, Frederick O.R., *Productivity in Local Government*. Lexington, Mass.: Lexington Books, D.C. Heath, 1977.

Hill, Michael, *The States, Administration and the Individual*. Glasgow, Scotland: Fontana/Collins, 1976.

Joint Financial Management Improvement Program, *Implementing a Productivity Program: Points to Consider*. Washington, D.C.: JFMIP, March 1977.

Public Administration Review 32 and 38 (1972 and 1978).

Schumacher, E.F., *Small is Beautiful: Economics as if People Mattered*. New York: Harper & Row, 1975.

Chapter 36
References

Brittain, John A., *The Payroll Tax for Social Security*. Washington, D.C.: The Brookings Institution, 1972.

George, Henry, *Progress and Poverty*. New York: Vanguard Press, 1929.
Knight, F.H., *The Ethics of Competition and Other Essays*. New York: 1935.
Lindahl, Erik, "Just Taxation—Positive Solution," in *Classics in the Theory of Public Finance* (ed. R.A. Musgrove and A.T. Peacock). London: Macmillan, 1958:168–176, 214–232.
Margolis, J., and Guitton, H., eds., *Public Economics: An Analysis of Public Production and Consumption and Their Relations to the Private Sector*. New York: Macmillan, 1969.
Musgrave, Richard A., and Musgrave, Peggy B., *Public Finance in Theory and Practice*. New York: McGraw-Hill, 1973.
Peckman, Joseph A., and Okner, Benjamin A., *Who Bears the Tax Burden*. Washington, D.C.: The Brookings Institution, 1974.
Phelps, E.S., "Taxation of Wage Income for Economic Justice," *Quarterly Journal of Economics* 87 (1973):331–354.
Rawls, John, *A Theory of Justice*. Cambridge, Mass.: Belknap Press of Harvard University Press, 1971.

Chapter 37
References

Advisory Commission on Intergovernmental Relations (ACIR), *The Case for State-Local Fair Play* 3 (Summer 1977). Washington, D.C.: ACIR, 1977.
Aljian, George W., *Purchasing Handbook*. New York: McGraw-Hill, 1973.
Braun, J. Peter, *Total Cost Purchasing*, Management Information Service Reports, 3 (S-4). Washington, D.C.: International City Management Association, 1971.
Cantor, Jeremiah, *Evaluating Purchasing Systems*. New York: American Management Association, 1970.
Council State Governments, *State and Local Government Purchasing: A Digest* RM-534 (June 1974).
Dyckman, John W., and Isaacs, Reginald R., *Capital Requirements for Urban Development and Renewal*. New York: McGraw-Hill, 1961.
Elkins, Eugene R., *Program Budgeting. A Method for Improving Fiscal Management*. Morgantown: West Virginia University, 1955.
Jernberg, James E., "Financial Administration," in *Managing the Modern City*, ed. James M. Banovetz. Washington, D.C.: International City Management Association, 1971.

Chapter 38
References

Advisory Commission on Intergovernmental Relations, *City Financial Emergencies*. Washington, D.C.: U.S. Government Printing Office, 1973:64–66.

Bahl, Roy W., and Jump, Bernard, "The Budgetary Implications of Rising Retirement Costs," *National Tax Journal* 27 (September 1974):479–490.

Bleakney, Thomas P., "Problems and Issues in Public Employee Retirement Systems," *The Journal of Risk and Insurance* 40 (March 1973):43–45.

_____, *Retirement Systems for Public Employees*. Homewood, Ill.: Richard D. Irwin, 1972.

Griffiths, Martha W., "Public Pensions: Growth and Impact," *Tax Review* 32 (January 1972):4.

Melone, J.J., and Allen, E.T., *Pension Planning*. Homewood, Ill.: Richard D. Irwin, 1966.

Tax Foundation, *Employee Pension Systems in State and Local Government*. New York: Tax Foundation, 1976.

_____, *State and Local Employee Pension Systems*. New York: Tax Foundation, 1969.

U.S. Bureau of the Census, *Finances of Employee-Retirement Systems of State and Local Governments*, series GF. Washington, D.C.: U.S. Government Printing Office, 1978.

_____, *Topical Studies* (6), Employee Retirement Systems of State and Local Governments. Washington, D.C.: U.S. Government Printing Office, 1973.

Chapter 39
References

Advisory Commission on Intergovernmental Relations, "Urban Policy: Initial Readings," *Intergovernmental Perspective* 4 (Spring 1978):4–19.

Barth, M., et al., *Toward an Effective Income Support System: Problems, Prospects and Choices*. Madison: Institute for Research in Poverty, 1974.

Danzigar, Sheldon, and Haveman, Robert, "Tax and Welfare Similification: An Analysis of Distributional and Regional Impacts," *National Tax Journal* 30 (September 1977):269–283.

Okner, Benjamin A., "Demogrnts as an Income Maintenance Strategy" in *Integrating Income Maintenance Programs* (ed. Irene Lurie). New York: Academic Press, 1975:79–107.

Ozawa, Martha N., *Jubilee for Our Times*. New York: Columbia University Press, 1977.

Packer, Arnold H., "Women's Roles and Welfare Reform," *Challenge* 20 (January and February 1978):45–50.

Rein, Martin, and Rainwater, L., "How Large is the Welfare Class?" *Challenge* 20 (September 1977):20–23.

Watts, Harold W., and Peck, J., "On the Comparison of Income Redistribution Plans," in the *Personal Distribution of Income and Wealth* (ed. J.D. Smith). New York: National Bureau of Economic Research, 1975.

426   Financing and Managing State and Local Government

Chapter 40
References

Advisory Commission on Intergovernmental Relations, *City Financial Emergencies*. Washington, D.C.: U.S. Government Printing Office, 1973:A-42.

_____, *Significant Features of Fiscal Federalism*. Washington, D.C.: U.S. Government Printing Office, 1977:M-113.

_____, *Federal Grants*. Washington, D.C.: U.S. Government Printing Office, 1977:A-61.

Cook, Gail C.A., "Toronto Metropolitan Finance: Selected Objectives and Results," *Metropolitan Financing and Growth Management Policies* (ed. George Break). Madison: University of Wisconsin Press, 1978:133–152.

Finkelstein, Philip, "Regional Land Value Tax Proposed to Support Transit," *Henry George News* (September–October 1975).

_____, "The Tax Base and the New York Economy," (unpublished paper), American Economic Association Conference, Dalals, Texas (October 30, 1975).

Sacks, Seymour, et al., "Competition Between Local School and Nonschool Functions for the Property Tax Base," *Property Taxation and the Finance of Education* (ed. Richard W. Lindholm). Madison: University of Wisconsin Press, 1974:147–161.

Chapter 41
References

Advisory Commisison on Intergovernmental Relations, *Community Development: The Workings of a Federal-Local Block Grant*. Washington, D.C.: U.S. Government Printing Office, 1977:A-57.

_____, *Block Grants: A Roundtable Discussion*. Washington, D.C.: Government Printing Office, 1976:A-51, M-113.

_____, *Significant Features of Fiscal Federalism, 1976–77*. Washington, D.C.: U.S. Government Printing Office, 1977:M-113.

_____, *Improving Federal Grants Management*. Washington, D.C.: U.S. Government Printing Office, 1977:A-53.

Caputo, David A., and Cole, Richard L., "General Revenue Sharing: Its Impact on American Cities," *Governmental Finance* 6 (November 1977):24–34.

Derthick, Martha, *Uncontrollable Spending for Social Services Grants*. Washington, D.C.: Brookings Institution, 1975.

_____, *Between State and Nation: Regional Organization of the United States*. Washington, D.C.: The Brookings Institution, 1974.

Kershaw, Joseph A., *Government Against Poverty*. Washington, D.C.: The Brookings Institution, 1970.

_____, eds., *Revenue Sharing: Methodological Approaches and Problems*. Lexington, Mass.: Lexington Books, D.C. Heath, 1976.

_____, *Urban Politics and Decentralization: The Case of General Revenue Sharing*. Lexington, Mass.: Lexington Books, D.C. Heath, 1974.

Porter, David O., et al., *The Politics of Budgeting Federal Aid: Resource Mobilization by Local School Districts*. Beverly Hills: Sage, 1973.

Saltzstein, Alan L., *Federal Categorical Aid to Cities: Who Needs It Versus Who Wants It*. Houston: Institute for Urban Studies, University of Houston, 1975.

Tax Foundation, *Monthly Tax Features* 22 (May 1978):1.

U.S. Department of Housing and Urban Development, *The Urban Development Action Grant Program*. Washington, D.C.: U.S. Government Printing Office, 1977.

U.S. Treasury, *Federal Aid to States, 1977*. Washington, D.C.: U.S. Government Printing Office, 1977.

Chapter 42
References

Axelson, Kenneth S., "Crisis in New York City: The Case for Municipal Accounting Reform," *Journal of Contemporary Business* 6 (Winter 1977):1–6.

Committee on Governmental Accounting and Auditing, *Audits of State and Local Governmental Units*. New York: Institute of Certified Public Accountants, 1974.

Enke, Ernest, "The Accounting Preconditions of PPBS," *Management Accounting* 53 (January 1972):33–37.

Granof, Michael H., "Operational Auditing Standards for Audits of Government Services," *CPA Journal* 43 (December 1973):1079–1085, 1088.

Kaiel, Michael L., "Performance Auditing in Portland, Oregon," *Governmental Finance* 5 (November 1976):38–43.

Moonitz, Maurice, "Obtaining Agreement on Standards in the Accounting Profession," *Studies in American Research* 8. Sarasota, Florida: American Accounting Association, 1974.

National Committee on Governmental Accounting, *Governmental Accounting, Auditing and Financial Reporting*. Chicago: Municipal Finance Officers Association, 1968.

Patton,, James M., "Standardization and Utility of Municipal Accounting and Reporting Practices: A Survey," *Governmental Finance* 5 (May 1976): 15–21.

Vatter, William J., *The Fund Theory of Accounting and Its Implications for Financial Reports*. Chicago: University of Chicago Press, 1947.

Zeikel, Arthur, "Pension Funds," *Journal of Acocunting Auditing and Finance* 1 (Spring 1978):249–256.

Chapter 43
References

Brazer, Harvey E., "Michigan's Single Business Tax-Theory and Background" in *Proceedings of the 69th Annual Conference of NTA/TIA*. Columbus, Ohio: NTA/TIA, 1977:62–69.

Ecles, Marriner S., *Beckoning Frontiers*. New York: Knopf, 1951:393–479.

Morris, Frank E., "The Case for Broadening the Financial Options Open to State and Local Governments," in *Financing State and Local Governments*. Boston: Federal Reserve Bank of Boston, 1970:125–146.

Plumb, William T., "The Priorities of Federal Taxes Over State and Local Taxes—Revisited," *National Tax Journal* 25 (June 1972):133–146.

Shannon, John, "Ways the Federal Government May Strengthen State and Local Financing," in *State and Local Tax Problems* (ed. Harry L. Johnson). Knoxville: University of Tennessee Press, 1969:103–111.

Strayer, Paul J., *Fiscal Policy and Politics*. New York: Harper, 1958.

Chapter 44
References

Advisory Commission on Intergovernmental Relations, *Profile of County Government*. Washington, D.C.: U.S. Government Printing Office.

Blair, George G., "Population Density as a Basis for Classifying Counties," *The County Officer* 23 (June 1958):121, 127.

Gilbertson, H.S., *The County, the Dark Continent of American Politics*, New York: National Short Ballot Organization, 1917.

Institute for Local Self Government, *Special Districts or Special Dynasties?* Berkeley: University of California, 1970.

National Association of Counties, *The County Yearbook, 1977*. Washington, D.C.: National Association of Counties, 1977.

Snider, Clyde F., *Local Government in Rural America*. New York: Appleton, 1957.

U.S. Department of Commerce, *County Government* (June 1958):121–127.
_____, *County Finances in 1975–76*. Washington, D.C.: U.S. Government Printing Office, 1976.

Chapter 45
References

Bohm, Peter, "Financing Methods and Demand for Education" in *Property Taxation and the Finance of Education*, ed. Richard W. Lindholm. Madison: University of Wisconsin Press, 1974:27–40.

Goetz, Charles J., "The Revenue Potential of User-Related Charges in State and Local Governments," in *Broad-Based Taxes: New Options and Sources* (ed. Richard A. Musgrave). Baltimore: Johns Hopkins Univerity Press, 1973:113–129.

Mushkin, Selma J., "User Fees and Charges," *Governmental Finance* 6 (November 1977);42–48.

National Tax Association Committee, "Local Nonproperty Taxation," *Proceedings of 67th Annual Conference, NTA/TIA 1974*:398–423.

Price, Willard, "The Case Against the Imposition of a Sewer Use Tax," *Governmental Finance* 4 (May 1975):38–41.

Shoup, Carl S., "Standards for Distributing a Free Governmental Service: Crime Prevention," *Public Finance* 19 (1964):383–392.

Stockfisch, J.A., "Fees and Service Charges as a Source of City Revenue: A Case Study of Los Angeles," *National Tax Journal* 13 (June 196):111–121.

Tawney, R.H., *Equality*. London: G. Allen and Unwin, 1931.

Wolff, R.P., *The Poverty of Liberalism*. Boston: Beacon Press, 1968.

Chapter 46
References

Anderson, Sven Axel, *Viking Enterprise*. New York: Columbia University Press, 1936:36–51.

Ayres, C.E., *The Theory of Economic Progress*. Chapel Hill: University of North Carolina Press, 1944:231–282.

Lindholm, Richard W., "German Finance of World War II," *American Economic Review* 37 (March 1947):121–134.

———, "The Farm: Misused Income Expansion Base of Emerging Nations," *Journal of Farm Economy* 43 (May 1961):236–246.

Petrie, W.M. Flinders, *Arts and Crafts of Ancient Egypt*. London: T.N. Foulis, 1923.

Polanzy, Karl, *Primitive, Archaic and Modern Economics* (ed. George Dalton). New York: Doubleday, 1968:xxiii–xxxi, 157–174.

Pirenne, Henri, *Economic and Social History of Medieval Europe*. London: Routledge and Kegan Paul, 1958):142–177.

Trevelyan, G.M., *English Social History*. London: Longmans, Green, 1944:1–13.

Index

About the Authors

Richard W. Lindholm is founding dean of the Graduate School of Management of the University of Oregon and is currently professor of finance at Oregon. He has previously held academic posts at Michigan State University, The Ohio State University, Texas A & M University, The University of Texas, and the College of St. Thomas.

Dr. Lindholm has been consultant to the finance departments of the state governments of Minnesota, Texas, Ohio, Michigan, and Oregon. In addition he has served as specialist in government finance to Pakistan, South Vietnam, Korea, Papua New Guinea, and Turkey.

He is editor and contributor to *Property Taxation—USA* and *Property Taxation and the Finance of Education*, both published by the University of Wisconsin Press. In addition he is author of *Introduction to Fiscal Policy*, *Public Finance and Fiscal Policy*, and *Value Added Tax and Other Tax Reforms*.

Hartojo Wignjowijoto has done empirical works in urban public finance, both in the United States and in selected developing countries, and has published and co-authored several papers that appear in the proceedings of the International Institute of Public Finance, the Urban Institute working papers, and the Lincoln Institute of Land Policy monographs.

Prior to joining M.I.T.'s Center for International Studies in 1976 as a research associate, he held research appointments at the Brookings Institution, the National Planning Association, and the Urban Institute, among others.

He is currently a research associate at the Center for International Studies and a member of the research staff at the Energy Laboratory, both at M.I.T. His works include optimal taxation of exhaustible natural resources and modeling financial aspects of long-term macroeconomic energy model.

Mr. Wignjowijoto has been consultant to the public utilities department of the state governments of Massachusetts and Hawaii, the Commonwealth of Puerto Rico, Skidmore, Owings & Merrill, and World Bank.